EMOTION AND CONFLICT

EMOTION AND CONFLICT

How Human Rights Can Dignify Emotion and Help Us Wage Good Conflict

Evelin Lindner

Foreword by Morton Deutsch

Contemporary Psychology
Chris E. Stout, Series Editor

PRAEGER

Westport, Connecticut
London

Library of Congress Cataloging-in-Publication Data

Lindner, Evelin, 1954–
    Emotion and conflict : how human rights can dignify emotion and
help us wage good conflict / Evelin G. Lindner ; foreword by Morton Deutsch.
        p. cm. – (Contemporary psychology, ISSN 1546-668X)
    Includes bibliographical references and index.
    ISBN 978-0-313-37237-7 (alk. paper)
    1. Emotions.   2. Humiliation.   3. Social conflict—Psychological aspects.
I. Title.
    BF531.L53   2009
    303.6—dc22   2008047567

British Library Cataloguing in Publication Data is available.

Library of Congress Catalog Card Number: 2008047567
ISBN: 978-0-313-37237-7
ISSN: 1546-668X

First published in 2009

Praeger Publishers, 88 Post Road West, Westport, CT 06881
An imprint of Greenwood Publishing Group, Inc.
www.praeger.com

Printed in the United States of America

∞

The paper used in this book complies with the
Permanent Paper Standard issued by the National
Information Standards Organization (Z39.48-1984).

10   9   8   7   6   5   4   3   2   1

Contents

Contents

FOREWORD

I first met Dr. Evelin Lindner in December 2001 when she was the speaker at a Colloquium of the Peace Education Program at Teachers College, Columbia University. I was attracted to the colloquium by the title of her talk, "Humiliation and the Roots of Violence." When she spoke, I was impressed by the importance and originality of her ideas. She showed how humiliation—a profound emotion that unfortunately has been little studied by psychologists—often plays a critical role in leading to destructive international and interpersonal conflicts. Her talk was illustrated by fascinating examples drawn from her rich and varied international experiences in such countries as Rwanda, Somalia, Egypt, Germany, and the United States.

As a result of her talk, she was invited to teach a course on the psychology of humiliation in the Program on Conflict Resolution at Columbia University's Teachers College. Her course was extremely well received by the students and faculty. During the summer of 2002, I read many of Dr. Lindner's papers and had an opportunity to talk with her about her work. I urged her to write a book that would present her ideas to a wider social science audience as well as to policy makers and the lay public.

Her book, *Making Enemies: Humiliation and International Conflict*, was a very valuable and original contribution to understanding how the experience of humiliation can lead to destructive interaction at the interpersonal and international levels.[1] The book was characterized as "path-breaking" and honored as CHOICE 2007 Outstanding Academic Title. After reading her book, I invited her to write a chapter on emotions and conflict for the second edition of *The Handbook of Conflict Resolution: Theory and Practice*.[2]

It was a brilliant chapter, but inevitably, a rather condensed presentation of her views. The present book is a much fuller, elaborated presentation of her original, thought-provoking ideas. More than most books on emotions, her writing is both broad and passionate. Broad in that it considers a great many factors that affect emotions: historical, cultural, and social, as well as neurological. For example, in her discussion of humiliation, she develops with great insight the important idea that our awareness of humiliation as a pervasive and powerful experience in human affairs has emerged only recently. She attributes this emergence to two phenomena: *egalization* and *globalization*. Egalization (a term coined by Lindner) refers to the development of the political ideal of equal dignity during the eighteenth century, as reflected in the American and French Revolutions. *Globalization* refers to the increasing interdependence and interconnectedness of peoples throughout the world. A woman in Afghanistan, for example, who has always accepted her husband's right to beat her, feels humiliated when she learns through television that in other parts of the global village, women are viewed as equal to men and husbands may be imprisoned for beating their wives.

Her book has a very passionate quality. It is a very strong and persuasive advocate for human dignity for all people. It is well grounded not only in science, but also in the highest moral values. It helps the reader transform destructive conflict and dignify his or her personal experiences. Dr. Lindner is a very thoughtful person who has read widely and deeply in the social sciences. She has also had a rich, varied experience in many countries as a psychotherapist, counselor, researcher, and global citizen, immersing herself in and embracing diverse cultures.

The book should interest a wide audience. Psychologists and other social scientists will find new ideas to enrich their understanding of how humiliation and other emotions contribute to destructive conflict and violence at the international as well as interpersonal levels. Policy makers will be exposed not only to these new ideas but also to their policy implications. Beyond the foregoing, all readers—whether they have a professional interest or not—will find much value to their personal lives.

Morton Deutsch
E. L. Thorndike Professor Emeritus of Psychology and Education, and
Director Emeritus of the International Center for Cooperation and
Conflict Resolution (ICCCR), Teachers College, Columbia University

Acknowledgments

This book builds on my global life of the past thirty years, and, more recently, on the attention I've focused on the study of dignity and humiliation. First, I wish to convey my profound thanks to Professor Morton Deutsch of Columbia University for his continuous strong support. He authored the foreword for my book *Making Enemies: Humiliation and International Conflict* (2006)—without his support, it would not have been completed.

Morton later invited me to write a chapter on emotion and conflict for the second edition (2006) of his renowned *Handbook of Conflict Resolution*. In preparation for this chapter, I updated myself on the latest research on emotion. This preparation was the starting point for this book.

I began studying dignity and humiliation in 1996, when I was preparing a four-year doctoral research project at the University of Oslo on *The Feeling of Being Humiliated: A Central Theme in Armed Conflicts* (1997–2001). This project was funded by the Royal Norwegian Ministry of Foreign Affairs and the Norwegian Research Council, and its task was to study the role of humiliation in the recent mass slaughters in Rwanda and Somalia, on the background of Nazi Germany, and other twentieth-century genocides. I am deeply grateful for the council's commitment to this critical issue.

During this research, I received generous international support from hundreds of academics and practitioners in anthropology, history, philosophy, political science, psychology, and sociology, and I thank them all. Among the very first to extend their kind support to me were, apart from Professor Deutsch, Dr. David A. Hamburg, president emeritus of the Carnegie Corporation; Alan B. Slifka, founder of the Alan B. Slifka Program in

Intercommunal Coexistence at Brandeis University; and Professor Lee D. Ross, co-founder of the Stanford Center on Conflict and Negotiation. I want to express my profound gratitude to my many generous collaborators in Europe, especially to Associate Professor Reidar Ommundsen, Professor Jan Smedslund, and the other dedicated members of the Department of Psychology at the University of Oslo.

The political insights offered in this book are the result of decades of living and working all over the world—in many countries within Africa, Asia, Europe, and America, among others for longer periods in Egypt, Somalia, the Great Lakes in Africa, the Middle East, China, Japan, Thailand, Australia, New Zealand, the United States, Norway, Germany, Switzerland, Belgium, or France. I extend especially warm thanks to all my international interlocutors, neighbors, and hosts, many of whom must struggle daily to carry on the work of peace, often under the most difficult circumstances.

As for my psychological insights, I owe them in large part to the many clients I have treated in my practice as a clinical psychologist (1980–1984 in Hamburg, Germany, and 1984–1991 in Cairo, Egypt) before moving on to social psychology as my main focus, and I am deeply indebted to them.

For this book, I would like to convey particularly deep-felt thanks to Linda M. Hartling for her untiring support and for connecting me with Jean Baker Miller and her work. Jean Baker Miller coined one of the central phrases of this book, "waging good conflict," and this book wishes to honor her life work.

I would like to thank Chris E. Stout, the editor of the Contemporary Psychology Series, and Debbie Carvalko, Senior Acquisitions Editor for psychology and health, for their never faltering belief in my work; Kathleen Morrow for her invaluable help in making the manuscript its most readable; and Sheryl Rowe for her generous support in editing.

Finally, I thank my parents, whose personal courage gave my work its direction and motivation.

INTRODUCTION

We live in times of crisis. This book describes a vision of an alternative future, a vision that aims to motivate us to strive for its realization and overcome the obstacles that wait on this path.

We live in times of dangerous global warming, or more precisely, overheating, not only in our physical environment but also in our social surroundings. As to the latter, we can observe two main trends or transitions—which, incidentally, are also responsible for the increasing importance of the topic of this book:

First, our world is shrinking as never before. Global interdependence binds us all together ever closer. When mutual respect is felt to be lacking, feelings of resentment and humiliation heat up. What is most needed in an increasingly interdependent world—cooperation—is hampered, while hot conflict is fueled.

Second, we live in the midst of a moral revolution—the human rights revolution. Formerly, underlings were expected to accept their lowly lot as god-given. In this day and age, people at the bottom are increasingly learning something new, namely, that their lowliness represents a violation of their human rights. Article 1 of the of the Human Rights Declaration states that every human being is born with equal rights and dignity (and ought not be humiliated). Consequently, scores of disadvantaged, downtrodden, and oppressed people around the world—lower class people, underlings, inferiors, or subalterns, whatever label—together with those who identify with them, "learn" to feel humiliated by conditions that formerly were often accepted as normal. Indeed, feelings of humiliation in victims, and those who witness their plight, are the fuel of the human rights movement. These feelings inspire some to embark on uprisings that—predictably—slide into stark conflict with traditional definitions of the situation. Hot emotions are fanned, risking malign runaway self-reinforcing processes that heat already burning emotions ever further.

Nelson Mandela has become the iconic name for a constructive transition out of humiliation (in my work I treat Mandela in the spirit of a Weberian ideal-type approach).[1] We must learn from him if humankind is to avoid all-out destructive conflict. We must learn and maximize Mandela's approach because there is also a Hitler way out of humiliation. The Adolf Hitlers of this world stand for cruel and cynical retaliatory humiliation—they are ready to turn the cycle of humiliation ever further, not hesitating to sacrifice even millions of lives. It is the Mandelas who hold the torch of wisdom and humility—virtues that can end cycles of humiliation.

In short, the shrinking of our world combined with the human rights message of equal dignity can work like an explosive gas and its trigger, if we do not handle the transition well. All this plays out at macro levels as much as at micro levels. If we wish to understand phenomena ranging from global terrorism to domestic violence, we are well advised to inquire about the role emotions play.

Let me share with you some introductory vignettes, one addressing the macro level of social interactions and a second from the micro level. As you will see, I always attempt to highlight larger patterns, because those larger patterns, albeit difficult to detect, can provide constructive guidance.

Japan

At its peak, in early 1942, Japan's Greater East Asia Co-Prosperity Sphere was huge. It stretched from the Aleutian Islands in the north, covered half of China, included Burma (Myanmar) and almost all of Southeast Asia. In Japan, the superiority of the Japanese "Yamato race" was praised, the emperor's war was hailed as holy, and his soldiers and sailors were expected to be invincible.

The rigorous samurai ethos of honor or *bushido* was revived. Japan would probably not have its characteristic culture today were it not for samurai courage and willingness to sacrifice their lives. Aided by divine intervention—*kamikaze*, or "divine wind" (speak: hurricanes)—samurai once saved Japan from losing its distinctness. Japan was on the verge of becoming part of Kublai Khan's empire, the most powerful empire of the world of its time. In 1258, Kublai conquered the Korean peninsula; in 1266, he crowned himself emperor of China; in 1274, he set his eyes on Japan. He sent more than nine hundred ships and forty thousand troops to Japan. The Japanese samurai fought bravely, and, supported by kamikaze, made the Mongols retreat. In 1281, Kublai tried again, now with an overwhelming force, a massive fleet of more than four thousand ships (though hastily and badly built), and more than one hundred forty thousand troops from China and Korea. Japan was in a seemingly hopeless situation.

Humankind has faced only a few junctures in history as stark as this one—another such life-or-death bifurcation happened when yet another army steeped in honor, the Spartan-led force, faced an impossible task at Thermopylae in 480 B.C.

Like the Spartans, the Japanese warriors, imbued by the ethos of faithful honor, gave their lives and succeeded.[2] Hit by another hurricane, the bulk of Kublai's army sank with the fleet, and Kublai lost, for a second time. His death spared Japan a third invasion.

Here we see the two faces of honor's role in conflict—first, its potential for rendering glorious success (in this case for the Japanese side), and second, its potential for dismal irrationality (on Kublai's side). If the Japanese samurai had not given their lives, the Japan of today would not exist, at least not as distinctly as we know it. Or, if the Spartans had not sacrificed themselves, the Europe of today would be drastically different, perhaps part of a Persian empire. These were the successes of honor-driven approaches.

However, there is also the second, much darker side. Japanese honor in the twentieth century—without compromise until death—brought Kublai's disastrous final failure also to Japan. The problem was that honor had become a psychological end in itself, divorced from reality. The emperor's warriors brought unspeakable cruelty and mayhem. Nearly three million Japanese died. In China, about fifteen million people perished. The Japanese empire was lost. Only humiliating defeat was reaped.

Why do I make this point? "Long after it had become obvious that Japan was doomed, its leaders all the way up to the emperor remained unable to contemplate surrender. They were psychologically blocked, capable only of stumbling forward."[3] The Japanese had "become prisoners of their own war rhetoric of holy war, death before dishonor, blood debts to their war dead, the inviolability of the emperor-centered 'national polity,' the imminence of the decisive battle that would turn the tide against the 'Chinese bandits' and stay the 'demonic Anglo-Americans.'"[4]

Is this rigid definition of honor a purely Japanese problem? No. John W. Dower, in his book *Embracing Defeat*, reminds us that the lessons to be learned from the Japanese experience are relevant to humankind at large: "neither the concepts, nor the debates, nor the weight of historical memory in these struggles are peculiar to Japan."[5]

The Japanese lessons are of acute importance today, everywhere around the globe. Unless we wish to be psychologically blocked, and end up compulsively committing suicide and homicide, we must learn to understand emotion and conflict and how they relate to changes in the environment.

We can also learn from the present state of affairs in Japan, which demonstrates how today's shrinking world is prone to intensify the tendency for honor to breed disaster, fanning ill feelings as never before in history. If Japan were isolated from the world—as it was until 1868—the nation's "inner affairs" would not be known to anybody else. In contrast, in 2005, modifications in Japanese school textbooks ("in order to make our children proud of Japan") triggered enraged mass demonstrations in China and Korea, who felt that Japan was trying to "gloss over its past." Floyd Rudmin explains what happened: "It is the humiliation of history. Japan's neighbors are now furious because Japan has again tried to gloss over its history of humiliating its neighbors, but Japan in turns finds it humiliating that it alone is required to continually account for and atone for its historical past."[6]

In short, honor (or, more precisely, the ranking order that is entailed in systems of honor and often in systems of power in general—read more in Chapter 5), driven by emotions, can have horrendous outcomes. Its potential for dismal destructiveness was always apparent, even in the past; however, its occasional successes worked to outweigh the perception of risk. Yet in today's interdependent world, the concept of honor (and concepts of power that define power as "power over others") is no longer suitable, and its outfall is even more negative. Destructive conflict is created unnecessarily when honor steers conflict resolution today. Today, global interdependence represents the ultimate deterrent for violent conflict resolution informed by honor—we need to learn much more constructive approaches to conflict.

This is the present human predicament, and it plays out everywhere. As I write these sentences, the news provides ample evidence, at local as much as at global levels. As a local example, in the February 2008 elections in Serbia, one candidate, Tomislav Nikolic, wished to turn back into the past of national honor, while the other, Boris Tadic, vowed to pull his people into the future of an interdependent world. Globally, two "credit crunches," a financial and an ecological one, make clear that the approaches of the past no longer work. The ecological crisis is the more serious of those two threats, because the loss from environmental degradation is higher than the loss from the banking crisis—a recent study puts the annual cost of forest loss at between $2 trillion and $5 trillion.[7] Human demands on the world's natural resources reach nearly a third more than Earth can sustain.[8]

Back into the familiar but outdated past, or forward into a yet unfamiliar future, this is always the question.

Adam and Eve

War and international relations play out conflict at a macro level, but all levels of conflict—from the macro to the meso to the micro—have been affected by emotions throughout history as the human species evolved new ways of ordering its societies. The following situation illustrates this relationship between emotion, conflict, and history at the micro level.

Imagine that you are a social worker and Eve is a woman in your district. She is regularly and severely beaten by her husband, Adam. You are afraid that Eve might not survive the abuse. Neighbors describe scenes of shouting and crying, and the bruises on Eve's body are only too obvious. You visit her as frequently as your schedule permits. You try to convince her to protect herself better, for example by leaving her unsafe home and seeking refuge in protected housing designed for cases like hers. You consider her a victim and her husband a perpetrator. You explain that "domestic chastisement" has long been outlawed. You suggest that Adam's behavior humiliates her and urge her to develop a "healthy" rage as a first step toward collecting sufficient strength to change her life for the better. In your eyes, this situation clearly represents a destructive conflict loaded with hot and violent emotion and you wish to contribute to its constructive resolution.

Sometimes, Eve is so exhausted that she seems to listen to you. At other times, however, she resists you, arguing: "Beating me is my husband's way of loving me! I am not a victim! It is all my fault! I bring it upon myself! My grandmother taught me that arrogant women sin against divine traditions! We have to respect our traditions!" Her husband, of course, adamantly refuses to be labeled a perpetrator. He accuses *you* of viciously disturbing the peace of his home, of violating his male honor. To Adam, there is no destructive conflict, no suffering victim, no violent perpetrator—except in your mind, the mind of the social worker, a third party.

You cannot help remembering the South African elite and its defensiveness about apartheid. You also think of the current attention to so-called honor killings and how this practice has recently moved from the neutral category of cultural practice to the accusatory category of violation of human rights. Or the Indian caste system, that has only recently been renamed "Indian apartheid." All such framings—unsurprisingly—do not meet with friendly acceptance from the supposed perpetrators.

Adam and Eve will accompany us throughout this book. I use their story to highlight my points. Let me begin with a bit of playful linguistic engineering. We are used to saying "Adam and Eve." In the spirit of the argument of this book, that those who are often invisible, including women, need to become more visible, let us place Eve's name first in the rest of this book: "Eve and Adam."

What to Expect from This Book

This book has no place in the old world of coercive hierarchies. Its very existence (for example, the fact that it found a publisher) is proof that the large-scale paradigmatic transition that it seeks to explain and to promote is already well under way.

This large-scale transition has to do with the two definitorial contemporary trends summarized at the outset of this book—the shrinking of our world, combined with the human rights message. The core ideal of human rights is that every human being is born with equal rights and dignity. Many human rights defenders concentrate on rights. This book focuses on dignity, or, more precisely, on the power and potential entailed in the ideal of equality in dignity, or nondomination,[9] to liberate the full range of our emotions, enable us to "wage good conflict,"[10] and help us transcend conflict and create a very different, much more benign world. This focus dovetails with the Lévinasian interpretation of human rights (the Kantian interpretation sees human rights as abstract principle, while the Lévinasian interpretation emphasizes care and respect for the other).[11]

This book brings the good news that capitalizing on the potential of the ideal of equality in dignity is the path to more well-being for individuals and communities, including the global society. This is a Mandela-book about dignity and how realizing its promise can help improve the human condition at all levels—from micro to meso to macro levels. Mandela was the inspiring spirit of his movement—he gave the task of institution building to experts as soon as he became the president of his country. Even though this process would have needed more of his guidance, partnering spirit with expertise is the recipe for successful social change.[12] Similarly, this is not a book on the technicalities of human rights. This book speaks to today's need for the spirit of Mandela to permeate our lives and our world, so that we find the way and the courage to empower and guide our experts to implement the appropriate solutions.

This book has two main audiences. First, those who have embraced the core ideal of human rights ethics of equality in dignity for all (including those who believe that through being born into a Western democratic country, their lives are automatically permeated with the necessary awareness and skills to realize equality in dignity), and, second, those for whom this ideal is less familiar and who condone a ranked world where "higher" beings dominate "lower" beings (for the sake of readability, I often use the term *honor* to connote such a world).

Both audiences need to learn more about the overt and covert effects of the traditional practice of ranking human worthiness, and how everybody is still affected today, even the most enlightened human rights defender. The reason is that in historical terms, the ideal of equality in dignity—albeit always around—moved to the forefront only very recently. The Declaration of the Rights of Man and of the Citizen, for example, was approved by the National Assembly of France as late as 1789. The ideal of equal dignity for all is still weak. The concept of unequal dignity, or ranked honor, is still making itself felt, overtly and covertly, all over the world. Even where the ideal of equality in dignity seems sufficiently influential, it is continuously in danger of being undermined (not least recent American foreign policy was legitimized by the American Southern honor[13] of "they want to humiliate us and we have to humiliate them"[14]). In other words, *rankism* is still rampant—Bob W. Fuller labels the abuse of rank "rankism," a practice that becomes humiliating with the rise of human rights ideals.[15]

Those who think that they have left behind the spirit of submission/domination that ranked honor breeds, those who believe they have safely embraced the ideal of equality in dignity and are immune to perpetrating rankism may gain unexpected insights from this book. Western citizens, Western scholars included, are largely shielded from the degree of pain that flows from the systemic domination that the majority of humankind knows only too well. This causes many Westerners to underestimate the cultural and social remnants of past domination in their own lives—in the absence of overt reminders, covert effects can lurk the more unimpeded.

This book attempts to show how the concept of ranked honor is the single largest "master manipulation" ever perpetrated (and still virulent, see more in Chapter 8). The driving force is the hideous suggestion entailed in ranked honor that it is unavoidable, either divinely ordained or nature's order, that dignity is not equal but that "higher" beings are meant to preside over "lower" beings who are expected to subject themselves to their masters' belief systems and decisions. In this way, ranked honor underlies and facilitates a host of other manipulations—it gives the power to define what is and what ought to be to a small master elite.

Only if we deeply understand the ideals of ranked honor versus equality in dignity can we forge a constructive transition to the latter. It is encouraging that slavery and apartheid are no longer regarded as legitimate almost everywhere on the globe. Or, for the most recent success on this path, it is a step forward that more than one hundred nations agreed in Dublin on May 30, 2008, on a treaty that will ban current designs of cluster bombs. Yet our psyches—even among the most enlightened human rights advocates—are still filled with bits and pieces of the emotional cluster bombs that our past cultural and social environments placed there. Inside ourselves and between ourselves, myriad destructive processes are still at work—we have yet to fully grasp the opportunities that human rights offer.

The old custom of foot binding is perhaps the most evocative example of the indirect impact of honor, showing how the pain of subjugation could become institutionalized into "what is appropriate." The tradition of painfully twisted deformed feet began late in the Tang Dynasty (618–906) and flourished until it was finally outlawed in the 1911 Revolution of Sun Yat-Sen. It began as a luxury among the rich but soon spread throughout society. For an entire millennium, millions of young Chinese women paid with a painful life to serve the honor of their husbands. The women were reduced to the status of dependent and helpless toys through this practice, while their husbands gained honorable status by imitating their elite.

Howard Levy describes the torturous details of feet bones being repeatedly broken, their growth stunted, to fit into the desired lotus shape.[16] It became a prerequisite for marriage and was especially hard on the poor, who could not afford servants.

Foot binding is now outlawed. The practice of so-called honor killing is slowly following suit, indicating increasing resistance against the traditional concept of ranked honor. However, the world is still permeated with "honorable" foot-binding practices. One of those practices—the denial of the significance of the full range of human emotions—forms the basis for much of this book.

The basic philosophy that produced Chinese foot binding reigned wherever hierarchical societies prevailed throughout the past ten thousand years. Underlings in coercive hierarchies were routinely forced into artificial incapacitation. Mutilation and handicap, physically and psychologically, were seen as normal for underlings. Health, as understood today, was beside the point (a recent example, the way the ruling elite tackled the 2008 cyclone Nargis in Burma, can illustrate this approach).

In *The Chalice and the Blade: Our History, Our Future*,[17] Eisler describes how otherwise widely divergent societies, from the samurai of Japan to the Aztecs of Meso-America, were characterized by very similar hierarchies of domination and a rigidly male-dominant "strong-man" rule, both in the family and state. Hierarchies of domination were maintained by a high degree of institutionalized (socially accepted) violence, ranging from wife and child beating within the family to aggressive warfare on the larger tribal or national level.

In the samurai bushido culture (or the Spartan military culture, for that matter) it was obligatory for males to maintain fitness and a ruthless willingness to be ready to die without fear and hesitation, while producing warriors was the role of women. Everything was subordinate to preparedness for defense against invaders, only the methods of enforcing this subordination varied. Sparta, for example, wanted its women to put their wombs at the service of the larger community, encouraging them to bear sons even for Spartans who were not their husbands. In most other cultures, women's wombs were the exclusive assets of their husbands. The traditional social construction of gender difference was predicated upon the anticipation of war.[18] *Biopolitique* (as described, for example, by Michel Foucault[19]) prepared the male body to become a soldier's body and the female body the reproductive body for preferably male offspring.[20] Nationalist discourse before and during World War II in Japan and Germany followed this strategy.[21]

Most if not all aspects of gender roles were forged within a submission/domination paradigm. During long stretches of human history, in most cultures, it was considered prosocial for a husband to use a "firm hand" on his wife and children. Such practices are still observed today. Wife beaters enjoyed acceptance and approbation both in law and in popular culture in many cultures around the world for almost as long as historians can remember.[22] Domestic chastisement was not yet dubbed domestic violence. *Coverture* is the legal concept that merges a woman's legal rights with those of her husband. It was part of the common law of England and the United States throughout most of the 1800s. Through marriage, a woman lost her existence outside of her husband and had no individual rights of her own. (I do not expand on the topic of gender in this book, but reserve this for *Gender and Humiliation: The Power of Dignity in Love, Sex, and Parenthood*.[23])

Gender roles were not the only ranked roles. Power-over structures permeated all walks of life. The overall cultural practice, since the inception of early civilizations some ten thousand years ago, was to "teach lessons" to underlings to "remind them of their place" and ensure "stability and order"—be it in countries, organizations, companies, or families.[24] Slavery, bondage, serfdom, feudalism, lords, and vassals, apartheid, coverture—terms abound to describe the various ways a person could be inserted into a ranked order.

Still nowadays, in many segments of global society, the pain of a beaten wife or a disciplined underling is regarded as good for them and for the social order as a whole, similar to a medical treatment that is good only when it hurts. By accepting painful treatment, the targeted person shows "respect" for the overall order. This kind of suffering is considered constructive, not a sign of a conflict that needs resolution. In such a context a loving husband may be expected to chastise his "disobedient" wife, and she might expect herself to love him for his devotion to duty. Trauma therapists, or other conflict experts, are not welcome in such contexts, because the situation is not defined as conflictual or traumatic.

The social worker, the human rights defender, and not least you the reader, I assume, are appalled. You cannot help think of the phrase "false consciousness," which has been coined to describe people who do not feel suitably humiliated and do not want to liberate themselves from humiliating living conditions.[25]

No doubt, we live in times of transition where traditional and new normative universes frequently clash. The changes in how emotion and conflict are framed—how "one ought to feel" and what "one ought to regard as a conflict"—contribute to fierce battles. Hot discord and conflict arise—seemingly where there was concord and "peace and quiet" before. Adam is not mistaken in saying that the social worker "disturbs" the "peace" of his house.

Virtually every social worker and human rights defender has been caught in this frustrating situation. Human rights defenders around the world face criticism for violating the cultural honor and private and national sovereignty of the people they seek to serve.

In this conundrum, questions arise such as: When can we label a situation as "conflict?" When and in what ways are emotions of suffering, pain and rage part of a conflict that calls for our attention? And when not? Who decides this?

The Adams of this world insist on respect for their culture of ranked honor and cry "humiliation" when criticized for cowing their underlings. On the other side are those who claim that ranked honor represents nothing but a deeply humiliating lack of respect for the equality in dignity that every human being ought to enjoy. In these head-on "clashes of humiliation," emotion and conflict reinforce one another. As a result, instead of arriving in a world of more dignity, humankind continues to spiral through violent cycles of humiliation.

If experts from another galaxy were to rate the quality of humankind's change management abilities, our species could well find itself at the bottom of the class. To use traffic as metaphor, the transition from ranking human worthiness to equal human dignity resembles switching from left-hand driving to right-hand driving (or vice versa), because ranking the essence of a person's worthiness as low or high cannot be achieved at the same time as unranking it as equal. If everybody drives on one side—either side—there are few problems. However, severe problems arise when some insist on driving on the left side and others drive on the right. Combining both sets of rules guarantees accidents. Unfortunately, today humankind lives in a global world where left-hand and right-hand driving occur together. Practices that rank human worthiness collide with those that unrank them. We must decide. Either all drive on the right side or all drive on the left side. Ranked honor and equal dignity are inherently irreconcilable. Ranking and unranking cannot be done concurrently (here I speak of the ranking or unranking of the core essence of a person, not of rankings that leave the core value of a person untouched, like functional hierarchies, humorous rankings, or rankings of humility—read more in Chapter 5).

The intergalactic experts would ask: Why does humankind accept so many accidents? Why do they carry out the transition from a traditional culture of submission/domination to a more contemporary culture of equality in dignity so inefficiently? The experts would have to concede that such stark phenomena as slavery and apartheid have been abandoned, at least on paper, however, that the transition is still managed in a dreadfully amateurish manner, unnecessarily heating up emotions in necessary conflicts.

There are many reasons for humankind's failure to manage the transition from ranked honor to equal dignity better. I emphasize three crucial reasons in Chapter 8: First, the transition proceeds both too slowly and too rapidly for people to understand that it is happening at all, and that they must influence it proactively and constructively. Second, those who have the resources to effect change are not sufficiently motivated to invest them, whereas those who have the motivation lack the resources. To me, the most insidious reason is the third one, namely, that cultural practices of the past linger on covertly. Covert manipulation exerts a stealth influence that is intricately linked to feelings, to the fact that they are strong and cannot be avoided. Humans need recognition and validation and they need to feel that they belong. This need motivates them to forge valuable connections with their fellow beings, but, as a side effect, it makes them also vulnerable to covert manipulation.

Those three reasons are linked to the fact that both traditional and new normative universes, with their diametrically opposed sets of values, evaluations, and scripts for action, are part of largely invisible "attitudes of everyday life." Therefore, many people are only dimly aware of the deep structure of the transition—they react haphazardly to its fallout, not to its causes—and are therefore unable to own and guide the change constructively.

We need a bird's-eye view to see larger patterns, patterns that can help us own the current transition. However, this is a much more difficult task than is generally believed. I learned it the hard way when I began to train to fly gliders (and later small airplanes) at the age of fifteen. I will never forget the panic I felt when I once failed to see the airstrip from the air. My glider sank, there was little lift, and I had no idea where to find the airstrip for safe landing. Prior to this incident, I was proud of having an excellent spatial orientation. Subsequently, I had to admit humbly that one needs to make a special effort to connect micro, meso, and macro levels.

Unfortunately, humankind has problems making the necessary emergency efforts to find suitable landing strips for our global problems.

Research in the field of intercultural communication offers help, because clashes that flow from the global normative transition toward human rights ethics are similar to clashes between local cultural mindsets. Intercultural research indicates that creativity is enhanced through interactions of mutually contradictory but equally compelling forces.[26] Disorienting dilemmas, those that unsettle our fundamental beliefs and call our values into question, can bring about transformative learning.[27] When cultural assumptions are called into question, a "stress-adaptation-growth" process unfolds.[28]

Regrettably, adaptation and growth can also fail. Violent conflict may ensue. Evidently, emotion and conflict, in their interaction, take up a core position in this contemporary historic transition, including meta-emotions, or how people feel about feelings.[29]

This book brings an optimistic message to all world citizens, East and West, North and South, and particularly to researchers of emotion and conflict: The human rights ideal of equality in dignity entails the potential to liberate the fullness of human emotions and dignify the entire human

condition, including conflict—human rights "unbind," so to speak. However, this liberation will not succeed unless it is proactively and constructively supported. Emotion and conflict researchers need to play a
central role.

From a bird's-eye view, we can see that an emergency is at hand for
humankind. Globally, the human sociosphere and biosphere are under
threat. This emergency is so urgent that sacrificing the normality of one's
life is warranted. Unfortunately, it is much easier to buy into being manipulated into the narrow views of "normality." This was the case in Nazi
Germany, when people ought to have stood up and not stood by.[30] It is the
case also in today's world. We need to invest our lives, as Mandela did, in
positive change. In times of mortal threat, clinging to our normal lives
might be fatal.

We need to instigate necessary conflict—not avoid it—and learn to wage
good conflict by investing our emotions in mature Mandela-like ways.

This book is organized in three parts. Part I: How Emotions Can Fuel
Conflict, examines the nature of emotion, how our emotions can generate
and perpetuate conflict, and how psychosocial contexts affect both emotion and conflict.

Part II: How Emotions Can Maximize and Minimize Conflict, examines
the nature of humiliation, how the humiliating effects of history and culture maximize conflict, and how the dignifying effects of human rights
have the potential to minimize conflict.

Part III: How We Can Dignify Emotion and Conflict, examines how we
can change our personal attitudes and reactions, as well as our political
and cultural contexts, to transcend conflict through dignifying emotions
and waging good conflict.

Margaret Mead said, "Never doubt that a small group of thoughtful,
committed citizens can change the world. Indeed, it is the only thing that
ever has."

This book is part of a growing movement of thoughtful, committed citizens. Let us join hands to liberate the full range of human emotions, un-
leash their creativity to wage good conflict, and invest them in creating a
better world.

The late Studs Terkel, famous oral historian based in Chicago, at the age
of ninety-six said in an interview, "I want to be remembered as a man who
made trouble where trouble was needed."[31]

PART I

How Emotions Can
Fuel Conflict

CHAPTER 1

WHAT ARE EMOTIONS?

Have you ever loved? And been betrayed? And felt like a fool? Then you know the strength of emotions and how treacherous they can be. I worked as a clinical psychologist in Cairo, Egypt, from 1984 to 1991. I watched the Western concept of love-marriage enter Egyptian culture. Egyptian grandparents warned against it. They told me that millennia of human experience had revealed to humankind that marrying a person with whom one had fallen in love was almost a guarantee for the failure of a marriage. To them, feelings were too unstable a foundation.

Are they so wrong? Divorce rates in the West indicate that basing an institution that should provide a secure environment for children on fragile feelings between the parents entails some inherent contradictions that can only be bridged if the partners are extremely emotionally intelligent. Unfortunately, not all are. Stability is more easily achieved by making institutions somewhat independent from feelings. Or not?

I frequently meet highly educated women in their thirties, all around the world, desperate to found a family. Those from traditional honor societies typically rejected their parents' wish to arrange a marriage for them—they put their education first, thus following their sisters in more individualistic Western societies. All wait for the "right" man. When he does not turn up, they gradually lower their requirements, step by step. At forty, many of these highly educated women sigh: "If only I could turn the clock back, be young again, and have somebody find a reliable father for my children for me! Forget about romantic love! It is much too fragile! Love for children is much deeper and I have now lost this love!"

These are emotions: hugely important, but also able to fool us. Only if we learn to guide our emotions constructively, can we hope to reap their rewards.

How This Book Belongs within a Larger Context

Research on emotions usually focuses on affect, feeling, emotion, script, character, and personality, while larger cultural contexts and an analysis of historic periods in human history are less emphasized. Dialogue with other academic fields and other cultural realms is not easy to achieve even in today's increasingly connected world.

I have lived as a global citizen for more than thirty years and have acquired an understanding of many cultural realms. The result is that I paint a broad picture that includes historic and transcultural dimensions. In this book, the usual approach is therefore inversed: larger cultural contexts as they were shaped throughout human history are used as lenses to understand emotion and conflict. This is not to deny the importance of research on affect, feeling, emotion, script, character, and personality but to expand it.

I began my work on humiliation in 1996 with my doctoral research on the genocidal killings that occurred in Rwanda in 1994 and in Somalia in 1988, on the backdrop of Nazi Germany. In 2001, I defended a dissertation thesis titled *The Psychology of Humiliation: Somalia, Rwanda/Burundi, and Hitler's Germany*.[1] Since then, I have expanded my studies in (among others) Europe, Southeast Asia, and the United States. I am currently building a theory of humiliation that is transcultural and transdisciplinary, entailing elements from anthropology, history, social philosophy, social psychology, sociology, and political science.[2]

In other words, my life is profoundly affected by the historical transitions that humankind is now enduring. Emotion and conflict—the topic of this book—are deeply inscribed into the same historical transition. Likewise, all researchers, including researchers on emotion and conflict, and their readers do not live in a vacuum. We are all part of our social contexts.

Let me briefly paint these contexts in a little more depth. Emotions were used as covert tools in the power dynamics of the past. Those in power manipulated emotions to win potential conflicts preemptively, before they could erupt openly. The powerful, as well as the "successfully duped" powerless, have great difficulties comprehending this manipulation, primarily because, as mentioned earlier, it is covert and we are typically blind to covert manipulation (read more in Chapter 8). Everybody is to a certain degree a victim, the powerless as much as the powerful, all born into preexisting cultural and social contexts that frame and define them. The stories of Eve and Adam and Japan's history are meant to illustrate the immense struggle that is associated with this liberation process.

In former times, power elites treated their underlings as lifeless tools, at best as domesticated animals. Tools made from nonliving material feel no emotions, and domesticated animals can reasonably be expected to be content when they receive sufficient food and shelter, possibly even when slaughtered. The full range of human emotions is perhaps the most significant component that distinguishes humans from nonhumans. And this range is precisely what has been denied to the majority of human beings during the past millennia almost everywhere on the globe. Interestingly, this has been achieved by coopting the victims. Even more astonishingly, it was only a few hundred years ago that this pain-generating tragedy began to be unmasked and changed. (Many religions teach that all human beings deserve to be treated as equals in dignity. However, in the past, these teachings were usually coopted into hierarchical institutions.)

Dictatorial regimes must fear one outcome more than anything: What if subalterns unmask the fact that they are held in bondage? What if they discover that they are treated like lifeless tools or domesticated animals? What if they wonder why they have to swallow humiliation? What if they doubt why they have no other options but to live and die by their masters' whims? What if they question why they do not enjoy respect as full human beings? What if they notice that those in power not only disregard the lives of others, but also display an astonishing lack of realistic view of their own interests?[3] What if underlings were to find out that their leaders engage in a march of folly?[4]

If we put ourselves into the position of totalitarian elites (using *realistic empathy*[5]), we may expect them to support research on emotions connected to the disobedient disturbance of calm and order. The goal of such research would be to help underlings manage anger better, so they can be more compliant. Or, they may fund research on the masters' own "rational" yearnings for security. Dictators usually prefer their conflict experts to focus on "safer" themes, on "harder" subjects, like food, shelter, or the strength of the enemies' weapons arsenals, in sum, on "resources."

Yet resources—even when they are scarce—do not automatically cause problems. It is a recurrent theme in peace psychology that environmental scarcity is fundamentally a psychological problem.[6] Everything can be negotiated pragmatically—everything, that is, except hot emotions. There have long been elaborate cultural scripts, for example, within families, for tackling the problem of dwindling resources with cooperation. These scripts focus on such divergent strategies as distributing resources equally to everybody, inventing new ways to increase the pie of resources, and finding alternative resources. This cooperation breaks down, however, when feelings get hostile, when in-groups define others as unfriendly out-groups with whom cooperation is "unthinkable," even if it would solve all resource issues and would serve everybody's survival.

This little word, "unthinkable," testifies how strong emotions can be. Addiction illustrates their strength. Many addictions are psychological. We all know that it is useless to say to addicted persons that much of their predicament is *only* psychological and therefore easily stoppable. If it were that simple, there would be no psychological addiction. Past experiences of humiliation, likewise, can be hard to shake. They are often remembered years later, hotly and often obsessively, and in great detail. Feelings of humiliation and fear of humiliation are what I call "the nuclear bomb of the emotions."

The current economic crisis may be inscribed into this dynamic, at least partly. Until recently, it was "unthinkable" to doubt the belief that the "free market," defined as unfettered profit maximization, would safely protect against future humiliation, and always be as "victorious" as over past Soviet humiliation.

Emotions can be more impervious causes of disaster than the need for survival: Emotions can even override survival, as the Kublai Khans of this world have shown. Why else would power elites give the lives of millions in duel-like violent conflicts, risk the loss of access to essential resources, and endanger national survival? Fear of dishonorable cowardice![7]

In other words, emotion and self-interested long-term survival do not necessarily go together. This contradiction becomes particularly visible when leaders mix the honor talk of "it is unthinkable to talk with the enemy," with survival rhetoric. This contradiction is starkest when elites, while making deadly decisions for their underlings, not only survive but live in luxury, gaining glory points paid for by the lives of their underlings. Throughout history, underlings have died for the honor of their masters, advised to define their own honor as faithful identification with their masters, without regard for their own health and survival and without questioning the reality of honor. Adolf Hitler required his followers to be ready to die for him "with enthusiasm" (*begeistert sterben*).[8] And at the end, even the powerful themselves may pay with their own lives. Hitler's "glory" ultimately ended in wretched death also for him personally.

The current global financial crisis offers yet another illustration. If we read David J. Rothkopf, a small number (approximately 6,000) of largely unelected powerful people around the globe have shaped the world during the past decades in ways that the financial meltdown became possible, and they did this by the same mixture of self-centered power play that lacks consideration for long-term survival to the degree that it is self- and other-destructive.[9] In other words, power seems to make arrogant to the point of blindness even for one's own self-interest. Former Federal Reserve chairman Alan Greenspan said that he was "in a state of shocked disbelief" and had been wrong in thinking that relying on banks to use their self-interest would be enough to protect shareholders and their equity.[10]

One of the premises of this book is that humankind needs to embark on an effort to guide self- and other-destructive power players, be it in the West or in the rest, from the oligarchs to the bin Ladens of this world, to let the Mandelas build lives of equality in dignity for all.

If we wish to create a decent world, this entails that not least scholars must be careful whose research they conduct. Funders wedded to traditional authoritarian paradigms may not like it, nevertheless, we need to study and understand emotions better and acknowledge their vulnerability to misuse. Only then we will be able to devise Mandela-like approaches to transform societies in constructive ways, so that all can live the fullness of their emotions and engange in nonviolent conflict. The question to be addressed is as follows: how to make a leap into a new world by dignifying emotions and waging good conflict.

New awareness must be fostered, new skills learned, and new institutions built. Humankind must enlarge its perspective in two dimensions—*up and wider* and *down and deeper*. First, a higher bird's-eye view needs to be developed, one that allows for a wider horizon, so that all humans learn to be stewards of their home planet. Second, we must go further down and deeper into detail—we have to look closer, differentiate more stringently, and refrain from sweeping generalizations and inflexible solutions.

Every aspect of human life needs scrutiny. Let me provide a brief example. Men and women need to recalibrate their definitions of rationality. As discussed, traditional honor trapped men (and their women) into a deadly dependency on "irrational" emotions. At a closer look, female "inferiority"—allegedly due to inappropriate and irrational female emotionality—may represent the true rationality of survival as opposed to the lure of deadly "higher" goals. Women often value the continued existence of the next generation over death for honorable glory—be it glory in history books or in heaven. This is not to say that women are necessarily more peaceable by nature or that they do not aspire to worthy higher goals. Freedom fighters sacrificing themselves for higher goals are widely regarded as heroes by women as well as men. What is destructive is "irrational" and counterproductive sacrifice, sacrifice informed by honor codes that are obsolete (including sacrifice invested in trying to achieve human rights through "honorable" methods of domination—human rights cannot be bombed into people's hearts and minds).

In short, emotions are worthy of the serious attention of all those who want to leave ranked honor behind, to meet in the middle, at the level of equality in dignity, where there are no more higher and lower beings.

We need to understand how emotion and conflict generate malign—or benign—self-perpetuating cycles and use that understanding to create more benign cycles of dignified cooperation. "Cooperation breeds cooperation, while competition breeds competition"[11]; this is the gist of Morton Deutsch's *crude law of social relations*, and cycles of cooperation are what we have to put in place of cycles of violence and humiliation.

In the following chapters, you will read about emotion research in more detail. The larger historic lenses that I use in my work are explained starting from Chapter 5.

If you are not interested in the details of emotion research, you can skip the following chapters and go to Chapter 5 now.

How Emotion Research Explodes

We learn from Joseph P. Forgas that "individuals who suffer certain kinds of brain damage to the prefrontal cortex that impairs affective reactions but leaves cognitive capacities intact tend to make disastrous social decisions, and their social relationships suffer accordingly, even though their intellectual problem-solving ability may be completely normal."[12]

If the preceding is true, we have to ask, "How could emotion ever be a less than burning topic for academic research?"

The answer is—as already alluded to—that cultural framings also define attitudes in academia. Until recently, the culture of the academic world favored research on cognition. Emotion is a relatively new focus. Emotions had a very bad press for a long time (see also the role of sophism discussed in Chapter 8). Emotions were seen as offensively irrational and uncontrollable, an aspect of human nature that was better denied or suppressed. Forgas said, "It is rather surprising that despite the longstanding fascination with the intriguing influence of feelings on thinking and behavior, much of the scientific research on this topic has been done only during the last two decades or so."[13]

Peter T. Coleman explains that "some scholars contend that extreme reactions seen in many conflicts are primarily based in emotional responses.[14] Yet, surprisingly, until recently researchers have paid little attention to the role that emotions play in conflict."[15] As Coleman recognizes, emotions and rationality cannot be divided. He states,

> In effect, the overall distinction between emotionality and rationality may be rather dubious when it comes to intractable conflicts, where they are often inseparable. Here, indignation, rage, and righteousness are reasons enough for retributive action. This is the essential dimension of human suffering and pain, of blood and sorrow, which in large part defines the domain of intractable conflict.[16]

However, times have changed. Words such as "revolution" or "explosion" have been used for the recent emergence of emotion as a topic for research. G. Terence Wilson prophesized, "Emotion will be to the turn of the century what the cognitive *revolution* was to the 1960s and 70s."[17] Or, "In the past twenty years, there has been a *revolution* in the study of emotion."[18] Or, "in recent years there has been an *explosion* of interest in questions concerning the nature of emotional experience,"[19] both in the scientific disciplines[20] and in lay domains.[21]

New research on mirror neurons underpins with hard evidence the recent emphasis on emotion, making headlines in such mainstream magazines as the *New York Times*: "Social emotions like guilt, shame, pride, embarrassment, disgust and lust are based on a uniquely human mirror neuron system found in a part of the brain called the insula, Dr. Keysers said."[22]

This trend co-occurs with new research that uncovers the extent to which *Homo sapiens* is a social animal that thrives on connection and cooperation rather than isolation and confrontation; see, for example, "The Human Brain: Hardwired for Connections"[23]—even rats are capable of generalized reciprocity, not just direct reciprocity.[24]

In "Why It Hurts to Be Left Out: The Neurocognitive Overlap between Physical Pain and Social Pain" we read, "Social connection is a need as basic as air, water, or food and that like these more basic needs, the absence of social connections causes pain. Indeed, we propose that the pain of social separation or rejection may not be very different from some kinds of physical pain."[25]

Scholars at the Jean Baker Miller Training Institute of Wellesley College, with their relational-cultural theory (RCT),[26] posit that relationships—specifically growth-fostering relationships—are a central human necessity. They challenge the dominance of individualistic perspective and propose a relational analysis of psychological development.[27]

Having friends (rather than money) is also at the core of happiness. Positive psychology has been catapulted into the limelight only very recently. Nobel Prize Laureate Daniel Kahneman, together with Martin Seligman and Ed Diener spell out the components of happiness.[28] *Stumbling on Happiness* is a telling prize-winning book title.[29]

In short, an optimistic view of emotion research—with many divergent approaches converging—is beginning to make significant contributions to understanding the human condition. We understand that history shapes human life (including emotions) and is in turn shaped by human interference. Increasingly we understand that we can and should intervene in this process proactively. Formerly, small elites held the ultimate power over how humans lived their lives. Today, every single individual has the potential to become a significant player. Let us become humble Mandelas who strive to optimize the human fit into a hugely complex universe, rather than Hitlers who maximize ultimately unsustainable hubris that seeks to maintain supremacy through humiliating domination.

Morton Deutsch is convinced that emotion is part of a triad that must receive attention equal to that given to cognition and motivation:[30]

It [the Lewinian way of thinking] emphasized the importance of theory; the value of experimentation for clarifying and testing ideas; the interrelatedness between the person and the environment; the interdependence of cognitive structures and motivation; the importance of understanding the individual in his or her social (group, cultural) context; the usefulness of theory for social practice; and the value of trying to change reality for the development of theory. These emphases are not unique to the Lewinian way of thinking; they characterize good social science and good social practice. But Lewin was the one who introduced them to social psychology.[31]

How the History of Research on Emotions Evolved

French Philosopher Blaise Pascal (1623–1662) believed that "the heart has its reasons which reason does not understand."[32] David Hume (1711–1776) developed a moral theory built on his belief that reason alone can not generate action. Desire or feelings are necessary to cause action. Therefore, he taught, morality is rooted in our feelings. "Reason is, and ought only to be, the slave of the passions, and can never pretend to any other office than to serve and obey them."[33]

Physicians, philosophers, poets, and priests, from Lao-Zi to René Descartes and William Shakespeare were masters of passion, however, they did not observe and define emotion in systematic ways. This was done only as late as the nineteenth century, by Guillaume Benjamin Duchenne de Bolougne, Charles Darwin, William James, and Walter B. Cannon, to name a few.[34]

A century ago, one of the fathers of psychology, William James (1842–1910), reflected as follows on emotions: "All we know is that there are dead feelings, dead ideas, and cold beliefs, and there are hot, and live ones; and when one grows hot and alive within us, everything has to recrystallize about it."[35] John Dewey (1859–1952) developed a theory of emotion, where he posited that self, object, mind, and bodily actions blend in a flow of action and interaction and that emotions interrupt this smooth flow when two tendencies to react stand in tension or conflict with each other. He places emotional experience at the core of rational behavior. For Dewey, emotion is the product of rationality, not its antithesis.[36]

More recently, other thinkers, among them Antonio R. Damasio, Gerald M. Edelman, and Robert B. Zajonc,[37] began to emphasize that emotions are central to the self: It is not just extended consciousness that props up the self but emotion and feeling.[38] William James spoke of a doer-watcher duality.[39] According to Damasio, there is a duality at the center of the phenomenal self: We can perform a task and at the same time be aware that we are performing it.[40] Arthur Deikman calls the component of the psyche that is aware of our actions the "observing self."[41] Jean Piaget posited cognition and affect within this duality.[42] "There is secondary action, the agent's reaction to his or her own action. This reaction takes the form of feeling or affect (emotion), and regulates primary action by assigning meaning and valence to the task, and subsequently prioritizing personal goals."[43]

In sum, even though there was early interest in emotion within the field of psychology, emotion was pushed into the background, first by psycho-analytic thought, then behaviorism, and then cognitive theory. In the 1960s and 1970s, only a few scholars worked on affect science—among them Silvan S. Tomkins, Magda B. Arnold, Paul Ekman, Carroll E. Izard, Klaus Scherer, and Nico H. Frijda.[44]

Readers who wish to delve deeper into the field of emotion may benefit from the following brief list of some of the debates, past and recent, which have dominated emotion research. We return to some of these debates later in this book:

- feeling and physiological theories;
- social neuroscience;
- cognitive theories;
- the affect/cognition debate;
- the question of "basic" emotions;
- the evolution of emotions;
- emotion and the brain;
- emotion and the emergence of an individuated self;
- the social construction of emotions;
- emotion and culture;
- control and emotion;
- morality and emotion;
- rationality and emotion;
- moods, temperament, and character traits;
- emotion and society;
- emotion and equality;
- emotion and economics;
- positive psychology.

What Are Emotions?

What are emotions? Are emotions cultural or biological or both? Perhaps they are nothing more than constructs of folk knowledge? Or are they merely bodily responses, nothing but hormones, skin conductance levels, and cerebral blood flows? Are there basic emotions? Affects? Feelings? Thoughts? Why do we have them? What functions do they serve? What of social emotions? Are there universal emotions across cultures? Do nonhuman animals have emotions? What are the relationships between emotions, moods, and temperament? Are emotions rational? Controllable? To which actions do emotions lead? Is there an automatic link between emotion and action?

A quote from Brian Parkinson illustrates the struggle that characterizes the very core of emotion research: "Unfortunately, the fact that psychologists have disagreed over which emotions are basic, about whether basic emotions exist, or even about whether basic emotions are emotions at all tends to detract from the credibility of the view that certain states are basically, irreducibly and inescapably emotional."[45]

In *A Framework for the History of Emotions*, William M. Reddy writes that "despite the many positive findings this new research has generated, the revolution has done little to clear up the vexed question of what, exactly, emotions are. Disagreements persist, uncertainties abound."[46] "We don't agree, as a discipline, on the nature of what we are studying."[47]

Jon Elster, as well, is skeptical of the prospects for a unified theory of emotions. He describes how emotions often transmute into one another: Love can turn to jealousy, jealousy to rage, rage to remorse, as the situation evolves.[48]

Jan Smedslund is just as skeptical. He offers a profound psychologic criticism of mainstream psychological research.[49] Smedslund warns social scientists against trying to appear scientific by mistaking "scientifically looking" methods for sound science in places where core rules are blatantly apparent. He writes: "The finding that all bachelors are in fact unmarried males cannot be said to be empirical." Smedslund warns that a lot of psychological research is as pointless as trying to make surveys to find out "whether bachelors really are all males."[50] This, Smedslund states, would be an inexcusable waste of time and resources, and in addition a basic confusion of "the *ontological* status" of psychology's research object.[51] He argues that "even though ordinary words have very variable meanings, they also have a stable core meaning, and many partly overlapping words may also refer to the same core meaning. In summary, it may be possible to explicate a skeleton system of important concepts underlying the complex surface of an ordinary language."[52]

Thomas J. Scheff cautions that, as long as clearly defined concepts are missing in emotion research, collecting data resembles pseudo-research. He uses astronomy as an illustration and suggests that as long as it was not understood that the sun—not the Earth—was at the center of our system, it was impossible to determine the position of the planets. Likewise, according to Scheff, most current research on emotion is stymied because clear definitions of emotions are missing. Scientists, falling victim to the assumptions made by their own cultures, merely grope in the dark and reiterate their cultural/social status quo, rather than doing substantive new research.[53]

Not only the discussions of emotions at the individual level are controversial and undecided, so are those of social and collective emotions at the macro level: "Our discourse about world politics is replete with 'angry' and 'fearful' states, 'traumatized' and 'resentful' societies, and so on."[54] Alexander Wendt asks, "How can we make sense of such emotions talk?" He responds with explaining that scholarship on collective emotions in the field of international relations studies is almost completely lacking. Talk about emotions is treated as an "as if" fiction, an approach that discourages deeper probing. Wendt proposes to push the quantum argument further, "to the conclusion that collectives do have a kind of consciousness."[55]

Paul Saurette agrees.

> Despite a growing awareness about the importance of emotions to global politics, the discipline of International Relations is still working towards adequate theorisations and investigations of their role. This is particularly noticeable in the fact that there has been little sustained, scholarly examination of the effects of various emotions on the shape and orientation of the US foreign policy reaction to 9/11.[56]

Robert Jervis seconds this. "Beliefs are central to political psychology, but in many ways remain undertheorized."[57] Jervis underscores how "over the past decade or so, psychologists and political psychologists have come to see (to 'believe'?) that a sharp separation between cognition and affect is impossible and that a person who embodied pure rationality, undisturbed by emotion, would be a monster if she were not an impossibility."[58] However, says Jervis, the problem is that beliefs have two functions, (1) understanding the world and reality testing, and (2) social and psychological functions of meeting the psychological and social needs to live with oneself and others.[59] When we want to understand "why people believe what they do, whether these beliefs are warranted by the available evidence, and whether they are correct,"[60] we need to differentiate these tasks, rather than fuse them. (To link back to our earlier discussion of honor, the belief in honor norms, for example, can be functional for "meeting the psychological and social needs to live with oneself and others," however, disastrous from the perspective of "reality testing.")

By using examples of World War I, Japan's involvement in World War II, and the 2003 Iraq war, Jervis illustrates how the lack of clarity and awareness that typically clouds our beliefs and emotions can lead to catastrophic misjudgments. See here another of his examples, Vietnam:

> Nixon and Kissinger told themselves, each other, and the South Vietnamese that this threat [that blatantly breaking the peace agreement would call forth an American military response] was credible enough to prevent major North Vietnamese violations and that they would carry it out if it were not. While it is impossible to be certain whether they believed what they were saying, my guess is that what they were expressing was something between a hope and an expectation. They partly believed it, or believed it on some days but not others, or believed it with some probability but less than certainty.[61]

We are tempted to conclude that speculation and uncertainty—or worse, blissful ignorance—reign at the very fundaments of large areas of social science. We are compelled to appreciate that not only consciousness and meaning but also our understanding of emotion are deeply affected by these ontological uncertainties.

Let us now turn to the brighter view that has already been evoked. Keltner and Haidt suggest that there is considerable convergence emerging in the field of emotion research and that recent findings have brought the field to new levels and provided new synergies. The authors argue that, for example, both evolutionary theorists and social constructivists are now regarded to be "right" in their views:

> Primordial emotions are universal, biologically based, coordinated response systems that have evolved to enable humans to meet the problems of physical survival, reproduction, and group governance. The creative process of culture, however, loosens the link between the primordial emotions and their functions, finding new solutions to old problems and new uses for old emotions.[62]

There is also convergence between emotion research and neuroscience. Cognitive psychologists such as Pierre Philippot and Alexandre Schaefer document that emotional processing occurs at several levels, from two to five.[63] Neuroscience mirrors this. Many therefore believe that an integrated theory of neuroscience structure and cognitive functioning of emotion will soon emerge. "We do not have to argue over whether emotions are discrete or dimensional, but under what circumstances they manifest as one or the other. The question of nature versus nurture becomes pedantic if automatic programs in the brain can be influenced by learning and active cognition."[64]

It may surprise many to learn that the field where phenomena such as consciousness are particularly hotly discussed is physics. Some physicists regard consciousness as no less than "the dominant force that determines the nature of existence."[65] The reason for this astonishing state of affairs is that quantum mechanics undermine the classical scientific paradigm that there is an objective reality "out there" independent of consciousness "in here." The fact that quantum mechanics may indeed represent a formidable challenge to contemporary notions of space, time, reality, and the nature of the human mind is currently increasingly discussed.[66]

Let me briefly deepen this point. Metaphysics is the branch of philosophy that reflects on "the study of being" (in Greek, *ontology*[67]). The dominant Western metaphysical orientation that underpinned the past centuries was *dualism*. Dualism holds that ultimately there are two kinds of substance. Descartes's dualistic view of a mind-body dichotomy is perhaps the most widely known expression of dualism.[68] Dualism is to be distinguished from *pluralism*, which holds that ultimately there are many kinds of substance. Dualism must also be differentiated from *monism*, which is the metaphysical and theological view that all is one, either the mental (idealism) or the physical (materialism and physicalism). Physicalism, the ontological orientation of most modern scientists, is thus a monist concept, holding that that there are no kinds of things other than physical things. Dualism must furthermore be distinguished from an orientation that many find difficult to grasp, that of *nondualism*, or "not-one, not-two."[69]

Many agree today that the dualism of Western thought created serious problems for the individual and society.[70] Dualism-Manichaeism-Armageddon (the DMA syndrome) is decried by peace researcher Johan Galtung as the core path from conflict to war.[71] Creating and firing up Manichaean self/other and good/evil dualisms in people prepares them for violence and convinces them that wars are worth fighting.[72] Recent forms of ecopsychology and transpersonal ecology hold that the dualistic split between planet and self must be healed.[73] Also economists and sociologists have become wary of dualism, criticizing it for exaggerating conceptual divisions and promoting an oversimplified, reductive outlook—the notion of duality has been suggested as an alternative to dualism.[74] Critical realists like Tony Lawson diagnose the world that mainstream economists study as out of phase with the underlying ontology of economic regularities.[75] Not least, the critique of the dualism of *binary oppositions* (a term coined by Ferdinand de Saussure) is an important part of postfeminism, postcolonialism, postanarchism, and critical race theory.[76]

Contemporary scientists usually are physicalists. However, since physicalism does not hold all the answers, at least not physicalism that is fashioned on Newtonian physics, quantum social science is being proposed—"human beings are in effect 'walking wave particle dualities,' not classical material objects."[77]

Anton Zeilinger, renowned physicist at the University of Vienna and director of the Vienna branch of the Institute of Quantum Optics and Quantum Information (IQOQI), explains in an interview:[78]

> I believe that quantum physics tells us something very profound about the world. And that is that the world is not the way it is independently of us. That the characteristics of the world are to a certain extent dependent on us." [I see two freedoms,] First the freedom of the experimenter in choosing the measuring equipment—that depends on my freedom of will; and then the freedom of nature in giving me the answer it pleases. The one freedom conditions the other, so to speak. This is a very fine property. It's too bad the philosophers don't spend more time thinking about it.[79]

Imants Barušs is a psychologist who works on quantum consciousness, altered states of consciousness, self-transformation, mathematical modeling of consciousness, and beliefs about consciousness and reality. He suggests that the problem of materialists is that they overlook the fact that materialism cannot even explain matter, let alone anomalous phenomena or subjective experience. Materialism, he contends, remains entrenched in academia largely for political reasons.[80]

At present, we observe growing fascination in so-called nondualistic approaches.[81] To the nondualist, reality is ultimately neither physical nor mental but an overwhelming state or realization beyond words. There are many variations of this view, with the gist of nondualism holding that while different phenomena are not the same, they are inseparable with no hard line between them. We see this approach in mystical traditions of many religions, particularly traditions originating in Asia. Ken Wilber describes the history of philosophy in general, especially in the West, as a continuous swinging between two poles of truth—be it subject-object, mind-body, culture-nature, or individual-group. While the West tended to conceptualize those dualities as solid, separate opposites, the East sees them as a continuum, arising simultaneously and mutually like a concave/convex line.[82]

Nondualism can be theistic or nontheistic. For nontheistic notions, consider, among others, "The All,"[83] or "The Absolute,"[84] or, simply, "The Nondual."[85] We find similar thoughts in various branches of psychology and psychotherapy, with Swiss psychiatrist Carl Gustav Jung (1875–1961),[86] or Gestalt therapy[87] coming to mind. Transpersonal psychology can be mentioned as well, with Erich Fromm (1900–1980) and his focus on "being" as opposed to "having."[88] Notions of an "observing self"[89] are related to the nondual approach.

Quantum social science is being proposed by some to solve the mind-body problem. "We know we have experience from, well, experience itself, but there is no apparent way to reconcile this fact with modern science. By rights it seems consciousness should not exist, and as such neither should meaning, which presupposes consciousness."[90] Wendt suggests that a quantum connection, justifying a "participatory epistemology" in social inquiry, would give additional force to critiques of the subject-object distinction, such as postmodernists or feminists.[91]

Let me end this section with two recommendations for how to conduct our inquiries. *Critical realism* is being recommended by Howard Richards, scholar of peace and global studies, as the most suited philosophy of perception approach. Critical realism brings the Enlightenment and postmodernism together.[92] Critical realists acknowledge the merits of Enlightenment to appreciate that not everything is self-referencing text, while postmodernism helps us admitting that the Enlightenment was not a discovery of eternal truth but a moment in the history of culture, he explains.

As appropriate epistemological orientation, Dagfinn Føllesdal[93] suggests the *reflective equilibrium*, or circular thinking,[94] which has been en vogue since the 1950s. Prior to that time, thinkers preferred to build their arguments from the ground up, placing each layer of logic firmly on the previous foundation. They were committed, in other words, to building their ships on secure ground. They could not conceive of "building their ships at sea" as do the modern practitioners of reflective equilibrium. Reflective equilibrium, therefore, can be described as a humble method of reasoning that avoids the hubris of trying to do the impossible or call for the impossible to be possible—an approach fitting for the humble dismantling of hierarchies of submission/domination that human rights stand for.

Are Emotions "Basic"?

The question of basic emotions has elicited hot conflict. In 1990, Andrew Ortony and Terence Turner asked in the title of an article "What's Basic about Basic Emotions," and concluded "very little."[95] This evaluation provoked a heated, conflicted discussion. In 1992, the *Psychological Review* published four articles by five scholars, in which Ortony and Turner were heavily criticized and tried to defend themselves (*Psychological Review*, vol. 99, no. 3).[96]

All authors agreed that certain biological preconditions are necessary for an individual to be able to feel emotions. However, definitions of different "basic emotions" differed widely. Jaak Panksepp criticized Ortony and Turner, saying that "their thesis was flawed by their failure to consider the available neurobehavioral data."[97] Paul Ekman stated, "the evidence on universals in expression and in physiology strongly suggests that there is a biological basis to the emotions that have been studied. Ortony and Turner's reviews of this literature are faulted, and their alternative theoretical explanations do not fit the evidence."[98] Carroll E. Izard made the point that "particular emotions are called basic because they are assumed to have innate neural substrates, innate and universal expressions, and unique feeling-motivational states."[99]

Ortony and Turner responded that according to their view, "a more promising approach to understanding the huge diversity among emotions is to think in terms of emotions being assemblages of basic components rather than combinations of other basic emotions."[100] They stressed that they did not deny that emotions are based on "hard-wired" biological systems, but felt that "the existence of such systems does not mean that some emotions (such as those that appear on lists of basic emotions) have a special status."[101]

Ortony and Turner suggested that the question "Which are the basic emotions?" is a misdirected question. It is, they said, "as though we asked, 'Which are the basic people?' and hoped to get a reply that would explain human diversity."[102] They insisted that "to believe otherwise is to adhere to an unsubstantiated and probably unsubstantiatable dogma—an air, earth, fire, and water theory of emotion."[103]

Table 1.1. A Selection of Lists of "Basic" Emotions[104]

Reference	Fundamental Emotions	Basis for Inclusion
Magda B. Arnold[105]	Anger, aversion, courage, dejection, desire, despair, fear, hate, hope, love, sadness	Relation to action tendencies
Paul Ekman, Wallace V. Friesen, and Phoebe C. Ellsworth[106]	Anger, disgust, fear, joy, sadness, surprise	Universal facial expressions
Nico H. Frijda[107]	Desire, happiness, interest, surprise, wonder, sorrow	Forms of action readiness
Jeffrey A. Gray[108]	Rage and terror, anxiety, joy	Hardwired
Carroll E. Izard[109]	Anger, contempt, disgust, distress, fear, guilt, interest, joy, shame, surprise	Hardwired
William James[110]	Fear, grief, love, rage	Bodily involvement
William McDougall[111]	Anger, disgust, elation, fear, subjection, tender-emotion, wonder	Relation to instincts
Orval Hobart Mowrer[112]	Pain, pleasure	Unlearned emotional states
Keith Oatley, and Philip N. Johnson-Laird[113]	Anger, disgust, anxiety, happiness, sadness	Do not require propositional content
Jaak Panksepp[114]	Expectancy, fear, rage, panic	Hardwired
Robert Plutchik[115]	Acceptance, anger, anticipation, disgust, joy, fear, sadness, surprise	Relation to adaptive biological processes
Silvan S. Tomkins[116]	Anger, interest, contempt, disgust, distress, fear, joy, shame, surprise	Density of neural firing
John B. Watson[117]	Fear, love, rage	Hardwired
Bernard Weiner and Sandra Graham[118]	Happiness, sadness	Attribution independent

Note: Not all the theorists represented in this table are equally strong advocates of the idea of basic emotions. For some it is a crucial notion;[119] for others it is of peripheral interest only, and their discussions of basic emotions are hedged.[120]

Ortony and Turner listed attempts to categorize emotion (see Table 1.1). Independent of the quarrel about the validity of the notion of basic emotions, this list provides an overview of the efforts to identify fundamental emotions.

Recently, scholars have begun to draw attention to cultural differences in emotions. Linguist Anna Wierzbicka wonders why the Polish language, for example, does not have a word for *disgust*. What if Polish was the language of psychologists working on the "fundamental human emotions" rather than English?[121] Batja Mesquita[122] reminds us of James A. Russell and his suggestion that "it is puzzling why a language would fail to provide a single word for an important, salient, discrete, and possibly innate category of experience—if such exists."[123]

As already reported earlier, Smedslund explains that psychologists often fail to analyze the conceptual relations between their independent and dependent variables. They "empirically" test hypotheses while forgetting that conceptually related variables are bound to be related.[124] Smedslund's *psychologic* is an axiomatic system intended to formulate the psychologically relevant conceptual relationships embedded in language and is an instrument for describing, explaining, predicting, and controlling intrapersonal and interpersonal processes. Smedslund[125] recommends Nico H. Frijda's twelve empirical "laws of emotion," formulated in 1988.[126] (In 2006, in *The Laws of Emotion*, Frijda expanded his earlier theory of emotions, examining the passionate nature of emotions, emotional intensity, and complex emotional realms such as sex, revenge, and the need to commemorate past events.[127])

Are Emotions Nonlinear, Dynamic, and Relational?

Nowadays, controversies about the basic emotions question have lost much of their heat. Evolutionary theorists are now regarded to be right when they claim cross-cultural similarity in (primordial) emotion,[128] and social constructivists are accepted as being equally right, when they highlight cultural variation in the uses and functions of (elaborated) emotions in human societies.

Researchers in the field no longer endorse a single emotion perspective. Instead, they call for nonlinear dynamic models[129] and adopt "a unified 'affect science' approach that is able to incorporate emotion's many aspects without making one function dominant."[130]

The new trend is a "fundamental readiness to treat emotion as a complex, multifaceted phenomenon that makes one most hopeful that the vision of a truly interdisciplinary affective science is more than a pious wish."[131] The current tendency is to conceptualize elaborated emotions as "the total package of meanings, behaviors, social practices, and norms that are built up around primordial emotions in actual human societies.

This approach integrates the insights of evolutionary and social constructivist approaches and points to the systematic role of emotion in social interactions, relationships, and cultural practices."[132]

A new cohort of emotion researchers include the contributors to *Emotions: Current Issues and Future Directions*.[133] Abandoned are the battles of the past concerning the relative merits of classic theories, the role of cognition in emotion, or the issue of the biological versus cultural nature of emotion. These younger scholars are interested in emotions in real life and concrete situational settings, and how emotions are embedded in social and cultural contexts.[134]

Are Emotions Interesting for Social Science?

Another trend to be observed is a rising interest in social phenomena. Attempts to model them mathematically are surging. So-called agent-based models are computational models that simulate the simultaneous operations of multiple agents, in an attempt to re-create and predict the actions of complex phenomena.[135]

Also social psychology is becoming a more "social" discipline.[136] Kenneth J. Gergen writes: "It is from the soil of critical appraisal that new attempts now spring to life, attempts to reconstitute the psychological terrain as a social one."[137] According to Gergen, such work is inspired by Lev Vygotsky's thesis of higher mental processes and in some degree by poststructural literary theory. Vygotsky made a strong case for mental processes being relocated social processes: One carries out a mental process called "thinking" in the terms of the community into which one is socialized. Thought is participation in relatedness.[138]

A relational perspective is developing in a number of ways,[139] with the need to belong recognized as a core characteristic of humanness.[140] John Bowlby has sparked important work on attachment.[141] Communal sharing, an elementary form of human relations, depends on the need to belong.[142] The relational-cultural theory (RCT),[143] mentioned earlier, posits that growth-fostering relationships are a central human necessity and that acute or chronic disconnections in or from such relationships (such as humiliation and human rights violations) cause psychological and social problems.[144] RCT emphasizes that all relationships are defined and influenced by the cultural context in which they exist. Relational development, rather than development of the self, is the primary focus of study in RCT.

The notion of social embeddedness is gaining importance in areas outside social psychology as well. The sociology of culture has experienced a striking revitalization in both Europe and America.[145] Research in several fields no longer stays "in the brain," explains Deutsch.[146] Early studies of emotion tended to focus on the intrapersonal aspects of emotion, mapping the determinants and characteristics of emotional response within the individual (except for the research on the interpersonal functions of facial expressions), and this has changed. Keltner and Haidt affirm that "the time is right for a more general discussion of the assumptions, claims, and empirical findings that can be brought together into a social functional perspective on the emotions."[147]

Many similar voices can now be heard. It is "imperative that we develop richer models of how our feelings about and around the members of other groups can influence and shape the course of intergroup relations."[148] Anthropologist Niko Besnier agrees, saying that "many emotions are collectively constructed and crucially dependent on interaction with others for their development."[149] The inherently social dimensions of the human brain are highlighted by psychiatrists,[150] as well as neuroscientists.[151] So-called social emotions (guilt, embarrassment, shyness, jealousy, shame, for example) play a crucial role in social situations, according to Ralph Adolphs and Antonio Damasio. They say: "One might predict a need for highly differentiated affective responses precisely in guiding cognition and behavior in those domains with the greatest complexity, and surely the social domain is the most complex of all."[152]

Keltner and Haidt make the point that "it may be time to study social interactions and practices that revolve around emotions."[153] The authors explain how cultural practices elaborate on more primordial emotions (for example, appeasement rituals) in ways that transform primordial emotions into new practices (for example, how primordial emotions such as disgust are often related to "unsavory" ideologies).[154]

Keltner and Haidt call on scholars to focus on emotions within social practice, treating the dyad or group as the basic unit of analysis rather than the individual and including cultural objects and practices (for example, etiquette manuals, religious texts, or institutions). They suggest that is it "precisely in looking at these sorts of interactions and practices where one will find culturally elaborated emotion."[155]

Galen V. Bodenhausen and his colleagues study affective influences on phenomena such as stereotyping and intergroup relations. They differentiate integral affect (chronic or episodic), and incidental affect.[156] They define incidental affect as arising for reasons outside of the intergroup context itself—carried over from other events. Integral affect, in contrast, is elicited by the group itself, either as chronic feelings about the group or as episodic affect, for example when one has a pleasant interaction with a member of an otherwise disliked group.[157] The authors call for more research:

We must . . . understand much more about the potentially distinct effects of various discrete types of integral and incidental affect (for example, guilt, pride, anger, resentment, envy, disgust). Research addressing the impact of affect on the earliest stages of person perception (i.e., category identification and stereotype activation) is clearly needed as well.[158]

The social functions of emotions, particularly anger, shame, and guilt have also been addressed.[159]

In sum, current emotion research embraces a broad, transdisciplinary focus. Researchers have begun to appreciate that interactional functions of emotion and their embeddedness into social and cultural contexts indicate that research on emotion must reach "beyond the confines of emotion psychology into other areas of psychology (cognition, motivation, personality, psychopathology, and development, to mention but a few of the most obvious ones) and to other disciplines (ranging from the neurosciences to cultural anthropology)."[160] We see a wave of research and theory in a variety of disciplines on the connections between emotions and the social environment.[161]

Are Emotions Interesting for Neuroscience?

Neuroscience documents the embeddedness of emotions into contexts of evolution and culture.[162] Emotions, according to Steven Pinker, reflect the structure of human ancestral conditions and evolutionary processes of tackling them.[163] For Pinker, emotions are adaptations serving our goals in a world of causes and effects.

The complex feelings we experience are a relatively late evolutionary development. Humans display the greatest variety of feelings and emotions among all species, reflected in the largest web of connections between the prefrontal area and the evolutionary older limbic structures. As Walter J. Freeman posits, consciousness initially came into being as group consciousness and only recently underwent an individuation process.[164] In evolutionary terms, the consciousness of a modern individual who says "I" is fresh—occurring as late as the seventeenth century.[165]

The brain is not a structure that has been "planned" in any systematic way. It has evolved through evolutionary advances. The communication and coordination between the various brain structures is imperfect and intertwined with learning and experience.[166] Stephen W. Porges wrote a chapter titled "Emotion: An Evolutionary By-Product of the Neural Regulation of the Autonomic Nervous System."[167] Whereas newborns may process basic affects in lower brain structures, more elaborate emotions evolve over time and are handled in different brain areas. "New" emotions, such as shame and embarrassment, emerge only when certain cognitive milestones have been reached.[168] In the second half of the second year of life, the cognitive capacity of objective self-awareness emerges, with emotions such as embarrassment, empathy, and envy.[169] Between two and three years of age, the more complex ability of evaluating one's behavior according to a standard (external or internal) emerges. Self-conscious evaluative emotions such as pride, shame, or guilt are now possible.[170] Schemas for emotions about what we believe, expect, and react evolve.[171] Finally, cognition and affect are powerfully bound together in cultural symbol and knowledge systems such as religions.[172] Bonanno and Mayne conclude that "given these multilevel structures and processes, one would be hard pressed to argue against either basic/universal or culturally determined emotions."[173]

According to component-process theory,[174] the perception of an external stimulus at first triggers fast and automatic emotional responses, such as changes in autonomic tone and heart rate. Then, knowledge is retrieved from brain structures more influenced by conscious volition, such as declarative memory and reasoning. Those different sets of emotional responses together change the somatosensory state of the body; its somatovisceral, endocrine, and neuroendocrine function; its autonomic tone; and global brain functioning.[175]

Comparative studies in neuroanatomy, neurophysiological, and neuropsychological research suggest that emotions at their most fundamental have something to do with homeostasis and are an affective representation that maps how changes in body state relate to the organism's survival and well-being.[176] Second, emotions also monitor the relationship with external sensory stimuli. The psychological concept of appraisal describes how we evaluate what happens around us, with our emotions telling us whether it be good or bad. Third, to many theorists emotions are associated with action, more precisely, with specific action tendencies.[177]

For example, "anger" is a comprehensive set of representations that unfold in a complex fashion in time:

> the neural correlates of anger directed at another individual would consist in multiple neural mappings that provide a comprehensive representation of the external stimulus (the sight of the other individual), of the organism's own body state (for example, readiness to fight), and of the relationship between the two (that the latter is a response toward the former, and that the former may have triggered the latter).[178]

By now, the reader may be confused by too many concepts and terms. Goals, beliefs, attitudes, affects, emotions, feelings, emotional states, moods, consciousness, self, psyche—how does this all work together? Unfortunately, various studies employ terms such as affect, emotion, and mood in ways that are difficult to distinguish.[179] For example, the Positive and Negative Affect Schedule[180] assesses experienced affect, but so does the Differential Emotions Scale.[181]

The terms *affect* (from Latin *ad* + *facere*, "to afflict," "to influence") and *emotion* (from Latin *ex* + *movere*, "to move out from") have often been used interchangeably. Yet some scholars differentiate them. Erika L. Rosenberg differentiates affective traits and states.[182] Affective traits refer to stable ways or predispositions to emotional responding, and affective states to moods and emotions.[183] Moods and emotions vary in intensity and duration,[184] with moods lasting longer than emotions. Emotions tend to be intense or short-lived; however, they may fade into general mood states over time. Furthermore, according to Norbert Schwarz and Gerald L. Clore, there is a difference in referent. Mood states have no specific referent, while emotions tend to respond to particular events or persons.[185]

Antonio R. Damasio, one of the world's leading researchers in neuroscience, differentiates feeling and emotion in three separates stages along a continuum: first, a state of emotion; second, a state of feeling; and third, a state of feeling made conscious. The first state can be triggered and executed nonconsciously; the second can be represented nonconsciously, while the third is known to the organism as having both emotion and feeling.[186]

The quaternity model, based on the work of Carl Jung, makes the following distinctions:

- Consciousness: a person's entire inner experience: thoughts, sensations of the body, emotions, visions of the spirit.[187]
- Being: sometimes called self; the integral state of all aspects of the self; may be cultivated to a higher than usual level of human functioning.
- Mind: the part of a person that reasons, thinks, remembers, imagines, feels, wills, perceives, judges, and so on; the part of a person that pays attention.
- Body: a person's physical structure and material substance; the body gives bounds to the personality and provides a vehicle for life.
- Emotion: a complex collection of chemical and neural responses forming a distinctive pattern, an automatic response to a stimulus, that changes the state of the body proper and the state of brain structures that map the body and support thinking. The result is to place the organism in circumstances conducive to survival and well-being.[188]
- Feeling: the perception of a certain state of the body along with the perception of a certain mode of thinking and of thoughts with certain themes. "Feelings let us mind the body."[189]
- Spirit: incorporeal, transcendent aspects of human being; connection with a larger creative source of meaning, the universe, or the divine.[190]

Let's revisit Eve and Adam as they seek counseling. Their marriage counselor believes that thought needs emotion to be effective and agrees with Vygotsky that thought is participation in relatedness. The counselor's first aim for Eve and Adam is to cool down and experience their emotions initially without acting on them. This, the counselor knows, will change their cognitions, which in turn will change their experience of their emotions.

CHAPTER 2

HOW EMOTIONS AFFECT CONFLICT

"How to seek shelter when it's raining fear" is the title of an article written by Joanna Bourke. She warns, "it seems clear to me that later generations will judge us by our responses not so much to acts of terror, but to the terror in our hearts," and explains that "since the Sept. 11 attacks, terrorism has provided many people with a convenient and coherent narrative with which they can make sense of the seemingly irrational, free-floating risks associated with modern life. For this reason, the politics of fear has become central to statecraft."[1]

We immediately associate conflict with emotions such as fear, hatred, and anger, rather than love and joy. Thus, we might ask: Are there fundamental differences between positive and negative emotions?

Yes, it seems so. Feelings can be hot or cold, and they can be positive or negative. A number of researchers and theorists have developed models distinguishing between valence (positive-negative) and arousal-activation (hot-cold).[2]

With regard to the brain's functioning, positive affect facilitates verbal fluency; it engages the left frontal cortex more than the right. Negative affect, in contrast, facilitates figural fluency; it engages the right frontal cortex more than the left.[3] Emotions like fear are processed in the amygdala via adrenergic neurons, whereas the processing of reward and positive valence takes place in the basal ganglia via dopaminergic neurons, and higher cortical structures allow for learning and adaptation, render self-consciousness, abstraction, and imagination.[4]

The Brain and Conflict

The amygdala is an almond-shaped lower cortical neurostructure which acts as a preattentive analyzer of the environment.[5] Emotion processing begins when "the amygdala and basal ganglia analyze internal and external inputs for the presence of threats and rewards."[6] When a stimulus is identified as threatening, the amygdala identifies shapes, sounds, and other perceptual characteristics, and, very quickly and automatically, responds, for example, with avoidance. If a stimulus, in contrast, shows itself to be rewarding, the basal ganglia encode and store what happens. There is thus a distinction between automatic and controlled emotion processing, and another distinction between two basic systems of approach and avoidance.[7] This constitutes the core affective life of each individual.[8]

The brain "wakes up" to controlled emotion processing as soon as the anterior cingulate (ACC, another brain structure) signals errors, conflicts, pain, uncertainty, anxiety, and violations of expectation. "These signals indicate that emotion knowledge may need to be deployed to consciously transform core affect into an emotion or that the trajectory of an ongoing emotional response (initiated via automatic knowledge activation) may be in need of regulation or alteration."[9]

Ochsner and Feldman Barrett present six brain structures that are involved in emotion processing.[10] Aside from the already-mentioned (1) *amygdala* and (2) *basal ganglia* (subcortical structures), we have (3) the *left prefrontal cortex*, for looking up abstract semantic and associative knowledge in (4) a *posterior area* where such semantic information is stored. Two cortical areas are involved, (5), the *anterior cingulate cortex* (*ACC*), which signals discrepancy, uncertainty, or violated expectancy; and (6) the *ventromedial frontal cortex* (*VMFC*) and *orbital frontal cortex* (*OFC*), which gauge current goals and the affective value of a given stimulus within this context.

The last subsystem is particularly important for conflict, because it enables the individual to regulate and take control of his or her emotional responses. When a person deliberately probes her emotional knowledge, this may change the way in which she interprets and draws inferences about her current affective responses.

Neurological changes in the mentioned brain regions may lead to conflict being sought rather than avoided, as described by diagnoses such as *attention deficit syndrome*, *poor impulse control*, and *intermittent explosive disorder*. It is interesting that controlled emotion processing influences both the generation and the regulation of emotion.

> Any act of regulation necessarily generates a new emotional response. Each time an emotion is inhibited, labeled, or reappraised, the input to the network of emotion processing systems changes and the emotional response that emerges therefore also is changed (i.e., knowledge and its associated language does not just represent the emotion but can also transform it). The term "controlled emotion processing" intentionally blurs the distinction between generation and regulation partly because we believe the line often is difficult to draw.[11]

Early childhood abuse, injury to the brain—usually the frontal lobes— combined with indifferent or cruel parenting can be found in the biographical backgrounds of serial killers. Furthermore, neurotransmitters seem to be altered in violent perpetrators.[12] There is also the monoamine oxidase A (MAOA) gene to be considered, located on the X chromosome; genetic deficiencies in MAOA activity have been linked with aggression. Furthermore, there is the gene to produce nitric oxide; when this gene was removed in mice, they became extremely aggressive. In nearly every experiment involving aggression, serotonin, dopamine, or norepinephrine are found to play a role; high testosterone levels combined with low serotonin levels seem to be particularly salient.[13]

Fear and Conflict

"The voice of intelligence is drowned out by the roar of fear. It is ignored by the voice of desire. It is contradicted by the voice of shame. It is biased by hate and extinguished by anger. Most of all, it is silenced by ignorance."

—(Karl A. Menninger)

Fear can lead to avoidance of conflict ("flight"), a counterphobic aggressive response ("fight"), or a desire to avoid disaster by reaching an agreement. (Here we find a gender difference—women tend to react with a "tend and befriend" reaction to stress, rather then "fight or flight."[14]) Fear can hamper constructive conflict resolution or enhance it when it sharpens our senses and alerts our thoughts.

As discussed earlier, fear is basic. Its seat in the brain is the amygdala. Fear warns us. It jolts us into alertness in a split second, sending stress hormones soaring, narrowing, and focusing our vision. Our old brain takes over to save us from immediate danger. We may gain short-term safety. However, there is a price to pay.

In 1998, I interviewed Adam Bixi in Somaliland. He described growing up in the Somalian semi-desert, learning as a very small boy to be constantly alert, even at night, for dangerous animals and enemies from other clans. He learned to be ready for fight or flight in a matter of seconds, at any time, day or night. Continuous emergency preparedness meant that all other aspects of life had to wait. Emergency trumped everything else. Bixi felt he had not lived life. Modern managers often feel the same way. Continuous emergency alertness diminishes our zest for life. It may even lead to cardiac failure. Essentials such as sound long-term planning and institution building are neglected.

Earlier, we saw that feelings can be hot or cold and automatic or controlled. We have a hot "go" system and a cool "know" system. The cool know system is cognitive, complex, contemplative, slow, strategic, integrated, coherent, and emotionally rather neutral. It is the basis of self-regulation and self-control. Fear, as well as acute and chronic stress, accentuates the hot go system. The hot system is impulsive and hastily reactive and undermines rational attempts at self-control. Intense fear causes "tunnel vision," reducing the range of one's perceptions, thoughts, and choices, putting us in danger of making suboptimal decisions.

In other words, the hot go system represents a double-edged sword. It may save us from immediate danger. However, in case of a complex conflict, fear easily operates malignly.[15] Fear and humiliation have the potential to link up in particularly disastrous ways. In Rwanda, fear of future humiliation, based on the experience of past humiliation, was used to justify genocide. In his speeches, Adolf Hitler peddled his fear of future humiliation by world Jewry. The Holocaust was his "solution."

To conclude, we are well advised to cool down when we experience fear during a conflict to avoid disastrous tunnel vision and reap the potential advantage of fear, enhanced alertness. Likewise, we should help our opponents in conflicts and in negotiations to calm their fears. In negotiations, operating with threats—making others afraid—may undermine constructive solutions rather than provide advantages.

In 1941, Erich Fromm wrote *Escape from Freedom*, pointing out that emotional distress makes people vulnerable to charismatic leaders.[16] Incidentally, the one emotional distress nobody can escape is awareness and fear of death—read, for example, *The Denial of Death* by Ernest Becker.[17] Terror management theory (TMT), first developed in the late 1980s by Sheldon Solomon, Jeff Greenberg, and Tom Pyszczynski,[18] analyzes how humans are terrorized by their awareness of their mortality, and how, as a remedy, they may overly cling to cultural belief systems.

Let's see how Eve and Adam are doing. Their counselor begins with reducing the level of threat and fear between them. The therapist works on transforming their fears into alertness and motivation for change. Adam is afraid to lose power, and Eve is afraid to be empowered. Approached in a calm manner, these fears can be translated into deep personal growth for both. However, this is possible only in an atmosphere of warm firmness that provides safety—an atmosphere of respect, love, understanding, empathy, and patience—all of which the therapist needs to make available, aided by the larger social support network.

Hate and Conflict

"Victory breeds hatred. The defeated live in pain. Happily the peaceful live, giving up victory and defeat."

—(*Gautama Buddha, Dhammapada, Sukha Vagga, verse 201*)[19]

We easily get angry when we feel hurt. Sometimes we even kick a chair that stood in our way and gave us a bruise. Yet anger is a more composite set of mental processes than fear. It unfolds in a complex fashion in time and entails cognitive and emotional elements. Our brain does three things. First, it maps a comprehensive representation of the thing, animal, or person who has hurt us; second, it maps the state of our body, for example, our readiness to fight; and third, it maps the kind of relationship we have to the perpetrator and how we might respond. For example, we usually refrain from hitting our boss or a sumo wrestler.

We react with anger—rather than sympathy—when we believe the other person, either through neglect or with intention, treated us with disrespect. The more we feel hurt, the more we get angry. We get angry when we deem that the person who hurts us has sufficient *control* over the situation to avoid harming us (the so-called *controllability* dimension; see more details shortly). We get even angrier when we infer that the other *intended* to hurt us. The quality of this inference is made less than optimal by the *fundamental attribution error* or the *actor-observer bias*, a tendency to paint the other darker than oneself (see more details in the next chapter).

Hate and Evil

Let us now look at how scholars have modeled hate and evil. Clearly, a full overview cannot be given here. Many works would merit more attention, for example, Israel W. Charny's mammoth work *Encyclopedia of Genocide*,[20] or Steven James Bartlett's *The Pathology of Man: A Study of Human Evil*,[21] or *Blood That Cries Out From the Earth: The Psychology of Religious Terrorism* by James W. Jones.[22] We will come to Vamik Volkan's work later in the context of humiliation; see here Volkan, "A Psychoanalytic Perspective on Intergroup Hatred."[23]

Seven Kinds of Hate

Robert J. Sternberg, psychologist and educator at Yale University, has developed a duplex theory of hate.[24] Sternberg differentiates seven types of hate: cool hate, hot hate, cold hate, boiling hate, simmering hate, seething hate, and burning hate. According to Sternberg, hate has two components, a triangular component and a story component. The triangular component entails the negation of intimacy, passion, and commitment. Burning hate, for example, combines all three triangular components: The individual cannot imagine intimacy with the target, passionately hates the target, and is cognitively committed to this hate. The vermin story, in which the hated object is equated with a pest, is common in this type of hate.

The Complexity of Hate

In her intensification theory of hating, Susan Opotow, social and organizational psychologist in New York, argues that hate is an understudied and underappreciated psychological construct, with great relevance to justice research.[25] "Hate is a simple word connoting extreme enmity and, as a construct, is readily understood, even by young children. Yet its prima facie obviousness is deceptive."[26] Hate, Opotow posits, is not only an emotion. She draws together four literatures—justice, psychology, psychoanalysis, and criminal justice—and describes the formation, perpetuation, and expression of hate as a dynamic process that moves from antecedents to emotions, cognitions, morals, and behaviors. "Violence has many forms. It can be obvious or hidden, direct or structural, and it can be narrowly focused or pervasive."[27] Hate can trigger injustice, and injustice has the capacity to trigger derogation, violence, and hate. Hate can become systemic when interactions among its components unfold over time to intensify it.

Evil as Egocentrism

According to Aaron T. Beck, psychiatrist and practitioner of cognitive therapy and author of *Prisoners of Hate*,[28] violence has its roots in over-stretched and unyielding egocentrism, which gives rise to hardened and fixed enemy images. Empathy is then annihilated, and the "enemy" is dehumanized and demonized. People attach themselves to the meaning they have created because meaning, Beck explains, is imbued with affect. It is difficult to withdraw from fixed ideological and self-interested positions, from what Beck calls "fight, flight, or freeze" responses. The remedy, following Beck, is to defuse anger and rage through reframing. Reframing means encouraging people to loosen emotional investment in previously established positions.

The Role of Bystanders in Evil

In his book *Roots of Evil*,[29] Ervin Staub, psychologist at the University of Massachusetts at Amherst, draws attention to the significance of the role of bystanders. The world's failure to protest the Armenian massacres, Staub argues, helped Hitler feel uninhibited in his plans to destroy the European Jewry. Staub lays out the entire field of social psychological scholarship and describes how both perpetrators and bystanders use the just-world hypothesis to assume that victims have earned their suffering. He also describes how both groups avoid empathetic distress by distancing themselves from the victim. Staub writes that both perpetrators and bystanders are "learning by doing." Perpetrators become more violent through violent actions; bystanders become more passive as they watch suffering without taking action.

The Inability to See One's Own Evil

Roy F. Baumeister, psychologist at Case Western Reserve University and author of *Evil: Inside Human Violence and Cruelty,* makes the point that almost no perpetrators of evil regard their actions as evil.[30] Nazi Germany, for example, saw their country as the victim. Contrary to the popular assumption that low self-esteem is a major source of criminality, Baumeister posits that perpetrators of violent crime combine a high but brittle self-esteem with poor self-regulation, particularly when it is challenged.

The Unlikeliness of Hate Crimes

Michael Harris Bond, cross-cultural psychologist at Chinese University of Hong Kong, and his colleagues have examined a wide range of genocides and highlight the fact that massacres (which often occur during wars, genocide, and political slaughter) are not "efficient" slaughter but generally more cruel. "Rape, torture, and mutilation typically precede killing. Many soldiers engage in these actions, although no information suggests they have propensities for rape, sexual sadism, or sadistic violence in civilian life. The extreme cruelty is therefore hard to explain using forensic trait theories."[31] The authors suggest a form of forensic ethology that draws together survivor reports, tribunal transcripts, and information on perpetrators.

Silence/Violence and Their Link to "Hypermasculinity"

Thomas J. Scheff, sociologist at the University of California, theorizes that an emotional/relational configuration that he calls *hypermasculinity* might be central to violence (mostly perpetrated by men).[32] He hypothesizes that four "vulnerable emotions," namely grief, fear, shame, and anger, play a crucial role at the emotional front of this configuration. The shame/anger spiral is the key mechanism of violence, both individual and collective, according to Scheff. The spiral begins with an absence of close bonds to others, and this plays out on the relational stage. The result is, according to Scheff, that men meet threats to self with either silence or violence because they are caught in isolation and have learned to suppress their vulnerable emotions.[33] For Scheff, *bypassed shame*—shame that is not acknowledged in particular—is the motor of all violence and the source of "humiliated fury" (a term coined by Helen Lewis[34]).

Dangerous Ideas

Roy J. Eidelson and Judy I. Eidelson, from the University of Pennsylvania, review in their article "Dangerous Ideas: Five Beliefs That Propel Groups toward Conflict,"[35] relevant literatures and identify five belief domains—superiority, injustice, vulnerability, distrust, and helplessness. These domains, they say, are central to both the core beliefs of individuals and to the collective worldviews of groups. Each of these issues can play an important role in triggering, maintaining, or escalating conflict between people and groups. Group leaders often call on these five concerns in their efforts to garner member support for their agenda, which may include violence against out-groups. Successful conflict resolution strategies frequently depend on effectively addressing these same key domains.

For both Eve and Adam, anger can lead to either destruction or personal growth. Adam is angry that Eve is not submissive enough. Eve does not dare be angry at Adam's wrath. She is frightened by him, as well as by the possibility and strength of her own anger. So she seeks relief in subservience. The therapist attempts to transform the explosive fury that Adam projects onto Eve into deeper reflection on his own growth. The therapist ultimately invites Adam to relinquish using anger as an escape route and face deeper feelings of hurt and pain. She explains to Eve and Adam that the new normative universe of mutual respect for equal dignity defines concepts such as love, loyalty, cooperation, attachment, connection, and relationship in profoundly new ways. She encourages Eve to embrace these new ways and no longer efface herself in front of Adam. It is important for Eve to dare to feel anger sometimes—not frantic rage and hatred—but a definite firmness that she can use for constructing a richer and more comprehensive repertoire for being a person.

If we consider intergroup or international relations, the world will benefit from everybody getting firmly angry in the face of abuse instead of disengaging and looking away. Anger must, however, be translated into Mandela-like strategies—rather than hatred and violence—to render constructive results.

Guilt and Conflict

"It has become appallingly obvious that our technology has exceeded our humanity. Technological progress is like an axe in the hands of a pathological criminal. I believe that the horrifying deterioration in the ethical conduct of people today stems from the mechanization and dehumanization of our lives, a disastrous by-product of the scientific and technical mentality. Nostra culpa!"

—(Albert Einstein)

Guilt is an elaborated emotion and a topic for psychology, psychiatry, ethics, criminal law, and other related fields. To feel guilty, we need self-awareness and the ability to measure our behavior in relation to standards. Self-conscious evaluative emotions such as pride, shame, or guilt are not possible earlier than the second or third year of life. However, as already discussed, elaborated emotions are very culturally dependent. Guilt as Westerners understand it might never evolve in some cultures, especially those that have no word for the concept.

In its simplest description, guilt may be understood as an affective state of regret at having done something one believes one should not have done. Humiliation, humility, shame, and guilt are related concepts (see more in Chapter 6).

Some scholars differentiate shame and guilt societies (Ruth Benedict, 1887–1948).[36] In a shame society, so goes the definition, "I seek to maintain my good name in the eyes of the others," whereas in a guilt society, "I have internalized moral norms into my super-ego and feel guilty when disobeying them."

"Face" and "face-saving" is often associated with Asian culture.[37] Indeed, shame is a powerful and prevalent emotion in Asian cultures, widely seen as a moral discretion and sensibility that people should desire to develop.[38] Shame and guilt, however, are not necessarily seen as separate but as shading into each other: both emotions "direct people into self-examination in social situations in order to recognize their own wrong doings, as well as to motivate people to improve themselves," contend Jin Li and Kurt W. Fischer.[39]

Guilt, like shame, is among those states of being that can be abused as a tool of social control, because guilty people feel less deserving and are less likely to assert their rights and prerogatives. As explained earlier, this tool has been used during the past millennia in hierarchical societies.

In sum, feelings of guilt can prevent people from doing evil. Feelings of guilt for past omissions and transgressions, if acknowledged and remedied by apology and forgiveness, can be a powerful healing force in conflict. What is needed for shame and guilt to be healing forces is the courage to face them and gauge them with candidness, humility, and warmth. If bypassed, feelings of shame and guilt can help maintain destructive conflict. In turn, conflict can impinge on feelings of guilt. Feelings of guilt can be pushed toward violence if conditions inhibit their acknowledgment and healing. Moreover, deliberately creating "pathological guilt" to weaken opponents may undermine long-term constructive solutions. Successful negotiation or solutions to conflict depend on firm commitments from strong players. Guilt can best work for healing if embedded in respectful restorative justice.

It's time to revisit Eve and Adam. Eve is kept in timid subservience in part because she is encouraged to feel guilty. She partly believes Adam's complaint that she ought to be more docile. Their counselor brings clarity into the normative confusion of the couple. Indeed, in traditional normative contexts of ranked honor, a woman is expected to efface herself. However, times have changed, and subservience no longer represents the same kind of virtue, at least not in cultural contexts influenced by the human rights message. Eve is entitled to develop a more comprehensive and expansive personal space—not arrogantly attacking Adam in retaliation but applying a spirit of firm and respectful humility. Adam, on the other hand, is no longer required to feel ashamed and guilty for not succeeding in keeping his wife meek and lowly—and he no longer needs to bypass his shame at his failure and cover up with violence. He is entitled to feel proud to be a male who supports a strong woman at his side. He may even come to feel guilty and apologize to his wife for not having grasped this insight earlier. An exchange of mutual respect for equal dignity, in a spirit of shared humility, may lead to a new and nourishing relationship between Eve and Adam.

CHAPTER 3

HOW CONTEXTS AFFECT EMOTION AND CONFLICT

It's late at night, and your spouse is snoring. You are utterly exhausted and cannot fall asleep. However, you know that he (or she) does not want to injure you. So you might get frustrated—but you do not get angry, at least not seriously. However, if your neighbor turns on loud music in the middle of the night, knowing that the walls between your apartments are thin and you do not like such nightly disturbances, the story is completely different. The noise level might be exactly the same, but not your appraisal of the situation and how you attribute control.[1]

This is the field of framing and meta-emotion, or how people feel about feelings, what their history is with specific emotions like pride, respect or disrespect, love, fear, anger, sadness.[2] Indeed, research shows that we want to harm others, either overtly or covertly, when we believe they could have avoided hurting us.[3]

Let us ask Eve and Adam: If Eve believes that Adam is hurting her with intention, she will get angry. As long as she believes that he chastises her out of love, she may love him more. The basic situation is the same, the physical hurt is the same, maybe even initial emotional reactions are the same. What differs is the *appraisal* of the situation and the final regulation of emotions.

The 2003 Iraq war is a contemporary example at macro levels. Pain inflicted for the sake of liberation from oppression is "good," pain inflicted as part of just another oppression is "bad." The pain is the same. The outcome is radically different.

What we understand is that it is crucial to probe intentions to appraise a situation. Currently, the world contains many camps that are riddled by the unfortunate outfall of interpretations of intentions that are arrived at "blindly." Israelis are pitched against Palestinians in the Middle East, Tamils against Singhalese in Sri Lanka, Turkish against Greek Cypriots in Cyprus, Western values against non-Western values; usually such controversies are regarded as head-on oppositions. However, research in social psychology suggests that such appraisals are ill informed. Many apparent divisions are in fact based on underlying agreements on values, a congruence that is almost systematically underestimated.

The problem is the phenomenon of *biases*, which distort our views (and are central to creating feelings of humiliation). Essentialization, attribution error (fundamental, ultimate), reactive devaluation, false polarization effect—the list of biases is long. Simplified, we tend to grant ourselves and members of our own group the benefit of the doubt, while we tend to assume the worst from members of other groups. We easily dismiss positive behavior by out-group members, merely because they are out-group members.

We can observe examples everywhere. We see them in the current Middle East conflict, the conflict in Sri Lanka, in the 2003 Iraq war, and in the global war on terrorism. We merely have to listen to any spokesperson's statement about the appalling behavior of others to understand how this link works. These spokespersons deplore an act of violence committed by the other side as "atrocity perpetrated in cold blood," implying that the other side's evil aim is to target innocent civilians. "Look how we are victimized by deep humiliation that cannot go unanswered, we have to retaliate!" is the message transmitted to the world by both sides. At the same time, each side confirms that civilian casualties that may have been caused by one's own actions to the other side are unintended and unavoidable side effects, and collateral damage, something the other ought to understand and excuse. The Israeli side insists their soldiers do their utmost to protect civilians. Palestinians, the Israelis say, use their compatriots as shields, again proving their moral worthlessness and evil. The Palestinian side explains that suicide bombers do not target civilians, but that as oppressed occupants they have no other weapons than their own bodies.

Bewildered, members of the international community ask, "Don't these adversaries see that all human beings basically want to live in peace and quiet, have some reasonable quality of life and offer their children a future? Don't they see that their distorted mutual perceptions are their biggest enemy? Why don't they change their perceptions?"

To compound the problem, we are not always aware of our biases. Much of our cognitive processing is beyond the reach of conscious thought (more in Chapter 8).[4] We often do not know why we act as we do. We then analyze our own behavior in the same way we analyze that of others and ask what beliefs and motives could have been responsible for it.[5]

These explanations may then misguide future behavior. Deborah Welch Larson writes about the psychological origins of American Cold War policy: "Truman was at first unsure of himself and inconsistent and his position hardened only after he came to interpret his hesitant steps as implying that the Soviet Union was aggressive and could only be countered by firmness. Having attributed these beliefs to himself, Truman then acted on them."[6]

Forming Emotions

One of the most relevant dimensions for triggering anger seems to be the so-called *controllability* dimension. We react with anger—rather than sympathy—when we believe that the person who hurts us has sufficient control over the situation to avoid harming us. Of course, the situation is even more severe when we infer that the other in fact *wants* to hurt us. Indeed, research shows that we want to harm others, either overtly or covertly, when we believe they could have avoided hurting us. It is one thing to be pushed accidentally by a drunk man, and another to be harmed deliberately by an apparently clearheaded man. As Keith G. Allred explains, it is crucial how we *attribute*—in the case of the pushing man, whether we attribute his behavior to drunkenness or to fully conscious malevolence.[7] Our beliefs as to why others behave as they do are being addressed by attribution theory, one of the dominant paradigms in social psychology.

The process of appraisal is intimately linked with attribution and framing. Fritz Heider (1896–1988) is thought to be the first attribution theorist. Attribution refers to the process by which people attempt to infer the cause of events in our world. Heider studied how we sometimes attribute other people's behavior to their internal dispositions (such as their personality traits, attitudes, or abilities), whereas on other occasions we attribute it to external circumstances.[8] This differentiation is central to whether hot emotions emerge, which in turn lead to conflict—or not. Our spouse has no control over his or her snoring; snoring is due to circumstances beyond a person's reach and thus snorers usually get exonerated and do not face wrath. Our neighbor, on the other hand, is clearly much more in control of his actions when torturing us with nightly blare.

Edward Ellsworth Jones, Keith E. Davis, and Harold H. Kelley suggest that two stages are involved when we appraise another person's behavior.[9] First, we ascertain whether the other person did what she did intentionally (stage 1A) and whether she is aware of the consequences of her behavior (stage 1B). Your snoring spouse does not snore intentionally (1A) and blissfully sleeps while having no clue as to how you suffer (1B). In contrast, your neighbor may not be that innocent. If we deem the other person's behavior to be intentional, we enter the second stage. The more we are hurt, the more we tend to believe that the other is disposed negatively; our neighbor might be a thoughtless person in our eyes (stage 2A) or even a mean person (stage 2B). If we were lovers of loud nightly music, we would be more lenient.

Interestingly, people from Western cultures are more prone to making systematic errors in this process than people of Asian socializations. People in the West tend to get unduly angry, more than people socialized in Asian cultures. In Western cultural contexts, people learn to highlight individual freedom and autonomy and thus have a tendency to commit the so-called fundamental attribution error, or the actor-observer bias, which leads them to prefer dispositional factors to situational ones. Jones and Harris gave people essays to read on pro- or anti-Castro feelings and asked them to assess the authors' stances. Even when they were told the authors had been directed to write pro- or anti-arguments, they still assumed the authors believed in what they were writing.[10]

The fundamental attribution error and the actor-observer bias refer to the tendency to attribute others' behavior (for example, hostile remarks) to the other's personality dispositions rather than to transient circumstances while attributing our own hostile remarks to circumstances rather than our own dispositions. During a contentious conflict this may lead each side to overestimate the other's hostility as well as one's own benignness.[11]

Thomas F. Pettigrew argues that the fundamental attribution error becomes the *ultimate* attribution error when people explain the actions of people in groups.[12] We tend to grant members of our own group the benefit of the doubt, and we tend to assume the worst from members of other groups. We tend to dismiss the positive behavior by out-group members, merely because they are out-group members. In an experiment, Galen V. Bodenhausen invited students to be part of a jury. All details were identical, only the name of the defendant differed. When the defendant's name was Carlos Ramirez, the jury found him guilty more often than when he was called Robert Johnson.[13]

This tendency must be expected to intensify as group members become more dependent on a group for addressing external crises and maintaining self-esteem. *Concurrence seeking* is close to the concept of *groupthink*.[14] Members of a decision-making group agree with the other members and set aside reservations, thus facilitating potentially perilous group decisions.[15]

Another human weakness relevant for conflict is the widespread belief in a just world that causes people to blame the victim. The belief in a just world gives the more privileged an alibi to be blind to the sufferings of the less privileged, because "everybody deserves what he gets." People who hold the just world belief are indifferent to social injustice not because they have no concern for justice but because they see no injustice.[16]

Lee D. Ross and his colleagues carried out interesting experiments.[17] Contrary to the assumption that it is the nature of human beings to grab as many resources as possible, these experiments show that people are willing to share resources equally. However, those who have more tend to justify this inequality. Human beings want a fair world; however, fairness in the future is judged differently from fairness in the past. We define fairness as equal sharing as long as the sharing lies in the future; when we have accumulated more than others, we tend to believe we deserve it. *Loss aversion*, the tendency of people to dislike losses significantly more than they like gains, plays into these psychological preferences—we don't mind sharing equally in the future, but we do not like to lose what we have. These psychological phenomena strengthen conservative stances, leading people to evaluate those who want another distribution of resources as aggressors.

The Irresistible Pull of Irrational Behavior is a telling title of a book by Ori and Rom Brafman,[18] which shows how rational action is undermined—from the desire to avoid loss to a failure to consider all the evidence.

Framing Emotions

Ervin Goffman, pioneer of the analysis of face-to-face communication, also analyzed how frames organize experience.[19] Many of his works form the basis for the sociological and media studies concept of *framing* (see also Chapter 8). Also, Ross and his colleagues worked on the role of the situation and of framing.[20] When students were told that a task they were asked to carry out was difficult, they were unable to complete it; however, when they received the explanation that the same task was usually handled very easily, they completed it. Or, when students were asked to play a game where they had the choice to cooperate or to cheat on one another (prisoner's dilemma game) and were told that this was a community game, they cooperated; however, they cheated on each other when told that the same game was a Wall Street game.

Quantum game theory has interesting contributions to make.[21] In quantum game theory players are "quantum decision makers" with indeterminate and entangled properties and strategies before action. The results are fascinating. Cooperation is much easier to achieve in this situation than it is in classical game theory. "This could help explain the finding that in real life people (and states) cooperate much more than they 'should' according to classical game theory."[22]

In conclusion, cooperation might have much more inherent strength than cynical "realists" might wish to concede. This is underpinned not least by archaeological evidence (for more, see later discussion). It is crucial to realize that we are not mere victims but creators of our world. As we read earlier, Morton Deutsch lays out what he calls Deutsch's *crude law of social relations*. This law says that "characteristic processes and effects elicited by a given type of social relationship (cooperative or competitive) tend also to elicit that type of social relationship." In short, "cooperation breeds cooperation, while competition breeds competition."[23]

This brings us to the norms that define the larger cultural realm within which emotional experiences are embedded. Robert Axelrod[24] explored computer models of the iterated prisoner's dilemma game (which gives two players the chance to cooperate or betray one another) and formalized the evolutionary tit-for-tat strategy. Axelrod's key finding is that the evolutionary tit-for-tat strategy—also known as reciprocal altruism—is remarkably successful and defeats all other strategies, increasing the benefits of cooperation over time and protecting participants from predators.

Following Deutsch and Axelrod, cultures that favor competition must be expected to breed more of it, and cultures favoring cooperation will expand the use of cooperation. As Deutsch reminds us, psychologists ought to pay more attention to these phenomena. He highlights that "psychologists have not yet acknowledged that there is a moral, normative feature to every type of social relation and that any reasonably full characterization of the psychological orientation associated with a social interaction (or its perception) will include the person's moral orientation as well as his or her cognitive and motivational orientation."[25]

Moral, cognitive, and motivational orientations vary according to cultural contexts, both across different cultural realms, and across historic time. Emotions and conflicts are part of these variations.

Framing Conflict

When a person suffers at the hands of other human beings, she has in principle four choices. (1) She may define this suffering as a kind of natural disaster (being beaten by a disturbed or drunk person, for example); (2) she may accept it as a "prosocial honorable lesson" or "prosocial humbling" (as discussed earlier, being beaten, in honor contexts, is often seen as equivalent to having surgery or a vaccination that "hurts but must be endured," see Chapter 5); (3) she may not accept it as prosocial honorable lesson (being beaten as a slight of honor that calls for retaliation with humiliation); or (4) she might see it as an illegitimate humiliation of dignity (being beaten as violation of dignity that ought to be opposed in a dignified Mandela-like fashion). Only in the third and fourth cases does a person see herself as traumatized victim.

This means that there is concord between me and my dominators as long as I accept being beaten as a prosocial honorable lesson. The word *concord* stems from Latin *cum* which means *with*, and *cord*, which means *heart*. *Concord* means that our hearts are with each other.

The word *conflict*, however, comes from the verb *flectere*, to bend, to curve. In conflict, *discord* displaces *concord* and may lead to confrontation. The word *confrontation* entails the Latin word *frons*, which means *forehead*. In a confrontation, foreheads are placed against each other, in opposition. Thus, the term *conflict*, similar to terms such as *victimhood* and *trauma*, is dependent on the particular framing of reality adopted by the players and the overall social mind-set within which the incident occurs.

Deutsch explains:

> Discontent and the sense of injustice may be latent rather than manifest in a subordinated group. Neither the consciousness of oneself as victimized or disadvantaged nor the consciousness of being a member of a class of disadvantaged may exist psychologically. If this be the case, consciousness-raising tactics are necessary precursors to the developing of group cohesion and social organization. The diversity of consciousness-raising tactics have been illustrated by the variety of techniques employed in recent years by women's liberation groups and black power groups. They range from quasi-therapeutic group discussion meetings through mass meetings and demonstrations to dramatic confrontations of those in high-power groups. It is likely that a positive consciousness of one's disadvantaged identity is most aroused when one sees someone, who is considered to be similar to oneself, explicitly attacked or disadvantaged and sees him resist successfully or overcome the attack; his resistance reveals simultaneously the wound and its cure.[26]

Every psychotherapist has seen divorce cases that evolve in the following manner. For years, a woman tries to make her husband understand that he must respect her dignity, while he thinks she is just a little sensitive or hysterical. For long periods, she suffers from psychosomatic symptoms and depression, seemingly supporting his views. When she finally files for divorce, he is surprised and hurt, while she tells him that she has talked to him for years, in vain. The woman probably does not call her private uprising conflict. If her husband were to understand her and apologize for being slow to embrace the ideal of equal dignity, there would be no conflict. If asked, she might say the man created the conflict by his loyalty to the old order that says a quiet woman is a good and happy woman. As long as she was quiet, he saw no need for change and was reluctant to bend to fit new worldviews.

As in the case of Eve and Adam, both sides experience irreconcilable types of humiliation—honor humiliation on the part of the husband, and dignity humiliation on the part of his wife. The husband shows defensive avoidance,[27] which is salient at micro levels as much as at macro levels. "Even highly credible threats by the adversary are likely to be missed, misinterpreted, or ignored. This is one reason why attempts to explain wars as the product of rational choices on both sides will often fail, just as the policies themselves fail," writes Robert Jervis.[28]

Shaping Emotions

What happens to the common ground that could be useful for developing cooperation instead of mayhem? It is squandered by feelings of humiliation that arise when I hear you misattributing my intentions. As long as communities live far away from each other and do not know about other communities misreading them, there is no problem. Everybody feels comfortable whitewashing their in-group and blackening out-groups. However, this becomes problematic when people learn how biased others' judgments about them are. In the introduction, we read about Japan's attempt to whitewash schoolbooks, and the violent reactions this triggered in China and Korea.

It is humiliating to learn about evaluations that place me in a less than advantageous light, particularly when I feel that those who levy such judgments lack any moral authority to do so. Thus, the attribution error, or the human tendency to treat out-groups less leniently than in-groups, can elicit feelings of humiliation in those out-groups who are on their way to becoming part of the in-group. The emergence of a global village, the merging of out-groups into one in-group, confronts people with humiliating and unwelcome out-group biases that they in former times never would have known existed.[29] Only when the transition toward one in-group is successfully completed can misreadings and confrontations of this kind be expected to wane.

These insights are crucial for building a world without terrorism. It is inherently impossible to win a war on terror with conventional weapons. Admittedly, missiles send powerful messages. Yet the recipients may not understand those messages in the intended way. They may not see them as inducements to humility, but rather as humiliation, reason to react with enraged defiance. Using ever more weapons could mean the eradication of humankind, rather than its rescue. The only way to win this war is to gain trust and turn enmity into neighborliness. The hearts and minds of the masses must be won to take away their incentive to resonate with those few humiliation entrepreneurs who instigate and organize terror. When the masses turn away from the few terrorist leaders, those can safely be policed, without fear that every dead or captured terrorist will be replaced with a new one within minutes.

PART II

How Emotions Can Maximize and Minimize Conflict

CHAPTER 4

WHAT IS HUMILIATION?

The Olympic Committee advertises the ideals of Olympism by sending the following message to all competitors about their opponents:

> You are my adversary, but you are not my enemy.
> For your resistance gives me strength.
> Your will gives me courage.
> Your spirit ennobles me.
> And though I aim to defeat you, should I succeed, I will not *humiliate* you.
> Instead, I will *honour* you.
> For without you, I am a lesser man.[1]

There is a "special sort of pain which the brutes do not share with the humans—humiliation," says American philosopher Richard Rorty.[2]

Thomas Friedman, *New York Times* columnist, states, "If I've learned one thing covering world affairs, it's this: The single most underappreciated force in international relations is humiliation."[3]

Aaron Lazare confirms: "I believe that humiliation is one of the most important emotions we must understand and manage, both in ourselves and in others, and on an individual and national level."[4]

The literature on conflict, featured in countless publications, is too vast to summarize here. However, protracted, intractable conflicts mark as new a research frontier in the field of conflict studies as is research on humiliation. This challenge has been taken up by Peter T. Coleman and his group at Columbia University, who study intractable conflict (for example, by including the significance of humiliation).[5]

Coleman writes: "Protracted, intractable conflict is a domain of human interaction that may very well determine our capacity to survive as a species."[6] He explains,

These intense, inescapable conflicts over issues such as critical resources, identity, meaning, justice, and power are complex, traumatic, and often resist even the most serious attempts at resolution. But why are they intractable? What characteristics distinguish intractable conflicts from more tractable, resolvable conflicts? Scholars have begun to identify a diverse array of interrelated factors.[7]

Coleman has developed a meta-framework for protracted, intractable conflict in the form of a broad conceptual framework for theory building and intervention.[8] Intractable conflicts are those that persist in a highly destructive state despite repeated good-faith efforts toward their resolution.[9] They are complex, multilevel, intertwined with other community problems (such as poverty, unemployment, and poor housing), and always in flux.[10] Coleman and colleagues suggest "that an essential step towards discerning the essence of intractability is to examine the role that moral emotions, such as humiliation, play in perpetuating them."[11]

What Is Humiliation?

In 2003, Tony Webb compiled an overview of some existing studies of humiliation in his doctoral dissertation *Towards a Mature Shame Culture*.[12] Table 4.1 represents the shame-related part of his compilation.

Another categorization, by W. Gerrod Parrott, places humiliation as tertiary emotion within a tree structure of emotions,[13] see Table 4.2.

There is not sufficient space here to discuss these categorizations in more depth; this overview is intended only to give the reader a taste of past research.

Julian L. Stamm proposes that humiliation is experienced when one feels "belittled or slandered, lowered in the eyes of others or in his own eyes."[14] Paul Gilbert suggests that humiliation occurs when one feels "criticized, degraded, and abused by a bad other."[15] He proposes that in cases of humiliation, the other is seen as bad and not the self (as in shame).

Coleman and his colleagues are among the first to bring humiliation research "into the lab,"[16] and they define humiliation as follows: "Humiliation is an emotion, triggered by public events, which evokes a deep

Table 4.1. Shame and Humiliation in Categories for Primary Affects[17]

Tomkins[18]	Ekman, Friesen, and Ellsworth[19]	Izard[20]	Darwin[21]
Shame-humiliation	Shame	Shame, shyness, guilt	Self-attention, shame, shyness, modesty, blushing

Table 4.2. Humiliation as Part of Emotions Categorized into a Tree Structure[22]

Primary Emotion	Secondary Emotion	Tertiary Emotions
Love	. . .	. . .
Joy	. . .	. . .
Surprise	. . .	. . .
Anger	. . .	. . .
	Suffering	Agony, suffering, hurt, anguish
	Sadness	Depression, despair, hopelessness, gloom, glumness, sadness, unhappiness, grief, sorrow, woe, misery, melancholy
	Disappointment	Dismay, disappointment, displeasure
Sadness	Shame	Guilt, shame, regret, remorse
	Neglect	Alienation, isolation, neglect, loneliness, rejection, homesickness, defeat, dejection, insecurity, embarrassment, humiliation, insult
	Sympathy	Pity, sympathy
Fear	. . .	. . .

dysphoric feeling of inferiority resulting from the realization that one is being, or has been, treated in a way that departs from the normal expectations for fair and equal human treatment."[23] Peter Coleman, Jennifer S. Goldman, and Katharina Kugler point out that as individuals and groups at the community, national, and international levels struggle with the effects of humiliation and aggression in protracted violence in schools, ethnopolitical conflicts, and global terrorism, this topic is of utmost importance today. From their research, they draw the conclusion that protracted conflict can be addressed by influencing the social norms (and/or how individuals perceive the social norms) regarding how people should respond, emotionally and behaviorally, when faced with a humiliating situation.[24]

Who Studied Humiliation?

Until very recently, the phenomenon of humiliation figured largely implicitly in the literature on violence and war. In the few instances in which it was treated explicitly, it typically was used interchangeably with shame or as a variant of shame.[25]

Very few scholars have focused on the role of humiliation per se. Among those is Donald C. Klein (1923–2007), one of the fathers of community psychology and late member of the board of directors of Human Dignity and Humiliation Studies network.[26] Klein edited two special issues of the *Journal of Primary Prevention*, in 1991 and 1992, devoted to the topic of humiliation.[27]

Linda M. Hartling pioneered a quantitative questionnaire on humiliation (Humiliation Inventory), which uses a scale of 1 to 5 to gauge the extent to which respondents feel harmed by humiliating incidents throughout life and how much they fear such events as "being teased, bullied, scorned, excluded, laughed at, or, harassed."[28] Hartling writes:

> Few people have engaged in any empirical analysis of the impact of humiliating experiences. My research convinced me that humiliation has a cumulative impact. Unless there is a healing, relational intervention—unless the individual is connected to family, friends, therapy, community connections, etc., to strengthen his/her resistance and resilience—I believe cumulative experiences of humiliation can suck individuals into a downward spiral of disconnection, depression, isolation, and, sadly, sometimes violence.[29]

Hartling lists some of the ways in which humiliation can be assessed:

1. from the perspective of the victim,
2. from the perspective of the witness,
3. from the perspective of the humiliator,
4. from any combination of the these relationships,
5. as an individual//internal experience,
6. as a relational//external experience,
7. as a traumatic relational violation,
8. as a narrative or reflection in response to an acute or a chronic experience of humiliation,
9. as a culturally dependent behavior or social practice (e.g., discrimination, micro-aggressions) in obvious or subtle forms,
10. as in individual incident or a systemic dynamic,
11. as an atmosphere or environment characterized by contempt, devaluation, denigration,
12. as a tool of social control, a tool of domination, a power-over tool,
13. from the perspective of a specific practice (e.g., using a single letter grade to describe the quality of a child's academic performance on a topic or using a number to signify a child's lifelong intellectual capacity), or
14. as a "resilience-triggering" experience.[30]

The role of humiliation and embarrassment has been studied in serial murder,[31] in sexual abuse,[32] poverty and exclusion,[33] education,[34] in the judicial system,[35] and resilience and aging.[36] Humiliation has also been studied in such fields as love, social attractiveness, depression, society and identity formation, sports, history, literature, and film.

Thomas J. Scheff and Suzanne Retzinger extended their work on violence and the Holocaust, studying the part played by "humiliated fury"[37] in escalating conflicts between individuals and nations.[38] Israel W. Charny analyzes excessive power strivings.[39] Psychiatrist James Gilligan focuses on humiliation as a cause for violence, in his book *Violence: Our Deadly Epidemic and How to Treat It.*[40]

Hegel's discussion of the struggle for recognition is the subject of an extensive literature in contemporary political theory.[41] German philosopher Max Scheler set out related issues in his classic book *Ressentiment* (similar to *resentment*).[42] He stated that a person at her core is a loving being, *ens amans*, who may feel *ressentiment* when not recognized.[43] Liah Greenfeld uses the example of Ethiopia and Eritrea and suggests that ressentiment plays a central role in nation building.[44] Also, Isaiah Berlin shows how nationalism is often motivated by some form of collective humiliation.[45] Dennis Smith was introduced to the notion of humiliation through Lindner's research and incorporated the notion into his work on globalization.[46]

The philosophy on the politics of recognition, building on Scheler, is a broader concept than the North American individualistic "need for positive self-regard."[47] In "The Politics of Recognition," Charles Taylor argues that identity politics are motivated by a deep human need for recognition, with the injurious effects of various forms of misrecognition.[48] He links the Romantic idea of authenticity and the authentic self with Enlightenment thinkers, such as Kant, for the modern notions of equality and dignity.[49] Identity is also the topic of Amin Maalouf, who links violence to identity and the need to belong.[50]

Social identity theory is a hotly discussed field,[51] for which dignity and humiliation are profoundly relevant topics. Michael Billig, who played a core role in developing social identity theory,[52] brought me to the Second International Conference on Multicultural Discourses in China,[53] for which I wrote the paper "How Multicultural Discourses Can Help Construct New Meaning." I discuss how feelings of humiliation have become the marker of the critical paradigm that guides the field of Multicultural Discourses. I draw on the work of Lu Xun (1881–1936),[54] who is considered the founder of modern Chinese literature. In his work, he unmasks the humiliating effects of feudalism. *Call to Arms (Na-Han)* (1922) was his first collection of stories,[55] which includes his most celebrated stories, such as "Diary of a Madman" and "The True Story of Ah Q," in which he depicts an ignorant farm laborer who goes through a series of humiliations before being executed during the revolution of 1911.

The notion of honor and humiliation is addressed by Richard E. Nisbett and Dov Cohen. They refer to the form of honor that operates in more traditional branches of the Mafia and in blood feuds.[56] Bertram Wyatt-Brown studied the history of American Southern honor and humiliation,[57] and William Ian Miller wrote a book titled *Humiliation and Other Essays on Honor, Social Discomfort, and Violence*,[58] where he links humiliation to honor as understood in historical and literary classics like *The Iliad* or Icelandic sagas.

More complex cases of humiliation, connected to the covert manipulation that will be discussed later in this book, include what I call self-humiliation,[59] or identification with the oppressor, or Ranajit Guha's definition of the term *subaltern*.[60] Ashis Nandy speaks of "hidden or disowned selves," or "subjugated selves," selves that represent both the non-West and the West and their encounters.[61] He asserts that all these selves must take part in cross-cultural dialogue if we want to avoid dogmatism, fundamentalism, or ultranationalism.

Finally, research itself can be affected by humiliation. In my article "How Research Can Humiliate: Critical Reflections on Method," I discuss how validity can be lost, if the objects of research, for example, interview partners, feel humiliated. Or the "truth" may be so humiliating that some researchers may wish to deny it.[62] *Action research* is one way out of this dilemma,[63] as is Maggie O'Neill's theoretical concept of *ethno-mimesis* (the interconnection of sensitive ethnographic work and visual representations), a methodological tool as well as a process for exploring lived experience, displacement, exile, belonging and humiliation.[64]

The relationship between guilt, shame, and aggression has been addressed,[65] as has the relationship between anger and aggression.[66] Culture differences have been highlighted.[67] *Facework* is a term associated with the work of Stella Ting-Toomey.[68] As mentioned earlier, face and face-saving are often associated particularly with Asian culture,[69] but is certainly relevant also outside of Asia. According to Goffman, "face" is the positive social value a person wishes to attain for herself in a social interaction; humiliation can be described as a loss of face—the picture one wishes to present is suddenly discredited.[70]

The term *avoidant personality* first appeared in the earlier writings of Theodor Millon.[71] Millon describes the avoidant individual as being hypersensitive to potential rejection and humiliation, highly socially avoidant, with a low tolerance for negative emotions.

The link between humiliation and aggression has received little attention among researchers. Among the few scholars addressing this topic are Louise Foo and Gayla Margolin, who found that feelings of humiliation serve as a justification for aggression in dating situations.[72] Walter Mischel and Aaron L. De Smet explain that rejection-sensitive men may get "hooked" on situations of debasement in which they can feel humiliated.[73]

Lately, the research group around Coleman has begun to work on this topic. They write: "As we look at the many violent conflicts around the globe today, it is not difficult to see the connections between severe emotions such as humiliation and rage with aggression. However, our understanding of how these emotions operate, and when they lead to repeated cycles of counter-humiliation and violence, is unclear."[74]

In our example of Eve and Adam, Adam may be a rejection-sensitive man. As long as Eve fades into subservience at his onslaught, no open destructive conflict and no cycles of humiliation occur. An unwise therapist could very well create such cycles of humiliation if she were to nurture feelings of humiliation in Eve that would lead to tit-for-tat retaliation, with Eve learning to use the same dysfunctional tools for handling humiliation as Adam. The therapist needs to lay out a vision for a Mandela-like handling of feelings of humiliation for both Eve and Adam.

There is also a link between help and humiliation. As we learn, for example, from Arie Nadler, helping can be both an expression of caring and a demonstration of superiority. Helping can be an effective instrument of dominance in the hands of a more advantaged group. As a result, help may be resented by low-status groups.[75] In international development, for example, trade may advance peace more than aid not least because it does not entail humiliation.[76]

Also, helpers themselves can suffer humiliation in many ways. When I carried out fieldwork in Africa in 1998 and 1999, virtually every helper I met had read Michael Maren's *The Road to Hell: The Ravaging Effects of Foreign Aid and International Charity*.[77]

Malignant narcissism has been linked to humiliation. Sigmund Karterud, Norwegian psychiatrist and specialist on malignant narcissism, suggests that humiliation leads to a partial fragmentation of the self and activates the grandiose self in people so disposed. The grandiose self, once activated, reacts with narcissistic rage and perpetrates revenge to restore itself. Karterud reports a higher propensity for narcissistic rage among individuals with personality structures of the paranoid, antisocial, borderline, and narcissistic types.[78]

Blema S. Steinberg suggests that feelings of humiliation and shame may lead to narcissistic rage, and acts of aggression meant to lessen pain and increase self-worth. Steinberg analyzes political crises and cautions that international leaders, when publicly humiliated, may in some cases instigate mass destruction and war.[79]

In the realm of psychology, sociology, and trauma, Ervin Staub's work, particularly the role of bystanders, already mentioned earlier, continues to be highly relevant.[80] And a special issue of the journal *Social Research* in 1997 was stimulated by *The Decent Society* by philosopher Avishai Margalit.[81] While Staub makes the point that bystanders need to stand *up*—and not *by*—when humiliation is perpetrated on their neighbors, Margalit draws our attention to the fact that we need to stand up not just against singular acts of humiliation but that we must build societies with institutions that do not humiliate their citizens.

Humiliation and rage have been classified as moral emotions, since they motivate moral behavior, even though in this case often negative and undesirable behavior, such as violence or aggression.[82] Margalit highlights the significance of the memory of such emotions and suggests that some people may become attached—almost addicted—to this emotion, as this secures the "benefits" of the victim status and an entitlement to retaliation.[83] In other words, the recollection of and rumination about such experiences can motivate the perpetuation of aggressive behavior.[84]

Similarly, Nadler shows that victimhood may provide an "exemption" from responsibility for being a perpetrator.[85] Goldman and Coleman posit that a humiliated person might feel morally justified to act aggressively against others: "To give up the status as a humiliated person would mean that the aggression would no longer be morally justified, and no further pleasure or catharsis could be derived from it. It would also mean having to face the reality of one's own perpetration, and one's own responsibility for the other's pain."[86]

Vamik Volkan and Joseph V. Montville carried out important work on psychopolitical analysis of intergroup conflict and its traumatic effects.[87] Vamik Volkan's theory of collective violence (put forth in his book *Blind Trust*) explains that a chosen trauma that is experienced as humiliation is not mourned, leading to the feeling of entitlement to revenge and, under the pressure of fear/anxiety, to collective regression.[88]

Earlier, new research on mirror neurons was mentioned. The human brain is hard-wired for connections,[89] social pain is processed like physical pain,[90] and we can also feel humiliated on behalf of others because we identify with other people's suffering via our mirror neurons.[91] This is an important insight for research on global terrorism, because it means that one can feel as humiliated on behalf of victims one identifies with, as if one were to suffer this pain oneself, a phenomenon that is magnified when media give access to the suffering of people in far-flung places.[92]

Psychoneuroimmunology studies are also relevant, as they look at interactions between behavioral/psychological factors, the central nervous system, the immune system, and health.[93] "I think that they [psychoneuroimmunology studies] also have obvious implication for humiliation studies: a person who is humiliated has probably a depressed immune system."[94]

To my knowledge, only Miller, Hartling, and the two above-mentioned journals explicitly used the word and concept of humiliation at the very center of their work, before I began my work. However, there may be research available of which I am unaware. The body of work on humiliation is just beginning to grow.[95]

What Is the Concept of Humiliation Used in This Book?

My book *Making Enemies: Humiliation and International Conflict* (published in 2006) was the product of ten years of work, resting on my entire life experience. It received the following evaluation: "This volume is a path-breaking work that skillfully explores the deeper intricacies between war and peacemaking from a social psychological lens."[96]

In 1994, after years of international experience—in the fields of medicine and psychology in Asia, Africa, the Middle East, America, and Europe—I began to ask, "What is the strongest obstacle to peace, to social cohesion, and to willingness to cooperate in our newly emerging interdependent world? What is the strongest force that disrupts, creates fault lines, and fuels destructive conflict?" My hunch was that the current coming together of humankind, along with the human rights revolution, has consequences for the balance of emotions felt by everybody. My intuition was that the dynamics of humiliation could be central. This conclusion was based on my clinical experience as well as other evidence. For example, there is a widely shared notion that Germany was humiliated by the Versailles Treaty to render it harmless. However, this strategy was counterproductive. It gave Hitler a platform for leading Germany into World War II and the Holocaust as a "remedy" for past and future national humiliation.

In 1996, I began to examine the literature and was surprised that humiliation had not received more academic attention. Search terms such as "shame" or "trauma" yielded innumerable hits, but "humiliation" produced very few. I was astonished—if humiliation could trigger World War II, certainly there should be enough interest in this subject to produce a large body of research, yet this is not the case. Because of this finding, I designed a doctoral research project on humiliation. In my work, humiliation is distinctly addressed on its own account and differentiated from other concepts.

Living globally, I observed that hope is increasing, linked to the two current trends of rising global interdependence and growing awareness of human rights ideals. The hope is that the human rights call will, in the near future, produce equal dignity for all, enabling humankind to live the richness of its diversity in new and dignified ways.

Three decades of living internationally gave me confidence to suggest that the human inhabitants of the Earth are more similar than different in their core needs and that there is ample common ground, common ground that entails the potential to bridge differences of personality[97] and culture,[98] mainly in the desire to be recognized. I like Alexander Wendt's observation that not security but "the struggle for recognition" may actually explain much of Realpolitik behavior.[99] I also resonate with Taylor's assertion that the need for recognition has become problematic during the transition from the premodern to the modern period, since identity that was once "automatic" must now be generated "inwardly," an attempt that can fail and generate feelings of humiliation.[100]

I suggest that the common ground—desiring recognition—connects people and draws them into relationships. Even more important, this tendency has the potential to turn divisive differences into precious diversities and sources of enrichment, as opposed to sources of disruption.

However, there is a condition. If this trend is badly managed, this very common ground can fuel new hot and conflictual fault lines.[101]

Understanding Emotion through the Twin Lens of History and Culture

The starting point for my research on humiliation was European history and the widely shared hypothesis that Germany's humiliation through the Versailles Accords ("The Treaty of Shame") after World War I provided Hitler with the fuel for World War II.[102] Marshal Foch of France said, in 1919, about the Versailles Treaties: "This is not a peace treaty—it will be a cease-fire for 20 years." World War I, as well, has been viewed through the humiliation lens; Mary Matossian made the point that late-developing industrial nations, experiencing military and imperial humiliation, as a response developed belligerent, bellicose, and nationalistic ideologies and regimes as a protective shell for modernization.[103]

From 1997 to 2001, I conducted a doctoral research project at the University of Oslo, with the fieldwork taking place in Africa and Europe. The project produced a thesis titled *The Feeling of Being Humiliated: A Central Theme in Armed Conflicts*.[104]

The questions that formed the starting point for my research where the following:[105] What is experienced as humiliation? What happens when people feel humiliated? When is humiliation established as a feeling? What does humiliation lead to? Which experiences of justice, honor, dignity, respect, and self-respect are connected with the feeling of being humiliated? What role do globalization and human rights play for humiliation? How is humiliation perceived and responded to in different cultures? What role does humiliation play for aggression? What can be done to overcome violent effects of humiliation?

From 1998 to 1999, I carried out interviews in Somaliland, Rwanda, Burundi, Nairobi, Kenya, and Egypt, as well as in Norway, Germany, Switzerland, France, and Belgium. Some of the interviews were filmed (ten hours of film and images of Somaliland and Rwanda), others were taped on mini-discs (over one hundred hours of audiotape). I made notes in situations in which it seemed inappropriate to use video or audiotape. The interviews and conversations were conducted in different languages—most were in English (Somalia) and French (Rwanda and Burundi in the Great Lakes region of Africa), many in German or Norwegian.

Both the conflict parties in Somalia and Rwanda/Burundi, as well as representatives of those who intervened were interviewed. Both in Somalia and Rwanda/Burundi, representatives of the "opponents" and the "third party" were approached. The results confirmed the original hypothesis that humiliation plays a role for war and genocide throughout the world and in the present, as well as the past.

Since 2001, I have continued working on a theory of humiliation,[106] and developed Human Dignity and Humiliation Studies,[107] a global network of like-minded academics and practitioners who wish to transcend humiliation and build a dignified decent world, and expanded my studies, so far in Europe, Southeast Asia, and the United States.

Definition of Humiliation

The definition of humiliation that I developed and use in my work is: Humiliation means the enforced lowering of a person or group, a process of subjugation that damages or strips away their pride, honor, or dignity. To be humiliated is to be placed, against your will (very occasionally with your consent as in cases of religious self-humiliation or in sadomasochism) and often in a deeply hurtful way, in a situation that is greatly inferior to what you feel you should expect. Humiliation entails demeaning treatment that transgresses established expectations. It may involve acts of force, including violent force. At its heart is the idea of pinning down, putting down, or holding to the ground. Indeed, one of the defining characteristics of humiliation as a process is that the victim is forced into passivity, acted on, and made helpless. People react in different ways when they feel that they are unduly humiliated. Some people may experience rage. When this rage is turned inward, it can cause depression and apathy. Rage turned outward can express itself in violence, even in mass violence when leaders are available to forge narratives of group humiliation. Some people hide their anger and carefully plan revenge. The person who plans for "cold" revenge may become the leader of a particularly dangerous movement.[108]

In everyday language, the word *humiliation* is used, at a minimum, in three different ways. First, it signifies an act, second, a feeling, and third, a process: "I humiliate you, you feel humiliated, and the entire process is one of humiliation." In this book, it is expected that readers understand from the context which meaning applies.

CHAPTER 5

How History and Culture Can Humiliate

In an immigrant family in Britain, or other Western countries, a girl who tries to live according to Western customs might risk being killed by her family to prevent the humiliation of family honor. The British police, however, define such killings as crimes, not as prosocial cures for humiliation. Human rights defenders stipulate that killing such a girl is equivalent to compounding humiliation, not remedying it. The immigrant family, in turn, might regard Western attitudes toward them as condescending, a humiliation of their cultural beliefs.[1]

Some of my Egyptian friends feel that the mere use of the case of so-called "honor killings" in my work betrays a humiliating mindset on my part. To their view, I am fanning anti-Arab feelings when I mention honor killings, depicting the West as "good" and the East as "primitive" and "evil." My Egyptian friends feel bitterly disappointed by me, their honor and dignity soiled.

The example of so-called honor killings is particularly stark; however, the world is riddled with such "clashes of humiliation," everywhere on the globe. I use this example—not to blacken anybody's reputation—but for its starkness and complexity. It comprehensively illustrates the numerous layers of humiliation and how they may be defined in ranked honor as opposed to equal dignity contexts. The starkness of honor killings illuminates the traffic metaphor introduced earlier, namely, that the ranking and unranking of human worthiness is as irreconcilable as right-hand driving is with left-hand driving: one side calls for the death of the girl, the other for her life.

During my international life, I have often faced outrage for standing up for human rights, from Western and Eastern "liberals" and "conservatives" alike. Clearly, as all arguments, human rights arguments are open to abuse.[2] However, my approach is different. To me, honor is not something to be found in the East alone; it is equally present in the West—see Wyatt-Brown's work on Southern honor.[3] The significant fault lines do not run between East and West but through the middle of all societies. There are human rights defenders everywhere, and they face opposition everywhere. This is my first point.

My second point is that people who are born into the honor code and adhere to it are not to be looked down on, not in the East and not in the West—the honor code evolved as a cultural adaptation to certain circumstances, not because some people are evil.

Third, I agree with Kishore Mahbubani that the West should not lecture the rest.[4] I do not lecture, and I do not define myself as part of the West. I am a global citizen, a member of the entire human family. To me, human rights represent a normative framework that is better adapted for the emerging and historically unique living conditions that the human species faces—namely, a budding one world. In this situation, human rights open space for people to unfold their full potential as human beings. This offer is valid for every single world citizen in all corners of the globe.

I discuss in Chapter 8 why I also reject the dichotomy of "liberal" relativism versus "conservative" rejection of relativism. My stance cuts across such categorizations. I agree with Riane Eisler, who proposes that we need new social categories that go beyond conventional ones, such as religious versus secular, right versus left, capitalist versus communist, Eastern versus Western, and industrial versus pre- or postindustrial.

As pointed out earlier, I paint a broad picture of large-scale historic and transcultural dimensions into which local cultural adaptations are embedded. In the spirit of Max Weber's ideal-type approach,[5] I use core cultural adaptations as they were shaped throughout human history as a lens to understand emotions. This is not to deny the importance of research on the brain or on the physiological and psychological details of affect, feeling, emotion, script, character, and personality but to expand the range of the angles and perspectives from which to analyze these phenomena.

My view resonates with William Ury's conceptualization of human history.[6] What anthropologists call the ingathering of the human family is a central force in the current historic shift. "Over the last ten thousand years, there has been one fairly steady trend in our history: the ingathering of the tribes of the earth, their incorporation into larger and larger groups, the gradual unification of humanity into a single interacting and interdependent community. For the first time since the origin of our species, humanity is in touch with itself."[7]

How Pride Was Once Pristine

In my theory of humiliation, therefore, I start with Ury's description of a historical development from hunting-gathering to complex agriculturalism and finally to the global information and knowledge society.[8]

Current brain research confirms that correlates with what human history teaches us—that "human nature" is not as inevitably aggressive as many believe. There is no archeological evidence for systematic war prior to ten thousand years ago. There is no archaeological proof of organized fighting among early hunter-gatherers. "The Hobbesian view of humans in a constant state of 'Warre' is simply not supported by the archaeological record."[9] The absence of evidence for homicide does not prove it never happened, but educated hunch indicates that organized killing started relatively late in history. Human nature does not, in other words, force humans unavoidably into destructive Hobbesian competition. On the contrary, older evolutionary roots seem to favor relationships and cooperation. As Ury indicates, the ingathering of humankind and the development of a global knowledge society reopens the door to the more benign frame of an egalitarian win-win era.

The point is not to idealize hunter-gatherers or romanticize them as the heroes of a lost harmonious golden age. Yet in the face of dissonance, conflict, disharmony, disease, or danger, the core ethos, the core moral sentiment, and moral economy among them seems to have been egalitarian. Or in other words, human worth and value were not ranked hierarchically in any deep institutionalized form. Every individual faced the world with considerable pristine unwounded pride, pride that had not yet tasted systemic humiliation.

The past ten thousand years—roughly from the introduction of complex agriculture until recently—were characterized by rather malign systematic war between hierarchically organized societal units, embedded in a win-lose frame. However, ten thousand years is a relatively short time period compared with the 90 percent of human history that humans spent in the comparably benign win-win situation of egalitarian hunting-gathering. A primordial "desire to dominate,"[10] or an "inherent will to power,"[11] or an "animus dominandi"[12]—all conceptualizations that we find at the core of many theories about human evil—appear to define human behavior only during the historically relatively short historic period of complex agriculture. The past ten thousand years may have passed in malign ways not because of human nature but despite it.[13]

It seems that we are justified in suggesting that humans have a stronger "desire to relate," or more precisely, "a desire to mutually connect and be recognized in a context of equal dignity." It makes sense, given the entirety of human history, to suspect that feelings of humiliation emerge when the human need for recognition is disappointed, with "evil" as possible response. This view—counting the past ten thousand years as a distortion of human nature, not as its essence—is more amenable to benign solutions and seems more appropriate in current historic times.

How the "Art of Domination" Was Perfected in Systems of Ranked Honor

Over as much as 90 percent of human history, hunter-gatherers populated the planet at their leisure, with pristine pride. However, there came a time when they were confronted with the fact that the globe has a limited surface and the abundance they were accustomed to was by no means guaranteed.

Cultural adaptations have two layers (at least): deep layers that stem from large-scale adaptations and more superficial layers that arise from local adaptations. Large-scale historical transitions have universal and global effects—forming the common ground that all humankind shares, on all continents, in all cultures to various degrees and handled with different cultural colorings. Learning the fact that the size of the planet is limited was (and still is) such a global and universal learning process. Humankind was spared learning this lesson only as long as its campaign of populating the planet had not yet reached these limits. This lesson began, however, to make itself felt roughly ten thousand years ago, even if only indirectly through unexpected systemic scarcity, and it continues its message today, among others, through climate change. Such lessons have profound consequences for the options humanity has to influence the human condition, with notions of pride, honor, and dignity—and humiliation as violation of honor or dignity—being deeply affected.

In some ways we could call the "hitting of the wall" ten thousand years ago humankind's first round of globalization, meaning that they had managed to populate the entire globe—or at least most of the known, easily habitable surface. In the language of anthropologists this set of circumstances is called *circumscription*.[14] Circumscription means that there was simply not enough for everybody anymore—not enough space that could easily be populated and not enough resources that could easily be consumed. Our planet is small, and it gives the illusion of being unlimited only as long as one has not yet reached its limits.

However, humankind adapted to this challenge. The experiment of intensification became possible and feasible. *Intensification* meant domesticating plants and animals, and developing agricultural systems[15] (with the ease of domestication deciding over whose civilization would flourish[16]). These systems provided an alternative way to increase resources when the old methods based on untouched abundance met their limits.

Agriculture requires land as a basic resource, by definition introducing a win-lose frame of "this is either my land or your land." Bloody competition is bound to emerge from mutual distrust, even if nobody is interested in going to war. The so-called security dilemma, as described in international relations theory, became *the* defining factor. The phrase "security dilemma" was coined by John Herz to explain why states that have no intention to harm one another may still end up in competition and war. Its very essence is tragic.[17] The security dilemma has been expanded on by many authors.[18] Jack Snyder's definition of the security dilemma, where one state requires the insecurity of another,[19] has been labeled by Alan Collins as a state-induced security dilemma.[20]

Under the conditions of the security dilemma, the Hobbesian fear of surprise attacks from outside one's nation's borders reigns. Barry Posen and Russell Hardin discuss these emotional aspects of the security dilemma and how they play out between ethnic groups as much as between states.[21] Constant preparations for war drain societal resources. Everybody has to be on continuously alert, dependent on leaders and governing organs. Stereotyped fear of out-groups permeates in-groups. For millennia, this fear became manifest in societal, social, and cultural institutions, from Ministries of War or Defense to identity constructs such as patriotism, or gender division.[22]

In the context of agriculture and the security dilemma, collectivist hierarchical societies emerged with ranked honor as a core value. Masters subdued underlings, higher beings stood above lower beings, men above women, and everyone subdued nature. The idea of subjugation and instrumentalization was not regarded as violation. On the contrary, making tools from nature was valued as useful and legitimate, as it was among hunter-gatherers. Within the context of the security dilemma, however, societies began to instrumentalize more than stones and bones. Animals and people became instruments. Underlings became tools in the hands of their masters. The core dynamic of humiliation, putting down and holding down, was expanded from the abiotic to the biotic world—and this was regarded as utterly useful and right.

Only some human communities were so out of the way that they remained untouched.[23] Others were left with nonarable land and developed pastoralism, whose in-built mobility lends itself to developing a culture of raiding as an alternative method of acquiring resources. (Somalia's fierce pastoralist culture, which is among the cultures I studied in considerable depth, serves as a contemporary illustration.) Yet others sought their livelihood in trade. Whoever took to trade, since trade means bridging borders, began weaving the web of global interdependence that characterizes contemporary world affairs. Unsurprisingly, traders experimented with the "partnership model" of civilization (Eisler's cultural transformation theory[24]) that the world needs to adopt today, preferring it to the "dominator model." The Minoans of Crete, for example, from 1700 B.C. onward, primarily a mercantile people engaging in overseas trade, allowed their men and women to hold rather equal social status. The mercantile city of

Florence in Italy nurtured the Renaissance, with its notion of humanism and dignity.

However, in most parts of the world, the dominator model with its ranked honor superseded the pristine pride of early hunter-gatherers. Ten millennia ago, collectivist societies of honor all around the globe began to subjugate people of untouched pride and put them into vertically stacked strata that ranged from elites at the top to slaves and outcasts at the bottom. As far back as in the fifth century B.C., Greek historian Thucydides identifies "fear, honour, and interest" as "the strongest motives" for war,[25] and more than two millennia later, Thucydides is still being quoted today.[26]

Pierre Bourdieu gave a lot of thought to honor,[27] connecting it to the concept of *méconnaissance* (misrecognition). He describes honor as a game of challenge and counterchallenge:

1. to challenge a person is to accord him a certain dignity, for it connotes a recognition of equality,
2. to challenge a person incapable of responding is to dishonor oneself,
3. only a challenge coming from an equal deserves to be taken up.[28]

I describe honor, or more precisely, ranked honor, as the "art of domination." Masters have different options to subjugate underlings. For example, they can use brute force. However, over the course of the past ten thousand years, a more devious application of domination evolved, replacing brute force by more subtle and covert approaches. One such art was for masters to let nobody forget the fear entailed in the security dilemma and instrumentalizing this fear for their advantage. Masters routinely instilled dread and apprehension in underlings and threatened them with violence and terror, from torture to killing. Over time, continuous humbling, shaming, and humiliating (honor humiliation, the form of humiliation that was seen as legitimate during the past millennia) became sufficient, particularly when underlings had learned to feel ashamed at failing their master's expectations.

As noted before, honor is not just honor but ranked honor. Its innermost core is to rank human worthiness, to justify that some beings are higher than others in their essence. Its antidote is not merely dignity but *equality* in dignity. The strategy to tacitly coopt underlings into accepting their lowly status has succeeded when underlings are proud of their honor and have forgotten and misrecognize that its core function is to rank people's worthiness.

In a system of submission/domination, the social bond that connects humans is usually a connection not between two equals but between the master's orders and the underling's self-effacing acquiescence. The human desire for connection and the need to belong, together with emotions such as love, hatred, and shame, are instrumentalized in ways that make domination easier and the application of brute force less necessary.

Gro Steinsland studies the power of rulers and the ideology of rulership in the Nordic societies from Vikings through the medieval age, from about 800 until 1200.[29] Because Christianity arrived relatively late in the North, the transition of ideologies in this region is well documented. Steinsland analyzes, for example, the eddaic poem *Skírnismál* and its depiction of the so-called myth of the sacred marriage (the Greek technical term is "hieros gamos"), or the erotic alliance between a god and a giant woman, which rendered the ruler special and gave him and his lineage a unique position with regard to other people. With Christianity a related, medieval ideology of rulership was imported, namely, the depiction of the king as an image of the Heavenly God.[30]

In other words, a system of submission/domination was enforced by way of myth, often made visible by grand edifices. These myths and their built expressions evolved over time, always designed to inspire awe so as to make underlings succumb without resistance.

This is not to deny that religion can be of high value, both for individuals and societies. However, whatever ontological status we wish to afford religion, both believers and nonbelievers can agree that the past millennia witnessed the instrumentalization of religion to rank human merit and value on a scale between higher and lower, rather than build a world of equality in dignity.

Here is another, more recent example for mass manipulation.[31] Adolf Hitler was very astute at putting into practice what he called the "correct psychology" of seduction. He wrote in *Mein Kampf*, "The art of propaganda lies in understanding the emotional ideas of the great masses and finding, through a psychologically correct form, the way to the attention and hence to the heart of the broad masses."[32] He spelled out in detail how he manipulated a whole nation into "total war" (causing millions of deaths):

> The broad mass of a nation does not consist of diplomats, or even professors of political law, or even individuals capable of forming a rational opinion . . . The people in their overwhelming majority are so feminine by nature and attitude that sober reasoning determines their thoughts and actions far less than emotion and feeling. And this sentiment is not complicated, but very simple and all of a piece. It does not have multiple shadings; it has a positive and a negative; love or hate, right or wrong, truth or lie, never half this way and half that way, never partially.[33]

To keep underlings subservient and reinforce their subjugation, to maintain their status as tools in the hands of their masters and keep them from disobeying, Hitler and many other leaders throughout the past thousands of years routinely manipulated their underlings into more or less enthusiastic obedience. Hitler was particularly adept; he became the "lover" of a nation that he describes as "feminine."[34] Others were less artful, yet to be sure, all kept underlings in awe, often in continuous fear for their lives, and they typically frustrated their underlings' desire for a secure mutual connection. Fear was the fuel masters used to keep their underlings docile. Therefore, masters tried to keep fear always looming, handy when needed. Not least religion and fear of God were used to legitimate this strategy with divine authorization.

In sum, over the past ten thousand years, manipulation, particularly the manipulation of emotions and feelings, became the very tool of the art of domination, or the art of covert penetration of honorable habitus so that it would be misrecognized. The art of domination rendered underlings helpless (more in Chapter 8).

How Egalization Can Undo Domination

We live in transitional times. The transition is marked, at least in part, by a shift in the meaning of the word *humiliation*. In the English language, the connotations of the verbs *to humiliate* and *to humble* parted around two hundred fifty years ago, going in opposite directions. Until that time, the verb *to humiliate* did not signify the violation of dignity. *To humiliate* meant merely *to lower* or *to humble* ("to remind underlings of their due place"), and this was widely regarded as a prosocial activity. William Ian Miller tells us that "the earliest recorded use of *to humiliate* meaning to mortify or to lower or to depress the dignity or self-respect of someone does not occur until 1757."[35]

It is interesting that the old meaning of the verb *to humiliate* was replaced by a new, much more negative meaning just prior to the American Declaration of Independence (July 4, 1776), the French Revolution (August 4, 1789), the emergence of the individuated self,[36] and the birth of a growing awareness that planet Earth is the home of one humankind. These were also the times that began the canonization of human rights ideals.[37]

In Ury's account, we are slowly entering a global knowledge society.[38] One reverberation of this transition is the change from traditional honor codes in hierarchical collectivist settings to new human rights codes based on equal dignity for all linked with more individualistic cultural ideals.

As the transformation of the verb *to humiliate* indicates, humiliation's role changes within this larger transition. Humiliation is important in both honor and dignity contexts, however, in profoundly different ways. In honor environments, humiliation is usually evoked by elites. Male aristocrats were called on to defend humiliated honor in duels, for example. In dignity contexts, in contrast, feelings of humiliation are encouraged in the downtrodden, those who formerly were expected to quietly bow in subservience.[39]

With the advent of human rights ideals, the concept of humiliation changes in terms of its social meaning and the people who experience it. It moves from the top to the bottom of pyramids of power, from the privileged to the disadvantaged. In a true human rights framework, the downtrodden underling is given the right to feel humiliated (the beaten wife, the girl who wishes to decide on her life herself, etc.). The masters, on the other hand, are called on to humble themselves and are no longer given permission to resist this call by labeling it humiliating.

The human rights revolution could be described as an attempt to collapse the master–slave gradient to the middel level of equal dignity and humility. The practice of masters arrogating superiority and subjugating underlings is regarded as illicit and obscene, and human rights advocates invite both masters and underlings to join in shared humility at the level of equal dignity. Feelings of humiliation, felt by the downtrodden and those who identify with them, are the very driving force of the human rights revolution.

The ability to feel humiliated, on behalf of oneself and others, in the face of violations of dignity, represents the emotional engine that can connect new awareness with conscientization, which can drive systemic change. Conscientization has been explored as a mediator between antecedent conditions and prodemocracy movements.[40] "Non-violent movements become increasingly powerful as conscientization becomes broadly networked" both locally and globally."[41] The ability to feel humiliated is a "bridge" to conscientization, a bridge on the path to giving life to the human rights ideal of equality in dignity for all.

It is important to note that equal dignity for all or the horizontal ranking of human worth and value in no way implies sameness as the antidote to inequality, hierarchy, or stratification. The significant point is not the absence or presence of hierarchy, inequality or stratification, but whether human worthiness is ranked. Functional hierarchies will always be necessary, and under conditions of equal dignity, difference and diversity can be celebrated. Primary is our shared humanity. Differences can be benign, however, only when regarded as secondary to our shared humanity. Otherwise they become destructive. Rank is not the problem—rankism is.[42]

The horizontal line in Figure 5.1 represents the middle level of equal dignity and humility. This line does not signify that all human beings are equal, or should be equal, or ever were or will be equal, or identical, or all the same. The horizontal line illustrates a worldview that does not permit the hierarchical ranking of existing differences of human worth and value. Masters are invited to step down from arrogating *more* worthiness, and underlings are encouraged to rise up from humiliation, up from being humiliated down to *lower* value. Masters are humbled and underlings empowered.

Globalization entails benign and malign aspects.[43] Globalization critics do not oppose all aspects of globalization. They do not oppose global civil society, for example, a benefit flowing from the coming together of

The Historic Transition to Egalization

Master in the traditional honor order (arrogation)		Top of the scale

New human rights order of humility   ⏐   Line of equal dignity

Underling in the traditional honor order (humiliation)   Bottom of the scale

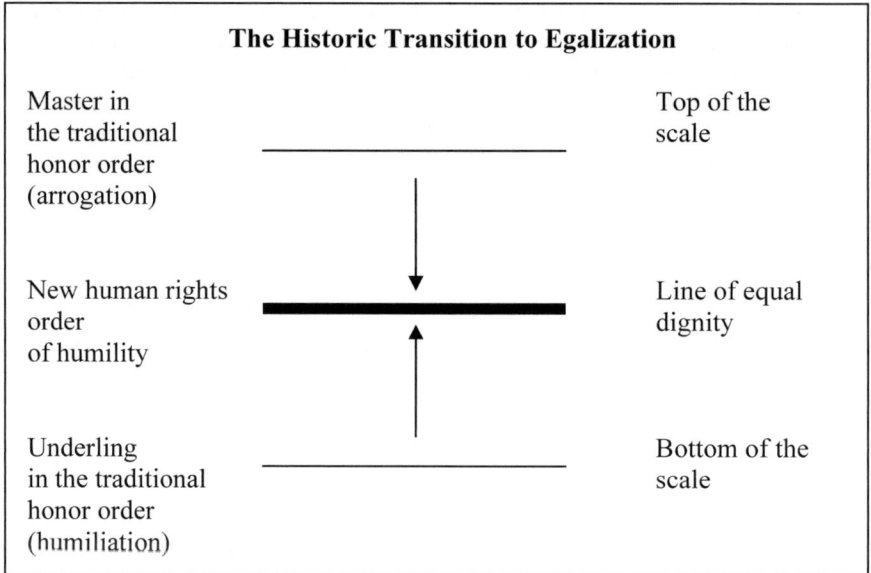

Figure 5.1. The Historic Transition to Egalization

humankind. However, they are uneasy about the possibility for humiliation, or what I call the lack of egalization. I coined the word *egalization* to match the word *globalization* and differentiate it from words such as equality.[44] Egalization avoids claiming that everybody should become equal and that there should be no differences between people. Egality can coexist with a functional hierarchy that regards all participants as possessing equal dignity; egality can not coexist, though, with a hierarchy that defines some people as lesser beings and others as more valuable.

> If we imagine the world as a container with a height and a width, *globalization* addresses the horizontal dimension, the shrinking width. *Egalization* concerns the vertical dimension, reminiscent of Hofstede's power distance. Egalization is a process away from a very high container of masters at the top and underlings at the bottom, towards a flat container with everybody enjoying equal dignity.
>   Egalization is a process that elicits hot feelings of humiliation when it is promised but fails. The lack of egalization is thus the element that is heating up feelings among so-called "globalization-critics." Their disquiet stems from lack of egalization and not from an overdose of globalization. What they call for is that *globalization* ought to marry *egalization*.[45]

If we recapitulate human history, we see that the species *Homo sapiens*, through its tendency to expand and wander, faced circumscription, or systemic global scarcity, for the first time ten thousand years ago, when wild food suddenly was no longer abundant, and "land" became a term for a scarce resource. This was a completely new situation—humankind unwittingly had reached the limits of the planet. Today, it is clean air, water, or biodiversity that follow suit—their abundance was taken for granted until very recently. Ten millennia ago, agriculture represented a viable adaptation, however, it brought fear, the security dilemma, and violent conflict. Even attempts to mitigate those malign effects by creating larger in-groups within which scarcity could be better managed usually created more overall scarcity in the long term (conquerors, for example, often were plunderers and left behind nothing but wasteland). Even when in-groups were formed to manage scarcity in cooperation, this was bought at the price of instrumentalizing people (for example, marriage being used to forge alliances precluded any freedom of choice of a partner).

"The Tragedy of the Commons," an article by Garrett Hardin,[46] spells out the potential vulnerabilities of communal sharing, and many economists drew the conclusion that is an unusable approach. However, even though communal sharing is vulnerable, both from within and particularly from outside, it does represent a key model for sharing the Earth's resources among all of humankind. Its vulnerabilities can be understood and adequately addressed, particularly in a situation where increasing global interdependence eliminates outsiders who otherwise could undermine its balance. Research shows that people are in fact willing to sign up to social norms of sharing.[47] The only true mitigation of the limits of the Earth's resources is a global alliance of a united humankind that creates new abundance by tapping into cooperative and creative knowledge management, rather than competing for land or other limited biosphere resources.

The Undoing of Ranked Collectivist Honor

The vision of a new world of equal dignity calls for individuals to develop as whole and dignified entities in and for themselves. Nobody should be regarded as a subservient part of the larger body of a group. Killing women or men is no longer legitimate. Using human lives as a means of sending messages of honor between groups is no longer condoned.

Today, human rights advocates around the world aim to invite formerly higher and lower beings to meet in the middle level of equal dignity. We read headlines such as "On the Obsolescence of the Concept of Honor."[48]

In the course of this large-scale transformation that is taking place, the mutilating effect of ranked collectivist systems of honor is being unmasked. The transition exposes the extent to which the ranking of people's worthiness had what I call foot-binding effects, as handicapping as the binding of women's feet in old China. Relegating fellow humans to the category of tools or cogwheels in the service and framework of the security dilemma was a form of mutilation.

Human rights defenders do not just talk about pride, honor, and dignity—these terms all connote worthiness and value. What is significant in the context of human rights is that the antidote to ranked honor, a ranking that subjugates untouched pristine pride, is not dignity in general but *equality* in dignity. Equality in dignity cannot bring back the untouched pride of the past—the memories of thousands of years of subjugation will never be erasable—but an unconcealment of the truth about the mutilating effect of this subjugation and its healing. German philosopher Martin Heidegger (1889–1976) reflected on the "call of conscience," and how *Dasein*'s (Being's) own Self is open to truth or unconcealment (Greek *aletheia*).[49] Incidentally, focusing on interest, not on position, as suggested in negotiation handbooks, can open a path to unconcealment, because positions often conceal tacit practices of mutilation, which can be unmasked by probing true interest.[50]

George A. Bonanno and John T. Jost studied survivors of the September 11 attacks in 2001 who were very near to the World Trade Center at the time of the attacks and exposed to high degrees of potential trauma. The researchers found that this exposure was followed by a shift toward more rigid and conservative beliefs. This shift, interestingly, however, appears to have been maladaptive (and psychologically mutilating):

> Despite its prevalence, we found relatively little evidence that embracing conservatism was related to improved well-being as measured either in terms of survivors' mental health symptoms or friends-relatives' ratings of their psychological adjustment. On the contrary, political conservatism, right-wing authoritarianism, and conservative shift were generally associated with the following: chronically elevated levels of posttraumatic stress disorder (PTSD) and depression, desire for revenge and militarism, cynicism, and decreased use of humor.[51]

This research indicates that the uncertainties of life are best mastered with a positive and flexible approach, not with rigidity and vengefulness. Good coping and favorable long-term adjustment are associated with genuine positive emotion (the so-called Duchenne smile is a marker).[52]

I would like to see more research analyzing the hypothesis that the maladaptive conservative shift described by Bonanno and Jost is stimulated by an honor tradition (where its maladaptiveness for human health is misrecognized).[53]

Ranked honor is still strong in two realms today: in certain world regions (for example, where women believe that being beaten is justified) and at certain macro levels, namely, at the level at which powerful international elites deal with each other. Honor often plays a stronger role in foreign policy matters, in armed services and diplomatic staffs, than among the lower echelons of the average citizen. A passion to retain a state's "honorable" preeminence, Donald Kagan proposes,[54] applies in today's world no less than it did earlier. This is true even when national honor is partly concealed by human rights rhetoric and no longer openly invoked as it was in the past. Certain segments of American society, for example, are still deeply entrenched in the Southern honor so well described by Wyatt-Brown.

By being demoted to the level of tools serving the security dilemma, living beings are robbed of the fullness of their capacities. This was not an overly apparent problem as long as humans lived on and worked the land. An agrarian world does not stop functioning when lords give obedient underlings orders. Underlings toiling in the fields did not have to enjoy their work to fulfill their roles. However, this changes in a modern knowledge society that depends on creativity. A human being reduced to being a tool cannot be creative (except perhaps in devising sabotage and other disruptive interventions that a master would not wish to foster). The growing need for creativity exposes the mutilation that comes with ranking humans beings.

Both masters and underlings in coercive hierarchies are forced into artificial incapacitation. Typically only master elites, usually males, can use the sword to defend humiliated honor. Underlings must swallow subjugation quietly. Masters use their sword arm, usually their right arm. Their left arm, the one responsible for caring and nurturing, metaphorically speaking, is not used or encouraged to develop. For lowly men and women, the inverse is true. Both elites and underlings function with only one arm. As noted earlier, the full range of human emotions—perhaps the most significant component distinguishing humans from nonhumans—was denied to the majority of human beings for the past millennia.

Arthur Koestler's term *bisociation* lends itself to illustrating how creativity, to be truly creative, requires the use of more than one "arm": "I have coined the term 'bisociation' in order to make a distinction between the routine skills of thinking on a single 'plane,' as it were, and the creative act, which . . . always operates on more than one plane."[55]

Morton Deutsch points out the advantages of leaving the distorted selves of the past behind. Dominators, Deutsch explains, must withdraw from processes of domination; reown and resolve their feelings of vulnerability, guilt, self-hatred, rage, and terror; and undo the projection of these feelings onto the oppressed. According to Deutsch, "psychologists, in their roles as psychotherapists, marriage counselors, organizational consultants, and educators have a role to play in demystifying the psychological processes involved in the dominators. So too . . . do the oppressed, by not accepting their distorted roles in the distorted relationship of the oppressor and the oppressed."[56]

In conclusion, we, as humankind, are part of a transition to a normative framework that frees everybody. The new normative framework of human rights invites everybody to use both arms, invest their full selves, and unfold their true potentials. It is a superior framework for an ever more interdependent world, a world that faces challenges that can only be addressed jointly, by unlocking creativity in a spirit of shared responsibility and mutual support. This transition is worth supporting and can and needs to be completed without vilifying adherents to the traditional paradigm, a paradigm that represented an adaptation to a different world.

However, there are problems. As I describe in greater detail later, the transition proceeds both too slowly and too rapidly, lacks clear support, and is hampered by the overt and covert persistence of outdated cultural scripts. Traditional honor norms and related feelings of humiliation are still alive and thriving. Many elites still feel entitled to supremacy and do not enter into the cooperation that is necessary to give the world a more even playing field. They still feel humiliated when asked to humble themselves. This can lead to head-on confrontations that undermine otherwise benign trends.

Other people resort to inherently contradictory strategies that are as harmful. They defend the traditional strategies of honor in one context, as honorable elites, while invoking the debasement of dignity in another context, as the victims of dignity humiliation. For example, a male head of family with a background in an honor culture may demand human rights defenders to walk their talk and treat his culture as equal, while disregarding that he is not treating his own wife and daughters as equals.

In other words, we live in a confused world where traditional honor norms linger, even where they stand in stark contradiction to new equal dignity norms. While the two moral universes are diametrically opposed—one condones ranked worthiness, the other equal worthiness for all—they are sometimes intertwined in ways that make it difficult for people to see their incompatibility. In all cases, this provides fertile soil for violent conflict. Therefore it is important to understand both normative universes: that of collectivist ranked honor and that of equal dignity for each individual human being.

The Undoing of Ruthless Individualism

The ideals of ruthless individualism in some Western cultural spheres, forced on fellow citizens with astonishingly collectivist fervor, share some commonalities with traditional honor codes. Like honor codes, overstretched individualism has yet to mature as an ideal of true equal dignity for all. Martha Albertson Fineman wrote a book titled *The Myth of Autonomy*, in which she stresses that "families bear the burdens of dependency, while market institutions are free to operate as though the domestic tasks that reproduce the society were some other institution's responsibility."[57]

Fineman concludes that by "invoking autonomy, we create and perpetuate cultural and political practices that stigmatize and punish those among us labeled dependent."[58] Linda Hartling identifies this practice as one of the root sources of destructive humiliation.[59]

Ruthless individualism could be described as another way of ranking human worthiness. Only the masters are different—those who elbowed their way up, legitimated by the might-is-right philosophy that was formerly reserved to honor elites, now extended to every individual.

The traditional world order is (1) collectivist and (2) ranked. Liberation from oppressive collectivist ranking cannot be achieved through a new kind of ranking, even if it is now individualistic ("Western" individualism). Nor can liberation be achieved through a new kind of oppressive collectivism, even though it is now uniformly unranked ("Eastern" communism). Ideologies of individualism and communism, in their liberation fervor, reform only one element, leaving the other to wreak havoc.

In a context where equality in worthiness is used as the structuring principle of relationships, liberation is two-tiered. Unity in diversity is a suitable guideline.[60] A unity in diversity approach fosters and is fostered by a nondualistic win-win frame, while a uniformity or division approach fosters and is fostered by a dualistic win-lose frame. The two-tiered liberation should not end in uniformity without diversity (so-called communism) or in division without unity (ruthless individualism). The most workable paradigm cherishes diversity and embeds it into the unity of relationships that are nurtured by mutual respect for equality in dignity. Only a two-tiered liberation gives humankind its full humanity and promises comprehensive personal and social health.

Incidentally, shame can play an important role in maintaining and developing personal and social health. Acknowledging (rather than masking) shame and using it constructively to maintain the human bond, can bring about personal change and help hasten cultural change towards a world of mutual respect for equality in dignity (more in Chapter 6).[61]

The Freeing of Dignity

How did ideas of dignity and equality in dignity emerge?[62] Undoubtedly, the ideas that feed into today's human rights ideas predate 1757. All the major religions include significant ideals of equality. Buddhism has a claim for equal dignity, as has New Testament Christianity, Islam, the Sikh faith, and so forth. However, these ideals were pushed into the background by the overall hierarchical structures of the larger social and societal environments. Only in the past couple of hundred years have these ideals begun to carry significant influence.

Medieval Christianity, for example, stressed the misery and worthlessness of *homo viator*, earthly man. Life on Earth meant suffering, which had to be accepted with dutiful and obedient humility and meekness. As suggested earlier, ruling elites found it convenient for their underlings to believe in such a worldview because it made it easier to bond them into ranked collectives. At best, rewards could be expected in the afterlife.

The concept of dignity opposes both the discourses of collectivism and this-worldly suffering. The concept of dignity embraces life on Earth as something positive and rejects collectivist hierarchy, instead emphasizing individual rights. Dignity has its basis in the pristine pride of the former, more benign hunting-gathering era of human history.

The term dignity has its etymological roots in the Latin words *decus* and *decorum* (Sanskrit *dac-as*, "fame"). For Cicero, dignity was a quality of masculine beauty. Even though it was discussed, the concept of dignity was not forged into an internally consistent set of ideas until the Renaissance. The Renaissance began in Florence, one of the first successful global players in what I call the second round of globalization (we are still in the midst of that second round today, although with a much broader understanding of globality than existed in emergent Florence). This round of globalization is connected to a new way of intensification, no longer through the exploitation of land and land ownership but through knowledge and skills thriving within a web of global relationships.

Giannozzo Manetti (1396–1459), son of a rich Florentine merchant, Marsilio Ficino (1433–1499), another Florentine humanist, and Giovanni Pico della Mirandola (1463–1494) gave philosophical and theological form to the importance of this-worldly dignity.

In the sixteenth century, the Protestant Reformation and the Catholic Reform, combined with the explosion of scientific studies, drastically impacted the concept of dignity, including a redefinition of the very role of the human being in the universe. What was called rationality was applied to every problem and thinkers and writers were no longer punished for violating established ideas. The Age of Reason, with the Enlightenment emerging in the eighteenth century, germinated ideas such as freedom, democracy, and the establishment of a contractual basis of rights. These ideas ultimately led to the scientific method, to the ideas of religious and racial tolerance, and to the concept of states as self-governing republics through democratic means.[63]

While the Enlightenment stands for the contractual basis of rights, Romanticism (an artistic, political, philosophical, and social trend arising out of the late eighteenth and early nineteenth centuries in Europe) celebrated what it perceived as heroic individuals. Romanticism is often seen as the antithesis of the Enlightenment, but together the two strengthened the role of the individual, protected by contract and enabled to exercise free choice.

The reverberations of these trends are still being felt today, the ideals generated through centuries of change still wait to be fully translated into the way humanity lives. *Dignity, Character, and Self-Respect*, an anthology edited by Robin Sleigh Dillon, gathers philosophical essays on self-respect and draws on Immanuel Kant, the Prussian philosopher, regarded as the last major philosopher of the Enlightenment.[64] It addresses the complexity of self-respect (even the moral duty to respect oneself), and its embeddedness into such concepts as personhood, dignity, rights, character, autonomy, integrity, shame, oppression, empowerment, and humility (with humility no longer meaning meek acceptance of lowliness).

The Freeing of Humility

Companies and countries around the world currently face activists who try to shame them into keeping their promises as protectors of the environment and human rights. Humbling and shaming with the aim to instill humility still works prosocially, while humiliation no longer does. We wish to be surrounded by people of confident humility, not by humiliated underlings or arrogant supremacists.

Nelson Mandela did not humiliate the white elites in South Africa—he taught them humility. He did not speak from a stance of arrogance but in a spirit of shared humility. In this way Mandela left behind ten millennia of human history. He humbled the masters, and he dismantled the hierarchical system together with its emotional expressions. He realized the two tiers of the human rights liberation.

Let us see whether Eve and Adam are making progress. Their predicament shows that human emotional reactions are embedded into broader historic transformations of normative contexts. The phrase "domestic chastisement" expresses positive valence—the "man of the house" has the right and duty to "chastise" his wife and children, and it is regarded as good for all involved to be reminded of their place. Nowadays, particularly in social contexts influenced by human rights values, this practice transmutes into the negative concept of domestic violence. In other words, the same sequence of behavior is no longer regarded as good for everybody but as bad for everybody. Eve and Adam are expected to leave behind domination and submission and share equality in dignity and humility. This is what their counselor explains to them.

CHAPTER 6

HOW HUMAN RIGHTS CAN DIGNIFY

The emergence of one single global knowledge society entails a number of benign promises. First, as William Ury argues, knowledge as a basis for livelihood brings back the more benign frame of the first 90 percent of human history. Second, as humankind perceives itself as one family, it is liberated from the malign grip of the security dilemma. These two developments open space for liberation—for a transition from coercive hierarchies of ranked honor to creative networks of equality in dignity. We need to grasp this historic opportunity and capitalize on it. This book is written to help in this process.

This liberation offers a number of "sub"-liberations. One such subliberation is the opportunity to free ourselves from the need to pit in-groups against "enemy" out-groups, which in turn liberates us from malign out-group biases. We also have the opportunity to become liberated from collectivist and ranked social models in which a few masters turn underlings into tools in the service of the security dilemma, robbing everybody of their humanity. We stand at a time in history in which we can free everyone on the globe, and we can all retrieve our humanity. In a world of one single human family, no longer do we need to dehumanize young men to become killers of "enemies." This does not mean that the world will become a rose garden—like in all villages, we will need police in the global village to apply the template of respectful social control.

Part of the liberation is to recognize that peace and happiness are more than simply conflict resolution. Peace and happiness are more than calm and quiet, more than supposedly peaceful subservience of underlings. Peace and happiness, to deserve their names, must allow for the fullness of human capacities. As discussed, unity in diversity is a helpful motto (rather than uniformity and division) for the two-tiered liberation described in Chapter 5.

In an interdependent world of limited resources, cooperation among equals is the only recipe for survival. Domination, the very approach that brought "victory" in the past, ensures collective failure today. Interdependence is the ultimate deterrent. In an interdependent world, security is no longer attainable through "keeping enemies out," or dominating them, but only through "keeping a fragmented world together."

What is needed for this task is the Lévinasian interpretation of human rights referred to in the introduction to this book. The Lévinasian interpretation goes further than the Kantian definition, emphasizing the liberation processes that are possible at the current point in human history.

How Human Rights Introduce New Definitions

Humility, shame, and humiliation, as they flow into affects, feelings, emotions, and acts, entail a spatial orientation, namely, a *downward* orientation. In their book *The Embodied Mind*, George Lakoff and Mark Johnson explain that the body and mind are linked by way of spatial metaphors.[1]

"Being down" is a state of being that carries basically three connotations: first, it can be "just right," second, "too far down," or third, "not sufficiently far down." All three states are defined in profoundly different ways in honor societies as compared to dignity societies.

"Just right," in a human rights context, is when a person is guided by a dignified sense of worth embedded into wise humility. "Too far down" is when self-depreciation and a sense of worthlessness depress a person. "Not sufficiently far down" is when arrogance, supremacist hubris, and haughtiness reign. Human rights–based societies endorse relationships that secure the connections between individuals as equals in dignity and rights.

In an honor society, in contrast, the rules for masters diverge from rules for underlings. Subaltern inferiors can almost never be too far down, are routinely warned to avoid being not sufficiently down, and know that their "right" place is wherever their masters want them. They bypass shame not least because they wish to avoid being lowered even more. Also, masters bypass shame, but they do this because they consider it shameful to feel shame; they are socialized to believe that masters ought not to bow or accept shame—they enter the "shame spiral"[2] or the "toxic shame bind."[3] Elites are socialized to believe that bowing or accepting shame humiliates them unduly.

In contemporary contexts, we find the former master's behavior wherever hypermasculinity is venerated, while many former underlings do not yet dare to accept the human rights message that they have gained the option to free themselves from shame and can carry their heads high. The story of Eve and Adam, who accompany us throughout this book, illustrates some aspects of this predicament.

Not only behavior, also institutions that entail humiliation are defined in profoundly different ways in honor societies and dignity societies. The most striking difference is that in an honor context, humbling, shaming, and humiliating are all legitimate acts when employed by masters on inferiors. White supremacists during apartheid were entitled by law to humble, shame, and humiliate blacks. In a human rights context of equal dignity, in contrast, the submission/domination gradient is dismantled, and humiliating others is no longer legitimate. Humiliation is isolated as an illegitimate act. Shaming and humbling remain socially useful, but only if applied in dignified and nonhumiliating ways and for worthy causes. In postapartheid South Africa, for example, corporations may be shamed into complying with their ethical standards, and overzealous politicians, who are in danger of arrogating supremacy (be it black or white supremacy), may be humbled. However, nowhere is humiliation legitimate—not as a spontaneous act, not as a routine action, and certainly not as an institutionalized agenda.

How Human Rights Delegitimize Humiliation

In human rights–based societies, humiliation becomes more hurtful (and therefore a more compelling research topic). This is because the *four* basic kinds of humiliation known to honor cultures become conflated into *one* kind of humiliation when viewed through a human rights lens.

Humiliation in honor societies—we may call it *honor humiliation*—can be categorized in four variants (see Table 6.1).[4] A master uses *conquest humiliation* to subjugate formerly equal neighbors into a position of inferiority. When the hierarchy is in place, the master uses *reinforcement humiliation*—ranging from seating orders and bowing rules to brutal measures, such as customary beatings or killings—to consolidate its power. A third form of humiliation, *relegation humiliation*, is used to push an already low-ranking underling even further down. *Exclusion humiliation* means excluding victims altogether, exiling, or even killing them.

Human rights turn all four types of humiliation into the latter one because all human rights violations exclude victims from humanity. This situation produces intense pain and suffering because losing one's dignity means being excluded from the family of humankind altogether. I call this *human rights humiliation* or *dignity humiliation*; it is a deeply destructive and devastating experience that attacks people at their cores. It is from this viewpoint that practices of humiliation once considered "normal," such as beating and "breaking the will," acquire medical labels such as *victimhood* or *trauma*.[5]

Table 6.1. Four Variants of Humiliation[6]

	Honor Humiliation	Human Rights Dignity Humiliation
Conquest humiliation: When a strong power reduces the relative autonomy of rivals, previously regarded as equals, and forces them into a position of long-term subordination. Creation of hierarchy or addition of a new upper tier within a hierarchical order.	X	–
Relegation humiliation: When an individual or group is forcefully pushed downward within an existing status hierarchy.	X	–
Reinforcement humiliation: Routine abuse of inferiors to maintain the perception that they are, indeed, inferior.	X	–
Exclusion humiliation: When an individual or group is forcefully ejected from society, for example, through banishment, exile, or physical extermination.	X	X

How Human Rights Can Free Shame

The human species' movement toward relationships of equal dignity opens opportunities to free emotions from their former instrumentalization. In the new context of equal dignity, former underlings can be liberated from continuous "voluntary" self-mutilating shame. Today we can set out to heal the hurt of the past ten thousand years, the mutilating instrumentalization of the human emotional and cognitive apparatus. We can call on people to acknowledge shame, not bypass or suppress it, and help them recognize that it is not necessary to live in continuous shame and fear of shame. Table 6.2 shows a short overview over the historic transition of human history and its relevance for shame and humiliation.

Thomas J. Scheff's concept of shame as a threat to the secure bond is informed by his advocacy of equality in dignity and his conviction that everybody needs to feel welcome in the human family. I am writing these sentences in Japan, where child murderers have shocked the nation. A girl just slit the throat of another, more popular girl. Most of the Japanese children who killed felt they were nothing—they were without what Scheff calls bonds.

Table 6.2. The Historic Transition of Human History and Its Relevance for Shame and Humiliation

	Large-Scale Frame	*Relevance for Shame and Humiliation*
Prior to 10,000 years ago	Wild food as resource for livelihood, no circumscription, win-win	Shame and humiliation developed as part of "a whole universe of cognates that . . . involve the feeling of a threat to the social bond."[7]
During the past 10,000 years	Land as resource for livelihood, security dilemma, win-lose	The human desire for a secure social bond was instrumentalized to build hierarchical societies of ranked honor. Humility, shame, honor and humiliation form a continuum that is put at the service of ranked honor.
Vision for the future: global knowledge society with equal dignity for every global citizen	Knowledge as resource for livelihood, global interdependence, win-win	Dignity humiliation is illegitimate and no longer part of the humility–shame continuum.

When we feel ashamed, we accept that we fell short. We may blush when we break wind inadvertently; we can be ashamed even if nobody notices it. Norbert Elias places the emerging skill of feeling shame at such transgressions at the center of his theory of civilization. Being able to feel shame is prosocial, as is the capability to feel guilt. When I feel guilty, I accept that I have committed a moral transgression (guilt may be defined as moral shame, shame over moral shortcomings). Somebody who is not capable of feeling shame and guilt is seen as a "shameless" monster with an unacceptable contempt for law. We all hope that shame will deter our neighbors from lying to us and that our neighbor will feel guilty and not try, for example, to have an affair with our spouse. In other words, we all hope that shame and guilt will safeguard social cohesion and foster humility before social and legal rules. We consider humility a virtue[8] and shame and guilt immensely valuable.

The dynamics of guilt and shame are very different in a culture of unequal honor as compared to a culture of equality in dignity. In traditional honor cultures, guilt and shame are instrumentalized to humiliate transgressing underlings. In human rights cultures, on the other hand, guilt is an internally motivated response by a person who recognizes that she has infringed on the rights or humanity of another.

Guilt can be remedied by interventions such as punishment, remorse, apology, forgiveness, or restorative justice. However, this can be achieved in dignifying ways only within a human rights–based context, because punishment, remorse, apology, forgiveness, or restorative justice all tend to have profoundly mutilating effects in a context of ranked honor. Human rights call for healing of human integrity in individuals and societies, for returning humanity to the pristine emotional status it enjoyed during the first 90 percent of human history. Ranked honor norms, in contrast, call for the maintenance of submission/domination by any and all means—including torture and execution—and continue the pain inflicted for the past ten thousand years.

Arne Næss, among the most renowned Norwegian philosophers, summarized the human rights approach to remedying guilt as follows: "There are no murderers; there are only people who have murdered." He explained his point at length at the Second Annual Meeting of Human Dignity and Humiliation Studies.[9] Næss described in rich detail how he would invite convicted murderers from prison into his philosophy class at Oslo University to demonstrate to his students that even murderers deserve and need to be dignified. He was adamant that only individuals who feel secure in their connection to humanity can admit to a crime, feel guilty, and show remorse. As long as people feel less than fully human, there is no reason for them to care that they have hurt others or society.[10]

As human rights ideals expand, space is opened for scholars such as Scheff and Webb, who teach the importance of learning the language of empathy (which entails unmasking shame). Room opens for a salutogenic rather than a pathogenic view of shame.[11] This accompanies the insight that there is a "need to re-evaluate the pathological (unhealthy, dysfunctional) aspects of shame, understanding these aspects as the result of both personal/developmental, and cultural distortions. These distortions stem from experiences in which the natural shame process was blocked, producing unresolved shame sequences."[12] No longer attacking others or self, no longer hiding from others or self,[13] is a healing step.

Former child soldier Ishmael Beah received help from a nurse called Esther. Esther untiringly repeated to Ishmael, "it is not your fault!" thus allowing him to feel shame and express it prosocially. Her selfless compassion rekindled the humanity that he could no longer find in himself. He recounts in an interview:

Well, after I'd been at the rehabilitation centre for quite some time, you know. I think it was you know the people who came into my life. There was a particular nurse at the centre called Esther who was just . . . patient and selfless and compassionate and was willing to look at me just as a child regardless of what I had been through. I would tell her the most vicious stories I could think of during the war just to kind of deter her from talking to me and that didn't go the way I wanted and she became closer and closer to me and because of her willingness to just look at me over and over as a child, it began to sort of make me feel that there was something more to me that even I had failed to see you know, that she was seeing.[14]

Tony Webb suggests that unmasking shame and changing scripts and patterns for reacting to shame need to receive priority as an integral part of any personal growth work. The new concept of shame needs to be part of everyday relationships at home and in the community. Relationship counseling needs to unmask shame in a wide range of fields and issues, including divorce and separation, domestic violence, school discipline, conflict education, bullying, restorative justice, conflict resolution, anger management, drug, alcohol and other addictions, recovery from trauma, suicide prevention, men's and women's support groups—the list is long.

Webb has developed an experiential education workshop titled Working *with* Shame (rather than seeing it, as so many therapists do, as something pathogenic). Webb ends his workshop with an exercise named "Unmasking shame and the empathic response." He invites one participant to choose one of the ways he or she traditionally avoids shame and dare to move away from the avoidance mechanism toward the feeling of shame. Once the shame is identified, the participant is asked to stay in the feeling, aided and supported by the rest of the group. Webb reports, "At this point the affect change can be quite profound—people often describe it as a lifting of the heavy/oppressive weight of shame. There is often surprise, curiosity (interest) and a smile (joy)—the transformation from shame to pride."[15] The group often reports that they see authentic pride emerge— "it has still a visible element of shame—shame-modesty or humility rather than 'up-himself' pride."[16]

An American friend wrote to me recently about what she sees as the healing effects of the more open conversation about race that has been part of Barack Obama's 2008 campaign for president of the United States.[17] "Since the Civil Rights unrest of the 1960s, race has been a subject that was spoken of only in the most veiled terms in public life. It was too dangerous to talk about race—a careless word could cause an explosion," she wrote. "But, all that began to change after the speech Senator Obama gave about race in April, 2008." In that speech, my friend explains, Obama said that his longtime minister had been correct in his very public diagnosis of America's historic racism, about the shame it called down on the entire culture. But Obama didn't end there; he continued to say: "But, the reverend is wrong in one very important way. He fails to understand that the great strength of our culture is that we can *change*. We *can* change and *when* we change, we do it very rapidly."

To illustrate the new relaxed atmosphere, my friend described a late-night news talk show. "It was mayhem—six hyper-dignified news commentators shouting one another down. They laughed, shouted, made silly faces at one another. It looked like a sixth grade party," she wrote.

> It took me a moment to realize that the subject was race, specifically "Can a black man *really* win the U.S. presidency?" The black commentators, who until very recently, were treated with exaggerated respect, were right in there in the thick of things, just as rambunctious as their white colleagues. This was a very elated, almost euphoric, group of people. A liberated group of people.

My friend found these changes to be relevant to my examination of emotion and conflict. "Somehow, the 'hot' emotions have been (or, rather, are being) defused on what was once the most divisive topic in the nation," she explains. "I suspect that the vehicle for that change was Obama's speech—which brought our hidden shame out into the open air, allowing us to accept it and begin to breathe."

In the context of human rights, a new approach to shame can heal not only subaltern meekness, but also arrogant supremacy. The arrogance of traditional elites can be transcended as much as the contemporary arrogance of ruthless individualists. Ruthless individualism could be described as a misunderstood uprising, an uprising that went too far. Subalterns, in a context of human rights, have two basic choices when they rise up—they can either try to emulate former masters, or they can learn true equality in dignity. Human rights call for the second (reflecting the two-tiered nature of the human rights revolution), while Western ruthless individualism resembles the first, in that it encourages former underlings to behave as autocratically as masters do in a world of honor. For human rights to be truly alive, ruthless individualism needs to mature into ideals of true equal dignity for all. Its adherents need to connect with fellow human beings in the context of equality in dignity and mutual care and consideration.

Somalia is a country of proud nobility. In the major clans, every man above a certain age is a sovereign. Somalia showcases relationships between fiercely proud masters in a system of honor. On December 3, 1998, I was a guest in a *khat*-chewing "focus group" session in Hargeisa, capital of Somaliland. Such sessions typically last for many hours, starting in the afternoon and running through half the night (such meetings are usually not attended by "respectable" women; I tried to remain "decent" by not chewing khat myself). I asked the men about humiliation or *quudhsiga* (belittling = humiliation). The hours were well invested and yielded many proverbs, such as the following: "Hadellca xun ayaa ka xanuun kulul xabada," meaning "Humiliation is worse than killing; in times of war words of humiliation hurt more than bullets" or "Rag waxaaa ku maamula agaan ama ku maamuusi," meaning "I can only be with people who are equal," or "Masse inaanu nahay oo tollim meerto no tahay," meaning "A man deserves to be killed; not humiliated."

Hassan Keynan, former secretary general of the Somali National Commission (1985–1988), explains that clan membership is all-encompassing and stultifying. The only liberation, he says, is to disown clan identity and adopt Somali identity—or even better, a global multi-identity.[18]

Western ruthless individualism resembles the fierce pride of Somalis. Overdone individualism generates the same negative side effects that can be observed in contemporary Somalia—the self-destructive devaluation and negligence of the caring and nurturing that is necessary to keep a society functioning in a dignified way. What Scheff describes as hypermasculinity is expressed in almost pure form in Somalia and is not much different from contemporary ideals of super-maleness in the West. Not surprisingly, testosterone-driven risk taking brought global economic downfall–testosterone and trading are linked in interesting ways.[19]

How Human Rights Can Prevent and Heal Humiliation

Acknowledging shame is important for healing it. In contrast, the coercive violation that is at the core of dignity humiliation cannot be translated into constructive channels by acknowledging shame. Should Nelson Mandela, when humiliated, have learned to feel ashamed and acknowledge that shame? No. Humiliators want their victims to feel ashamed. Resilience in the face of humiliation, therefore, means resisting feelings of shame. Refusing to feel shame, to insist on one's self-worth in the face of humiliation is not the same as suppressing shame.[20]

Succumbing to (rather than resisting) humiliation produces one of the most unbearable kinds of shame. I have spoken with people in Rwanda (and in Germany who lived through the Nazi era), who say that the worst suffering, the most painful form of humiliation, is to be forced to choose between two loves—and afterward recognizing that this was the wrong choice. In Kenya, I heard stories of Hutu *genocidaires* who were in hiding and needed psychotherapy because they could not eat without seeing the small fingers of children on their plates. Many Hutus had been forced to kill their own families, their Tutsi spouses and Tutsi-looking children, to show their allegiance to the Hutu cause. Their love for the Hutu cause became pitted against their love for their family. After the genocide, they were alone, deprived of their beloved family—and the killers were none but themselves. The International Panel of Eminent Personalities confirms: "Hutu women married to Tutsi men were sometimes compelled to murder their Tutsi children to demonstrate their commitment to Hutu Power.

The effect on these mothers is . . . beyond imagining."[21] The humiliation of being forced into barbarism can be so unbearable that unmasking this shame is almost impossible.

A person who considers herself a victim of undue humiliation (in contrast to appropriate shaming or humbling) has basically the following options:

1. Particularly if she has no means to resist within or outside of herself, she might turn her rage inward and become depressed or apathetic. Such a person might even turn to drug abuse (like a depressed wife suffering from psychosomatic symptoms)—a recourse that is likely to only increase the sense of shame and compound the depression.
2. If this person turns her rage outward, several outcomes are possible:
    a. This person might explode in hot, desperate, self- and other-destructive rage, abandoning rational self-interest and survival as her guiding principles. Passionate murder and/or suicide can be the result.
    b. Following Hitler's example, this person might organize large-scale humiliation entrepreneurship, attempting to redress humiliation by inflicting humiliation on the supposed humiliators. This is the traditional honorable master's method for managing humiliation and it achieves nothing but continuing spirals of humiliation. Hitler urged Germans to feel ashamed at accepting humiliation from the victors of World War I, and from what he saw as the future humiliation emanating from world Jewry. He led Germans out of their underling shame to become masters by assuming their supposed Aryan master race essence. He asked them to get angry to overcome being humiliated. He called on them to subjugate their enemies, as masters do.[22] Also in Rwanda, feelings of humiliation were systematically incited. Contemporary terrorists, as well, attract followers with humiliation narratives. Expensive weapons become unnecessary when feelings of humiliation are hot: Neighbors will kill neighbors with knives (Rwanda); civilian planes can be turned into missiles (September 11, 2001). I call feelings of humiliation the "nuclear bomb of the emotions."
    c. By following Mandela's example, a humiliated person can pour the energy that fuels her rage into constructive social change. Mandela facilitated the birth of a new social order based on respect for individual dignity. Central to his effort was the inclusion of the humiliators, members of the white upper class, as co-protectors of human rights. In other words, Mandela solved the conflict by peacefully but firmly making Frederik Willem de Klerk and his followers understand that the old order was dying. Mandela attempted to attain shared humility without humiliation. He himself did not feel ashamed and therefore did not have to acknowledge suppressed or bypassed shame, even though he had been systematically put down and humiliated. He had freed himself from the master's message. He carried his head high. He did not translate humiliation into shame. He rejected humiliation, like a master; and he refrained from walking the traditional path of honor. He did not force the white elite of South Africa into submission but humbled them into equality in dignity. He rejected humiliation by translating it into a force for profound constructive social change within the context of human rights call for equal dignity for all.

How Human Rights Meet Resistance

Times of transitions are difficult times. Paradigm shifts are painful. It is very hard for people who believe themselves to be good people (and that includes just about everybody) to accept that they have harmed others, even unintentionally. Cognitive dissonance may cause discomfort when there is discrepancy between what we already know or believe and new information or interpretations.[23] Both shame and humiliation are thorny issues; many choose self-justification instead of admitting to change.[24] Traditional elites feel entitled to supremacy and resent being labeled oppressors, violently repressing shame when they lose superiority, while underlings are caught between self-disparaging humility and angry humiliation.

In 1843, the book *The Contagiousness of Puerperal Fever* was published.[25] Thomas Watson was a professor of medicine at Kings College Hospital in London. He suggested in 1842 that obstetric attendants should wash their hands with chlorine solution "to prevent the practitioner becoming a vehicle of contagion and death between one patient and another."[26] A well-known obstetric professor in America, Charles D. Meigs, embodying the authoritarian myth of his time and disparaged hand disinfection, incensed by the suggestion he may himself be transmitting disease. His logic was: "Doctors are gentlemen, and gentlemen's hands are clean."[27] Many a patient had to die until the paradigm shift was complete—and this is only one example out of myriad similar trajectories.

Adherents to the traditional order of honor typically reject the call for humility regard it as humiliation to be asked to let go of their worldview that humiliation is prosocial. "Employees need to be humiliated, otherwise they do not work! Humiliation is an important tool in the workplace! It teaches people the right work ethics! Don't take this tool away from us!" is an argument frequently voiced in the corporate sector in many parts of the world. I was reprimanded in this way by a celebrated Indian economy professor in 2002 and by a renowned Chinese organizational consultant in 2006. In the same vein, some contemporary researchers still place humiliation into the traditional humility–shame–humiliation continuum. Maury Silver and colleagues, for example, suggest that humiliation functions as a form of social control, which can also be used positively, not just negatively.[28] In many schools around the world, this message is still being heard.[29]

Basically, the more a person identifies with so-called right-wing political positions, the more this person will either reject research on shame and humiliation or try to instrumentalize it. This is valid for the political spectrums within and even between countries. It is no accident that my research on humiliation was initially funded in Norway, where the ideal of equal dignity (*likeverd*) represents a traditional cultural value and human rights have a particularly strong anchoring. Altogether, the political spectrum of Europe, particularly Scandinavia, is located left of that of the

United States. Many people labeled left in the United States would fit into the right-wing spectrum in Scandinavia. Research on shame and humiliation, for its own merit and not in the service of honorable confrontations, is therefore more welcome in Scandinavia than elsewhere.

I encountered resistance to research on humiliation among the right-wing political spectrum in the United States, those who pride themselves on a "no-nonsense" approach to life and ridicule research on humiliation as either "dreamy" or "dangerous." They subscribe to the view that it is a person's own fault—a weak psyche—that causes him or her to feel humiliated. From this perspective, humiliation may be interpreted as a product of envy, and the values and power of the United States trigger envy and feelings of humiliation in those pitiable souls who are not tough enough to work their way up to success—invoking humiliation as cheap excuse for poor people and poor countries to explain their own laziness, so to speak. From that point of view, people who research humiliation cater to these disgraceful souls and put bandages on their wounds. By "understanding" why they become "lazy and cowardly" terrorists, humiliation researchers even contribute to condoning terror.

From this perspective, research on humiliation is abominable. Instead, research on shame is called for, so we can all understand better how the world's lazy freeloaders can be made to feel ashamed of their misguided conduct, acknowledge their own weakness, and stop evading responsibility by accusing others of humiliation. In sum, advocates of the no-nonsense approach reject research on humiliation and welcome research on shame.

In other words, my experience indicates that research on both humiliation and shame is requested or rejected depending on whose interest is at stake. Those who feel wrongly accused as perpetrators of humiliation call for research on shame to make victims go away and face their own responsibilities. Certainly, this approach is at times very much to the point. Accusing others of humiliation to avoid acknowledging one's own shame is nothing to be encouraged. Conversely, those who feel wrongly debased call for research on humiliation to make the perpetrators learn to be ashamed. They also often have a very valid point. Apartheid fell when the call became louder for white supremacists to acknowledge that their system represented institutionalized humiliation, something to be ashamed of, rather than proud.

Research on shame and humiliation are both important and difficult. Both have their supporters and critics, depending on their place in the game. Alleged oppressors and humiliators rebuke accusers by calling for research on shame, and unhappy underlings call for research on humiliation.

To me, the term *humility* is central. Humility and acknowledged shame connote the descent of superiors and ascent of inferiors to shared humility and equality in dignity (see also the two theories of intelligence, mentioned later). I recommend taking it seriously that the meaning of the word *humiliation* changed, as it did in the English language in 1757. I suggest we refrain from conceptualizing humiliation as a variant of shame and abstain from advocating "mild humiliation" as possible prosocial intervention. In this book, I engage in linguistic engineering when I write "humankind" instead of "mankind," because I wish to include all humans, not only men. Likewise, I suggest that "humbling" and "humility," in a human rights context, ought not be labeled "mild humiliation" since "mild violation" of dignity also remains violation. Humbling and humility are important terms that we can use to highlight the crucial significance of humility in human rights contexts, while we can apply the term *humiliation* to indicate violation. In an emerging human rights context, we can reserve the term *humiliation* for the illegitimate lowering of a person's worthiness that violates the ideal of equality in dignity, while we can use *humbling* to describe kinds of lowering that address arrogance and transform it into humility.

Eve and Adam struggle hard. It is not easy to let go of familiar worldviews and the feelings that underpin them. How can Adam cool down from supremacist rage and reach out to Eve in shared humility? Initially, he can't. He feels that by doing so he would fail his sense of masculinity. Not only that, it is too painful for him to acknowledge the many variants of shame he harbors, shame that he fears would only be heightened and cause him to collapse if he allowed himself to feel it openly. And Eve? For her it is also easier to cling to the familiar. Her struggle to gain a sense of confident humility is as hard. The counselor's message is also the message of this book: The rewards for these efforts are so rich that they are worth it.

PART III

HOW WE CAN DIGNIFY EMOTION AND CONFLICT

CHAPTER 7

HOW WE CAN REGULATE
OUR EMOTIONS

Jean Baker Miller, a pioneer in women's psychology, suggests that conflict is a necessary part of growth and change. She stipulates that conflict is not the problem—the way we engage in conflict is. Miller encourages us to learn how to "wage good conflict."[1]

As discussed in Chapter 2, when we hear the words "conflict" and "emotion," we usually think of conflicts that have become "stranded" in a host of negative emotions such as anger, rage, and hatred (which, in turn, are born out of other negative emotions, like fear, disappointment, or humiliation). In our imagination, we see people at each other's throats, shouting and hurling insults in violent flare-ups of hot and dramatic emotion—or, even more frightfully—onslaughts of hatred that have solidified into coldly applied gruesome Machiavellian strategies—Mafia methods, for example, can certainly be labeled as ritualized cruelty. We can all draw from our memories vivid pictures of abuse, ranging from violent marital quarrels at an interpersonal level to tragedies such as the conflict in the Middle East at intergroup and international levels.

Intuitively, we believe that conflict is connected with strong negative emotions and that positive emotions only blossom in the absence of conflict. Yet this is not necessarily so. On reflection, we all know that Miller is right and that sometimes it is important to "take up" a conflict, instead of "pushing it under the carpet." As Miller stresses, the word "conflict" ought to stand not for destruction but for opportunities for creative change and emotional growth. Using the constructive potential in conflict requires courage, empathy, and creativity, along with a certain confidence, all of which are quite positive faculties. Often a conflict turns sour only because it has been left unattended for too long, because we lacked the courage to use it creatively.

We might conclude that if we boost our positive emotions, we can avoid the trap of destructive conflict. However, overindulgence in positive feelings is no solution either. To keep smiling does not protect us from destructive conflict; it may even make us perpetrate what we want to avoid. Aaron Lazare writes about "blissful unawareness":

> Some offenders may be generally insensitive to the impact of their behaviors. These are bulls in China shops; they manage to say and do the wrong things much of the time and offend many people by remaining blissfully unaware of their actions. The offended people, in order to get the attention of the offenders, may have to shout at and confront them about their behaviors.[2]

Where do we go from here? What do we have to learn to wage good conflict? How can we use negative and positive emotions constructively?

Mental "Toolkits" Can Help Us Dignify Our Emotions and Transcend Conflict

Rage, wounded pride, despair, or anxiety can make us undermine our best interest when we strive for constructive conflict management. When we are angry we misperceive the situation and fall prey to biases. In the heat of conflict, norms of cooperation are easily violated and negative emotions introduced and allowed to spiral out of control. "You're stubborn," "you're selfish," "you're unreasonable," "you're inconsiderate," "you're narcissistic," "you're paranoid!" Morton Deutsch advises: "Recognize when you start to do this, stop, apologize, and explain what made you angry enough to want to belittle and hurt the other. If the other starts to do this to you, then interrupt, explain why you are interrupting, and try to resume a mutually respectful dialogue."[3]

We might agree with Deutsch but wonder how it is possible to behave as maturely and wisely as he asks us to.

To start, we need effective self-regulation. In Chapter 2, the ventromedial frontal cortex (VMFC) and orbital frontal cortex (OFC) were identified as particularly important brain areas enabling us to regulate and take control of our emotional responses by changing the way in which we interpret and draw inferences about our current affective responses. Theoretical and empirical studies of self-regulation (SR), self-regulated learning (SRL), and closely related constructs such as volition are areas of lively research in applied psychology.[4]

The capacity for self-regulation has profound consequences on intellectual functioning.[5] With successful self-regulation, an optimal state of flow can be achieved,[6] while intellectual functioning can become degraded when we switch into coping mode.[7] Some emotions involve high arousal and mobilize the autonomic nervous system (ANS) to rush into action, while others demobilize the ANS, facilitating serene contemplation.

Let's look at the inner structure of self-regulation.

Respecting Regulatory Feedback Loops

In "Emotion Self-Regulation,"[8] George A. Bonanno explains that regulatory feedback loops are organized hierarchically, with *subordinate loops* embedded within *superordinate loops*.[9] Superordinate loops tend to be linked to longer term, abstract goals, while subordinate loops are associated with proximal, immediate mechanisms.[10] Dysregulation occurs, when lower order mechanisms supersede higher order mechanisms.[11] "In terms of emotions, this may occur when phylogenically more immediate and automated emotional processes are instigated that temporarily override more abstracted regulatory processes."[12]

To keep superordinate loops operative, we need to step outside the frameworks within which we understand experience, and slow down our thinking processes so that we can critically assess them. We need to get in touch with deeper feelings, thoughts, and factors that lie outside of our "current mental and sensory models."[13]

Appreciating the Dualities of Mental Life

Examining some of the dualities that characterize mental life[14] will give us insight into how we can regulate our emotional lives more efficiently.

The Duality of Attention and Processing

Earlier, we mentioned the doer-watcher duality or the "observing self." The duality of attention and processing is the phenomenon that allows us to perform a task while watching ourselves performing this task.[15] Emotions have the potential to interfere in this duality and disturb task focus and performance. Many theoretical models build on this duality. In their resource allocation theory, Henry C. Ellis and Patricia W. Ashbrook, for example, explain that depression is detrimental to cognitive performance.[16] The problem with stress and cognitive performance has been mentioned earlier.[17]

The Duality of Conscious versus Unconscious Processing

Yun David Dai makes distinctions concerning the duality between conscious and unconscious activities. Conscious mental activity is effortful serial (capacity-limited) processing. Unconscious processing is largely automatic and parallel distributed.[18] Unconscious (or largely unconscious) processing is crucial to managing emotion and conflict, since creativity is at the core of successful conflict resolution and the art of cooling depends on skillfully interacting with these processes. Dai explains that in creativity research, the "mind-popping" or sudden-insight phenomenon has puzzled psychologists for decades[19] (interestingly, sudden insight is at the center of nondualistic teachings, on the leap of consciousness, that is necessary to "realize" the nondual).

The Duality of the Task and the Self

The duality between the task and the self is related to two contrasting beliefs about intelligence and learning that are widespread.[20] Some people believe that intelligence is fixed (the entity theory of intelligence); others think that intelligence is malleable (the incremental theory of intelligence). These two beliefs precipitate two kinds of goals—ego-oriented performance goals versus task-oriented learning-mastery goals. People with performance goals aim to look smart and avoid mistakes; they have an ego orientation and try to satisfy high expectations of others by performing well. Those with learning-mastery goals, on the other hand, desire to learn new things, even if they might get confused, make mistakes, and look less than smart; they are intrinsically motivated toward achieving mastery in the task.

Research results show that students with mastery goals are generally more successful, because they are more likely to search for and find successful alternative strategies "than are those with concerns about validating their ability."[21] This indicates that a task orientation is preferable to an ego orientation.

Incidentally, constructively managed shame may be the core ingredient for achieving a successful task orientation, because the clumsiness involved in mastering a task requires the ability to feel shame without being overwhelmed by it.

Double-Swing or Pendulation

Muneo Yoshikawa has developed a *double-swing* model for how individuals, cultures, and intercultural concepts can blend in constructive ways.[22] The model is graphically presented as the infinity symbol, or Möbius strip (∞). For this model, Yoshikawa brought together Western and Eastern thought. He draws on Martin Buber's idea of "dialogical unity" in *I and Thou*—"the act of meeting between two different beings without eliminating the otherness or uniqueness of each."[23] Also *Soku*, the Buddhist nondualistic logic of "Not-One, Not-Two," describes the twofold movement between the self and the other that allows for both unity and uniqueness.[24] Yoshikawa calls the unity that is created out of the realization of differences "identity in unity." The dialogical unity does not eliminate the tension between basic potential unity and apparent duality. Judith Martin, Thomas Nakayama, and Lisa Flores's dialectical approach, the third source of Yoshikawa's model, emphasizes the processual, relational, and contradictory nature of intercultural communication.[25]

The double-swing model shares common ground with Peter A. Levine's *pendulation*.[26] Successful pendulation can produce solidarity and social integration; without it, we have alienation and lack of social integration. Thomas J. Scheff commends the idea of pendulation, through which "we swing back and forth between our own point of view and that of the other."[27] "It is this back and forth movement between subjective and intersubjective consciousness that allows us the potential for understanding each other."[28] As Scheff explains, good attunement is achieved when pendulation is successful—then intersubjectivity is lived to its full potential. When pendulation succeeds, the result is a relationship of interdependence, not dependence, and not independence.

Clearly, Yoshikawa, Levine, and Scheff are imbued with and promote the ideal of equality in dignity. Theirs are not the ideals of the traditional honor order, where husbands were not required to build a mutually shared identity with their wives, who, in turn, had to buy into his identity and live in what Scheff calls engulfed love. This was the situation of Eve and Adam.

Marshall Rosenberg holds workshops on nonviolent communication. Also he suggests that maintaining empathetic connectedness is the first priority in personal relationships. Scheff recounts:

> In Rosenberg's workshops, this question often arises in parent-child relationships, when a mother or father complains about a child's behavior. For example, a mother may repeat a dialogue between her and her son about getting his homework done before watching TV or playing electronic games. Rosenberg begins by explaining that the child has a need for autonomy, for being his own person, as well as a need for remaining connected with the parent.
>
> This idea seems to be lost on the parent. She will ask: "So how do I get him to do the homework?" The parent seems to have the idea that what is involved is a test of wills, and that the way to go is to have a stronger will than the child. Rosenberg then goes on to explain that the parent needs to show that empathic connectedness is more important to her than getting the homework done. That is, that she respects the child's need for autonomy.[29]

As we see, Rosenberg encounters parents who still believe that "what is involved is a test of wills, and that the way to go is to have a stronger will than the child." (Read more on models of parenting further down.)

In the traditional order, subjugation was the name of the game; help and love were associated with the stick rather than with mutually shared identity or pendulation. *Egalization* ideals are new and call for skills that have not yet been incorporated as culturally transmitted knowledge. Old recipes vie with new ones, different definitions of help and love elicit humiliating "misunderstandings." The confusion is great.

To conclude, to wage good conflict, we must learn to design our efforts in ways that do not "walk over" recipients. Healthy identity-in-unity pendulation is interdependent—neither independent and isolated nor engulfed.

Both parties in conflictual relationships must avoid going too far, neither walking over the other, nor allowing the other to walk over them. This entails a vote for the ontological orientation of nondualism.

Cooling

Parents know that their children can appear to be quite calm and grown-up at times. However, under pressure they may suddenly regress and act very immature. Competent parents know how to assist their children without belittling them, using cooling strategies to restore a more adult posture. Mischel and De Smet write on cooling:

> Between six and eighteen months of age, infants begin to learn to regulate their emotions. Six-month-olds approached by a stranger tend to cope with their fear and anxiety by averting their eyes and "fussing." Twelve- and eighteen-month-olds, on the other hand, use other strategies, such as self-distraction and self-soothing, to deal with an anxiety-producing stranger. These more sophisticated cooling strategies allow children to effectively cope with their hot fear and anxiety reactions. Because conflict elicits similar fight-or-flight emotional responses, self-distraction, self-calming, and other cooling strategies are equally important skills for adults.[30]

What are good cooling strategies for adults? New research provides scientific validation for the benefits of meditation practice. Modern brain imaging is yielding evidence of the effectiveness of meditation techniques.[31] Goleman reports on Owen Flanagan's studies of the Tibetan Buddhist claim that destructive emotions can be greatly reduced (contrasting with the common Western assumption that our biological programming for emotions is fixed).[32] "Some Tibetan Buddhists," as he puts it, "think it possible and advisable to overcome, even eliminate emotions such as anger or hostility, which Western philosophers see as natural and immutable."[33]

How did Mandela survive twenty-seven years in prison without becoming enraged and vindictive? How did he acquire his unique mixture of humility and pride? Perhaps there is no recipe, but we still can learn from his experience. Maybe he developed what Robert Jay Lifton calls the flexible protean self.[34] Flexible and weak ties to one's emotions and past experiences and flexible and weak ties to a great number of fellow beings seem to be advantageous for social peace. Perhaps he drew on something that Buddhists call mindfulness[35] and sukha?

> For instance, Buddhism posits the possibility of sukha, "a deep sense of serenity and fulfillment that arises from an exceptionally healthy mind"—a concept with no parallel word in English, nor a direct equivalent in psychology (though some psychologists have recently begun arguing for a more "positive psychology," which might embrace such concepts). Moreover, Buddhism

posits that the capacity for experiencing sukha can be developed . . . and offers a set of methods for attaining this state. That training starts with positive shifts in fleeting emotions that lead to more lasting changes in moods, and eventually to a shift in temperament.[36]

The sense of serenity expressed by the word *sukha* is similar to the *third factor* proposed by Eileen Borris. She describes this factor as an element of strength and faith that can be labeled in a variety of ways, such as closeness to divinity, appreciation of compassion, or faith in shared humanity.[37] Victor Frankl's concept of *self-observation* in the framework of logotherapy is related, as well.[38] *Self-remembering*, as advocated by George Ivanovich Gurdjieff, is a similar concept.[39] *Being awake*, a concept from transpersonal psychology has related implications.[40]

A sense of serenity can be an effect of either mature self-cooling training or third-party cooling strategies. Debriefing and short-term counseling are among the interventions designed to restore and strengthen the inner balance and self-regulation of traumatized people.

However, people cannot always cool down effectively. Physicians, lawyers, or police personnel are usually taken off the case when they cannot be trusted to be in control of themselves. Broader social networks should be responsible for taking this practice to levels where it has not yet been institutionalized. Leaders of countries, who are "too hot," ought not to be allowed by their larger social environment—the international community— to remain in power when they face situations that are too emotionally demanding and endanger thousands or even millions of lives. The world community has not yet fully embraced this responsibility.

We must also remember that those living in regions of protracted conflict, with continuous cycles of violence, unremitting stress, and chronic trauma have almost no chance to live "normal" emotional and intellectual lives. People under conditions of continuous trauma require comprehensive ongoing support. Providing "emergency help" when emergency is the norm and preparing people for a normality that does not exist is— apart from insulting—extremely ineffective.

David R. Matsumoto has coined a label for the person who is skilled in using potential conflict not as a crisis but as a chance: the *voyager*. The voyager uses the challenge of cultural diversity and intercultural conflicts as a stage for forging new relationships, new ideas, and new people.[41] The world of the voyager is neither a panacea nor a utopia. Being an intercultural voyager does not mean that one has to like or accept everything one encounters. Intercultural voyagers do not necessarily value the conclusions arrived at but the process by which this is achieved. The distinction between voyagers and another type—Matsumoto calls them *vindicators*—is based primarily on the processes they engage to draw their conclusions.

Those people who cannot control their emotions reinforce and crystallize their pre-existing ethnocentric and stereotypic ways of dealing with the world that are limited. This is a no growth model, and these individuals are not engaged in a journey. This is a model of stagnation, with no growth potential inherent in such a process. We call these people "Vindicators," because their worldviews are established solely to vindicate their pre-existing ethnocentrism and stereotypes, not to challenge them and grow.[42]

Matsumoto and colleagues explain that many models of intercultural communication have focused only on the cognitive aspects of communication, including cultural knowledge, language proficiency, and ethnocentrism, neglecting the emotional aspects. The authors caution: "We believe that no matter how complex or advanced our cognitive understanding of culture and communication are, this understanding does no good if we cannot regulate emotions that inevitably occur in intercultural communication episodes."[43]

The ability to constructively channel and manage particularly negative emotion is the "gatekeeper"[44] of communicative effectiveness, particularly in an increasingly interconnected world that requires superior communication skills for tackling the negative emotions that are bound to be elicited in intercultural encounters.

In essence, the field of intercultural communication applies to national and international levels the core components of all psychotherapies at the personal level—"experience the emotion, change the cognition."[45] We must learn to experience our emotions, while we change our cognitions, which in turn changes the experience of our emotions.[46]

To revisit Eve and Adam, in the course of their growth process, they slowly become voyagers. They no longer focus on judging the other or themselves to be right or wrong in the style of vindicators; they increasingly enjoy the process of accompanying each other on the journey of personal self-realization that in turn feeds back into their relationship and strengthens and enriches it.

Cultural Frames Can Help Us Dignify Our Emotions and Transcend Conflict

Is our species an antisocial or a prosocial animal?[47] Primate behavior is varied, including a full range of cooperative, confrontational, and territorial behaviors. As discussed earlier, during the first 90 percent of human history, *Homo sapiens* seems to have developed as a rather prosocial animal. The long and formative period of hunting-gathering demanded a basic capacity for cooperation. However, beginning roughly ten thousand years ago, the large-scale shift from a win-win frame for the human condition to a win-lose frame favored and fostered confrontation and a sense of borders—cultural pressure nudged people to adopt a readiness to confront, overriding hard-wired tendencies to cooperate. In that way, the last 10 percent of history led us to believe that "human nature" is aggressively predatory (see Chapter 5).

Certainly, there will always be a minority of people predisposed to cruelty, out of whatever reasons. However, for the majority, killing others is not easy; it does not come naturally to most humans. Soldiers are trained not to look their victims in the eyes, lest this stops them from killing, and the youths used as militia forces all over the world are typically drugged. Incidentally, this is also why feelings of humiliation are so dangerous. These feelings can grow so strong that they have an addictive drug effect, overriding psychological barriers that otherwise inhibit human beings from perpetrating mayhem.

In other words, cultural frames may be more instructive than human nature studied in a vacuum. The dichotomy of human "nature" versus "culture" is misleading. Human nature is neither savage nor noble, because human nature *is* culture. Neither nature nor culture, with all their baggage, be it genes that shape individual dispositions or cultural scripts that shape cultural dispositions, acts autonomously. Humans do not have the option of a "nakedly natural" relationship with their environment; culture always mediates this relationship. It mediates the environment that humans inhabit in a variety of ways, both driving emotions and being driven by them.[48]

This means that neither emotions nor conflicts occur automatically. It is therefore insufficient to study the contemporary individual in a few cultural contexts to understand emotions and their interplay with conflicts. It is essential to be aware of the global historical and cross-cultural scaffolding into which emotions are inserted as they play out in the individual's relationships with others. With this knowledge, we can devise new and more constructive cultural frames.

Optimizing Cooperation

As already discussed in Chapter 3, game theorists have found that populations in which people help others, but refuse to help people who cheat, are more stable than populations in which kindness is unconditional or cheating is the norm. Cooperating is the most intelligently selfish strategy people can employ (when they are involved in long-term relationships, see one another often, and know that they may depend on each other in the future). The rule is simple: Do not help unconditionally, do not cheat, help those who reciprocate.[49]

In the *crude law of social relations*, Deutsch stipulates that "cooperation induces and is induced by a perceived similarity in beliefs and attitudes, a readiness to be helpful, openness in communication, trusting and friendly attitudes, sensitivity to common interests and deemphasis of opposed interests, an orientation toward enhancing mutual power rather than power differences, and so on."[50] In contrast, competition induces and is induced by coercion, threats, deception, suspicion, self-serving biases, poor communication, and attempts to enhance the power differences between oneself and the other.

In other words, what we learn from Deutsch is that by collecting systematic knowledge of the effects of cooperation and competitive processes, we can also learn more about how to address conflict constructively. Thus, it pays for groups of people to create cultural frames that systematically encourage cooperation and creative problem solving.

Coleman and Deutsch have developed guidelines for creative problem solving. They emphasize that it is important to avoid such simple traps as, for example, rushing. To adequately define the problem, opening it for alternative perspectives, takes time.[51] We need to develop cultural practices that encourage a patient approach to conflict resolution, allowing time for the emergence of creative solutions. Also numerous other skills enhance cooperation, among them constructive controversy (deliberate discourse in Aristotle's terminology) rather than debate (which depends on the presence of an authority to declare a winner[52]). Western individualist societies, which have a tendency to deify confrontational debate, might benefit from acknowledging its disadvantages.

Investing in Hope

C. Richard Snyder, who developed hope theory, defines hope as "the perceived capability to derive pathways to desired goals, and motivate oneself via agency thinking to use those pathways."[53] Snyder's work partially overlaps with theories of learned optimism, optimism, self-efficacy, self-esteem, and coping. He reports that hope is consistently related to better outcomes in academics, athletics, physical health, psychological adjustment, and psychotherapy. Hope theory "involves an interrelated system of goal-directed thinking that is responsive to feedback at various points in the temporal sequence."[54]

When high-hope people see that their goals are blocked, they remain flexible and find alternative goals, similar to individuals who have the task-oriented learning-mastery goals already discussed. "Low hopers," in contrast, ruminate about being stuck[55] and entertain magical escape fantasies, all counterproductive.[56] "Preoccupied with avoidance thoughts, low-hope persons continue their passivity because they do not learn from past experiences."[57] Low hopers will resemble those with ego-oriented performance goals.

"A high-hope person should have enduring positive emotions, with a sense of affective zest about the pursuit of goals. A low-hope person, on the other hand, should have negative emotions, with a sense of affective lethargy about the pursuit of goals."[58] High hopers' emotions consistently are characterized by "friendliness, happiness, and confidence," representing the residue from myriad previous goal pursuits and reflecting positive and active feelings about engaging in future goal pursuits, while the low-hope person's emotions "tap into a reservoir of negative and passive feelings about task pursuit endeavors."[59]

Research on personality as a moderator of affective influences on cognition supports Snyder's work:

> High-neuroticism individuals and those who exhibit ruminative tendencies may be particularly prone to negative mood-congruent thinking. Extraverted individuals and those who are adept at regulating negative emotions through distraction (and other effective strategies) may be particularly prone to positive mood-congruent thinking.[60]

The guiding assumption for Snyder is that human actions are goal-directed. The *goal* is the cognitive component that anchors hope theory.[61] Snyder's theory emphasizes pathway thinking. High-hope people are more decisive about the pathways for their goals. The motivational component in hope theory is *agency thought*, the perceived capacity to use one's pathways to reach desired goals. High-hope people embrace such self-talk agency phrases as, "I can do this," and "I am not going to be stopped."[62]

Snyder hypothesizes that positive emotions flow from perceptions of successful goal pursuit, not vice versa. In other words, the goal-directed thinking process takes precedence over emotions. Indeed, perceived lack of progress in the pursuit of important goals has been found to be the cause for reduction in well-being, rather than vice versa (this is related to our earlier discussion of the significance of framing for emotions).[63]

Likewise, according to Snyder, self-esteem is secondary, not primary; hope effects esteem and not vice versa. "Self-esteem is the personal judgment of worthiness."[64] Hope also relates to meaning and self-actualization. Hope and meaning "should be companions because it is through the self-reflections about personal goals, and the perceived progress in reaching those goals, that meaning is constructed in a person's life."[65]

Most people are insufficiently hopeful, Snyder points out,[66] because they were not taught appropriately during childhood or had their nascent hopeful thinking strategies destroyed. Snyder recommends the building of cultural and institutional frames that incorporate insights from hope theory, such as sound democratic institution building: "When laws are implemented so as to allow a maximal number of people to pursue goal-directed activities, then citizens should be less likely to become frustrated and act aggressively against each other."[67]

As a result, public health and general well-being is likely to increase. Higher hope is associated with better social adjustment, both with friends and extended family. Snyder quotes physician Leonard Sagan who, in his book, *The Health of Nations: The Causes of Sickness and Well Being*,[68] concludes, "It is the brain that is the true health provider,"[69] and, "more important in explaining the decline in death worldwide is the rise of hope and the decline in despair and hopelessness."[70]

Clearly, humankind would benefit from learning more of Snyder's kind of hope and developing cultures of hope and institutions for hope. This means creating more alternative goals, more potential pathways, and more endurance. If we succeed, we will have people gravitating to wider social networks that benefit everyone. Positive emotions will follow.

Ironically, pessimists are oblivious to these insights (see more discussion on that point in Chapter 9). By lamenting, they indulge in increasing the burden of conflict instead of lessening it. We have to learn constructive optimism and hope, because only this will render beneficial framings. A cancer patient, told she is in deep crisis, might survive if she can mobilize all her hope resources. She might die if surrounded by pessimists. For the world, we need constructive hope that models emergency and crisis as a challenge and not as the end of the world.

Let us revisit Eve and Adam here. Initially, Adam undermines Eve's social support network. She is to live for him alone. He systematically humiliates her and destroys whatever confidence she has left by telling her that nobody but him could love her. She is worthless without him. Both believe that this strategy, if intensified sufficiently, will lead to a happy relationship, but it brings only violence and tears. Their therapist reformulates their definitions and strategies of hope. Slowly, Adam understands that when he induces hopelessness in Eve, they both lose. The therapist rekindles Eve's confidence in herself, and her life begins to flourish. The therapist also helps Adam gain confidence in his ability to keep a strong woman as a partner and enjoy her fresh zest for life. Both learn to nurture higher hopes for their relationship and work for newly defined, share goals.

Learning New Ways of Speaking

If we wish to build new cultural frames within which emotion and conflict can be managed constructively, we need to change how we use language.[71] Sharon Ellison describes "the art of powerful non-defensive communication" in her book *Taking the War Out of Our Words*.[72] She campaigns for no less than a change in deep-seated cultural habits. She highlights the advantages of nondefensive communication—that we need to develop an art of asking questions in genuine curiosity to learn what the other person is communicating. She explains the advantages of communicating in ways that are transparent, open, and vulnerable—instead of guarded and closed—to attain a deeper sense of the connection and to convey a sense of security to the other.

Designing New Models of Parenting

Alice Miller explained that in the period that led up to the two World Wars, leading pedagogues regarded breaking the will of the child an essential task of childrearing.[73] Lakoff and Johnson describe an underlying framework they call the *strict father* model, in which the father expects his commands to be obeyed and enforces his moral rules through reward and punishment. Children must not be coddled, lest they become spoiled. Through their obedience they are expected to learn the discipline and self-reliance that is necessary to meet life's challenges.[74]

The strict father model "tends to produce children who are dependent on the authority of others, cannot chart their own moral course very well, have less well-developed consciences, are less respectful of others. Interestingly, these children have no greater ability to resist temptations than children raised in more liberal environments."[75] The strict father model produces what Theodor Adorno called the *authoritarian personality*, whose principal characteristic is obedience and readiness to follow orders blindly, irrespective of their moral contents.[76]

The *nurturant parent* model of rearing children, on the contrary, describes a parenting style that abides by the emerging human rights ideals. What formerly was regarded as good for children turns into abuse and neglect in the new nurturant framework. Lakoff and Johnson write,

> Nurturant Parent morality is not, in itself, overly permissive. Just as letting children do whatever they want is not good for them, so helping other people to do whatever they please is likewise not proper nurturance. There are limits to what other people should be allowed to do, and genuine nurturance involves setting boundaries and expecting others to act responsibly.[77]

The point with the nurturing parent model is that "lessons" are taught with firm love and humility, not by applying humiliation. The presently unfolding transition from a strict father model to the nurturant parents model is part of the emergence human rights ideals, and only the nurturant parent will produce children who can stand up for them.

Finding a Place for Romantic Love

Let us think back to the introduction to Chapter 1. Can modern societies which base marriage on romantic love between spouses build successful marriages? Can fragile romantic love between parents provide a stable frame for the love between parents and children? Is not humiliation the very force that makes romantic love so incompatible with stable parenthood—romantic love, when disappointed, so easily transmutes into cycles of humiliation? And those cycles can tear everybody apart and take innocent children hostage.

Is the concept of arranged marriages the best, after all? What can a society do that wishes to enjoy romantic love *and* healthy offspring? How can the stability that children need be wedded with the sense of freedom that makes romantic love flourish?

New cultural frames must be promoted. One way to succeed would be to weave some of the wisdom entailed in the practice of arranged marriages into individualistic notions of romantic love. One solution would be to conceptualize the roles of spouse and parent as independent from each other, at least to a certain degree. When the bond of love between the parents turns out to be too fragile to keep them together as a couple, their parental love could be maintained. A good test for young couples wishing to wed would be to think of their divorce. Only those couples who can promise each other that they will continue to cooperate as good parents after divorce should be encouraged to marry. Shared custody for children could be an obligatory pledge prior to any wedding celebration (or any other marking of a joint decision of a couple to commit to having a family, including same-sex couples).

Humankind—at least those who have the necessary resources—has gained control over procreation, by way of contraceptives. This, however, is not enough. We have to take more control of our cultural frames so that our feelings can flourish in constructive ways. Parental love must be protected against the fragility of romantic love. (Please see more in *Gender and Humiliation: Power and Dignity in Love, Sex, and Parenthood*.[78])

The cultural model of shared custody, incidentally, is a suitable frame not only at the micro level. Also at macro levels we need new kinds of cooperation, cooperation even across fault lines of people who hate each other (like after divorce).[79]

Personal Skills Can Help Us Dignify Our Emotions and Transcend Conflict

Attending to Positive Emotions

Probably due to their dramatic impact, negative emotions have received much more scholarly attention than positive emotions. Negative emotions (anger, fear, and distress) have been studied in their association with destructive processes ranging from violence and war to morbidity and mortality in connection with chronic disease such as cancer, asthma, and cardiovascular disease.[80]

Barbara L. Fredrickson and Christine Branigan, on the other hand, focus on positive emotions.[81] They offer a new theoretical perspective which they call the *broaden-and-build* model. This model questions common assumptions of contemporary emotion theory,[82] namely, that emotions must necessarily entail action tendencies and lead to physical action. Rather than action, positive emotions seem to facilitate changes in cognitive activity.

What negative emotions are to threat, positive emotions are to opportunity. Traditional action-oriented models for negative emotions indicate that negative emotions narrow a person's momentary thought–action repertoire, an effect that is adaptive in life-threatening situations that require quick action. In contrast, positive emotions broaden a person's momentary thought–action repertoire.[83] Joy and contentment, for example, widen the array of our thought–action repertoire, while fear and anger shrink it. Constructive coping is associated with positive emotions even under the chronic stress of caregiving and bereavement.[84]

Fredrickson's work relates to motivational psychology and Kuhl's theory of volitional processes. Kuhl and colleagues[85] propose that two earlier discussed dualities, namely, positive versus negative emotions and intuitive-holistic versus analytic-serial processing, are interdependent and form part of an affective-cognitive regulatory (dialectical) system. Positive affects and emotions promote intuitive-holistic (right hemisphere, RH) mental strategies, while negative affects and emotions further analytic-serial (left hemisphere, LH) mental strategies.[86]

We might conclude that negative emotions are maladaptive and ought to be avoided. However, negative emotions are functional in emergency situations and for effective learning. Successful conflict resolution often requires a certain amount of conceptual change for which negative emotions can be instrumental (earlier, we discussed the traps of blissful unawareness). Elizabeth A. Linnenbrink and Paul R. Pintrich explain that too much positive emotion may hinder effective learning. "Under situations requiring conceptual change, positive affect may both enhance (based on the mood-and-general-knowledge structure theory) and hinder (based on the dual-process theory) cognitive processing resulting in no clear relation between positive affect and conceptual change, as was found in our studies."[87]

Does this mean that conflict experts should try to induce negative affect in people in order to promote conceptual change? Linnenbrink and Pintrich recommend that we diminish positive affect when conceptual change is at stake. They do not recommend, however, enhancing negative affect.

What we learn is that both negative and positive feelings can be functional and that both need to be calibrated carefully. Negative emotion must always be managed first, then positive emotion is needed to avoid hasty retaliatory reactions and access a broader range of mature responses. *Beyond Reason: Using Emotions as You Negotiate*, a book by Roger Fisher and Daniel L. Shapiro, is of great help, not just in difficult negotiations.[88]

Learning Communicative Virtuosity

"If we are to live in a better social world, we will have to make it."[89] Barnett Pearce calls for *cosmopolitan communicative virtuosity*. Pearce believes that "modernity has been the primary force in the development of the contemporary, postmodern world, but that, as a form of communication, modernity is ill equipped to deal with the conditions that it has created."[90] One of the most important misconceptions of early modernists was to dismiss communication as "immaterial" and inconsequential.[91]

Earlier, we examined regulatory feedback, which stipulates that subordinate loops are embedded into superordinate loops.[92] Pearce suggests that we differentiate acts, actions, episodes, patterns, and forms, where the former is embedded in the latter. An act is part of an action, which is part of an episode, which is part of a pattern. Patterns are part of forms of communication. Of the latter, Pearce differentiates the following: monocultural, ethnocentric (and its modern variant, neotraditional), modernistic, and cosmopolitan forms of communication.[93]

Pearce's *cosmopolitan communicator*—similar to Matsumoto's voyager—is a person who acknowledges that others are both different and similar, that we all have different resources at hand yet use them for similar functions. For a cosmopolitan communicator, disagreement is an opportunity for learning and constructing new realities. Disagreements are dilemmas that call for further exploration to find creative solutions (this links up to the disorienting dilemmas mentioned in the introduction).

"Our chances of making a better social world will improve if we develop 'communicative virtuosity'—the ability to discern and differentiate among forms of communication, and to call into being preferred forms of communication."[94] Virtuosity means (1) a "grand passion" for what we are doing, (2) an ability to make insightful distinctions, and (3) the ability to engage in skilled performance.

Earlier, I mentioned Norwegian philosopher Arne Næss. He developed the notion of the *depth of intention*, or the *depth of questioning*, or *deepness of answers*. Næss writes, "our depth of intention improves only slowly over years of study. There is an abyss of depth in everything fundamental."[95] Warwick Fox, in his paper "Intellectual Origins of the 'Depth' Theme in the Philosophy of Arne Næss," explains: "The extent to which a person discriminates along a chain of precizations (and, therefore, in a particular direction of interpretation) is a measure of their depth of intention, that is, the depth to which that person can claim to have understood the intended meaning of the expression."[96] Greater depth means continuing to ask questions at the point at which others stop asking.[97]

What we learn is that we need a grand passion for developing new forms of communication that entail a careful and skilled balance between the broaden-and-build capacity of positive emotions and the conceptual-change capacity of negative emotions so that we can transcend conflict by "asking questions that others stop asking."

Engaging in Compassionate Witnessing

Kaethe Weingarten calls for *compassionate witnessing* to build a more sustainable social world. "Compassionate witnessing helps us recognize our shared humanity, restore our sense of common humanity when it falters, and block our dehumanizing others."[98]

Compassionate witnessing does not mean that we ought to feel that we are all similar or that we should uncritically identify with the other; it is about caring bridge-building. Weingarten proposes four tasks: we need to support mourning and grief, rehumanize the enemy, enter into dialogue, and be a witness to individual and collective pain.

The significance of mourning to halt cycles of violence has been widely acknowledged.[99] Age-old enemy images can be adjusted—dialogue is a tool with which to achieve the rehumanization of the enemy and foster reconciliation.[100] Being a witness builds on the duality of attention and processing. We can witness ourselves and others. The awareness flowing from this duality is crucial for halting cycles of violence, because by being aware we avoid repeating the past. "To develop the capacity to witness the self, the infant and young child must be treated with kindness and respect by someone who recognizes that the child's needs are different from her own. Later, the capacity to witness the self is linked to having an appreciative listener, someone with whom one can share honestly."[101]

Developing True "Subjectivity": Shutaisei

Emiko Ohnuki-Tierney, in her book *Kamikaze, Cherry Blossoms, and Nationalisms: The Militarization of Aesthetics in Japanese History*, explains that the *tokkotai* operations (*tokkotai* is a more correct term than *kamikaze*) were "phantasmagorical."[102] The fascist Japanese state created a phantasm in the hearts and minds of young men about how beautiful it would be to die for the emperor and the country. Among the most hideous strategies was to make the tokkotai operation a "forced voluntary" system instead of an imperial order, creating such an elaborate network that nobody had to declare direct responsibility for an operation of utter insanity. "The pilots were coerced either by their superiors, by the circumstances

on the base, or by the atmosphere of the society at large."[103] Ohnuki-
Tierney explains:

> At the level of the individual, the question of what constitutes "volunteering"
> is almost too complex to narrow down to certain factors. It involves the gen-
> eral circumstances of society as well as the specific context. Given the patriotic
> fervor of the time, many young men were willing to fight for their country,
> especially before they experienced the reality on the base or before their deaths
> were imminent. However, after they were drafted and had spent some time
> on the base, to take the next step of volunteering to be tokkotai pilots was
> never a clear-cut "decision." Most remained undecided about the step they
> had already taken until the last moment. "Volunteering" in the pilots' cases
> was far removed from such factors as motivation, intentionality, or rational
> decision-making in a simplistic sense.[104]

John W. Dower, in his book *Embracing Defeat: Japan in the Wake of World
War II*, describes the Japanese struggle for genuine *shutaisei*—true subjectivity or autonomy at the individual level—to resist the indoctrinating
power of the state.[105] Dower writes about Natsume Soseki (1867–1916),
one of the premier philosophers and novelists of modern Japan, who
called for a spirit of individualism vis-à-vis the state. Also the novelist and
essayist Sakaguchi Ango (1906–1955) affirmed the need for genuine shutaisei. For Sakaguchi, each individual needs to create his or her own "samurai ethic," his or her own "emperor system."[106]

The call for true subjectivity or autonomy dovetails with John Dewey's
call for *critical thinking* to make democracy viable.[107] *Postconventional moral
reasoning* is a related concept.[108] Paulo Freire calls for *critical consciousness*.[109] Elena Mustakova-Possardt, in building on Freire's work, proposes
a life span developmental model of mature critical moral consciousness,
achievable by a deepening lifelong integration of moral motivation, agency
and critical discernment.[110]

Soseki's call for shutaisei also echoes Ervin Staub's call to stand up and
not by in the face of injustice and atrocities.[111] Staub argues that the significant element in the atrocities perpetrated by Hitler's Germany was that
bystanders stood idly by instead of standing up and getting involved.

As already discussed, the individuation process and the emergence of a
mediated doer-watcher "sense of self" are historically recent.[112] The self-
consciousness of the symbolic "I" is historically new. Earlier, consciousness was consciousness of one's biological autonomy and separateness
within the context of what Norbert Elias called the "survival unit,"[113]
namely, the group, family, clan, tribe, or society. Paul Stokes writes, "Feelings which began as immediate sensations would have evolved into mediated emotions with the development of a psychological sense of self. The
sensation of fear, for example, became an emotion with the advent of
consciousness."[114]

How can the mediated doer-watcher "sense of self" be of help in constructive conflict management? The well-known Milgram experiments[115] show how ordinary people, not harboring any particular hostility, became perpetrators. People gave electric shocks to others because those with authority in the lab, those leading the experiment, told them to. Even when the destructive effects of their work became clear, and their actions were incompatible with fundamental standards of morality, few people were able to resist authority.[116]

Can religion help make people more resilient? Samuel P. Oliner and Pearl M. Oliner wrote *The Altruistic Personality: Rescuers of Jews in Nazi Europe*.[117] They point out that religious belief played a lesser role than personal values and psychological orientations. These values were altruism, universalism, care, compassion, empathy, equity/egalitarianism, justice, respect, fairness, and patriotism. Interestingly, rescuers—as opposed to nonrescuers— described their parents as benevolent, loving, kind, tolerant, compassionate, nonabusive, prone to explain rather than punish, and extensive rather than restrictive in their orientation toward others. Drawing on such parenting, the rescuers enjoyed a sense of basic strength, autonomy, and independence (this links up to the nurturing parenting model discussed earlier).

Honoring Dignity, Self-Respect, and Humility

Without respect, relationships falter, writes John Gottman: "Respect and affection are essential to all relationships working, and contempt destroys them. It may differ from culture to culture how to communicate respect, and how to communicate affection, and how not to do it, but I think we'll find that those are universal things."[118] Gottman is not alone—many share his view. Among them is Jan Smedslund; also for him it is respect that plays the central role, particularly in the analysis of trust.[119]

We have a duty for self-respect. As mentioned earlier, Robin Sleigh Dillon addresses the complexity of self-respect. We cannot be moral citizens if we violate our own dignity. Dillon draws on Kant, who defines three forms of self-respect, with the third form having two components: "Humility, on the one hand, and true, noble pride (Stolz) on the other are elements of proper self-respect."[120] Kant explains that humility is the recognition that we always fall short in our moral behavior and must therefore limit our opinion of our moral worth, while positive self-assessment and noble pride flow from a consciousness of having "honored and preserved humanity in one's own person and in its dignity."[121]

Dillon explains that self-understanding lies at the heart of self-respect. She writes,

> self-understanding can be self-respecting rebellion against subordination. For as Jean Baker Miller explains, there is a relationship between self-ignorance

and domination . . . striving to understand oneself is reclaiming oneself from oppression through one's insistence that one is worthy of being known, that self-understanding is appropriate, warranted, indeed called for what any self-respecting person must do.[122]

Never Forgetting Apology

The numbers of publications on apology, forgiveness, and reconciliation are currently exploding. In 1958, Fritz Heider wrote on *The Psychology of Interpersonal Relations*.[123] More recently, Nicolas Tavuchis authored *Mea Culpa: A Sociology of Apology and Reconciliation*.[124] Jan Smedslund wrote "The Psycho-Logic of Forgiving."[125] Ardith J. Meier focuses on "Conflict and the Power of Apologies."[126]

Aaron Lazare, in his book *On Apology*, asserts that one of the most profound human interactions is the offering and accepting of apologies. "Apologies have the power to heal humiliations and grudges; remove the desire for vengeance, and generate forgiveness on the part of the offended parties."[127] For the offender, he states, apologies can diminish the fear of retaliation and relieve the guilt and shame, and ideally, the result is the reconciliation and restoration of broken relationships.

Rumination is among the major obstacles to forgiveness. Ruminating on the experience of emotions like humiliation can motivate the perpetuation of aggressive behavior.[128] Research suggests that rumination impedes forgiveness by rekindling initial levels of anger (and fear) toward the transgressor. Frequent rumination on the wrongs done to oneself or one's group and attempts to restore respect by avenging past wrongdoings create significant barriers to ending conflict.[129] Leonard L. Martin and Abraham Tesser define rumination as the rehearsal of conscious thoughts about a particular theme in the absence of immediate environmental demands requiring the thought.[130] Mental ruminations come about by induction of emotion through mental imagery.[131]

Earlier, we discussed Margalit, who shows how the memory of humiliation may be held onto as a means to keep victim status and an entitlement for retaliation.

In related research, Michael Harris Bond studied how long emotions are felt by people in different cultures. He found a correlation between longer holds on emotion and the level of homicide in that culture. He writes, "countries populated by persons who experience emotions for greater lengths of time would, on average, commit more homicide."[132]

Lazare explains that the globalization of the world increases the importance of the apology process:

First, neighbors who interact on a continual basis have more disputes to settle than those who live, literally, "oceans apart." As neighbors in this global village, we use apology as an essential method of conflict resolution. Second, the very nature of our instant global communications, our being continually exposed to the world, diminishes the possibility of secret behaviors that others regard as offensive. These uncensored communications can reveal thoughts and attitudes that the originator would rather have kept secret, and for which an apology may now be expected.[133]

The example of Japanese textbooks mentioned in the introduction illustrates Lazare's point. As for Germany, it has certainly gained international respect by apologizing to the world and acknowledging that Hitler's strategy was disastrous. Instead of ruminating on past humiliations, and thus remaining caught in the past, Germany opened a new chapter in its history.

New Consciousness Can Help Us Dignify Our Emotions and Transcend Conflict

"What sets worlds in motion is the interplay of differences, their attractions and repulsions. By suppressing differences and peculiarities, by eliminating different civilizations and cultures, progress weakens life and favors death."

—(Octavio Paz)

As long as we live in isolated, homogenous cultural spheres, we can often guess correctly what our fellow human beings are trying to tell us with their words and actions. We tend to behave with a certain amount of confidence, secure in our environment. However, this definition of confidence is not always beneficial, particularly in times during which the world's cultures move closer.

In an increasingly interdependent world, we have to learn to float confidently in uncertainty rather than cling to assumed certainties. We have to become confident voyagers and not rigid vindicators. We must learn to tolerate uncertainty and ambiguity. Without these strengths, we may be tempted to jump to conclusions when we fail to understand our counterpart. Such hasty decisions may give the short-term illusion of certainty but are almost guaranteed to produce long-term miscommunication. Hastily guessing what others "want" and basing our actions on such guesswork is doomed to fail—this approach often does not even work with our spouses and children, so how can it succeed with "terrorists?" We have to learn to stay calm and use frustration creatively, with imagination and inspiration, so as to gain safer ground. To do that, we need curiosity, courage, and patience.[134]

How do we attain the higher consciousness that is needed for patience, kindness, truthfulness, humility, and forgiveness? The notion of *higher consciousness* has different names in various spiritual traditions, for example "super consciousness" (yoga), or "cosmic consciousness" (Sufism and Hinduism).[135] William James (1842–1910), American psychologist and philosopher, describes the stream of consciousness as the "I" using the "me" as a vehicle for the control and regulation of its own behavior.[136] James wrote on higher consciousness as the consciousness of a human being who has reached a higher level of evolutionary development and who has come to know reality as it is.[137]

We spoke earlier about Yoshikawa's double-swing model and Levine's pendulation, the swinging back and forth between our own point of view and that of the other. Double-swing pendulation—from you to me, back to you, back to me, and so on—must be managed with respect and warmth for all conflict parties. This respect and warmth is particularly important because the so-called negativity bias must be overcome, or the tendency to discount the positive—painlessness is so much more "pale" an experience than pain.[138] This effect is compounded for men. As discussed, men tend to react to stress with a fight or flight reaction, women gravitate to tend and befriend.[139] Men find it therefore more difficult to calm down from a state of vigilance. It is hence crucial to proactively build positivity into relationships.

Mandela-like respect and warmth is the glue that can keep individuals together while they move back and forth in the double-swing movement. Community conflicts and global conflicts can be conceptualized along similar lines.

But respect and warmth do not come automatically—they must be learned. A host of tools and very specific strategies of approaching the world are available and have already been discussed. One such strategy is to maintain the "glass is half full" approach, rather than immaturely smashing the glass whenever it appears to be half empty. Lamenting over what has yet to be accomplished only drains energy, making it harder to see the exciting challenge ahead, the challenge that will respond when approached with enthusiasm, motivation, and courage in a joint effort.

We can learn a lot from couples therapy. Marriage counselors teach couples a new balance: no longer constantly criticizing or feeling criticized, no longer overreacting emotionally when being criticized; no longer being domineering or unassertive; no longer undercommunicating positive emotion or feeling unloved by default.

Gottman and colleagues have done extensive research on the question of why some marriages last and others do not.[140] For several decades, he and his colleagues have watched couples interact at the Family Research Laboratory in Seattle. Using video cameras, one-way mirrors, and body sensors, Gottman and his associates have collected a wealth of data. They can predict divorce that will occur many years later very early on in marriage.[141] "Successful conflict resolution isn't what makes marriages succeed."[142]

Gottman's approach is to work primarily on increasing positive couple interactions and strengthening the friendship that is at the heart of any marriage.[143] Relationships begin to head downhill when the ratio of positive to negative interactions falls below five to one—couples seem to need at least five positive interactions to every negative one.

Gottman proposes seven principles, with the first three primarily relating to relationship building: (1) know each other, (2) focus on each other's positive qualities, and (3) interact frequently. The last four are traditional conflict resolution principles, such as (4) let your partner influence you, (5) solve your solvable problems (communicate respectfully, etc.), (6) overcome gridlock, and (7) create shared meaning.

Jean Baker Miller describes "five good things" that reward us when we succeed with forging growth-fostering relationships:[144]

1. increased zest (vitality),
2. increased ability to take action (empowerment),
3. increased clarity (a clearer picture of oneself, the other, and the relationship),
4. increased sense of worth, and
5. a desire for relationships beyond that particular relationship.

Eve and Adam learn from therapy that when all players in a conflict invest respect, warmth, and calmly floating confidence rather than frantic righteousness, conflict can be framed benignly. In the beginning, Eve and Adam threw monologues at each other and tried to prove to the therapist that the other was evil. Slowly, they learn to listen to each other. They try to grasp the other's feelings and thoughts, using both sides of the double swing. They emerge mutually enriched, recognizing that their conflict was based on solipsistic misperceptions of the other, with each looping in only one side of the double swing. Their conflict, they begin to understand, grew because of their immature and self-defeating conflict-solving strategies.

Finally, they see also that they suffered from a high degree of normative confusion. They had jumbled together the contradictory normative frames of ranked worthiness and equal dignity, helplessly oscillating between the contradictory emotional scripts that are related to those normative universes. Today, Eve and Adam no longer wish to participate in an order of higher and lesser beings (with Adam at the top and Eve at the bottom), but to treat each other as worthy of equal dignity.

Adam originally believed that only a weak partner would need him, so he kept Eve weak. Eve tried her best to fit Adam's definition of her. Both have learned that love flourishes best between two confident and strong partners who mutually enrich each other. They understand now that they must nurture their love in a proactive way. It is a long learning process for Eve and Adam. It is like mastering a totally new language. They have to redefine all their hypotheses about "what works" and "what does not work." Time and again they "fall back." However, they do not give up. The rewards, when they succeed, are too great.

Eve and Adam envisage with excitement the experiences of growth that lie ahead of them. For Eve and Adam, panicky actionism, fueled by pain, has given way for calm reflection and firm resolve in an atmosphere of hope and courage.

CHAPTER 8

HOW WE CAN REINVENT OUR CONTEXTS

Many of the problems of the global village need "no passport"[1] because they are impervious to borders and boundaries. Therefore they require "solutions without passports." In an interdependent world, there is less distinction between self-interest and common interest. We, humankind, have to cooperate. We cannot afford to misdirect our energies into destructive squabbles. Interdependence is the ultimate deterrent to violent conflict. Violent conflicts which formerly may have stayed local, now rapidly become global, diffusing insecurity in an unprecedented manner.[2] Terrorism is the most visible outfall of the globality of destructive dynamics.

We must learn to view ourselves as part of a larger entity—a humankind facing unprecedented challenges jointly. Emotion, also in relation to conflict, has to be tackled in new ways, globally and locally, in relationships between groups and individuals, including in our dealings with ourselves.

Even though we all hope for a world where everybody learns to love everybody else, humankind does not have to reach its highest dreams to survive. We must simply avoid pushing the planet over the edge, both socially and ecologically. This is the mandatory minimum requirement for the survival of our species. In many countries, parents increasingly receive joint custody for their children after divorce (see Chapter 7). Humankind has joint custody for the planet—irrespective of any interpersonal or international falling out.

We currently live in a ramshackle global village. John Stuart Mill coined the phrase *ramshackle states* for those that fail to build sound institutions; Robert Jackson describes them as *quasi-states*.[3] Even worse, in many ways the global village of today faces the world that Robert Kaplan describes in *The Coming Anarchy*,[4] in which he prophesizes overpopulation, resource scarcity, crime, and disease as compounding cultural and ethnic identities to create a chaotic world.

Since cooperation begets cooperation, we should be able to create constructive globalization that begets constructive globalization and decreases the likelihood of destructive conflict. Research indicates that the only remedies for humanity's strong splitting tendencies[5] are common superordinate goals that are attainable and determined by common consent among equals.[6]

In *Creating Super-Ordinate Goals*, Michael Harris Bond writes:

> Social polarizations may be transcended through groups' and their members' uniting successfully around a common purpose or goal.[7] This might involve local tasks such as constructing community facilities. Community service projects, especially if involving younger students from various ethnic groups serving members of various other ethnic groups, may be especially effective in building trust and good-will across group lines. . . . National tasks, such as protecting the shared environment or indeed, fighting off an invader, will accomplish the same unification. Social capital will then develop out of the experience of working together and subsequently out of shared pride in the ongoing benefit from the actual accomplishments themselves.[8]

The broaden-and-build model by Fredrickson and Branigan and research by John F. Dovidio and colleagues demonstrate that positive affect increases our ability to create broader kinds of categorizations.[9] If groups that chronically view one another with suspicion are brought together in structured ways that create positive feelings, former in-group/out-group demarcations weaken. Positive affective states promote inclusive categorizations; former out-groups merge into new in-groups.

> For example, there may be a greater likelihood of conflict between Korean-Americans and African-Americans in a particular community if they define themselves in terms of their distinct ethnic identities. However, if they define themselves in terms of a shared superordinate identity (for example, "resident of New York," "people of color," or simply "Americans"), there is a greater likelihood of positive relations.[10]

In other words, if we frame our identities in ways that put priority on our membership in the *one* human family of Earth, we may reap positive feelings, which in turn will strengthen cooperation and help avoid destructive conflict. Paul Lederach,[11] Herbert C. Kelman,[12] William Ury . . . the list of people who travel the world to bring people together across fault lines is huge. Norway is among the most sought-after mediators.

The problem, however, is that coming together in a common in-group (such as a global village) does not automatically create positive feelings, since, as mentioned earlier, humans share a strong tendency to split into in- and out-groups. New closeness may bring not joy but negative feelings, creating whole new fault lines. The *contact hypothesis*, or the hope that mere contact can foster friendship, is not necessarily true.[13] People might experience, for example, anxiety in the context of intergroup interactions.[14] Anxiety might be fueled by (1) general uncertainty about unfamiliar situations, (2) negative stereotypic expectancies about the out-group, and (3) concern about acting inappropriately or appearing to be prejudiced.[15] Anxiety has negative effects, arousing the sympathetic nervous system and amplifying stereotypic responses to out-groups.[16] Anxiety also limits processing capacity,[17] so that the out-group is viewed in undifferentiated, stereotypic ways. Anxiety makes people less likely to notice when out-group members behave in positive, constructive ways.

Charles Taylor theorizes that recognition becomes a problem with the transition from the premodern to the modern period, since identity is no longer "automatic" but generated "inwardly," an attempt that can fail.[18] I posit that the likelihood for negative feelings increases even further when the ingathering coincides with the emergence of new ideals—particularly such revolutionary ideals as the human rights ideals of equal dignity. The reason is that increasingly, people expect everybody's equal rights and dignity to be recognized. When people increasingly expect everybody's equal rights and dignity to be recognized, feelings of humiliation replace the fear that dominated the world as long as it was caught in the security dilemma. Perhaps the strongest forces that hinder cooperation are feelings of humiliation that flow from failed recognition of equal dignity, because they may lead to "humiliated fury" and, in extremis, to "mindless" mayhem.

We need better psychological, social, and cultural social mindsets, and must foster systemic change that provides us with global decency. The task has three core aspects, and requires two core loops (using the ideal-type approach explained earlier[19]): we must create (1) new awareness in every single human being for our global responsibility, (2) new personal skills of cooperation, and (3) new global institutional frames that enable global and local cooperation. Institutions (3) have preeminence because decent institutions can drive feedback loops that foster (1) and (2) in a systemic rather than haphazard way. The first loop, the initial realization of new institutions, depends on a few Nelson Mandela–like individuals, who "nudge" the world's systems into a more constructive frame (remember Nobel Peace Laureate Jody Williams's campaign to ban personal landmines).[20] The second and subsequent loops will have the advantage of enjoying the support from the system, no longer only depending on a few gifted individuals.

Interestingly, new studies underline the preeminent role of systemic structures. Within nations, economic, ethnic, and regional effects have only modest impact on political stability.[21] Rather, stability is determined by a country's patterns of political competition and political authority. In "How to Construct Stable Democracies," Jack Goldstone and Jay Ulfelder explain that liberal democracy is a powerful means of enhancing a country's political stability. The authors stipulate that we have to learn more about "how some emerging democracies manage to foster free and open competition without descending into factionalism and why some leaders are more willing to accept meaningful constraints on their authority."[22] Goldstone and Ulfelder recommend (and this advice could be heeded also by global society) that "the focus must be shifted from arguments over which societies are ready for democracy toward how to build the specific institutions that reduce the risk of violent instability in countries where democracy is being established."[23]

Scholars such as Stanley Milgram and Philip Zimbardo underpin Goldstone and Ulfelder's message. They have shown through their experiments how important it is to create systems that allow people to be good, rather than limit our efforts to attempts to reform individuals who have to function in less than nurturing systems.[24] Zimbardo explained how "a system" creates "a situation," which brings "good" people to behave "badly."[25] Since the Inquisition, he argues, we have been dealing with problems at an individual level—the individual only was addressed, with its propensities and culpability. The influence of the situation was neglected.

If we apply Milgram's and Zimbardo's results to the real world, we learn that even the "best" people may succumb to pressure—they may be nudged, perhaps not to the extreme but far enough so that dictators can get their way and abusive systems can last. In Nazi Germany, a whole people was being placed into a horrifying system by Hitler and his helpers. Not surprisingly, post–World War II German crime series on television (*Tatort, Soko 110, Rosa Rot, Derrick*, etc.) have at their core the nuanced description of unfolding moral dilemmas wherein people who are not necessarily evil are nudged to become perpetrators.[26]

If we follow Zimbardo, it is wiser to systematically nurture Mandela-like behavior than to wait for exceptional personalities to emerge against all odds and by chance. It is wiser to heed Jean Baker Miller's advice and create "alternative arrangements" rather than accept false choices.[27] It is wiser to systematically promote an alternative climate of trust rather than a climate of fear.[28]

Even if we were inclined not to believe Zimbardo and Miller, the presently unfolding global crises amply make the same point. Troubled teens are helped by being placed in constructive systemic frames or "rehabilitation" camps. It seems that troubled humankind is ready to build global institutions for itself that compel everybody to behave in ways that ameliorate the overall situation. What Goldstone and Ulfelder teach us about countries pertains also to the global village. We, as humankind, need to coalesce under a more benign global frame, modeled on the pattern of democratic institutions. In a decent global village under the roof of new superordinate institutions, local settings can become more benign—global and local situations can express a climate of trust between people from different groups, and nudge all world citizens to behave "good."

To build such global superordinate institutional structures, we can draw on expertise from all walks of life. We can heed the expertise of the European Union, who uses the *subsidiarity principle*—meaning that local decision making and local identities are retained to the greatest extent possible.[29] *Regulatory pyramids* can be put in place.[30] In agriculture, *integrated pest management* maintains homoeostatic balance. As discussed earlier, even our brains can teach us how to embed subordinate loops into superordinate loops.[31] In short, we are well advised to use nondualistic unity in diversity as ontological fundament for all our future undertakings.

Wherever I go, I hear that the solutions are all on the table, that the experts know how to "rescue" humankind. What is lacking is global political leadership. United Nations Secretary-General Ban Ki-Moon said: "We often say that global problems demand global solutions. And yet . . . Today, we also face a crisis of a different sort. Like these others, it knows no borders. It affects all nations. It complicates all other problems. I refer, here, to a challenge of global leadership."[32]

Where does humankind's current faint-heartedness come from? Why are billions invested in war, while the fraction that is necessary to forge a decent global village is so reluctantly forthcoming?

What are the challenges we face?

Own the Transition You Are Part Of

The transition from the traditional order to a new order of equality in dignity does not progress consistently: It moves too fast and too slowly at the same time. It requires a bird's-eye view to see larger patterns. This is much more difficult to achieve than is generally believed. Let me illustrate this point with a story.

In 1971, the Aswan Dam was completed in the south of Egypt. A huge new lake, Lake Nasser, formed behind the dam over the subsequent years. In 1985, I met an Egyptian anthropologist who worked in the sun-dried and wind-beaten desert around Lake Nasser, studying the proud Bedouin tribes that have roamed these vast stretches of land in south Egypt for millennia. She told me the following story.

> One day I visited the tribesmen deep in the desert, far away from the world as we know it. I had visited them before. We went through the lengthy greeting rituals that these Bedouins have practiced since the dawn of time. After a while I was told about the hottest news—the Nile was behaving very strangely. The water was not receding anymore; instead it was forming a kind of lake.

I said that this was to be expected; it was nothing to be astonished about. It was merely the new Lake Nasser. The Nile would never be back to its former bed again, at least not as long as the dam was there.

I should never have said that! The reaction was amazing! Anger and pity! The old wise men of the tribe told me that I was much too young to be able to judge such phenomena and that I should curb my tongue. Of course the Nile would go back to its former shape; it was just a matter of time! How could I be so foolish as to believe that age-old nature would change just like that!

There I was, reprimanded by wise men who knew "better"! There I was confronted with age-old wisdom! Yes, I understood that I was young and immature; still, I was sure that I was right and they were wrong. Their judgment was based on a "database" that was simply too narrow. Their wisdom did not protect them against profound misjudgments. I did not know what to do.

The dilemma of the Egyptian anthropologist reminds me of the well-known anecdote about how to cook a frog. If Mr. Frog were suddenly dropped into a saucepan of hot water, he would swiftly jump out; the water is hot and he does not want to be cooked. But if Mr. Frog is placed in a saucepan of comfortably warm water that is heated very slowly, he does not notice that he is being cooked. Likewise, the moderate speed of change can mask its significance. The Bedouins were like frogs; they were being "cooked" without knowing. The process of change was slow enough to make them miss how dramatic it was—the change was still powerful enough to change their lives forever.

If change had occurred faster, in a matter of days or weeks, it would have been so unsettling that the Bedouins would perhaps have sought help and explanations from a wider world. But the process took months and years, allowing Bedouin thinking to remain within their age-old frames of understanding. These frames were now so inaccurate that they were more or less deadly for these people. Waiting for the Nile to go back to its former bed was just not a viable response to the situation. If the change had occurred even more slowly, over many centuries, generations of Bedouins would have had the chance to adapt without being alarmed much. The Bedouins were cooked by the moderate speed of the change they were part of.

Nazi Germany illustrates the importance of being able to assume a bird's-eye view to avoid missing larger patterns and trends, particularly in times of complex transition. Jewish families who did not flee were killed—in other words, potential Holocaust victims paid with their lives if they failed to understand the bigger picture. Bystanders also paid, with their moral integrity—the German families who blissfully appropriated property left behind by Jewish families ended up having to hide this, in shame, from their children and grandchildren; their failure to question the legitimacy of the practices of their times, including legal practices, had facilitated the most atrocious of human immoralities, the Holocaust. Germans did not grasp in time that they had to resist Hitler; instead they elected him. They did not understand that the experiments of the Weimar Republic with democracy were not a failure but an achievement that had to be built on; instead they fell back into traditional familiar *Obrigkeitsdenken* or "blind trust in superiors and voluntary submission."

What happened in the Egyptian and German examples progressed too slowly to be identified as profoundly new and urgent, and too fast to be treatable with familiar tools. This is also the problem facing the human rights movement. Many do not grasp the significance and urgency of the situation, and those who do often fail to recognize the need to shape this transition constructively and fail to refrain from outdated responses. Inability to see the emergency threatens the human rights movement from outside. But human rights defenders themselves endanger it also from within when they endorse outdated solutions (like using dominating methods to overcome domination). All this is aggravated by the fact that individuals and societies, who do accept the ideals of human rights, do so at different paces. Those who are farther ahead, those who wish to see human rights implemented much faster, are in danger of losing patience and getting into heated battles with those who need more time to process this enormous change in thinking. This inner fragmentation handicaps the human rights movement in its aim to convince the adherents of the traditional orders to join hands to create a new world, a world where every human being enjoys equal rights and dignity.[33]

Why do human beings have problems adapting quickly and appropriately to new situations? Mark Gerzon asks, "why does one person, walking on the beach, stroll blindly to her death without realizing that a lethal tsunami wave is about to strike—while another person takes action and saves herself and a hundred other people?"[34] Clearly, there is a need to intensify the study of the interplay of emotions and cognition in conflict, if we wish to understand this conundrum.

Research on emotions and conflict is needed in many fields: in decision making,[35] risk perception,[36] how paradigms shift,[37] on leadership;[38] on the cultural shaping of emotions,[39] on the science of conflict,[40] on power and conflict,[41] on resistance and rebellion,[42] to name only a few of the many relevant fields.

We need a new breed of humble[43] and selfless leaders,[44] so-called *outside-inside* leaders,[45] who forge innovative ways of organizing our lives and our world, with collaborative teams[46] and a flexible network orientation, rather than rigid organizational structures.[47] We need to be cautious in accepting "the way it's done by experts," because these methods might be counterproductive for promoting new goals.[48]

Gerzon proposes eight tools leaders might use to transform differences into opportunities:

- Integral vision: committing ourselves to hold all sides of the conflict, in all their complexity, in our minds—and in our hearts.

- Systemic thinking: identifying all (or as many as possible) of the significant elements related to the conflict situation and understanding the relationships between these elements.
- Presence: applying all our mental, emotional, and spiritual resources to witnessing and transforming the conflict.
- Inquiry: asking questions to elicit essential information about the conflict that is vital to understanding how to transform it.
- Conscious conversation: becoming aware of our full range of choices about how we speak and listen.
- Dialogue: communicating to build trust and knowledge that maximizes the human capacity to bridge and to innovate.
- Bridging: building partnerships and alliances that cross the borders that divide an organization or community.
- Innovation: catalyzing social or entrepreneurial breakthroughs that foster new options for moving through conflicts.[49]

Leaders may draw on Neil J. Smelser's value added theory (or strain theory) to gauge what is necessary for a new social movement to emerge:

- Structural conduciveness—things that make or allow certain behaviors possible (e.g., spatial proximity).
- Structural strain—something (inequality, injustice) must strain society.
- Generalized belief and explanation—participants have to come to an understanding of what the problem is.
- Precipitating factors—spark to ignite the flame.
- Mobilization for action—people need to become organized.
- Failure of social control—authorities not clamping down.[50]

Remind Those Who Have the Resources to Invest Them

Another obstacle to the advancement of the human rights movement is the division of motivation and resources. A child soldier with no option but to kill or die cannot change the overall context of misery within which he suffers—he may have the motivation, but not the resources. Readers of this book may have the resources, but since they do not suffer as directly, they may overlook the degree of pain in the rest of the world, and may not be sufficiently motivated to step out of their normal lives to invest their resources into large-scale change.

A friend in the United States told me that she responds to allegations that human rights are a Western imperialist project by being careful not to come across as an arrogant Westerner. She explains human rights as something she has learned to appreciate through growing up in her American family. Moral values based on human rights are therefore, she says, neither inferior nor superior to other cultural normative universes, just different. She espouses moral relativism to show respect.

I appreciate the respect. However, to me, such a stance entails a logical fallacy which can be deeply humiliating, even if unintentionally. This stance advocates the impossible—to use a metaphor from traffic management—the combination of right-hand driving with left-hand driving in the same place (see the introduction). My American friend wishes to respect those who drive on either side. This is laudable. However, the problem is that she is closing her eyes to the fact that her solution preprograms accidents.

Even more important, her stance undermines the efforts and humiliates human rights defenders who risk their lives around the world. They don't put themselves in harm's way for some arbitrary cultural difference that can be casually dismissed. They do so because they believe fervently in the possibility of human liberation. Human right ideals entail a release from past bondage. More precisely, in terms of the theme of this book, human rights ideals offer a liberation from instrumentalization of emotion and conflict by power elites. This liberation entails the potential to dramatically dignify the entire human condition, and it is open to every world citizen. (The traffic metaphor ends here, it does not hold up in this situation—driving on the left and on the right are not equally healthy options.)

To speak for myself, I do not stand up for human rights because I want to humiliate the non-West by denigrating passé honor codes of ranked human worthiness. As mentioned earlier, first, honor is not the reserve of the non-West (see Southern honor in the United States[51]).

Second, to my view, people who endorse codes of ranked honor should not be looked down on. Those codes had their respected place before the gathering of humankind into one single family. I agree with Robert Jervis, who reminds us how difficult but important it is to appreciate beliefs that underpin views that are now morally unacceptable. Using slavery as an example, he explains the temptation to avoid "the difficulty and the pain of reconstructing a worldview in which slavery appeared appropriate, effective, and beneficial for all. The line between understanding and approving is too thin to make this a comfortable task."[52] I concur with Jervis that it "is not only a mistake, it is also disrespectful of the people we are trying to understand"[53] to disparage beliefs that have passed their time.

We live in a new reality, an increasingly interdependent world, with the emerging reality of a global village. This new reality can best be tackled with human rights norms. I am convinced that human rights not only promise to liberate and dignify the entire human condition, including all living creatures and the natural world that supports life, but also represent a normative framework that is better adapted to our present reality of global interdependence.

To conclude, the ideal of equality in dignity is worth our sacrifices. Those who enjoy material privileges in today's world have an obligation to invest and sacrifice their resources for the complete implementation—beyond mere rhetoric—of human rights. Those who risk their lives for human rights deserve the full support from those who already enjoy the privilege of living in much more benign contexts.

Many may think my position smacks of neoconservatism. Other passages of my work may raise criticisms that I am too liberal. My position cross-cuts such definitions, which I believe should be left behind. We need both unity *and* diversity. To return to the traffic metaphor and how it can be managed more effectively by using traffic lights, equal dignity means that every driver, no matter the size or quality of his or her vehicle, has the same rights before traffic lights. Governments and police are required to enforce traffic laws. However, it would be overkill to put traffic lights at every corner or to build institutions that regulate traffic in authoritarian ways. Balanced regulation is the answer; neither too much nor too little—balanced regulation regards the essence of each person as equal in dignity with all others, and it dignifies nature, while at the same time celebrating diversity, even diversity that entails inequality, be it expressed in functional hierarchy, the humility of wisdom, or the humor of irony.

We need to build just enough interventions and institutions, both locally and globally, so that we can safeguard the unity, the common ground that is necessary to enable diversity in equality in dignity.

Unmask Covert Manipulation

Perhaps the most insidious reason for humankind's failure to better manage the transition from ranked honor to equal dignity is that cultural practices of the past linger both overtly and covertly. We sometimes consciously cling to wrong beliefs to conform to pressures from our environment: "Wrong Beliefs May Be Sensible and Sincere" is the heading of a section in Jervis's article "Understanding Beliefs."[54]

However, much of our cognitive processing is beyond the reach of conscious thought,[55] and we may not be aware of how we adapt our beliefs to covert manipulation. We may be blind to the effects overt manipulation from the past have on us today, obstructing the emergence of new paradigms.

Though cognitive bias surely plays a role, our vulnerability to covert manipulation is also due to our needs, emotions, and feelings.[56] Humans need to feel recognized and validated. They need to know they belong. This is a wonderful need, a need that provides common ground for cooperation. However, it also makes us vulnerable to covert manipulation.

Let me first give you a feel for this manipulation and how covertly it can work. Emiko Ohnuki-Tierney, already introduced, explains the eerie ways in which young and brilliant Japanese students were coaxed into dying as suicide bombers in World War II.[57] Ohnuki-Tierney was motivated to write her book because she was deeply moved by the diaries of these students. These diaries show how these highly educated young men were torn. Most did *not* want to die. Ohnuki-Tierney shows how they were "persuaded" to "volunteer" by ways of *méconnaissance*. She explains, in detail, how the aesthetics of Japan's cherry blossom symbolism were used—more precisely, abused. The cherry blossom symbolism originally signified life and birth, rather than death. Aestheticization was abused to make ugly cultural practices appear visually and conceptually beautiful. Slowly, as the country grew more militaristic, cherry blossom symbolism was circumspectly transformed to aestheticize death.

Another notion abused to aestheticize deaths on the battlefield was the image of "a shattering crystal ball" (*gyokusai*). Originated in *The Chronicle of Beiqi*, completed in 636 during the Tang Dynasty in China, the term refers to the beautiful way in which a crystal ball shatters into hundreds of pieces. The Japanese military government adopted the term to encourage mass suicide when faced with a hopeless situation. The expression appeared as early as 1891 in a school song that declared that Japanese soldiers would fight until they died like a shattering crystal ball, irrespective of how many enemies there were. The most dramatic use of this term occurred when the Japanese military headquarters decided to abandon their men on an island, which was too heavily surrounded by U.S. ships to allow the Japanese to send in support. Twenty-nine Japanese soldiers were captured, 2,638 died or committed suicide (there were 550 American casualties).

Ohnuki-Tierney tells of a Japanese kindergarten song, published in 1887, that prepared children to "die for the emperor." The children learned to sing: "Mountain cherry blossoms, mountain cherry blossoms, even when they fall, it is for His Majesty."[58] It was their quest for aesthetics, beauty, meaning, their sincerity and dedication that doomed brilliant young students to volunteer to die as tokkotai pilots. Those who volunteered were the idealistic and earnest ones, those who did not try to evade what they perceived to be their noble duty. (Some of their less idealistic comrades managed to survive the war by holding on to less lethal tasks in the military.) Many believed that a new peaceful world would rise from the ashes, giving meaning to their sacrifices.

Why did these dedicated students, with their noble feelings and desire to bring peace to the world, not fight against the political nationalism orchestrated by the state? Ohnuki-Tierney believes that they would have resisted if the coercion had been more blatant. But the insane tokkotai operation was made palatable by hideously manipulated symbols of beauty—cherry blossoms and crystal balls. To make the tokkotai operation a "forced" voluntary system instead of an imperial order compounded its character as a trap. It exonerated those directly responsible (who, interestingly, never volunteered to die themselves!). The young students were coerced by their superiors, by the circumstances on the military bases, and by the atmosphere of the society at large. The best young people were willing to die, yes, but only because those in leadership positions, including intellectuals, teachers, and professors, sent them to their deaths.

As it seems, beauty can easily be abused to covertly be instrumentalized to serve ugly evil. Beauty touches people deeply, consoles and uplifts them, helps them manage even the fear of death. Nigel Spivey shows how art has always been instrumentalized as a means of mass persuasion and was essential to the creation of hierarchical societies around the world.[59] Spivey draws on a wide range of material: From Paleolithic cave paintings to contemporary visions of propaganda and social control, and from ancient Egyptian to classic Greek sculptures, and images of the divine created in medieval Europe and Buddhist Asia.

In Nazi Germany, Göbbels's propaganda machine peddled the abuse of the beauty of pathos and thus succeeded in making evil seem "normal." In her world-renowned book, *Eichmann in Jerusalem: A Report on the Banality of Evil*,[60] Hannah Arendt analyzed how evil actions may not necessarily be the result of evil intentions but rather of the perpetrators' banal lack of critical distance to this normality. In Rwanda, officials employed Radio Mille Collines the same way Göbbels did. And Willem Van Vuuren and Ian Liebenberg show how South Africa was "governed by illusion."[61]

Clearly, we need to overcome being duped into powerlessness and mayhem—no longer should we play the role of useful idiots but assume responsibility, as humankind as a whole.

You might think that the ugliness of war and genocide, though very important, are far removed from you, and that apartheid is of the past. Other readers may feel that this topic is significant only for policy makers at national and international levels, or that a few experts are sufficient to take care of victims who still get manipulated into cults and sects at local levels. Many may also think that they themselves are above manipulation, both as victims and perpetrators.

It takes true humility and the willingness to look more closely to overcome these beliefs. After all, the experiments by Milgram and Zimbardo demonstrated that respectable people were ready to bow to authority, even to the point of perpetrating evil when that authority asked it of them. And the Chinese practice of foot binding was embedded into normality for as long as a thousand years.

The very concept of ranked honor lasted for ten thousand years and is still part of normality in many places today. As explained earlier, the concept of ranked honor is perhaps the single biggest master manipulation ever perpetrated by humankind. By creating helpless underlings, it facilitates manipulation itself. Introducing the concept of ranked honor is a master manipulation because it legitimates and underpins might-is-right supremacy. Anybody who ever succeeded in subjecting others, by whatever effort or accidental circumstances, could turn *might* to seem *right* by invoking divinely ordained ranked honor.

During the past ten thousand years, all over the world, millions of young men were socialized to believe in honor, and they suffered much more than broken and bound feet—they had no lives at all because they died premature deaths. Throughout all history the Kublai Khans of the world have proven the potential destructiveness inherent in honor. The slaughter of World War I wrote the intrinsic contradiction between "rational" choices that secure survival and "irrational" norms of glorious honorable death, for the first time in large bloody letters so that it became very difficult to overlook.

As explained throughout this book, honor is still definitive of every detail of life in many parts of the world at all levels—from the macro to the meso to the micro. Even in contemporary times, genocides and violent intractable conflicts around the world follow the same logic. American Southern honor[62] has guided recent American foreign policy. Many would also place the development of nuclear weapons in this category of the irrational. Even Chernobyl, or the so-called peaceful use of nuclear energy, can be seen as symbols of glorious honorable grandeur for which humankind risks survival, either through all-destructive war or disastrous accident.

The same irrationality permeates our private lives also. The Eve and Adam vignette shows how norms of ranked honor can operate also at the interpersonal level. The Eves of this world still accept foot binding–like self-injury, physical and psychological, to serve the honor of their men.

Even the intrapersonal sphere is not spared. I know from my practice as a clinical psychologist that we all have Eve-and-Adam voices in our minds, struggling with each other, both above, but often below the level of full consciousness.

At the present juncture in human history, all spheres of human life are permeated by an uncoordinated unraveling of past covert manipulations and their resistance.

Let us have a closer look at the inner workings of these covert manipulations to be better prepared for overcoming them.

How Reason and Emotion Slid into Opposition

In ancient Greece and Rome, it was well recognized that feelings can be misused to trap people. It started rather harmlessly with an emphasis on rhetoric to confront conflict-causing situations. In the fifth century B.C., Thrasybulus, the tyrant of Syracuse, seized the land and property of many common citizens. An "art of rhetoric" was developed to permit ordinary people to make their cases in the courts.[63] Sophism was rhetoric's extension; however, the sophists were already regarded as much less harmless, indeed as querulous and even dangerous.

Many renowned philosophers—Socrates (470–399 B.C.[64]), Plato (424/ 423–348/347 B.C.[65]), Isocrates (436–338 B.C.[66])—struggled to remove the potentially "evil" manipulative effects from rhetoric. Plato was altogether skeptical about the art of rhetoric and therefore made it a point to define himself as a philosopher, not a rhetorician. He wanted rational reason to dominate, not feelings. Aristotle (384–322 B.C.), on his part, recognized that one cannot avoid rhetoric, since it is an inherent and important part of all communication, and tried to mitigate its negative effects by reconciling it with philosophy.[67]

Ernesto Grassi points out that humans must have something to believe in if language is to have meaning at all. There must be a kind of axiomatic understanding of the world, and "passion and logic" must stay connected.[68] It is impossible to protect against falling prey to manipulation through rhetoric that abuses emotion (Grassi calls this "false speech"[69]) by simply cutting out feelings, emotions, and passion. Worse even, removing feelings may do away with the very bulwark against manipulation that mature emotion management can provide. Reason and emotion can and need to be fused constructively, not be regarded as opposites.

However, removing passion was precisely what was attempted in historic Europe, and the legacy of this solution still lingers on—particularly in the West people find it difficult, even nowadays, to include feelings in a constructive way.

For a long time, rhetoric remained discredited as the effort to talk people into something by way of abusing of feelings. For many centuries, a kind of "indoctrinating monologue" replaced rhetoric in education. To know the field of logic, for example, students had to learn Aristotle's *Organon* by heart. In physics, Aristotle's *Physic* and *Parva Naturalia* had to be studied. To study meant to read or hear a book (*legere librum* or *audire librum*). In Paris around 1128, Hugo of St. Victor, in his *Didascalicon*, urged lecturers not to be diverted by rhetoric but follow the book.[70] The ideal of academia was similar to the role of priests—it was to inculcate knowledge, not discover it. Strict discipline and the whip were the rule. Emile Durkheim illustrates this discipline in his story about Pierre Tempête, the "pupil flogger."[71]

The pupil flogger had the Dutch humanist Erasmus of Rotterdam (1466/ 1469–1536) in his class. Clearly, love for reason and aversion to rhetoric had gone too far. The European cultural and intellectual movements of Renaissance and humanism which began in Florence in the last decades of the fourteenth century—which also brought the notion of dignity to the forefront[72]—liberated knowledge from its "slavery" to a few canonical books (helped by advances in printing, which gave students access to many more books). *Libertas philosophandi*, or the freedom of philosophizing, became an academic ideal.[73] Many of the most renowned humanists built their careers outside of universities, which they felt, produced people with useless qualifications. Erasmus, for example, declined offers to accept a permanent position at a university.

However, as could be expected, the liberation movement also suffered setbacks. Petrus Ramus, or Pierre de la Ramée (1515–1572), a French humanist, logician, and educational reformer, developed Aristotle's dialectic to serve freedom of thought. He was killed during the St. Bartholomew's Day massacre—it is believed his death was at the hands of jealous academic rivals, who saw him as too provocative and unconventional, infusing students with too passionate a love for libertas philosophandi. Ramée's life and death marked a short rise and fall for the legitimacy of feelings for reason to be reasonable.[74]

Yet the liberation could not be halted altogether. In the eighteenth century, the Enlightenment movement demanded that knowledge be useful and efficiently taught to audiences who were encouraged to *mitdenken* or "co-reflect" with the teacher or lecturer.[75]

As reported in Chapter 5, the year 1757 marked the transition of the meaning of the verb *to humiliate* in the English language from prosocial humbling to the antisocial violation of dignity. This was the beginning of a tipping point for the ideal of equality in dignity, away from ranked honor. The ideal of equality in dignity began to open space for passion to be invested into reason without falling prey to linguistic seduction. However, and this is the message of this book, this does not mean that the abuse of emotions for covert manipulation has disappeared; it still permeates our lives and can rise its head again in disastrous ways if not met with informed resistance.

This discussion is extremely important not least for today's academic institutions.[76] In the article "The Educational Environment as a Place for Humiliating Indoctrination or Dignifying Empowerment,"[77] I highlight the importance of academia in fostering genuine *shutaisei* (Chapter 7)— true subjectivity or autonomy at the individual level—the ability to resist manipulation.

Let us look now at more recent analyses of how covert manipulation works.

Unwittingly Manipulated into Self-Humiliation

Norbert Elias argues that what we experience as "civilization" is constituted by a particular *habitus* or psychic structure that is embedded within broader social relationships.[78] For Pierre Bourdieu, habitus is "socialized subjectivity," our second nature, the mass of conventions, beliefs, and attitudes which we share. Habitus is the part of culture which is so taken for granted that it is virtually invisible to its members. Rules are unnecessary in homogeneous societies, and are replaced by habitus, the "orchestrated improvisation of common dispositions."[79]

Common sense as an "organized body of considered thought,"[80] is a related concept. According to Peter L. Berger and Thomas Luckmann's *social constructionism*, all knowledge, including the most basic, taken-for-granted common sense knowledge of everyday reality, results from social interactions, which, over time, are regarded to be "natural."[81] Michel Foucault's *discourse* and *discursive formation* are related.[82] Sociologist Talcott Parsons used the concept of *gloss* to discuss the idea how "reality" is constructed.[83] Social constructionism is often regarded as a sociological construct because it conceptualizes the development of social phenomena in relation to social contexts, while social constructivism is a more psychological construct, addressing how the meaning of knowledge is relative to social contexts.[84]

Terms such as *horizon* (Immanuel Kant, Edmund Husserl, William James), *tacit knowledge*,[85] or *zero-order beliefs*,[86] or the term *truthiness*[87] speak to the same phenomena. Hugh Mackay introduced the *invisible cage* as a metaphor for the tacit effects of life experience, cultural background, and current context on an individual's view of the world.[88] We have *mental models*[89] on which we base "preferences without inferences,"[90] and frames "that allow human beings to understand reality—and sometimes to create what we take to be reality."[91] We have *cultural mindsets*, or *cultural scripts*, which means that we have "structures within which we store scenes," or "sets of rules for the ordering of information about Stimulus-Affect-Response Sequences (SARS)."[92] Eric Berne illuminates script theory in his book *What Do You Say After You Say Hello?*[93]

Benedict Anderson explains how communities can be ideated and imagined.[94] *Zeitgeist* and *paradigm* are important terms—Thomas S. Kuhn describes how paradigms can shift.[95] Before they shift, they rigidify, with some people identifying with them strongly and standing up for them. Then they are toppled by a new generation of people who ask new questions that undermine the edifice. The already-mentioned psychological phenomenon of *defensive avoidance* plays a role here.

The "automaticity" of all such defensive processes is astounding.[96] We use *rapid cognitions*, in other words, we "think without thinking."[97] An impulsive system exists,[98] and attitudes, including stereotypes, are activated "automatically,"[99] in a rapid interplay of implicit and explicit attitude changes.[100]

The country that brought the Declaration of the Rights of Man and of the Citizen to the world in 1789 has subsequently seen its scholars dissecting how the covert nature of habitus can be abused for covert domination. Concepts such as méconnaissance (misrecognition) and naturalization were used by Roland Barthes, Pierre Bourdieu, and Michel Foucault (among others). They address how power structures use the concealed nature of habitus to manipulate not just overtly but covertly and stealthily, making it much more difficult to rid oneself of these manipulations.

In his work on mythology (1954–1956), Barthes discusses socially constructed reality and how it is perceived as "natural."[101] Barthes describes how opinions and values can be introduced by a certain power group and then held up as "universal truths." Those who try to question this socially constructed reality (what Barthes calls *le cela-va-de-soi*) are ridiculed and rejected. They are accused of lacking "bon sens." Power relations are glossed over and their political threat obscured. In other words, Barthes exposes the artificiality of realities which disguise their historical and social origins.

Bourdieu makes the point that knowledge can never be disinterested. It is in the interest of certain groups to impose meaning, as a continual enactment of symbolic violence. In his theory of practice, Bourdieu describes social behavior as the continual accomplishment of actions. He explains the process through which the arbitrariness of an established order is "naturalized"—*cultural* arbitrariness is transformed into the *natural*.[102] An entire system of schemes of perception, appreciation, and action constitutes the habitus of a society. It is this habitus, explains Bourdieu, which lends order to customary social behavior by functioning as "the generative basis of structured, objectively unified practices."[103]

The imposition of meaning and its incorporation into habitus is achieved in covert ways, via what Bourdieu calls *second-order* or *officializing* strategies. Those strategies make behavior appear to be pure and disinterested by "ostentatiously honouring the values the group honours."[104] In Bourdieu's usage, misrecognition is not just a lack of awareness of the objective reality of a particular cultural practice but a strategic misconstruing of practice. He uses gift-giving is an example. Even though everybody knows that reciprocity is expected, "collective bad faith" is maintained.[105] Everybody holds on to a "sincere fiction of a disinterested exchange."[106] In analogous fashion, a manipulated habitus is both the product of history and produces history.

Foucault, in *Discipline and Punish*,[107] exposes the naturalization of the "criminal character." Brenton Faber discusses *intuitive ethics*,[108] suggesting that intuition is the naturalization of dominant values and beliefs. He bases his theory of intuition on the sociological terms of habitus as used by Bourdieu, as well as Giddens's *routinization*,[109] and Fairclough's naturalization concept.[110]

Foucault coined the term *governmentality*,[111] describing a novel kind of governing that emerged in Europe during the sixteenth century when feudalism (an earlier form of governmentability) was failing. Governmentability was made possible again through the creation of specific (expert or professional) "knowledges" as well as the construction of experts, institutions and disciplines (for example, medicine, psychology, psychiatry).

I call it *voluntary self-humiliation*, when elite "expertise" is followed blindly (which is as destructive as rejecting it blindly).[112] Johan Galtung forged the related notion of *penetration*, or "implanting the topdog inside the underdog,"[113] illustrating the fact that acceptance of subjugation may become a culture of its own. The term *subaltern* is related,[114] as is the already mentioned Obrigkeitsdenken. Also Jürgen Habermas's concept of the *colonization of the lifeworld*[115] may lend itself to describing the covert manipulation of habitus. Patricia Hill Collins's concept of *controlling images*[116] is related, describing images being imposed by a dominant culture, images that are voluntarily or involuntarily accepted by disempowered subordinate groups.

The *authoritarian personality*[117] is a personality that slides easily into subservience. Certain child-rearing methods lend themselves to producing such personalities; indeed they facilitated the rise of Hitler's Nazism.[118] As referred to earlier, the *strict father* model (as opposed to the *nurturant parent* model) is the underlying pedagogical framework that generates obedient inferiors.[119]

Many colonized subjects (*jacere* is Latin for *to throw*, and the prefix *sub* means *under*) deemed their colonizers to be more "civilized" than they were themselves. Many yearned to become "more French than the French," or "more British than the British." Frantz Fanon wrote a book entitled *Black Skin, White Masks*,[120] wherein he describes how he was once very proud of being almost "French," of climbing *up* the scale of human value. What he initially overlooked was that his newly won pride validated his former lowliness. You cannot be proud of being up without judging your former status as low.

There are many terms describing this identification with the oppressor. *Learned helplessness* is a term coined by Martin Seligman to define that helplessness can be a learned state produced by exposure to noxious, unpleasant situations in which there is no possibility of escape or avoidance.[121] Likewise, the *Stockholm syndrome* is "an emotional bond between hostages and their captors, frequently observed when the hostages are held for long periods of time under emotionally straining circumstances. The name derives from the instance when this was first publicly noted, namely, when a group of hostages was held by robbers in a Stockholm bank for five days."[122] *Cognitive dissonance* is another relevant term here (see also Chapter 6), because it highlights how, when a system is enforced by way of oppression, attempts to alleviate dissonance can lead to adopting a belief system rather than merely adapting to it pragmatically.

Identification with the oppressor is not always an individual process; it can also be a societal process. As discussed before, many underlings turned their lowliness into a "culture." Galtung's notion of penetration illustrates the fact that acceptance of subjugation may become a culture of its own. Ranajit Guha's understanding of the term *subaltern* also points to this process.[123] Ashis Nandy's work was mentioned earlier.[124]

A caveat: Lowliness does not necessarily connote meek helplessness—it can also be an expression of proud humility. A monk choosing poverty to live closer to God, for example, may accept lowliness to realize humility. It would be arrogant to frame everybody as passive and weak victim who appears to hold a lowly position. Likewise, it would be wrong to attribute evil intentions to everyone in a place of power—truly benevolent patronage exists (see Chapter 5 and the discussion that egalization can coexist with functional hierarchies). The important point here is that during the past ten thousand years, nobody could escape a world framed malignly by the security dilemma. Everybody was a victim of this large-scale tragedy, those with power as much as those without. The aim of this book is not to blame victims but to enable us all to capitalize on the current large-scale transformation and undo the shackles from the past.

Researchers who focus on emotion and conflict need to ask, Where does this human vulnerability to covert manipulation come from? Why are people sometimes willing to put status higher than health and survival? Why do they voluntarily humiliate their own humanity? Is this a mechanism of addiction? Is status addictive? Does it provide a kind of emotional gratification that is worth more than health and survival? Does it operate, perhaps, like drug addiction, which overrides any awareness of its potentially destructive consequences?

Let us summarize what we learned so far. The success of covert manipulation rests on the human dependence on tacit knowledge, which, in turn, makes humans inherently vulnerable to méconnaissance. And méconnaissance can be efficiently enforced by the manipulation of emotions and meta-emotions. Whoever has sufficient power-over leverage will find it advantageous to introduce ranked honor as master manipulation, because it makes might seem right, and inferiors susceptible to more manipulation. If done cleverly, these manipulations will penetrate, and underlings will debase their dignity, damage their health, and risk death "voluntarily." The overall strength of emotions and the human need for belonging and recognition figure as powerful liabilities in this process (they overlap with the phenomenon of affordance, which I will discuss later). This need makes people vulnerable to being malignly and stealthily turned into handicapped and thus harmless inferiors in ranked systems—if people believe that they can increase their sense of belonging by climbing up the ladder in a ranked system, even at the cost of mutilating themselves, they may fall for this trap and do so (foot binding as stark example). I call this process voluntary self-humiliation to highlight that it can be unmasked and undone, even though I am aware that it would be more correct to say that people are unwittingly manipulated into self-humiliation.

As repeated throughout this book, this manipulation is not something of the past. Allow me to look at some contemporary examples.

Advertisement and Spin

Industrial mass production—including that of unhealthy products—was, and still is, made palatable through covert manipulation. For example, to widen the market for cigarettes, women were coopted into smoking by the image of women smokers as torches of freedom.[125] This was done by Sigmund Freud's nephew Edward Louis Bernays (1891–1995), who combined Freud's psychoanalytical concepts with the work of Gustave LeBon on crowd psychology and Wilfred Trotter's ideas on the instincts of the "herd."[126]

The latest expression of this manipulation, as every reader will recognize in contemporary politics, is spin.

The Newtonian Machine Paradigm

Among the most recent large-scale occurrences of covert manipulation that spills its ill effects everywhere, even in the most modern and allegedly informed society, is what I call the *Newtonian machine paradigm*, or the idolization of misunderstood physicalism.

It is the mistaken belief that human health and quality of life are best described with Newtonian physicalism and best served by being forced into Newtonian frames. This belief overlooks that it is wrong to conclude that it is healthy for humans to function like Newtonian machines only because those machines operate well. As noted earlier in connection with quantum social science, humans are much more complex creatures than Newtonian physics indicate—they are living organisms who are organically embedded within a hugely intricate biosphere. Designing the human-made world according to inappropriately crude Newtonian principles and forcing humans into such worlds—worse even, looking down on those who fail to fit—spells disaster. Examples of this disaster abound, from architecture to how we design our social lives, or how we expect us to perform psychologically. Touching reflections on this problem were recorded by American philosopher Alan Wilson Watts (1915–1973).[127]

The machine paradigm is virulent not least because it maximizes profit if a large enough number of people can be manipulated into accepting it—the leverage that earlier could be derived from conquering land can now be derived from mass production and huge industrial projects. To simplify, when employees strive to become cog wheels, and consumers pay money for mass produced uniformity, and all believe that it is virtuous to ignore the impact such dehumanization might have on their health and the biosphere, a few entrepreneurs profit.

The machine paradigm still dominates the world everywhere—it is currently exported from the West to the rest. We still have to understand that it is not enough that China has outlawed foot binding, that apartheid as ended, or that our governments have signed human rights covenants. We still unwittingly socialize one another into mutilating ways of dealing with lives and emotions, our own and those of others.

Human Affordance to Entrepreneurs

Another phenomenon that makes humans vulnerable to covert manipulation is *affordance*. The notion of affordance was introduced by James

Gibson.[128] It was later slightly changed by Donald Norman's ecological approach (akin to systems-theoretic approaches in the natural and social sciences), which made the concept relational, rather than subjective or intrinsic.[129] The term is used in perceptual psychology, cognitive psychology, environmental psychology, industrial design, human–computer interaction, interaction design, and artificial intelligence. A door handle, for example, "affords" or invites pulling.

For hunter-gatherers honey was a delicacy, which they craved. Honey "invited" consumption. Yet since honey was scarce, there was no danger of obesity or diabetes due to overconsumption of sugar—nature invited hunter-gatherers to enjoy honey, however, in a limited and thus harmless way. The global market order of the past decades, in contrast, turned the tables: Entrepreneurs not only scrutinized nature as to how it invites humans, they also scrutinized how nature, human nature included, invites entrepreneurs. For example, entrepreneurs regarded the human preference for honey as an invitation to earn a profit by making food more sugary—they thus capitalized on human affordance, and by doing so, they eliminated nature's restrictions.

In all spheres of life, be it human nature or nature in general, restrictions that keep a regulatory balance in place risk being destroyed when a market system "accepts invitations" without considering the need for restrictions. As a result, a few entrepreneurs make a profit by destroying the overall interdependent system, be it the homeostasis of the global climate[130] or global social cohesion. In this way, humankind sells out its resources and thus undermines its own life support.

Coming back to ranked honor as master manipulation, humans afford and invite this manipulation through their strong emotional needs for belonging and validation. As soon as a ranked system is in place, elite status is craved. Nothing is more characteristic of elite status than the consumption of scarce products—only the rich can afford meat and sugar or big cars, and everybody wishes to ascend in rank by following suit, opening the gates for unfettered maximization to overrun limiting regulations. Current times amply demonstrate this effect. Even the most sophisticated economists and politicians were "dazzled" by the promise of an unregulated market and, collectively and blindly, they ran into global financial meltdown.

Affordance works as a two-tiered trap for humankind: Entrepreneurs have an interest in disregarding nature's restrictions, and buyers do not oppose this, on the contrary, those manipulated into believing in rank support the maximization of profit, including the mass production of what was once scarce, because having the money to be able to consume scarce products signifies higher status.

The consequence is that nature's homeostasis is destroyed. Complex interdependent systems need a certain amount of regulation to function and are best nurtured by optimizing nondualism (Chapter 1). Runaway maximization of dualism (for example, "we" against "nature") wrecks such systems. As we learn from Jared Diamond, for civilizations to collapse, the one factor that all had in common, during all of human history, was their mismanagement of natural resources.[131] This time it is all of humankind that will collapse.

From global warming to the current financial crisis, all such crises point at a core fault in the system: Runaway maximization of singular aspects destroys the optimization of an interdependent complex system, with the effect that all humankind manipulates itself into humiliating self-destruction.

Unmasking Covert Manipulation

Yet change is under way. The entire world is currently engaged in unmasking covert manipulations, and this process forms the core of the human rights movement. We can observe this process unfolding everywhere, in many variations. Japanese architect Kisho Kurokawa summarizes this new spirit, when he calls for a shift from a "machine principle" to a "life principle," not just in architectural designs.[132]

To pick one example among many, *social identity complexity* is currently gaining legitimacy. In the past, such complexity was unwelcome. Social identity was supposed to be monolithic, shaped by power elites.[133] In the context of the security dilemma, the dualism of "good in-group" versus "evil out-group," if maximized, paved the path to "victory." The West used this method with great success and conquered the world as colonizers. At the current point in history, even though this approach becomes increasingly dysfunctional, the West still draws on accumulated power from colonial times in many ways (from unfair global trade rules to using up the world's resources, the list is long).

Not surprisingly, power elites fear complex social identities, because they make for disloyal underlings. Sonia Roccas and Marilynn B. Brewer show how our identity structures become more inclusive and our tolerance of out-groups increases when we acknowledge and accept social identity complexity.[134]

Michel Serres advocates mixing and blending. He suggests that it is not by eliminating and isolating that we grasp the real more fully. It is by combining, by putting things into play with each other, by letting things interact. In his book *The Troubadour of Knowledge*,[135] he uses the metaphor of the "educated third," which, to Serres, is a "third place" where a mixture of culture, nature, sciences, arts, and humanities is constructed. Michalinos Zembylas explains, "this 'educated third' will blend together our multiple heritages and will integrate the laws; he/she will be the inventor of knowledge, the eternal traveler who cares about nature and his/her fellow human beings."[136]

Philosopher Kwame Anthony Appiah makes a "case for contamination."[137] He says "no" to purity, tribalism, and cultural protectionism, and "yes" to a new cosmopolitanism. Emmanuel E. Lévinas highlights the Other, whose face forces us to be humane.[138] Terms such as *métissage*, or *intermingling*, mean that both "I" and the "other" are changed by our contact. Werner Wintersteiner, a peace educator in Austria, builds on Lévinas and uses the term of métissage in his *Pedagogy of the Other*.[139] Wintersteiner suggests that the basis for peace education in the future must be the stranger, and that we must learn to live with this permanent strangeness as a trait of our postmodern human condition and culture.

Earlier, I referred to German TV crime series and their focus on nondualistic nuance. Without being labeled as such, these series represent an educational program that teaches its audiences Yoshikawa's double-swing approach. Currently, many more media campaigns follow suit. Al Gore and the UN's Intergovernmental Panel on Climate Change won the 2007 Nobel Peace Prize. Programs such as *Earth Report*,[140] or IRIN Film & TV,[141] to name only a few, attempt to open the eyes of humankind. Queen Rania of Jordan,[142] Omar Amanat,[143] Bono[144]—influential individuals begin to use their media clout. The idea of a Peace Star aims to turn media campaigns into a large-scale paradigm shifting force.[145]

Eve and Adam are encouraged by their counselor to capitalize on the ideal of equality in dignity, enshrined in human rights, to unmask and undo past manipulations. It takes time, but slowly they gather the courage to accept that an alternative normative frame can liberate them from the belief that damaging themselves (and others) may protect or increase their rank. They understand that equality in dignity does not mean that people cannot still gain in stature—but they are relieved from having to pay with their health for higher rank and status. Eve and Adam begin to understand that they can gain stature by not falling for the trap of ranked status.

CHAPTER 9

HOW WE CAN DIGNIFY OUR
EMOTIONS AND CONFLICTS

At the current point in history, humankind faces a unique window of opportunity. Never before has humankind understood how small and vulnerable their habitat is. Michio Kaku, renowned physicist, concludes his book *Parallel Worlds* with the following paragraph:

> The generation now alive is perhaps the most important generation of humans ever to walk the Earth. Unlike previous generations, we hold in our hands the future destiny of our species, whether we soar into fulfilling our promise as a type I civilization [meaning a civilization that succeeds in building a socially and ecologically sustainable world] or fall into the abyss of chaos, pollution, and war. Decisions made by us will reverberate throughout this century. How we resolve global wars, proliferating nuclear weapons, and sectarian and ethnic strife will either lay or destroy the foundations of a type I civilization. Perhaps the purpose and meaning of the current generation are to make sure that the transition to a type I civilization is a smooth one. The choice is ours. This is the legacy of the generation now alive. This is our destiny.[1]

David A. Hamburg, president emeritus of Carnegie Corporation of New York and author of *No More Killing Fields*,[2] warns, in *Learning to Live Together*, that the central challenge of our time is that our predispositions toward hateful beliefs have acquired destructive powers which dwarf those of our ancestors. "There must be many responses, involving many sectors of society, and many kinds of governments, institutions, and organizations. But scholarship and practice in international relations, including war and peace issues, have gravely neglected both the crucial psychological aspects and the educational opportunities of these terrible problems."[3]

An American friend's recent letter to me[4] illustrates how far we still have to go—even in societies that pride themselves of providing freedom for self-realization. My friend wrote of the unintended humiliations she sustained as a middle-class child in postwar America: "I was saddled with the burden of being a child who cried easily," she recalls.

> There was a fat girl named Margaret. The kids made fun of her when she tried to run. When that happened, I'd cry. Then, the kids made fun of me. There was a girl named Gloria, who wet her pants whenever she had to take part in a spelling bee. Every time she wet her pants, I'd get to thinking about how embarrassed she must be and cry. Then, the kids made fun of me. There was a boy named Tommy, who was bad. I'd watch his face, his lips twisted to keep from weeping, when he got punished. (The nuns were heavy into corporal punishment.) I'd feel so bad for him that I'd cry in his place. It was common in any classroom in which I was a student, to hear: "Sister, Sister, Kathy's crying again!"

My friend went on to say that she can find no "villains" in her story. "No one tried to shame me," she said. "But, what's to be done with an eight-year-old who weeps her heart out because another child wet her pants in public?"

Reading an earlier draft of this book, my friend realized that as a child she experienced another person's humiliation as her own, a type of empathy she insists is natural to all human beings (see the discussion of mirror neurons in Chapters 1 and 4).

Her suggestion is that children need to learn early that there is no crime in being empathetic, that it's okay to feel hurt when another person bleeds. "A society truly dedicated to human dignity would build into its educational system lessons on how to manage the very strong emotions humiliation arouses in both the victims and the witnesses," she concludes. "Such a society would teach children that when they see another human suffering, they are being called to take action. They are being called to stand up, not sit by and hope no one notices that they are crying."

In Chapter 7, the concept of the *depth of intention*, or *depth of questioning*, or *deepness of answers* by Norwegian philosopher Arne Næss was introduced.[5] In Chapter 1, I discussed that humankind must enlarge its perspective in two dimensions—*down and deeper* and *up and wider*. This is also what my American friend wishes to tell the world, namely, that we, as humankind, need to add depth and width to all realms of human life on planet Earth.

Many domains offer blueprints, from medicine to environmental protection. To make industrial production sustainable, for example, it is not sufficient to tinker with the symptoms of the malaise at the "end of the pipe."[6] The entire production process needs to be taken apart, each detail has to be looked at in more detail (deeper differentiation), and reassembled in more comprehensive ways (wider perspective).

Tinkering with emotion and conflict is, likewise, not enough. A decent world is not the same as a world without conflict. Studying emotions and conflict so as to "eradicate" conflict and hatred is not the solution; neither is teaching everybody lessons such as resilience and forgiveness, important as they are. These "solutions" intervene too closely to the end of the process. A "de-contextualized trauma-based approach" (achieving 'resilience' within the status quo) does not address the systemic and endemic factors of collective violence," warns peace psychologist Daniel J. Christie.[7]

To emphasize this point, just imagine—would it, for example, help improve the institutions of the world if all Holocaust survivors forgave all those Jews who were forced to lead fellow Jews into the gas chambers for not preferring to be killed? It would certainly heal individuals and their offspring, but would it bring about systemic change? The entire Nazi system was responsible, not the individual Jew who was coerced into becoming a co-perpetrator—the individual Jew had no freedom but was forced into the horrible dilemma of either death or cooperation. Or can we believe that a child soldier, who is coerced into becoming a killer, is nothing else but personally responsible? Or can the individual citizen of the Western world, who contributes to her region's overuse of the world's resources, be expected to act single-handedly to undo the damage?

In December 2007, I saw a play titled *Masked* that dramatizes this dilemma.[8] An Israeli playwright put on stage three Palestinian brothers and throws into stark light the conflict between, within, and around a family caught in the conundrum of the Middle East situation. The play's Web site features the message: "There are no bystanders."[9]

In Chapter 8, Miller, Milgram, Zimbardo, Goldstone, and Ulfelder explained the significance of larger contexts for human behavior. We, as humankind, have two core choices: either to build horrifying boot camps for ourselves that throw everybody into inhumane dilemmas, or create constructive frames within which people can exercise personal responsibility without facing unacceptable punishment or death.

This is the fundamental conundrum of humankind today: The whole contemporary world system forces individuals into dilemmas that humiliate them and humiliate the humanity of all human beings. More comprehensive approaches to worldwide problems are necessary. The entire system needs deep reform. The true perpetrators are we who have the resources to stand up instead of standing by. We have to stop valuing our normal lives over the advancement of the human race. We have to stop believing that we can be bystanders. We who have the resources must step up to the challenge.

We Must Create a Decent Global Village!

There is need for large-scale systemic change, powered by a new human awareness of global unity. We need to build a decent global village, in the spirit of Avishai Margalit's call for a decent society, a world in which institutions do not have humiliating effects.[10] We have to create global framings that teach everybody that the stewardship of our world is a joint task, that it is a community game and not a "Wall Street game" (Chapter 3). And we need to proactively increase positivity, not just resolve conflicts (Chapter 7).

Current peace psychology summarizes the need for systemic change as follows: "In particular, three themes are emerging in post–Cold War peace psychology: (1) greater sensitivity to geohistorical context, (2) a more differentiated perspective on the meanings and types of violence and peace, and (3) a systems view of the nature of violence and peace."[11]

What is systemic change? Christie explains that episodic peace-building often involves the promotion of intergroup contact and nonviolent management of conflict, while structural peace-building is characterized by large-scale social justice movements that promote equitable political and economic arrangements in a society. Taken together, he argues, episodic and structural peace-building can yield "an increase in cooperative and equitable relationships across levels, from interpersonal to intergroup."[12]

Milton Schwebel has invested his life work in promoting human development and functioning through societal, organizational, and educational change and therapy. His systems perspective of violence and peacebuilding distills three elements,[13] (1) political reality, (2) realistic empathy, and (3) active nonviolence. To approach contemporary political reality, where those in power tend to equate their interests with national interests to justify direct and structural violence, peace-building is a process that alters political reality toward socially just ends through the application of *realistic empathy* and nonviolent social activism.

How do we build a decent global village? What kinds of large-scale structural tools are available? At the nation-state level, individuals submit to state power. We have a social contract, as discussed by philosophers such as Thomas Hobbes (1588–1679) in *Leviathan*, John Locke (1632–1704) and Jean-Jacques Rousseau (1712–1778). Rousseau's *Social Contract* became a textbook for the French Revolution and influenced the history of the entire Western world.[14]

Current global problems call for a global social contract where individuals and states submit to common superordinate global institutional structures. The notion of *subsidiarity* (Chapter 8) needs to be central to these institutions. Subsidiarity allows for safeguarding and celebrating diversity in ways that do not separate and divide but embed diversity into a unifying context of respect for equal dignity. The European Union uses the subsidiarity principle and is praised, among others by global critics such as Kishore Mahbubani, for having reached the "gold standard" of peace within its borders.[15]

We can observe many processes of coalescence, both historic and current. The United States went through such a process and Europe is currently undergoing one. The European Union (EU), the Asia-Pacific Economic Cooperation (ASEAN), the Asia-Pacific Economic Cooperation (APEC), the Latin American common market (MERCOSUR), or the North American Free Trade Agreement (NAFTA), are all examples of processes in which certain elements of local sovereignty are placed at a higher level and are slowly and carefully transferred to commonly accepted superordinate structures.

United Nations institutions, so far, are the highest level of superordinate institutions. However, the influence of the institutions of the United Nations is limited by national sovereignty. Despite lofty rhetoric, the United Nations was created primarily to cater to national interest, not necessarily to the common good of the individual citizens of our planet. So far, few people have the common good of humankind at heart, and even fewer institutions hold the common good as its ultimate goal. Our generation's task is to develop the global village so that the common good of all humanity, including its habitat, is protected—the Human Dignity and Humiliation Studies network I founded (Chapter 4) is but one contribution.

Emotion and conflict are and must be involved in this process at all levels. Even inner dialogues need to be adapted to assist. Emotions must be managed in ways that make them support waging good conflict and building new institutional frames. New ways of negotiating emotions and related beliefs at personal and group levels must drive better institution building, and this, in turn, will feed back into better emotion management. As Robert Jervis writes, "actions not only produce beliefs, but, once formed, these new beliefs influence later actions."[16]

We Must Humble Globalization with Egalization!

Currently the global village is a pyramid—a few rich on top of masses of poor. Even if we could close our eyes to the moral obscenity of this situation, the problem with asymmetries is that they are not stable. One set of players satisfies their desire for recognition by denying full recognition to another.[17] Those who do not have full recognition fight for it, often dissolving the social order. "If the choice is between a world of growing threats as a result of refusing to fully recognize Others versus a world in which their desires for recognition are satisfied, it seems clear which decision rational Great Powers should make."[18]

How can we build a new sustainable world, or what Kaku calls a type I civilization? How can we persuade all world citizens to define their personal health in ways that entail an obligation to create access to dignifying living conditions for all fellow human beings? How can we realize *egaliza-tion* (Chapter 5)?

Humiliation is an important factor, both negative and positive. In an asymmetric world, particularly when inequality is thrown into even starker contrast by human rights ideals of equal dignity, dynamics of humiliation permeate all aspects of social life. Subalterns feel humiliated by the lack of recognition for equal dignity, while those at the top feel humiliated when they see the gratitude they think their underlings owe them as lacking. Feelings of humiliation in turn may be played out in mayhem. This is the negative effect of feelings of humiliation.

However, humiliation is also the emotional fuel that drives the human rights movement, which is at the core of this project. As discussed earlier, in the human brain, negative emotions serve as eye-openers—that something is wrong and needs to be addressed (Chapters 2 and 7). Therefore, feeling humiliated by the failings of the current state of affairs of the world is crucial. The ability to feel humiliated, on behalf of one's own suffering and that of others, serves like a fire sensor—it drives *conscientization* (Chapter 5).

Yet sensing danger, feeling negative emotions, and experiencing scruples are not enough. This may lead to apathy, depression, helplessly empty rhetoric, or even violence. For constructive change to occur, Mandela-like action must emerge from negative emotions. The sickening feeling of humiliation can and ought to be healed by promoting equality in dignity for all, in a proactively caring, enabling, and nurturing manner. To stay in the metaphor of fire, the fire sensor has to expand into a fire alarm, and ultimately call people to go out to build a world better protected against fire. Whenever equal dignity is violated, humanity itself is humiliated, and we need people to feel this humiliation and to act on these feelings in constructive ways.

The long-term future of the global village can be benign, if we steer clear of the short-term malignancies. We can link our hopes to a global village of social and ecological sustainability. Our fears need to keep an eye on—not alone but pivotally—the phenomenon of humiliation. Feelings of humiliation that are translated into hatred and violence hamper the cooperation that is needed to tackle the pressing problems of the globe, and, unfortunately, dynamics of humiliation are brought to the fore in the course of globalization that lacks egalization. If not curbed, they risk undermining in malignant ways otherwise benign tendencies.

Which insights and practices can feed a benign and helpful vision for a healthier future, both collectively and individually? What are Mandela-like approaches to building a healthier world for healthier individuals, embedded in a more appropriate understanding of biological, physical, and chemical underpinnings of health and its embeddedness in global social and ecological interdependence?

Howard Richards, founder of the Peace and Global Studies and Philosophy at Earlham College, writes, "Think of the diverse human beliefs and practices of the past and the present as cultural resources available to be employed in the construction of a world that works for everybody."[19]

In other words, we must harvest all Mandela-like approaches from all cultures, past and present.[20] This is why maintaining cultural diversity is as crucial for the survival of humankind as protecting biodiversity. Biodiversity may hold yet unknown medical remedies in store for humankind, and cultural diversity may provide essential social remedies.

Yet we need to be selective. When we look back in history, we can identify myriad cultural practices. Mutilating foot-binding practices are destructive—they are not remedies but poisons. We need to harvest the liberating and dignifying practices that humankind developed around the world, practices that free the fullness of human capacity and creativity.

Living well is a suitable heading for constructive harvesting. On June 5, 2008, more than a thousand representatives from indigenous communities across the Americas, gathering in Lima, Peru, agreed on a new social system that focuses on reciprocity between people and the Earth, and they called it "Living Well."[21]

If we look at the world's large cultural realms, they all entail strengths that we can combine[22]—Asian know-how of nondualism and harmony can serve the proactive creation of global cohesion, if carefully combined, with, for example, Anglo-Saxon emphasis on action, European strengths in systemic planning, and all other nondualistic, dignifying philosophies from around the world.

I propose founding a new field, *global interhuman communication* (supplementing the field of intercultural communication). This field would need to explain why traditional ranked honor norms are as unhelpful as "Western" ruthless individualism in efforts to foster a harmonious global society that offers equality in dignity to all world citizens in a proactive and nondualist fashion, and why a new way must be found.

As a species, we have had many experiences that indicate that we can overcome problems. At the national level, Hobbesian anarchy has been tamed in many places. This can serve as a template for success at the global level. The idea and reality of one single interdependent in-group is more benign than the idea and reality of many in-groups that view one another as enemy out-groups. This is the promise of globalization. And every move toward marrying globalization with egalization is a benign one, notwithstanding the current obscene lack of egalization that profoundly humiliates the humanity of every world citizen.

We Must Humanize Globalization with Egalization!

Peace is more than resolved conflict, like love in a marriage is more than the ability to solve quarrels or dignity is more than the absence of humiliation. Egalization is not just about rights, it is about more—about dignity, caring, enabling, and nurturing.

How can we create this *more*? How can we attain not just liberté and égalité, but also fraternité, or harmonious[23] social cohesion,[24] and how can we achieve this globally?

We can do this through applying the Lévinasian interpretation of human rights and humanize globalization with egalization through the proactive creation of *positivity* (Chapter 7). In this way, we can build the inclusive decent world that Margalit calls for.

To create positivity, we must develop new ways to live in the world, including new definitions and skills. Many traditional conceptualizations are outdated. It is time to rectify a number of misconceptions. As Ury indicates, the ingathering of humankind and its movement toward a global knowledge society reopens the door to a more egalitarian and humane win-win era.

Let us begin with politics. Politics need to be imbued with new definitions. Sir Samuel Brittan is one of the United Kingdom's foremost political economists. In the Hinton Lecture of 1999,[25] he makes the point that perhaps the time has come to question the old dichotomy between "realists" and "idealists." Clearly, both are "wrong" and "right" simultaneously. Realists are impressed by Thomas Hobbes's description of the world as a dark place and, indeed, they are often "right." Undoubtedly, people "seeking Rousseau, are finding Hobbes," as Ralf Dahrendorf coins it. Realists feel superior to frivolous "idealists," who naively dream of a better world. However, "idealists" might be "right" when they call for goals more ambitious than mere survival. They may be justified when they accuse Hobbesian realists of merely covering up their jaded supremacy and lack of willingness to share.

Deutsch's *crude law of social relations* has been discussed earlier, as has Axelrod's *reciprocal altruism strategy*, also known as *evolutionary tit-for-tat*. Both are reflected in many world philosophies, for example in the African *ubuntu*, the traditional philosophy for living together and solving conflict in an atmosphere of shared humility ("I am because of you").[26]

Reciprocal altruism is the only successful approach in an interdependent world, where everybody depends on everybody else as they move toward their shared future. Reciprocal altruism outshines all other strategies. It increases the benefits of cooperation over time and protects the participants from deceivers and tricksters. Interdependence forces self-interest and common interest into the same boat. Cost-benefit and pay-off calculations in the name of self-interest flow together with common interest, the common interest in a health-sustaining world.

In an interdependent world, it pays to approach other people in a spirit of cooperation and not try to win at the expense of others. It pays to learn to enjoy human contact for its own sake. It pays to heed Jean Baker Miller's view that our health depends on our relations.[27] It pays to follow Martin Buber and define meeting a fellow human being in a real dialogue as a reflection of the human meeting with God. Also, atheists can make the world a better place by taking pleasure in the quasi-divine nature of human relationships.

We can call this approach *metta* (Pali) or *maitri* (Sanskrit), translated as "loving-kindness," "friendliness," "benevolence," "amity," "friendship," "good will," "kindness," "love," "sympathy," or "active interest in others." Or we can label it as *agape*, an adjective and adverb that means, in Greek, "gaping, as with wonder, with expectation, or with eager attention"—or, as a noun, we can translate agape as spiritual love for God and human-kind. Or we can call it *philia*, which in Greek means love between friends. All these words mean we can touch the beauty and mercy of the universe in a way that goes beyond all religious explanations.

We can also turn to Rudolf Otto (1869–1937) and his notion of the *myste-rium*.[28] Otto was one of the most influential thinkers in the first half of the twentieth century in Europe. In his view, an experience of a *mysterium tremendum et fascinans* (fearful and fascinating mystery) underlies all religions. It is an experience of a Wholly Other (Mysterium), that we perceive with blank wonder, combined with a sense of our own nothingness in contrast to divine power (tremendum), which we find attractive in spite of our fear (fascinans). Otto's numinous experience, while still a form of otherness or alterity, can be characterized as the breakdown of subject-object dualism and understood in nondualistic (Chapter 1) and nontheistic terms.[29]

Otto's notion of the mysterium relates to teachings of Donald C. Klein, one of the fathers of community psychology. He criticizes psychology for being a psychology of projection.[30] Klein speaks about awe and wonderment and the human ability to live in awe and wonderment not just when facing a beautiful sunset or the majesty of the ocean but always. The psychology of projection is like a scrim, a transparent stage curtain, he explains, where we believe that what we see is reality only as long as the light shines on it in a certain way. However, it is not reality. It is a projection. To live in awe and wonderment, we have to look through this scrim and let go of all the details that appear on it. When we do that, we can see the beauty of the sunset, the majesty of the ocean, always, in everything.

Another misconception to rectify is the notion that we are merely observers or reactors. We are always actors. As Deutsch teaches us, by cooperating we nurture a culture of cooperation. Ironically, pessimists increase the burden instead of lessening it. We must learn constructive optimism and hope, because these attitudes generate more beneficial framings.

Furthermore, we need to learn how to avoid biases. For example, it is important to understand that human nature is not inherently "aggressive"

(Chapter 5), and that we usually share much more common ground with our adversaries than we think we do (Chapter 3).

It is crucial that we build a global culture of *task orientation*, discouraging *ego orientation* (Chapter 6), which promotes covering up mistakes. More than one hundred people were killed and almost five hundred injured when a train crashed into a house in Japan in 2005, mainly due to the engineer's desire to cover up earlier blunders. In 2004, a building at the Charles de Gaulle Airport in Paris collapsed because of errors in its design and construction. Do our nuclear engineers have a task or an ego orientation? What about our leaders? Safeguarding our ego facades can lead to colossal fatalities and block reasonable conflict management. Ego orientation undermines good governance and transparency.

Last, we need to learn how to regulate emotions. Negative emotions are the gatekeeper (Chapter 7). However, we must not go to extremes. Blissful ignorance is no solution. A certain amount of negative emotion is necessary to master conceptual change, since anxiety is a component of learning. Much refusal to change and learn may stem from the avoidance of necessary negative emotion.[31] What we need most, however, are positive emotions, because they broaden our problem-solving capacities.

We Need More Emotion Research!

Emotion research cannot escape the wider changes in society (Chapter 1). Research influences change and is influenced by it. Earlier emotion research focused on studying stimulus-response sequences, but increasingly a need is recognized to study the interactional functions of emotion within their social and cultural contexts. There is a new cohort of emotion researchers today, "who turn to the phenomenon and attempt to design pragmatic approaches, both in theory and research design, that allow better understanding of the underlying processes."[32] This new cohort of researchers insists on the dynamic nature of emotion and the need to adopt suitable theoretical models and research strategies. This gives "rise to hopes that the days when emotion psychologists paid mostly lip service to the idea of emotion as a process are over."[33]

One of the results of the new emotion research is that the very definition of emotion has become more comprehensive. In "Social Functions of Emotions," Keltner and Haidt conclude:

> Emotions are part of systems that solve problems related to physical survival, reproduction, and group governance. Biologically based, universal primordial emotions involve experience, perception, physiology, and communication that solve these problems in the context of ongoing social interactions. Elaborated emotions are the total package of meanings, behaviors, social practices, and norms that are built up around primordial emotions in actual

human societies. This approach integrates the insights of evolutionary and social constructivist approaches and points to the systematic role of emotion in social interactions, relationships, and cultural practices.[34]

Hitler and Mandela led their people out of shame by using two diametrically antithetical ethical and moral frames—the frame of ranked honor versus that of equal dignity. Hitler attempted to lead Germans out of shame into the traditional honorable master's way of handling humiliation, while Mandela led his downtrodden brothers and sisters out of shame by applying human rights ideals. Mandela carried his head high, even though he had been the target of humiliating treatment and felt humiliated. He did not translate humiliation into shame or violence. He rejected humiliation, like a master, but refrained from walking the traditional path of honor. He did not subjugate the white elite of South Africa but humbled them into equality in dignity, translating humiliation into a force for profound constructive social change.

Today's world needs Mandelas. Emotion researchers have a responsibility to explore and further the emotional maturity that Mandela was able to wield. The Mandelas of this world transcend the narrow confines of the fear that the security dilemma had instilled for millennia and the stark alternatives of either losing or winning. The Mandelas embed their strategies within the much wider scope of the human rights ideal of mutuality.

During the past ten thousand years, humiliation was imposed on the majority of humans by power elites (Chapter 5). At present, those of us who live in societies that call themselves free have the freedom to undo this humiliation, including self-imposed "self-humiliation" (Chapters 6 and 8). However, we typically fail to act on this freedom, as individuals and as cultures. We impose self-humiliation on ourselves, seemingly willingly and voluntarily. We do that because we are not aware that it is self-imposed, and that we have the freedom to undo this practice.

This book aims to bring more clarity, and it calls on academia to intensify their efforts. Most people are still uninformed and believe the ways they usually learn to deal with emotions are natural. For more than a thousand years, Chinese mothers never questioned the convention that said their daughters' feet had to be bound. Today, many of us still think that being treated as a more or less emotionless tools in the hands of masters is normal. Too many people do not yet truly live their own lives but allow their relationships to be defined by traditional scripts of submission and domination. The ideal of ruthless individualism is not a solution, merely a variation on the same old might-is-right model. The way out of submission is not to become dominators, it is to build caring relationships of mutuality, embedded in equality in dignity.

The result of the prevalent lack of clear understanding and suitable action plans is a widespread malaise, ranging from depression to domestic violence within Western societies, akin to the threat of global terrorism from outside.

This book is meant, among other things, to be an eye-opener for people who believe they are "free" individuals, and who think they have fully realized the promises entailed in human rights ideals. There is much more for them still to gain—an unparalleled zest of life—Jean Baker Miller's "five good things" (Chapter 7). Our hearts and minds are still "foot bound" in many ways, still waiting to be unbound. Liberating the full range of our emotions and understanding the inner workings of this process is crucial knowledge. It is vital for ourselves, our loved ones, our wider social circles, culture as a whole, our choice of politicians, and how we treat other world regions.

This knowledge is particularly critical if we want to explain the advantages of unbinding emotions to those who still are living in contexts where their mutilation is regarded as legitimate.

To succeed, however, the liberation of our emotions requires more than individual attention to emotions, and research on emotions is not enough. As emphasized, we need to invest our time and energy into systemic change and create a more suitable global frame, within which all citizens can enjoy the liberating space that is promised by human rights. At the global level, institutions are still "bound," and this inflicts binding also on citizens of societies that otherwise embrace human rights. It is an illusion to believe that human rights can be fully functional anywhere, even within societies who for themselves embrace them, if they are not operational at the global level.

Two yet-to-be achieved liberations are the focus of this book, liberations that enforce each other mutually: liberation of the highest global systemic level—a liberation that will have the effect to draw also those societies into the realm of human rights who are not there yet—thus aiding the second liberation, that of our emotions. And vice versa.

We Must Transcend Optimism and Pessimism!

What is "realistic" Realpolitik? So-called realists doubt that humankind can come together and create world peace, since, they say, the world is caught in Hobbesian anarchy and condemned to endless conflict and war.[35] So-called liberals are more optimistic, believing that international cooperation can make peace prevail over anarchy.[36]

I am both more optimistic than many liberals and more pessimistic than many realists. I am more optimistic, because I believe William Ury is right and the historically unprecedented ingathering of humankind into one single knowledge society is more benign than ever. At the same time, I am more pessimistic than realists because, according to my view, the dynamics of humiliation, if not taken seriously, may have such malign effects that they could cancel out the benign tendencies.

Reasons for Optimism

Optimism appears justified in the face of the power of the human desire to connect, bond, belong, cooperate, and receive recognition and acknowledgment, and the potential of those desires to bring people together. As mentioned, "human nature" is not inevitably aggressive but hard-wired for cooperation and mutual bonding. Optimism is justified when we consider the benign effects of people learning to regard all humankind as jointly responsible for its survival on earth. Optimism may even emanate from the threat of global climate change, or of "nuclear one-worldism"[37]—the growing destructiveness of these threats may persuade states to do what individuals do in states and submit to a higher superordinate institutional frame. In the case of the global village, that common frame would be represented by viable global superordinate institutional structures that overcome Hobbesian anarchy.

American philosopher Richard Rorty believes in moral progress, understood as development "in the direction of greater human solidarity . . . the ability to see more and more traditional differences (of tribe, religion, race, customs, and the like) as unimportant when compared with similarities with respect to pain and humiliation—the ability to think of people wildly different from ourselves as included in the range of 'us.'"[38]

Rorty could be right. The global village is currently acquiring a life of its own, beyond McLuhan's initial connotations.[39] Citizens increasingly relate to each other across borders, states are losing their status as more or less isolated entities that constrain and define their citizens' global relationships. A global "supranational We-feeling" is in the making, and the "struggle for recognition" by individuals alongside that of states is emerging as a force at the system level.[40]

At times, we have the sense that humankind remembers philosopher Plotinus (204–270 A.D.), who reminded us not to forget our soul's origin in the realm of the One.[41] We see *postindividual consciousness* emerge,[42] or *unity consciousness*.[43]

We feel a "Kantian culture" of collective security or "friendship" coming closer,[44] a global civic culture,[45] a world society.[46] Even a world state may be imminent[47]—Alexander Wendt, with his self-organization theory, argues that the coming-into-being of a world state is "inevitable" because of the "interaction between a self-organizing, bottom-up process and a structural, top-down one: struggles for recognition mediated by technological change at the micro-level, conditioned by the logic of anarchy at the macro."[48] It is predicted that even businesses of the future, to be successful, will have to move away from what Martin Buber calls the "I-It" relationship to an "I-Thou" relationship based on mutual respect.[49]

A growing number of people are now joining the so-called *cultural creatives* movement and refuse "cynical realism."[50] Ray and Anderson identify three main cultural tendencies: first, *moderns* (endorsing the "realist" worldview of *Time Magazine*, the *Wall Street Journal*, big government, big business, big media, or past socialist, communist, and fascist movements); second, the first countermovement against moderns, the *traditionals* (the religious right and rural populations); and third, the most recent countermovement, the *cultural creatives* (valuing strong ecological sustainability for the planet, liberal on women's issues, personal growth, authenticity, and anti–big business). In the United States, traditionals comprise about 24–26 percent of the adult population (approximately 48 million people), moderns about 47–49 percent (approximately 95 million), and cultural creatives about 26–28 percent (approximately 50 million). In the European Union, the cultural creatives are about 30–35 per cent of the adult population.

The United Nations' agencies occupy the highest level of superordinate institutions. Though currently only a "club of jealous nations," the United Nations does represent the embryonic seeds that may mature into stabile good governance at the highest global level, governance that has the common interest of the global—not national—citizen at heart.[51]

Since states are hesitant to lose sovereignty, this unifying process meets strong resistance whenever institution building needs to get serious. The discourse on how to best build good world governance and institutions is always in danger of dying down, in need of revival. Yet people do step up to the challenge—Joseph Preston Baratta has recently taken up this crucial discussion.[52] Worldwide, new discourses do indeed emerge.[53] A global culture of solidarity is being advocated—Howard Richards offers a list of alternative names, such as love ethic, or servant leadership, or production for use, or de-alienation, or mobilizing resources to meet needs, or a higher form of pragmatism, or economic democracy.[54] We could add that the practice of communal sharing[55] will have to be expanded to embrace the community of all of humankind at global levels, and that "money" will have to *serve* this global communal sharing (instead of dominating our agenda).

Optimism can also be drawn from the fact that many authors explain that building a better world is not utopian.[56] The ways to secure global sustainability, ecologically and socially, are all surprisingly simple and even inexpensive. The Millennium Development Goals[57] are not impossible to reach.

All we lack is the political will to embark decisively on those solutions. The necessary energy can emerge when the broad masses abandon their belief in their powerlessness. Change is possible when every citizen of the world grasps that in today's connected world the individual has enormous potential power to force the political system to stand up to the global challenges that humankind faces. "Yes, we can," Barack Obama's call, needs to be a global motto. The task is difficult, but difficulty can serve as a spur to action, not a deterrent.

Reasons for Pessimism

Pessimism, on the other side, is justified by the fact that the strength of the desire for recognition is also its weakness. Thwarted desire for recognition and disappointed expectations can generate feelings of humiliation, which represent what I call the "nuclear bomb of the emotions." Feelings of humiliation can create and deepen fault lines that hamper what is most needed in the global village, namely, cooperation. In an increasingly globalizing and interdependent world, in a world that at the same time wakes up to the call for equal dignity, no longer is it the fear entailed in the security dilemma, but feelings of humiliation which play the key role. These emotions have the power to turn human beings into creators and users of weapons of mass destruction and into perpetrators of terrorist acts.

Coming closer to one's fellow human beings does not necessarily lead to merry friendship. The so-called *contact hypothesis*, or the hope that mere contact can turn enemies into friends, is not necessarily true (Chapter 8). New relationships raise new expectations, which have the potential to turn sour, even very sour. Newly emerging in-group relationships in the global village are vulnerable to new fault lines, which emerge particularly when new expectations are disappointed. The human rights message does, indeed, raise significant expectations: It renders conditions of unequal dignity obscene.

International relations used to be dominated by the established hierarchies of a few rulers and their diplomats, caught in the security dilemma. In place of those hierarchies we now see the emergence of a hot web of relationships between millions of global villagers, who desire recognition and respect in equal dignity.

The coming together of humankind provides new opportunities for comparison that turn absolute into relative deprivation.[58] When I sit in the Egyptian desert in my mud brick house with only one or two dresses to wear and watch American soap operas, it is as if I am going to school to learn to feel humiliated. Inequalities that were not clear to me before become apparent. I learn about my relative deprivation. At the same time the message of human rights reaches me, teaching that relative deprivation is an illegitimate violation of human rights. This removes traditional justifications for inequality, eliciting my rage and anger. Human rights transmute deprivation into injustice and perceived injustice into humiliation.

It is inevitable that impoverished people will feel humiliated when they see the amenities of modern life in Western soap operas on television. It is inevitable that being invited into the family of equal human beings by human rights advocacy while being deprived of those amenities will produce feelings of humiliation and anger. First comes a deep sense of betrayal and hypocrisy, then emerges the question, "Why do these people preach empty human rights rhetoric to us?" Double standards can be deeply humiliating.

"Humiliated fury,"[59] although it may transform people into wise Mandela-like elders, may also create atrocious humiliation entrepreneurs like Hitler, the instigators of the 1994 genocide in Rwanda, and other people who engage in acts of terror.

People who have set their minds on humiliating their perceived humiliators do not need much military training or expensive equipment. Instigating feelings of humiliation in followers is far more cost-effective. Victims can even be brought to pay for their own destruction. In the 1994 Rwandan genocide, some victims paid for bullets to be shot instead of being hacked to death by the household knives and machetes of their neighbors who were set to cut them down from alleged arrogance. Also on September 11, 2001, the "weapons" were not paid for by the perpetrators—passenger airplanes were hijacked and turned into missiles to bring down and humiliate the symbols of pride of the world's purportedly arrogant superpower.

Transcending Pessimism and Optimism

Pessimism is a luxury we can afford only in good times. In difficult times pessimism easily transmutes into a self-inflicted, self-fulfilling death sentence: This is the conclusion of a dear friend of mine, an Auschwitz survivor.[60] By their lamentations, the pessimists among us may tip the delicately balanced world situation toward failure. Pessimists seem to be unaware that nobody is merely an observer, nobody is merely a reactor. We are all actors, and we need everybody to cooperate and contribute, if we are to make a constructive difference. We have to learn constructive optimism and hope (Snyder's kind of hope, see Chapter 7) because these attitudes will foster beneficial framings.

We live in times of greater threat than ever but also of greater promise. We can grasp the promise only if we act now. If we choose not to act, we are left with nothing but the threat.

Never before in human history has anything comparable occurred. Never did a unification process comprise the entire globe and touch so many hearts and minds. Never before did a concurrent continuous revolution— the human rights revolution—call into question so radically traditional norms.

Social emotions felt by millions of people are no longer defined, channeled, and regulated by a few elites. They are now relevant to internal conflicts in the global village in unprecedented ways, affecting everybody's emotional universe, down to the micro level, even intrapersonally. For traditional elites (and coopted subalterns) to close their eyes to these new realities, to overlook the new significance of the feelings of millions of people and to cling to traditional Realpolitik of elite-to-elite strategizing is living a delusion that can only humiliate and enrage these very millions of people.

According to international relations theory, the current increase in inter-dependence weakens *classical realism,* and opens space for a more benign reality, but only if humankind grasps the opportunity.[61] Let us capitalize on this new situation and replace traditional concepts of Realpolitik with new, more constructive concepts.[62]

These days, global awareness of the need to protect the Earth's climate is rising dramatically. We need, however, to extend the same attention to social sustainability. Global tariff negotiations, such as the Doha Develop-ment Round, are at the core of building a truly level playing field for all globally.[63] Let us make the Doha Round a household name. The current bank crisis, as well, calls for comprehensive global solutions and not a few local bandages. The intractable conflicts of this world, equally, will only whither in the face of strong global institutions.

I believe that we can harness the power of globalization with egaliza-tion. However, in times of emergency, a hands-off approach will not work. The only viable approach is hands-on, even if we fail. The reward will be much more benign than the past ten thousand years—a new world where men and women together can engage in nurturing relationships with se-cure and caring connections embedded into mutual respect for equality in dignity.

We Must Stand Up! Not By!

Hunter-gatherers prior to ten thousand years ago may have enjoyed untouched pristine pride (Chapter 5). Yet roughly ten thousand years ago, the party was over. In the grip of the security dilemma, malign hierarchies evolved. The majority of people became underlings, tools in the hands of a few masters. They were taught shame and helplessness, by overt brute force or by covert misrecognition, naturalization, and penetration (Chap-ter 8). This was labeled "civilization."

If we use the language of dialectics, the thesis was pristine pride, the antithesis was the subjugation of pride into systems of ranked honor. Dur-ing the past ten millennia, the only "synthesis" underlings could achieve was either subserviently accepting inferiority or replacing the oppressors in uprisings. Revolutions typically toppled oppressive elites only to re-place them. Any ambition to achieve a true synthesis—the creation of a different and better world—typically stopped short and turned back into the former antithesis of submission/domination.

Today, the thesis is still pristine pride and the antithesis is inequality in dignity. That setting can now be seen for what it is, as illegitimate humili-ation, rather than divinely ordained. Today, space opens for attempts for a synthesis at a new level—resistance to humiliation and constructive social change toward a world of equality in dignity. Equality in dignity reaches back to the experience of pristine pride, only that it is no longer pristine.

After ten thousand years of oppression, the taste of humiliation will always inform and reinforce the yearning for equal dignity.

However, even though space opens for resistance to humiliation today, this does not guarantee a constructive outcome. Resistance to humiliation can go two ways, even today, either back into the past, or forward into the future—the Hitler-path of returning into the past by retaliating with humiliation in a duel-like honorable fashion, or the Mandela-path of transcending anger toward a new synthesis of mutual respect for equality in dignity for all. We must stand up for this new kind of synthesis if we wish to go forward.

We can also use the concept of unity in diversity to summarize humankind's predicament. During the past ten thousand years, unity meant agreeing that honor should be ranked within in-groups and that there was a division between in-groups and out-groups. There was no conflict within—unity meant uniformity and was achieved through ruthless oppression and routine subjugation/humiliation of underlings.

Today unity means "difference on an equal footing." Again, there is no destructive conflict within; there is unity, but that unity is now achieved through waging good conflict, with the aim to celebrate complexity and lovingly embed diversity into unity.

Destructive conflict occurs when the transition is incoherent, when the first definition of unity weakens but does not die, while the second strengthens. The second definition cannot be achieved in the face of the first; irreconcilable conflict is the result.

The solution is a Mandela-like transition from the first to the second definition of unity. The answer is embedding the social and ecological diversity of our world into the unity of our vow to work for the common good of all humankind, for a decent world where everybody can live a dignified life and is equal in dignity.

The Eves and the Adams of this world, all its citizens, need to stand up, in the spirit of Ervin Staub's call for bystanders to get involved and stand up and not by, develop true subjectivity—*shutaisei* (Chapter 7)—and pour it into an effort to build this decent global village for everybody, thus transcending the old "us" against "them."

How do we stand up? Albert Bandura did important work on moral disengagement and how aggression can be learned—or unlearned[64]—emphasizing those mechanisms that make it "easier" to perpetrate atrocities or accept their occurrence. Bandura calls on the members of the global community to avoid those mechanisms and take action when they see those mechanisms being applied by others. This is what we must steer clear of and resist: obscuring causal agency; blaming and devaluating the targets; moral justification of counterterrorist measures; public intimidation and judgments of retaliatory violence; euphemistic labeling; and disregard for, or distortion of, consequences.[65]

How do we measure success? In development work or disaster management, the way to measure success is to determine output, not input.[66] Merely counting how many thousands of blankets were distributed, how many millions of bags of food were provided, or how many millions of dollars were spent, is insufficient. Those dollars may have been misspent. What needs to be assessed is the outcome, for example, children's survival. As to the entire globe, long-term survival is the crucial figure, not shareholder value or the growth of the gross national product.[67] As to conflict, the significant parameter is whether the situation improves—all parties reiterating their right of self-defense, if this defense only turns spirals of tit-for-tat retaliations, is too weak a measure. In sum, we need to abandon input that does not render valid output.

My personal life may serve as an example of the fact that we must do more than merely nod our heads and subscribe to the new human rights vision in theory.[68] I heed Elise Boulding, one of the most influential peace researchers and activists of the twentieth century, and devote my entire life to looking for new solutions, finding new solutions in old ones, and making the leap into the unknown of innovation.[69] I try to be aware of my biases and vulnerabilities to covert manipulation (Chapter 8). I try to recognize that I typically am afraid of novelty, even when it would serve me well, and that I may be blind to what is good for me—I hear Daniel Gilbert, author of *Stumbling on Happiness*,[70] when he says that we are often wrong when we try to predict what will make us happy.

I became aware of the depth of this counterintuitive insight when I wrote my doctoral dissertation in medicine on quality of life.[71] I realized that I would not have chosen my personal path that I now cherish had I not been forced into it by the hurtful experience of being born into a displaced family (from Silesia in Central Europe) and pained by feeling excluded from humankind as I grew up. I healed this pain by widening my definition of health, becoming a global citizen, and accepting global responsibility. Being embedded into global connections heals me.[72] In my studies, I realized that the development of the concept of humiliation in the course of human history illustrates and is part of the expanding process that also I experienced and that humiliation can be and needs to be prevented and healed.

I adhere to the Lévinasian interpretation of human rights. I wish to help build Margalit's decent world that enables every human being to live a dignified life. I also adhere to Buber's I-Thou framing of human relationships, resisting I-It approaches. I feel that I-Thou meetings are indeed meetings with God, in a way that combines reciprocal altruism with a notion of love without dogma, against the background of a mysterium tremendum. It gives me an immense sense of health and well-being when I say with pride and dedication that my family is all humankind. I embrace that family with metta, agape, and philia. My health flows from being embedded into relational communion and mutuality, locally, globally, and universally.

I design my life as a global citizen so as to be able to build one of the seeds of a global alternative community, Human Dignity and Humiliation Studies (HumanDHS), a global network of like-minded academics and practitioners who wish to build a decent world of equality in dignity and transcend humiliation (Chapter 4).

In Chapter 8, I referred to Neil J. Smelser's list of six conditions that are necessary for a new social movement to emerge. We, as HumanDHS, address all six of his points: We react to structural strain (humiliation causing general well-being to diminish, or even fueling terrorism); we use the structural conduciveness of the Internet; we contribute to efforts to develop a shared understanding of what the problems are; we try to ignite the flame of dignity, and mobilize action; while using the inclusive approach that human rights call for.

As for action, I propose a "moratorium on humiliation," similar to the Moratorium on Trade in Small Arms (see the Human Dignity and Humiliation Studies Web site for many more ideas).

Our experience with our HumanDHS work indicates that, after initial hesitation, people are thrilled when they see that it is possible to create what our forefathers of the past ten millennia would have dismissed as an illusionary utopia—a web of I-Thou relationships of mutuality and equality in dignity, where a sense of fulfillment is increased for all involved. This is a historically new form of group cohesion, more inclusive than ever in human history. In former times, groups typically held together *against* "others," we in HumanDHS attempt to draw our cohesion from our dedication to work *for* a decent future for all. This web of the relationships extends a sense of meaning and forms the vehicle for diverse applied projects (in our research, education, and intervention branches).

I do not expect everyone to live as I do in all its practical details. However, the leap I encourage us all to make is to integrate philia for all humankind into our overall life designs, our daily lives, and our minute-to-minute definitions of well-being and health.

Let us conclude this book by revisiting Eve and Adam one last time. Initially Adam was enraged when the social worker told him that beating his wife was a violation. He shouted and accused the social worker of befouling his honor and infringing on his freedom and sovereignty as master of his home. He saw the social worker as bringing conflict into his house and heating up feelings where there was calm and quiet before. Today, Adam has learned new humility, and Eve new pride. Both understand that sovereignty and freedom do not include wife-beating. Eve and Adam have learned to place their emotions into a new cognitive frame, and they experience their emotions in new ways. They have learned new social skills,

skills that enable them to respect and love each other as equals in dignity. Both know that waging good conflict is essential. They have even joined global civil society and help promote stronger global legislation against domestic violence. They contribute now to building not only a decent life but a decent world for all, with dignified emotions and good conflict.

NOTES

Notes to the Foreword

1. E. Lindner, *Making Enemies: Humiliation and International Conflict* (Westport, CT: Greenwood/Praeger Security International, 2006).

2. E. G. Lindner, "Emotion and Conflict: Why It Is Important to Understand How Emotions Affect Conflict and How Conflict Affects Emotions," in *Handbook of Conflict Resolution: Theory and Practice*, ed. M. Deutsch, P. T. Coleman, and E. C. Marcus, 2nd ed. (San Francisco: Jossey-Bass, 2006), 268–293.

Notes to the Introduction

1. I use Weber's third kind of ideal type when I focus on Mandela's constructive core strategies, which are not minimized by otherwise possibly valid criticisms. Please read about ideal types in Coser: "Weber's three kinds of *ideal types* are distinguished by their levels of abstraction. First are the *ideal types* rooted in historical particularities, such as the 'western city,' 'the Protestant Ethic,' or 'modern capitalism,' which refer to phenomena that appear only in specific historical periods and in particular cultural areas. A second kind involves abstract elements of social reality—such concepts as 'bureaucracy' or 'feudalism'—that may be found in a variety of historical and cultural contexts. Finally, there is a third kind of *ideal type*, which Raymond Aron calls 'rationalizing reconstructions of a particular kind of behavior.' According to Weber, all propositions in economic theory, for example, fall into this category. They all refer to the ways in which men would behave were they actuated by purely economic motives, were they purely economic men." L. A. Coser, *Masters of Sociological Thought: Ideas in Historical and Social Context*, 2nd ed. (Fort Worth, TX: Harcourt Brace Jovanovich, 1977), 224.

2. T. D. Conlan, *In Little Need of Divine Intervention: Takezaki Suenaga's Scrolls of the Mongol Invasions of Japan* (Ithaca, NY: East Asia Program, Cornell University, 2001).

3. J. W. Dower, *Embracing Defeat: Japan in the Wake of World War II* (New York: Norton, 1999), 22.

4. Ibid., 22.

5. Ibid., 30. See also C. Tavris and E. Aronson, *Mistakes Were Made, but Not by Me: Why We Justify Foolish Beliefs, Bad Decisions, and Hurtful Acts* (Orlando, FL: Harcourt, 2007).

6. Personal communication, April 11, 2005.

7. N. Stern, *Review of the Economics of Climate Change* (Cambridge: Cambridge University Press, 2006).

8. World Wildlife Fund, *Living Planet Report 2008* (London: World Wildlife Fund, 2008), assets.wwf.org.uk/downloads/lpr_2008.pdf.

9. See P. Pettit, *Republicanism: A Theory of Freedom and Government* (Oxford: Clarendon Press, 1997).

10. This term was coined by Jean Baker Miller, *Toward a New Psychology of Women*, 2nd ed. (Boston: Beacon Press, 1986).

11. A. Badiou, *Ethics: An Essay on the Understanding of Evil* (London: Verso, 2001).

12. J. Goldstone, *Conflict among Civilizations 500 BC–2030 AD* (Oslo: Paper presented at the 11th Annual Meeting of Humiliation Studies in Norway, June 23–July 1, 2008).

13. B. Wyatt-Brown, *Southern Honor: Ethics and Behavior in the Old South* (New York: Oxford University Press, 1982).

14. Henry Kissinger said, "They want to humiliate us and we have to humiliate them," see M. Danner, "America Defeated: How Terrorists Turned a Superpower's Strengths Against Itself," *Alternet*, March 26 (2008), 3, www.alternet.org/story/80547. This essay was adapted from an address first delivered in February at the Tenth Asia Security Conference at the Institute for Security and Defense Analysis in New Delhi.

15. R. W. Fuller, *Somebodies and Nobodies: Overcoming the Abuse of Rank* (Gabriola Island, Canada: New Societies Publishers, 2003).

16. H. S. Levy, *The Lotus Lovers: The Complete History of the Curious Erotic Custom of Footbinding in China* (Buffalo, NY: Prometheus Books, 1992).

17. R. Eisler, *The Chalice and the Blade: Our History, Our Future* (London: Unwin Hyman, 1987).

18. See J. S. Goldstein, *War and Gender: How Gender Shapes the War Systems and Vice Versa* (Cambridge: Cambridge University Press, 2001). See also P. G. Allen, *The Sacred Hoop: Recovering the Feminine in American Indian Traditions* (Boston: Beacon Press, 1992), and C. Ueno, *Nationalism and Gender* (Melbourne, Australia: Trans Pacific Press, 2004).

19. M. Foucault, *Discipline and Punish. The Birth of the Prison* (Harmondsworth: Allen Lane, 1977).

20. See also G. L. Mosse, *The Image of Man: The Creation of Modern Masculinity* (New York: Oxford University Press, 1996). See also work on emotional roles (for instance, a grieving widow, a jealous lover, an angry young man, a nervous, expectant father, and so forth) in J. R. Averill, "The Emotions: An Integrative Approach," in *Handbook of Personality Psychology*, ed. R. Hogan, J. Johnson, and S. Briggs (San Diego, CA: Academic Press, 1997).

21. E. Ohnuki-Tierney, *Kamikaze, Cherry Blossoms, and Nationalisms: The Militarization of Aesthetics in Japanese History* (Chicago: University of Chicago Press, 2002), 151.

22. With the exception of certain religious groups, especially groups such as Quakers, Methodists, and Baptists, who used to punish, shun, and excommunicate them.

23. E. Lindner, *Gender and Humiliation: The Power of Dignity in Love, Sex and Parenthood* (Westport, CT: Greenwood/Praeger Security International, 2009).

24. W. Ury, *Getting to Peace. Transforming Conflict at Home, at Work, and in the World* (New York: Viking, 1999).

25. Read, among many others, M. Augoustinos, "Ideology, False Consciousness and Psychology," *Theory & Psychology*, 9, no. 3 (1999): 295–312.

26. K. Hayashi, "Current Intercultural Issues and Challenges in Japanese Business Interfaces: Blending Theory and Practice," *Management Japan*, 35 (2003), www.iijnet.or.jp/imaj/mj/hayashi35.pdf.

27. See, for example, J. Mezirow, *Transformative Dimensions of Adult Learning* (San Francisco: Jossey-Bass, 1991). See also B. Fisher-Yoshida, "Coaching to Transform Perspective," in *Transformative Learning in Action*, ed. J. Mezirow and E. W. Taylor (San Francisco: Jossey-Bass, 2008).

28. Y. Y. Kim and B. D. Ruben, "Intercultural Transformation: A Systems Theory," *International and Intercultural Communication Annual*, 12, (1988): 299–321.

29. J. M. Gottman, L. F. Katz, and C. Hooven, *Meta-Emotion: How Families Communicate Emotionally* (Mahwah, NJ: Erlbaum, 1997).

30. E. Staub, "The Psychology of Bystanders, Perpetrators, and Heroic Helpers," *International Journal of Intercultural Relations*, 17 (1993): 315–341.

31. In BBC World's *HARDtalk* with Stephen Sackur on February 4, 2008.

Notes to Chapter 1

1. E. Lindner, *The Psychology of Humiliation: Somalia, Rwanda / Burundi, and Hitler's Germany* (Oslo: University of Oslo, Department of Psychology, doctoral dissertation in Psychology, 2000).

2. See www.humiliationstudies.org/whoweare/evelin02.php. See here some selected publications: E. G. Lindner, *The Relevance of Humiliation Studies for the Prevention of Terrorism* (Budapest, Hungary: Paper presented to the NATO Advanced Research Workshop "Indigenous Terrorism: Understanding and Addressing the Root Causes of Radicalisation among Groups with an Immigrant Heritage in Europe," March 7–9, 2008); E. G. Lindner, "Humiliation, Trauma, and Trauma Recovery in a Globalizing World," in *Peacebuilding for Traumatized Societies*, ed. B. Hart (Lanham, MD: University Press of America, 2008); E. G. Lindner, "Avoiding Humiliation—From Intercultural Communication to Global Interhuman Communication," *Journal of Intercultural Communication, SIETAR Japan*, 10 (2007): 21–38; E. G. Lindner, "In Times of Globalization and Human Rights: Does Humiliation Become the Most Disruptive Force?," *Journal of Human Dignity and Humiliation Studies*, 1, no. 1, March (2007), available at www.humilliationstudies.upeace.org; E. G. Lindner, "Dynamics of Humiliation in a Globalizing World," *International Journal on World Peace*, 34, no. 3, September (2007): 15–52; E. G. Lindner, "Humiliation and Global Terrorism: How to Overcome It Nonviolently," in *Encyclopedia of Life Support Systems (EOLSS), Theme 6.120: Nonviolent Alternatives for Social Change*, ed. R. Summy (Oxford: Developed under the Auspices of the UNESCO, EOLSS Publishers, www.eolss.net, 2007); E. Lindner, *Making Enemies: Humiliation and International Conflict* (Westport, CT: Greenwood/Praeger Security International, 2006); E. G. Lindner,

N. R. Walsh, and J. Kuriansky, "Humiliation or Dignity in the Israeli-Palestinian Conflict," in *Terror in the Holy Land, Inside the Anguish of the Israeli-Palestinian Conflict*, ed. J. Kuriansky (Westport, CT: Greenwood/Praeger Security International, 2006), 123–131; E. G. Lindner, "Humiliation, Killing, War, and Gender," in *The Psychology of Resolving Global Conflicts: From War to Peace. Volume 1: Nature vs. Nurture*, ed. M. Fitzduff and C. E. Stout (Westport, CT: Greenwood/Praeger Security International, 2006), 137–174; A. C. Hudnall and E. G. Lindner, "Crisis and Gender: Addressing the Psychosocial Needs of Women in International Disasters," in *Handbook of International Disaster Psychology (Vol. 4): Interventions with Special Needs Populations*, ed. G. Reyes and G. A. Jacobs (Westport, CT: Greenwood/Praeger Publishers, 2005), 1–18; E. G. Lindner, "Humiliation or Dignity: Regional Conflicts in the Global Village," *International Journal of Mental Health, Psychosocial Work and Counselling in Areas of Armed Conflict*, 1, no. 1, January (2003): 48–63, see also www.transnational.org/forum/meet/2002/Lindner_RegionalConflicts.html; E. G. Lindner, "Healing the Cycles of Humiliation: How to Attend to the Emotional Aspects of 'Unsolvable' Conflicts and the Use of 'Humiliation Entrepreneurship,'" *Peace and Conflict: Journal of Peace Psychology*, 8, no. 2 (2002): 125–138, available at www.informaworld.com/smpp/ftinterface~content=a785828772~fulltext=713240930; E. G. Lindner, "Humiliation—Trauma That Has Been Overlooked: An Analysis Based on Fieldwork in Germany, Rwanda/Burundi, and Somalia," *TRAUMATOLOGYe*, 7, no. 1 (2001): Article 3 (32 pages), tmt.sagepub.com/cgi/content/abstract/7/1/43; E. G. Lindner, "Humiliation and the Human Condition: Mapping a Minefield," *Human Rights Review*, 2, no. 2 (2001): 46–63; E. G. Lindner, "Were Ordinary Germans Hitler's 'Willing Executioners'? Or Were They Victims of Humiliating Seduction and Abandonment? The Case of Germany and Somalia," *IDEA: A Journal of Social Issues*, 5, no. 1 (2000), www.ideajournal.com/articles.php?id=31.

3. Krippendorff Ekkehart, *Staat und Krieg. Die historische Logik politischer Unvernunft* (Frankfurt: Suhrkamp Verlag, 1985).

4. B. W. Tuchman, *The March of Folly: From Troy to Vietnam* (New York: Knopf, 1984). Tuchman sees "stupidity" as an unavoidable historic fact, while Krippendorf identifies it as an incurable pathology in states.

5. R. K. White, *Fearful Warriors: A Psychological Profile of U.S.-Soviet Relations* (New York: Free Press, 1984).

6. D. J. Christie, "What Is Peace Psychology the Psychology Of?," *Journal of Social Issues*, 62, no. 1 (2006): 1–17, retrieved on August 14, 2007, from www.blackwell-synergy.com/doi/pdf/10.1111/j.1540-4560.2006.00436.x, 9.

7. Henry Kissinger said, "They want to humiliate us and we have to humiliate them," as quoted in the Introduction. Gore Vidal, American author with a background in a prominent political family, has the distance and courage to unmask the self-destructiveness of such approaches. G. Vidal, *The Selected Essays of Gore Vidal*, ed. J. Parini (Toronto: Doubleday, 2008).

8. Interview with Paul Lindner, July 22, 2008.

9. D. J. Rothkopf, *Superclass: The Global Power Elite and the World They Are Making* (New York: Farrar, Straus and Giroux, 2008).

10. BBC NEWS, October 10, 2008, news.bbc.co.uk/go/pr/fr/-/2/hi/business/7687101.stm.

11. M. Deutsch, *The Resolution of Conflict: Constructive and Destructive Processes* (New Haven, CT: Yale University Press, 1973), 367.

12. J. P. Forgas, "Introduction: Affect and Social Cognition," in *Handbook of Affect and Social Cognition*, ed. J. P. Forgas (Mahwah, NJ: Erlbaum, 2001), 1–24, 3.

13. Ibid., Preface.

14. W. B. Pearce and S. W. Littlejohn, *Moral Conflict: When Social Worlds Collide* (Newbury Park, CA: Sage, 1997).

15. B. Barry and R. L. Oliver, "Affect in Dyadic Negotiation: A Model and Proposition," *Organizational Behavior and Human Decision Processes*, 70 (1996): 175–187, quoted by P. T. Coleman, "Characteristics of Protracted, Intractable Conflict: Toward the Development of a Metaframework—I," *Peace and Conflict: Journal of Peace Psychology*, 9, no. 1 (2003): 1–37, 25.

16. P. T. Coleman, "Characteristics of Protracted, Intractable Conflict: Toward the Development of a Metaframework—I," *Peace and Conflict: Journal of Peace Psychology*, 9, no. 1 (2003): 1–37, 25.

17. In T. J. Mayne and G. A. Bonanno, eds., *Emotions: Current Issues and Future Directions* (New York: Guilford Press, 2001), Preface, xviii, emphasis added.

18. K. W. Fischer and J. P. Tangney, "Introduction: Self-Conscious Emotions and the Affect Revolution: Framework and Overview," in *Self-Conscious Emotions: The Psychology of Shame, Guilt, Embarrassment, and Pride*, ed. K. W. Fischer and J. P. Tangney (New York: Guilford Press, 1995), 3–24, 3, emphasis added.

19. K. N. Ochsner and L. Feldman Barrett, "A Multiprocess Perspective on the Neuroscience of Emotion," in *Emotions: Current Issues and Future Directions*, ed. T. J. Mayne and G. A. Bonanno (New York: Guilford Press, 2001), 38–81, 39, emphasis added.

20. See, for example, P. Ekman and R. J. Davidson, *The Nature of Emotion: Fundamental Questions* (New York: Oxford University Press, 1994), M. Lewis and J. M. Haviland, *Handbook of Emotions* (New York: Guilford Press, 1993).

21. See, for example, A. R. Damasio, *Descartes' Error: Emotion, Reason, and the Human Brain* (New York: Putnam, 1994); D. Goleman, *Emotional Intelligence* (New York: Bantam Books, 1995); J. E. LeDoux, L. M. Romanski, and A. E. Xagoraris, "Indelibility of Subcortical Emotional Memories," *Journal of Cognitive Neuroscience*, 1 (1989): 238–243.

22. S. Blakeslee, "Cells That Read Minds," *New York Times*, January 10 (2006), Section F, Column 2, Science Desk, retrieved on January 10, 2006, from www.nytimes.com/2006/01/10/science/10mirr.html?ei=5088&en=4b525f923a669928&ex=1294549200&partner=rssnyt&emc=rss&pagewanted=print, 3. Christian Keysers was a leading investigator in the research group in Parma that made the original discovery of mirror neurons from 2000 until 2004. Today, he is the scientific director of the Neuroimaging Center and Professor for the Neurobiology of Empathy at the medical faculty of the University Medical Center Groningen. See, for example, C. Keysers and V. Gazzola, "Towards a Unifying Neural Theory of Social Cognition," in *Progress in Brain Research, vol. 156*, ed. S. Anders, G. Ende, M. Junghofer, J. Kissler, and D. Wildgruber (Amsterdam: Elsevier, 2006), www.bcn-nic.nl/txt/people/publications/keysersgazzolapbr.pdf. See, furthermore, C. D. Frith and D. Wolpert, eds., *The Neuroscience of Social Interaction: Decoding, Influencing, and Imitating the Actions of Others* (Oxford: Oxford University Press, 2004); M. Hopkin, "How We Judge the Thoughts of Others: Brain Division Could Help Explain Stereotyping, Religious Conflict and Racism," *Nature*, (2008), retrieved on April 28, 2008, from www.nature.com/news/2008/080317/full/news.2008.677.html;

M. Iacoboni et al., "Cortical Mechanisms of Human Imitation," *Science,* 286, no. 5449 (1999): 2526–2528; D. McNeill, *Gesture and Thought* (Chicago: University of Chicago Press, 2005); V. S. Ramachandran, *Mirror Neurons and Imitation Learning as the Driving Force behind "the Great Leap Forward" in Human Evolution,* Edge Foundation, 2000, retrieved on August 14, 2006, from www.edge.org/documents/archive/edge69.html; G. Rizzolatti and L. Craighero, "The Mirror-Neuron System," *Annual Review of Neuroscience,* 27 (2004): 169–192; M. A. Umilta et al., ""I Know What You Are Doing": A Neurophysiological Study," *Neuron,* 31 (2001): 155–165; B. Wicker et al., "Both of Us Disgusted in My Insula: The Common Neural Basis of Seeing and Feeling Disgust," *Neuron,* 40, no. 3 (2003): 655–664.

23. A. Banks and J. V. Jordan, "The Human Brain: Hardwired for Connections," *Research & Action Report,* 28, no. 2, Spring/Summer (2007): 8–11, retrieved on July 20, 2007, from www.wcwonline.org/joomla/index.php?option=com_content&task =view&id=1358&itemid=198. See also R. I. M. Dunbar, "The Social Brain Hypothesis," *Evolutionary Anthropology,* 6 (1998): 178–190.

24. See T. Pfeiffer et al., "Evolution of Cooperation by Generalized Reciprocity," *Proceedings of the Royal Society of London, Series B,* 272 (2005): 1115–1120, retrieved on July 8, 2007, from www.journals.royalsoc.ac.uk/content/u47987fqkfy74u7p/ fulltext.pdf.

25. N. I. Eisenberger and M. D. Lieberman, "Why It Hurts to Be Left Out: The Neurocognitive Overlap between Physical Pain and Social Pain," in *The Social Outcast: Ostracism, Social Exclusion, Rejection, and Bullying,* ed. K. Williams, J. P. Forgas, and W. v. Hippel (New York: Psychology Press, 2005), 109–127, 110.

26. See, for example, J. V. Jordan and L. M. Hartling, "New Developments in Relational-Cultural Theory," in *Rethinking Mental Health and Disorder,* ed. M. Ballou and L. Brown (New York: Guilford Press, 2002), 48–70; J. V. Jordan, M. Walker, and L. M. Hartling, *The Complexity of Connection* (New York: Guilford Press, 2004); J. B. Miller and I. P. Stiver, *The Healing Connection: How Women Form Relationships in Therapy and in Life* (Boston: Beacon Press, 1997); and M. Walker and W. Rosen, *How Connections Heal: Stories From Relational-Cultural Therapy* (Wellesley, MA: Guilford Press, 2004).

27. See also G. Wheeler, *Beyond Individualism: Toward a New Understanding of Self, Relationship & Experience* (Hillsdale, NJ: Analytic Press, 2000).

28. See, for example, D. Kahneman, *Daniel Kahneman: The Sveriges Riksbank Prize in Economic Sciences in Memory of Alfred Nobel 2002* (Stockholm: Nobel Foundation, 2002), retrieved on January 7, 2007, from nobelprize.org/nobel_prizes/economics/ laureates/2002/kahneman-autobio.html; M. E. P. Seligman, *Authentic Happiness: Using the New Positive Psychology to Realize Your Potential for Lasting Fulfillment* (New York: Free Press, 2002); or N. Schwarz, D. Kahneman, and E. Diener, eds., *Well-Being: The Foundations of Hedonic Psychology* (New York: Russell Sage Foundation, 1999).

29. D. T. Gilbert, *Stumbling on Happiness* (New York: Knopf, 2006).

30. M. Deutsch, "A Personal Perspective on the Development of Social Psychology in the Twentieth Century," in *Reflections on 100 Years of Experimental Social Psychology,* ed. A. Rodriguez and R. V. Levine (New York: Basic Books, 1999), 1–34, 23.

31. Ibid., 10. See also E. Frydenberg, *Morton Deutsch: A Life and Legacy of Mediation and Conflict Resolution* (Brisbane: Australian Academic Press, 2005).

32. B. Pascal, *Pensées* (Harmondsworth: Penguin Books, original work published in 1643, 1966), 113.

33. D. Hume, "A Treatise of Human Nature, Book 2: Of the Passions, Part 3: Of the Will and Direct Passions," in *The Complete Works and Correspondence of David Hume*, (Charlottesville, VA: InteLex, 1996), section 3, paragraph 4/10, 414.

34. G. A. Bonanno and T. J. Mayne, "Preface," in *Emotions: Current Issues and Future Directions*, ed. T. J. Mayne and G. A. Bonanno (New York: Guilford Press, 2001), xvii–xx, xix.

35. W. James, *Selected Writing (The Varieties of Religious Experience)* (New York: BookoftheMonth Club, 1997), 219.

36. As explained by Lloyd Gordon Ward in "Editor's Notes" at spartan.ac .brocku.ca/~lward/Dewey/Dewey_1895.html. See J. Dewey, "The Theory of Emotion (l) Emotional Attitudes," *Psychological Review*, 1 (1894): 553–569, J. Dewey, "The Theory of Emotion (Ll) The Significance of Emotions," *Psychological Review*, 2 (1895): 13–32.

37. A. R. Damasio, *The Feeling of What Happens: Body and Emotion in the Making of Consciousness* (New York: Harcourt Brace, 1999); G. M. Edelman, "Memory and the Individual Soul: Against Silly Reductionism," in *Nature's Imagination: The Frontiers of Scientific Vision*, ed. J. Cornwell (Oxford: Oxford University Press, 1995), 200–206; and R. B. Zajonc, "Feeling and Thinking: Preferences Need No Inferences," *American Psychologist*, 35 (1980): 151–175.

38. D. Y. Dai and R. J. Sternberg, "Beyond Cognitivism: Toward an Integrated Understanding of Intellectual Functioning and Development," in *Motivation, Emotion, and Cognition: Integrative Perspectives on Intellectual Functioning and Development*, ed. D. Y. Dai and R. J. Sternberg (Mahwah, NJ: Erlbaum, 2004), 3–40, 14.

39. W. James, *The Principles of Psychology (Vol. 1)* (New York: Dover, 1950).

40. A. R. Damasio, *The Feeling of What Happens: Body and Emotion in the Making of Consciousness* (New York: Harcourt Brace, 1999), A. R. Damasio, "A Neurobiology for Consciousness," in *Neural Correlates of Consciousness*, ed. T. Metzinger (Cambridge, MA: MIT Press, 2000), 111–120.

41. A. J. Deikman, *The Observing Self: Mysticism and Psychotherapy* (Boston: Beacon Press, 1982).

42. J. Piaget, *Intelligence and Affectivity: Their Relationship during Child Development* (Palo Alto, CA: Annual Reviews, 1981), J. Piaget, *The Origins of Intelligence in Children* (New York: International University Press, 1950).

43. D. Y. Dai, "Putting It All Together: Some Concluding Thoughts," in *Motivation, Emotion, and Cognition: Integrative Perspectives on Intellectual Functioning and Development*, ed. D. Y. Dai and R. J. Sternberg (Mahwah, NJ: Erlbaum, 2004), 419–432, 421.

44. G. A. Bonanno and T. J. Mayne, "Preface," in *Emotions: Current Issues and Future Directions*, ed. T. J. Mayne and G. A. Bonanno (New York: Guilford Press, 2001), xvii–xx, xvii.

45. B. Parkinson, *Ideas and Realities of Emotions* (London: Routledge, 1995), 12.

46. W. M. Reddy, *The Navigation of Feeling: A Framework for the History of Emotions* (Port Chester, NY: Cambridge University Press, 2001), ix.

47. L. Feldman Barrett, "The Future of Emotion Research," *Affect Scientist*, 12 (1998): 6–8, 6.

48. J. Elster, *Strong Feelings: Emotion, Addiction, and Human Behavior* (Cambridge, MA: MIT Press, 1999); J. Elster, *Alchemies of the Mind: Rationality and the Emotions* (Cambridge: Cambridge University Press, 2003); J. Elster, "Emotion and Action,"

in *Thinking about Feeling: Contemporary Philosophers on Emotions*, ed. R. Solomon (New York: Oxford University Press, 2003).

49. J. Smedslund, *Psycho-Logic* (Berlin: Springer, 1988); J. Smedslund, *The Structure of Psychological Common Sense* (Mahwah, NJ: Erlbaum, 1997); J. Smedslund, "Social Representations and Psychologic," *Culture & Psychology*, 4, no. 4 (1998): 435–454; J. Smedslund, *Dialogues about a New Psychology* (Chagrin Falls, OH: Taos Institute Publishing, 2004).

50. J. Smedslund, *Psycho-Logic* (Berlin: Springer, 1988), 4.

51. Ibid., 4, emphasis in original.

52. Ibid., 5.

53. T. J. Scheff, *Strategies for the Social Science of Emotion* (St. Barbara, CA: www .soc.ucsb.edu/faculty/scheff/31.html, 2004), T. J. Scheff, *Toward a Web of Concepts: The Case of Emotions and Affects* (St. Barbara, CA: www.soc.ucsb.edu/faculty/scheff/41.html, 2004).

54. A. Wendt, *Social Theory as Cartesian Science: An Auto-Critique From a Quantum Perspective* (Columbus, OH: www.humiliationstudies.org/documents/Wendt AutoCritique.pdf, 2004), 37, an early text in preparation for S. Guzzini and A. Leander, *Constructivism and International Relations: Alexander Wendt and His Critics* (New York: Routledge, 2006).

55. Ibid., 37

56. P. Saurette, "You Dissin Me? Humiliation and Post 9/11 Global Politics," *Review of International Studies*, 32 (2006): 495–522, Abstract.

57. R. Jervis, "Understanding Beliefs," *Political Psychology*, 27, no. 5 (2006): 641–663, 641, Abstract.

58. Jervis recommends as good summaries R. McDermott, "The Feeling of Rationality: The Meaning of Neuroscientific Advances for Political Science," *Perspectives on Politics*, 2 (2004): 691–706; G. E. Marcus, "The Psychology of Emotion and Politics," in *Oxford Handbook of Political Psychology*, ed. D. O. Seares, L. Huddy, and R. Jervis (New York: Oxford University Press, 2003), 182–221; and R. B. Zajonc, "Emotions," in *The Handbook of Social Psychology, Vol. 1*, ed. D. T. Gilbert, S. T. Fiske, and G. Lindzey (Boston: McGraw-Hill, 1998), 591–632.

59. Jervis suggests going back fifty years, revisiting the typology introduced by M. B. Smith, J. S. Bruner, and R. W. White, *Opinions and Personality* (New York: Wiley, 1956).

60. R. Jervis, "Understanding Beliefs," *Political Psychology*, 27, no. 5 (2006): 641–663, 643.

61. Ibid., 644.

62. D. Keltner and J. Haidt, "Social Functions of Emotions," in *Emotions: Current Issues and Future Directions*, ed. T. J. Mayne and G. A. Bonanno (New York: Guilford Press, 2001), 192–213, 204.

63. P. Philippot and A. Schaefer, "Emotion and Memory," in *Emotions: Current Issues and Future Directions*, ed. T. J. Mayne and G. A. Bonanno (New York: Guilford Press, 2001), 82–121.

64. K. N. Ochsner and L. Feldman Barrett, "A Multiprocess Perspective on the Neuroscience of Emotion," in *Emotions: Current Issues and Future Directions*, ed. T. J. Mayne and G. A. Bonanno (New York: Guilford Press, 2001), 407–408.

65. M. Kaku, *Parallel Worlds: A Journey through Creation, Higher Dimensions, and the Future of the Cosmos* (New York: Doubleday, 2005), 349.

66. See, for example, E. L. Mayer, *Extraordinary Knowing: Science, Skepticism, and the Inexplicable Powers of the Human Mind* (New York: Bantam Books, 2007).

67. See, for example, M. J. Loux, *Metaphysics: A Contemporary Introduction*, 3rd ed. (London: Routledge, 2006).

68. See also the term *binary opposition*, which has its origins in Saussurean structuralist theory.

69. The nondualistic Buddhist logic of "soku"or "not-one, not-two," has been used by Muneo Yoshikawa to develop a concept of dialogue—read more in chapter 7.

70. G. Bateson, *Steps to an Ecology of Mind* (Scranton, PA: Chandler, 1972).

71. J. Galtung, C. G. Jacobsen, K. F. Brand-Jacobsen, and F. Tschudi, *Searching for Peace: The Road to TRANSCEND* (London: Pluto Press in association with TRANSCEND, 2000).

72. L. LeShan, *The Psychology of War: Comprehending Its Mystique and Its Madness* (Chicago: Noble Press, 1992).

73. See, for example, D. D. N. Winter, *Ecological Psychology: Healing the Split Between Planet and Self* (New York: HarperCollins, 1996).

74. "A possible alternative to dualism is the notion of duality, derived from Giddens's structuration theory, whereby the two elements are interdependent and no longer separate or opposed, although they remain conceptually distinct." W. A. Jackson, "Dualism, Duality and the Complexity of Economic Institutions," *International Journal of Social Economics*, 26, no. 4 (1999): 545–558, retrieved on March 26, 2008, from www.emeraldinsight.com/Insight/ViewContentServlet?Filename= Published/EmeraldFullTextArticle/Pdf/0060260406.pdf, 545, A. Giddens, *The Constitution of Society: Outline of the Theory of Structuration* (Berkeley: University of California Press, 1984).

75. T. Lawson, *Economics and Reality* (London: Routledge, 1997), 22.

76. Jacques Derrida argues that the binary oppositions that create abusive hierarchies must be deconstructed—see J. Derrida, *Of Grammatology* (Baltimore, MD: John Hopkins University Press, a translation from the original French edition *De la grammatologie* first published in 1967, 1976).

77. A. Wendt, *Social Theory as Cartesian Science: An Auto-Critique From a Quantum Perspective* (Columbus, OH: www.humiliationstudies.org/documents/Wendt AutoCritique.pdf, 2004), 7, an early text in preparation for S. Guzzini and A. Leander, *Constructivism and International Relations: Alexander Wendt and His Critics* (New York: Routledge, 2006).

78. A. Zeilinger, M. Plüss, and R. Hügli, *Spooky Action and Beyond: Viennese Physicist Anton Zeilinger Talks about Teleportation, the Information Stored in a Human Being and Freedom in Physics* (Berlin: Perlentaucher Medien, signandsight.com, 2006), retrieved on April 16, 2008, from www.signandsight.com/features/614.html.

79. Ibid.

80. I. Baruŝs, "Can We Consider Matter as Ultimate Reality? Some Fundamental Problems with a Materialist Interpretation of Reality," *Ultimate Reality and Meaning: Interdisciplinary Studies in the Philosophy of Understanding*, 16, no. 3–4 (1993): 245–254, I. Baruŝs, "The Art of Science: Science of the Future in Light of Alterations of Consciousness," *Journal of Scientific Exploration*, 15, no. 1 (2001): 57–68.

81. J. Katz, ed., *One: Essential Writings on Nonduality* (Boulder, CO: Sentient Publications, 2007).

82. K. Wilber, *No Boundary* (Boston: Shambhala, 1979), 25.

83. Plotinus, circa 205–270 B.C., philosopher of the ancient world, born in Egypt, later teaching in Rome—see Plotinus, S. MacKenna, and B. S. Page, *The Enneads,* 2nd ed. (London: Faber and Faber, 1956).

84. German philosopher Schelling (1775–1854) was influenced by German writer Johann Wolfgang von Goethe (1749–1832), see F. W. J. v. Schelling, *System des transcendentalen Idealismus* (Tübingen: Cotta, 1800), F. W. J. v. Schelling, *System of Transcendental Idealism,* new April 1, 1993 ed. (Charlottesville: University Press of Virginia, 1978).

85. British philosopher Francis Herbert Bradley (1846–1924)—F. H. Bradley, *Appearance and Reality: A Metaphysical Essay* (New York: Macmillan, 1893).

86. B. Wittine, "Jungian Analysis and Nondual Wisdom," in *Sacred Mirror: Nondual Wisdom & Psychotherapy,* ed. J. J. Prendergast, P. Fenner, and S. Krystal (New York: Paragon House Publishers, 2003), 268–289.

87. D. A. Leupnitz and S. Tulkin, "The Cybernetic Epistemology of Gestalt Therapy," *Psychotherapy: Theory, Research & Practice,* 17, no. 2 (1980): 153–157, retrieved on March 27, 2008 from psycnet.apa.org/index.cfm?fa=main.showContent&id=1980-30800-001&view=fulltext&format=pdf.

88. E. Fromm, *To Have or to Be?* (New York: Harper and Row, 1976).

89. A. J. Deikman, *The Observing Self: Mysticism and Psychotherapy* (Boston: Beacon Press, 1982).

90. A. Wendt, *Social Theory as Cartesian Science: An Auto-Critique From a Quantum Perspective* (Columbus, OH: www.humiliationstudies.org/documents/Wendt AutoCritique.pdf, 2004), 10, an early text in preparation for S. Guzzini and A. Leander, *Constructivism and International Relations: Alexander Wendt and His Critics* (New York: Routledge, 2006).

91. Ibid., 7.

92. H. Richards, *Foucault and the Future* (Richmond, IN: unpublished work in progress, 2007), see, for example, Chapter 10, "More Philosophical Contributions to Building Non-Authoritarian Cultures of Solidarity." For an overview over critical realism, see M. S. Archer, R. Bhaskar, A. Collier, T. Lawson, and A. Norrie, eds., *Critical Realism: Essential Readings Roy Bhaskar, Andrew Collier, Tony Lawson, and Alan Norrie* (London: Routledge, 1998).

93. For his publications, see, for example, Føllesdal, "Husserl on Evidence and Justification," in *Edmund Husserl and the Phenomenological Tradition: Essays in Phenomenology. Proceedings of a Lecture Series in the Fall of 1985, in Studies in Philosophy and the History of Philosophy,* ed. Robert Sokolowski (Washington, DC: Catholic University of America Press, 1988), 107–129, and D. Føllesdal, *Intersubjectivity and Ethics in Husserl's Phenomenology* (Oslo: Seminar organized by the Norwegian Ethics Programme at the Research Council of Norway, Oslo, February 19–24, 1996).

94. D. Føllesdal, *How Can We Use Arguments in Ethics?* (Oslo: Presentation at Det Norske Vitenskaps-Akademi [Norwegian Academy of Science], January 30, 1996).

95. A. Ortony and T. J. Turner, "What's Basic about Basic Emotions?," *Psychological Review,* 97 (1990): 315–331.

96. C. E. Izard, "Basic Emotions, Relations among Emotions, and Emotion-Cognition Relations," *Psychological Review,* 99, no. 3, July (1992): 561–565; P. Ekman, "Are There Basic Emotions?," *Psychological Review,* 99, no. 3, July (1992): 550–553;

J. Panksepp, "A Critical Role for 'Affective Neuroscience' in Resolving What Is Basic about Basic Emotions," *Psychological Review*, 99, no. 3, July (1992): 554–560; T. J. Turner and A. Ortony, "Basic Emotions: Can Conflicting Criteria Converge?," *Psychological Review*, 99, no. 3, July (1992): 566–571.

97. J. Panksepp, "A Critical Role for 'Affective Neuroscience' in Resolving What Is Basic about Basic Emotions," *Psychological Review*, 99, no. 3, July (1992): 554–560, Abstract.

98. P. Ekman, "Are There Basic Emotions?," *Psychological Review*, 99, no. 3, July (1992): 550–553, Abstract.

99. C. E. Izard, "Basic Emotions, Relations among Emotions, and Emotion-Cognition Relations," *Psychological Review*, 99, no. 3, July (1992): 561–565, Abstract.

100. T. J. Turner and A. Ortony, "Basic Emotions: Can Conflicting Criteria Converge?," *Psychological Review*, 99, no. 3, July (1992): 566–571, Abstract.

101. Ibid.

102. A. Ortony and T. J. Turner, "What's Basic about Basic Emotions?," *Psychological Review*, 97 (1990): 315–331, 329.

103. Ibid.

104. Adapted from A. Ortony and T. J. Turner, "What's Basic about Basic Emotions?," *Psychological Review*, 97 (1990): 315–331, 316.

105. M. B. Arnold, *Emotion and Personality* (New York: Columbia University Press, 1960)

106. P. Ekman, W. V. Friesen, and P. C. Ellsworth, "What Emotion Categories or Dimensions Can Observers Judge from Facial Behavior?," in *Emotion in the Human Face*, ed. P. Ekman, 2nd ed. (Cambridge: Cambridge University Press, 1982), 39–55.

107. Personal communication, September 8, 1986.

108. J. A. Gray, *The Neuropsychology of Anxiety* (Oxford: Oxford University Press, 1982).

109. C. E. Izard, *The Face of Emotion* (New York: Appleton-Century-Crofts, 1971).

110. W. James, "What Is an Emotion?," *Mind*, 9 (1884): 188–205.

111. W. McDougall, *An Introduction to Social Psychology* (Boston: Luce, 1926).

112. O. H. Mowrer, *Learning Theory and Behavior* (New York: Wiley, 1960).

113. K. Oatley and P. N. Johnson-Laird, "Towards a Cognitive Theory of Emotions," *Cognition & Emotion*, 1 (1987): 29–50.

114. J. Panksepp, "Toward a General Psychobiological Theory of Emotions," *Behavioral and Brain Sciences*, 5 (1982): 407–467.

115. R. Plutchik, "A General Psychoevolutionary Theory of Emotion," in *Emotion: Theory, Research, and Experience: Vol. 1. Theories of Emotion*, ed. R. Plutchik and H. Kellerman (New York: Academic Press, 1980), 3–31.

116. S. S. Tomkins, "Affect Theory," in *Approaches to Emotion*, ed. K. R. Scherer and P. Ekman (Hillsdale, NJ: Erlbaum, 1984), 163–195.

117. J. B. Watson, *Behaviorism* (Chicago: University of Chicago Press, 1930).

118. B. Weiner and S. Graham, "An Attributional Approach to Emotional Development," in *Emotions, Cognition, and Behavior*, ed. C. E. Izard, J. Kagan, and R. B. Zajonc (New York: Cambridge University Press, 1984), 167–191.

119. For example, C. E. Izard, *Human Emotions* (New York: Plenum Press, 1977); J. Panksepp, "Toward a General Psychobiological Theory of Emotions," *Behavioral*

and Brain Sciences, 5 (1982): 407–467; R. Plutchik, "A General Psychoevolutionary Theory of Emotion," in *Emotion: Theory, Research, and Experience: Vol. 1. Theories of Emotion*, ed. R. Plutchik and H. Kellerman (New York: Academic Press, 1980), 3–31; S. S. Tomkins, "Affect Theory," in *Approaches to Emotion*, ed. K. R. Scherer and P. Ekman (Hillsdale, NJ: Erlbaum, 1984), 163–195.

120. For example, O. H. Mowrer, *Learning Theory and Behavior* (New York: Wiley, 1960), B. Weiner and S. Graham, "An Attributional Approach to Emotional Development," in *Emotions, Cognition, and Behavior*, ed. C. E. Izard, J. Kagan, and R. B. Zajonc (New York: Cambridge University Press, 1984), 167–191.

121. A. Wierzbicka, "Human Emotions: Universal or Culture-Specific?," *American Anthropologist*, 88 (1986): 584–594, 584. See also A. Wierzbicka and J. Harkins, eds., *Emotions in Crosslinguistic Perspective* (Berlin: Mouton de Gruyter, 2001).

122. B. Mesquita, "Culture and Emotion: Different Approaches to the Question," in *Emotions: Current Issues and Future Directions*, ed. T. J. Mayne and G. A. Bonanno (New York: Guilford Press, 2001), 214–250, 223.

123. J. A. Russell, "Cultural Variations in Emotions: A Review," *Psychological Bulletin*, 112, no. 2 (1991): 179–204, 440.

124. J. Smedslund, "From Hypothesis-Testing Psychology to Procedure-Testing Psychologic," *Review of General Psychology*, 6, no. 1 (2002): 51–72, Abstract.

125. Personal communication, February 1, 2008. See J. Smedslund, "Are Frijda's 'Laws of Emotion' Empirical?," *Cognition & Emotion*, 6, no. 6 (1992): 435–456.

126. N. H. Frijda, "The Laws of Emotion," *American Psychologist*, 43 (1988): 349–358.

127. N. H. Frijda, *The Laws of Emotion* (Hillsdale, NJ: Erlbaum, 2006).

128. See, for example, P. Ekman, "An Argument for Basic Emotions," *Cognition and Emotion*, 6 (1992): 169–200.

129. T. J. Mayne and J. Ramsey, "The Structure of Emotion: A Nonlinear Dynamic Systems Approach," in *Emotions: Current Issues and Future Directions*, ed. T. J. Mayne and G. A. Bonanno (New York: Guilford Press, 2001), 1–37.

130. G. A. Bonanno and T. J. Mayne, "Preface," in *Emotions: Current Issues and Future Directions*, ed. T. J. Mayne and G. A. Bonanno (New York: Guilford Press, 2001), xvii–xx, xix.

131. K. R. Scherer, "Foreword," in *Emotions: Current Issues and Future Directions*, ed. T. J. Mayne and G. A. Bonanno (New York: Guilford Press, 2001), xiii–xv, xv.

132. Ibid., xv.

133. T. J. Mayne and G. A. Bonanno, eds., *Emotions: Current Issues and Future Directions* (New York: Guilford Press, 2001).

134. K. R. Scherer, "Foreword," in *Emotions: Current Issues and Future Directions*, ed. T. J. Mayne and G. A. Bonanno (New York: Guilford Press, 2001), xiii–xv, xiii–xiv.

135. See, among others, R. McElreath and R. Boyd, *Mathematical Models of Social Evolution: A Guide for the Perplexed* (Chicago: University of Chicago Press, 2007); E. Fehr, U. Fischbacher, and M. Kosfeld, *Neuroeconomic Foundation of Trust and Social Preferences* (London: Centre for Economic Policy Research, 2005); E. Fehr, M. Naef, and K. Schmidt, *The Role of Equality and Efficiency in Social Preferences* (London: Centre for Economic Policy Research, 2005); R. Sun, ed., *Cognition and Multi-Agent Interaction: From Cognitive Modeling to Social Simulation* (Cambridge: Cambridge University Press, 2006).

136. N. Schwarz, "Warmer and More Social: Recent Developments in Cognitive Social Psychology," *Annual Review of Sociology*, 24 (1998): 239–264.

137. K. J. Gergen, "Technology and the Self: From the Essential to the Sublime," in *Constructing the Self in a Mediated World*, ed. Grodin and Lindlof (London: Sage, 1996), draft of chapter retrieved January 6, 2000, from www.swarthmore.edu/SocSci/kgergen1/text11.html, 9.

138. L. S. Vygotsky, *Mind in Society: The Development of Higher Psychological Processes* (Cambridge, MA: Harvard University Press, 1978). See also J. S. Bruner, *Acts of Meaning* (Cambridge, MA: Harvard University Press, 1990).

139. See an overview in R. Spencer, "A Comparison of Relational Psychologies," *Work in Progress, No. 5* (Wellesley, MA: Stone Center Working Paper Series, 2000).

140. See, for example, R. F. Baumeister and M. R. Leary, "The Need to Belong: Desire for Interpersonal Attachments as a Fundamental Human Motivation," in *Motivational Science: Social and Personality Perspectives*, ed. T. E. Higgins and A. W. Kruglanski (Philadelphia: Taylor and Francis, 2000), 24–49, or A. Maalouf, *In the Name of Identity: Violence and the Need to Belong* (New York: Arcade Publishing, 2001).

141. J. Bowlby, *Attachment and Loss* (New York: Basic Books, 1969). There is a vast body of literature to draw from.

142. See A. P. Fiske, *Structures of Social Life: The Four Elementary Forms of Human Relations—Communal Sharing, Authority Ranking, Equality Matching, Market Pricing* (New York: Free Press, 1991).

143. See, for example, L. M. Hartling and J. Ly, "Relational References: A Selected Bibliography of Research, Theory, and Applications," *Work in Progress, No. 7* (Wellesley, MA: Stone Center Working Papers Series, 2000); L. M. Hartling and E. Sparks, "Relational-Cultural Practice: Working in a Nonrelational World," *Work in Progress, No. 97* (Wellesley, MA: Stone Center Working Papers Series, 2000); L. M. Hartling, "Prevention through Connection: A Collaborative Response to Women's Substance Abuse," *Work in Progress, No. 103* (Wellesley, MA: Stone Center Working Papers Series, 2003); L. M. Hartling, "Strengthening Resilience in a Risky World: It Is All about Relationships," *Work in Progress, No. 101* (Wellesley, MA: Stone Center Working Papers Series, 2003); J. V. Jordan and L. M. Hartling, "New Developments in Relational-Cultural Theory," in *Rethinking Mental Health and Disorder*, ed. M. Ballou and L. Brown (New York: Guilford Press, 2002), 48–70; J. V. Jordan, M. Walker, and L. M. Hartling, *The Complexity of Connection* (New York: Guilford Press, 2004); J. B. Miller and I. P. Stiver, *The Healing Connection: How Women Form Relationships in Therapy and in Life* (Boston: Beacon Press, 1997); M. Walker and W. Rosen, *How Connections Heal: Stories from Relational-Cultural Therapy* (Wellesley, MA: Guilford Press, 2004).

144. J. V. Jordan and L. M. Hartling, "New Developments in Relational-Cultural Theory," in *Rethinking Mental Health and Disorder*, ed. M. Ballou and L. Brown (New York: Guilford Press, 2002), 48–70.

145. See, for example, R. Munch and N. J. Smelser, eds., *Theory of Culture* (Berkeley: University of California Press, 1992).

146. Personal communication, December 2004.

147. D. Keltner and J. Haidt, "Social Functions of Emotions at Four Levels of Analysis," *Cognition & Emotion*, 13, no. 5 (1999): 505–521, 506.

148. G. V. Bodenhausen, T. Mussweiler, S. Gabriel, and K. N. Moreno, "Affective Influences on Stereotyping and Intergroup Relations," in *Handbook of Affect and Social Cognition*, ed. J. P. Forgas (Mahwah, NJ: Erlbaum, 2001), 319–343, 338.

149. N. Besnier, "The Politics of Emotion in Nukulaelae Gossip," in *Everyday Conceptions of Emotion*, ed. J. A. Russell, J. M. Fernández-Dols, A. S. R. Manstead, and J. C. Wellenkamp (Dordrecht: Kluwer Academic Publishers, 1995), 221–240, 236.

150. See, among others, L. Brothers, *Friday's Footprint: How Society Shapes the Human Mind* (New York: Oxford University Press, 1997).

151. J. T. Cacioppo, G. G. Berntson, R. Adolphs, C. S. Carter, R. J. Davidson, M. K. McClintock, B. S. McEwen, M. J. Meaney, D. L. Schacter, E. M. Sternberg, S. S. Suomi, and S. E. Taylor, eds., *Foundations in Social Neuroscience* (Cambridge, MA: MIT Press, 2002); J. T. Cacioppo and G. G. Berntson, eds., *Essays in Social Neuroscience* (Cambridge, MA: MIT Press, 2004); T. R. Insel and R. D. Fernald, "How the Brain Processes Social Information: Searching for the Social Brain," *Annual Review of Neuroscience*, 27 (2004): 697–722; J. Panksepp, *Affective Neuroscience: The Foundations of Human and Animal Emotions* (New York: Oxford University Press, 1998); D. J. Siegel, *The Developing Mind: Toward a Neurobiology of Interpersonal Experience* (New York: Guilford Press, 1999).

152. R. Adolphs and A. R. Damasio, "The Interaction of Affect and Cognition: A Neurobiological Perspective," in *Handbook of Affect and Social Cognition*, ed. J. P. Forgas (Mahwah, NJ: Erlbaum, 2001), 27–49, 43.

153. D. Keltner and J. Haidt, "Social Functions of Emotions," in *Emotions: Current Issues and Future Directions*, ed. T. J. Mayne and G. A. Bonanno (New York: Guilford Press, 2001), 192–213, 207.

154. Ibid.

155. Ibid.

156. G. V. Bodenhausen, "Emotions, Arousal, and Stereotypic Judgments: A Heuristic Model of Affect and Stereotyping," in *Affect, Cognition, and Stereotyping*, ed. D. M. Mackie and D. L. Hamilton (San Diego, CA: Academic Press, 1993), 13–37.

157. G. V. Bodenhausen, T. Mussweiler, S. Gabriel, and K. N. Moreno, "Affective Influences on Stereotyping and Intergroup Relations," in *Handbook of Affect and Social Cognition*, ed. J. P. Forgas (Mahwah, NJ: Erlbaum, 2001), 319–343, 320–321.

158. Ibid., 338.

159. See, for example, N. H. Frijda and B. Mesquita, "The Social Roles and Functions of Emotions," in *Emotion and Culture: Empirical Studies of Mutual Influence*, ed. S. Kitayama and H. R. Markus (Washington, DC: American Psychological Association, 1994), 51–87; B. H. Rosenwein, *Anger's Past: The Social Uses of an Emotion in the Middle Ages* (Ithaca, NY: Cornell University Press, 1998); C. Z. Stearns and P. N. Stearns, *Anger: The Struggle for Emotional Control in America's History* (Chicago: University of Chicago Press, 1986); see for love, for example, F. Amini, R. Lannon, and T. Lewis, *A General Theory of Love* (New York: Vintage, 2001).

160. K. R. Scherer, "Foreword," in *Emotions: Current Issues and Future Directions*, ed. T. J. Mayne and G. A. Bonanno (New York: Guilford Press, 2001), xiii–xv, xiv.

161. See, among many others, T. D. Kemper, "Sociological Models in the Explanation of Emotions," in *Handbook of Emotions*, ed. M. Lewis and J. M. Haviland (New York: Guilford Press, 1993), 41–51; C. A. Lutz and L. Abu-Lughod, eds., *Language and the Politics of Emotion* (Cambridge: Cambridge University Press, 1990);

J. Tooby and L. Cosmides, "The Past Explains the Present: Emotional Adaptations and the Structure of Ancestral Environments," *Ethology and Sociobiology,* 11 (1990): 375–424.

162. K. N. Ochsner and L. Feldman Barrett, "A Multiprocess Perspective on the Neuroscience of Emotion," in *Emotions: Current Issues and Future Directions,* ed. T. J. Mayne and G. A. Bonanno (New York: Guilford Press, 2001), 38–81.

163. S. Pinker, *The Blank Slate: The Modern Denial of Human Nature* (London: Allen Lane, 2001).

164. W. J. Freeman, *Societies of Brains: A Study in the Neuroscience of Love and Hate* (Hillsdale, NJ: Erlbaum, 1995).

165. See the note explaining "emotion and the emergence of an individuated self."

166. P. D. MacLean, *A Triune Concept of the Brain and Behavior: Hincks Memorial Lectures* (Toronto: University of Toronto Press, 1973).

167. S. W. Porges, "Emotion: An Evolutionary By-Product of the Neural Regulation of the Autonomic Nervous System," in *The Integrative Neurobiology of Cognition,* ed. C. S. Carter, I. I. Lederhendler, and B. Kirkpatrick (Annals of the New York Academy of Sciences, Volume 807, New York: New York Academy of Sciences, 1997), 62–77.

168. M. Lewis and L. Michalson, *Children's Emotions and Moods: Developmental Theory and Measurement* (New York: Plenum Press, 1983). See also J. Elison and S. Harter, "Humiliation: Causes, Correlates, and Consequences," in *The Self-Conscious Emotions: Theory and Research,* ed. J. L. Tracy, R. W. Robins, and J. P. Tangney (New York: Guilford Press, 2007), 310–329.

169. M. D. Lewis, "Emotional Self-organization at Three Time Scales," in *Emotion, Development, and Self-organization: Dynamic Systems Approaches to Emotional Development,* ed. M. D. Lewis and I. Granic (New York: Cambridge University Press, 2000), 37–69.

170. G. Labouvie-Vief and M. M. González, "Dynamic Integration: Affect Optimization and Differentiation in Development," in *Motivation, Emotion, and Cognition: Integrative Perspectives on Intellectual Functioning and Development,* ed. D. Y. Dai and R. J. Sternberg (Mahwah, NJ: Erlbaum, 2004), 237–272, 243.

171. H. Leventhal and K. R. Scherer, "The Relationship of Emotion to Cognition: A Functional Approach to a Semantic Controversy," *Cognition and Emotion,* 1 (1987): 3–28.

172. T. A. Pyszczynski, J. Greenberg, and S. Solomon, "Toward a Dialectical Analysis of Growth and Defensive Motives," *Psychological Inquiry,* 11 (2000): 301–305.

173. G. A. Bonanno and T. J. Mayne, "The Future of Emotion Research," in *Emotions: Current Issues and Future Directions,* ed. T. J. Mayne and G. A. Bonanno (New York: Guilford Press, 2001), 398–410, 407.

174. K. R. Scherer, "On the Nature and Function of Emotion: A Component Process Approach," in *Approaches to Emotion,* ed. K. R. Scherer and P. Ekman (Hillsdale, NJ: Erlbaum, 1984), 293–318.

175. R. Adolphs and A. R. Damasio, "The Interaction of Affect and Cognition: A Neurobiological Perspective," in *Handbook of Affect and Social Cognition,* ed. J. P. Forgas (Mahwah, NJ: Erlbaum, 2001), 27–49, 29.

176. A. R. Damasio, *Descartes' Error. Emotion, Reason and the Human Brain* (New York: Avon Books, 1994), 1999; J. Panksepp, *Affective Neuroscience: The Foundations of Human and Animal Emotions* (New York: Oxford University Press, 1998).

177. N. H. Frijda, *The Emotions* (Cambridge: Cambridge University Press, 1986); N. H. Frijda, P. Kuipers, and E. ter Schure, "Relations among Emotion, Appraisal, and Emotional Action Readiness," *Journal of Personality and Social Psychology*, 57, no. 2, August (1989): 212–228; R. S. Lazarus, *Emotion and Adaptation* (New York: Oxford University Press, 1991); R. W. Levenson, "The Intrapersonal Functions of Emotion," *Cognition & Emotion*, 13, no. 5 (1999): 481–504; J. Tooby and L. Cosmides, "The Past Explains the Present: Emotional Adaptations and the Structure of Ancestral Environments," *Ethology and Sociobiology*, 11 (1990): 375–424.

178. R. Adolphs and A. R. Damasio, "The Interaction of Affect and Cognition: A Neurobiological Perspective," in *Handbook of Affect and Social Cognition*, ed. J. P. Forgas (Mahwah, NJ: Erlbaum, 2001), 27–49, 28–29.

179. L. Feldman Barrett and J. A. Russell, "The Structure of Current Affect: Controversies and Emerging Consensus," *Current Directions in Psychological Science*, 8 (1999): 10–14.

180. PANAS; D. Watson, L. A. Clark, and A. Tellegen, "Development and Validation of Brief Measures of Positive and Negative Affect: The PANAS Scales," *Journal of Personality and Social Psychology*, 54 (1988): 1063–1070.

181. DES; C. E. Izard, *Patterns of Emotion: A New Analysis of Anxiety and Depression* (San Diego, CA: Academic Press, 1972).

182. E. L. Rosenberg, "Levels of Analysis and the Organization of Affect," *Review of General Psychology*, 2 (1998): 247–270.

183. See social psychological research on affective states and cognitive processing, for example, J. P. Forgas, "Feeling and Thinking: Summary and Integration," in *Feeling and Thinking: The Role of Affect in Social Cognition*, ed. J. P. Forgas (New York: Cambridge University Press, 2000), 387–406.

184. N. Schwarz and G. L. Clore, "Feelings and Phenomenal Experiences," in *Social Psychology: Handbook of Basic Principles*, ed. E. T. Higgins and A. W. Kruglanski (New York: Guilford Press, 1996), 433–465.

185. See for alternative perspectives, for example, C. D. Batson, L. L. Shaw, and K. C. Oleson, "Differentiating Affect, Mood, and Emotion: Toward Functionally Based Conceptual Distinctions," in *Review of Personality and Social Psychology: Vol. 13. Emotion*, ed. M. S. Clark (Newbury Park, CA: Sage, 1992), 294–326, or W. N. Morris, "A Functional Analysis of the Role of Mood in Affective Systems," *Review of Personality and Social Psychology: Vol. 13. Emotion*, ed. M. S. Clark (Newbury Park, CA: Sage, 1992), 256–293.

186. A. R. Damasio, *The Feeling of What Happens: Body and Emotion in the Making of Consciousness* (New York: Harcourt Brace, 1999), 37.

187. A. Nelson, *Living the Wheel: Working with Emotion, Terror, and Bliss through Imagery* (York Beach, ME: Samuel Weiser, 1993).

188. A. R. Damasio, *Looking for Spinoza: Joy, Sorrow, and the Feeling Brain* (Orlando, FL: Harcourt, 2003).

189. A. R. Damasio, *Descartes' Error. Emotion, Reason and the Human Brain* (New York: Avon Books, 1994), 151.

190. A. L. Nagata, "Bodymindfulness for Skillful Communication," *Rikkyo Intercultural Communication Review*, 5 (2007): 61–76, 66. See also A. L. Nagata, *Somatic Mindfulness and Energetic Presence in Intercultural Communication: A Phenomenological/Hermeneutic Exploration of Bodymindset and Emotional Resonance*, Dissertation Abstracts International, 62 /(12), 5999B. (UMI No.3037968), 2002), A. Nelson, *Living*

the Wheel: Working with Emotion, Terror, and Bliss through Imagery (York Beach, ME: Samuel Weiser, 1993).

Notes to Chapter 2

1. J. Bourke, "How to Seek Shelter When It's Raining Fear," *International Herald Tribune,* February 8 (2005), www.commondreams.org/views05/0208-26.htm.

2. See, for example, J. T. Cacioppo, W. L. Gardner, and G. G. Berntson, "The Affect System Has Parallel and Integrative Processing Components: Form Follows Function," *Journal of Personality and Social Psychology,* 76, no. 5 (1999): 839–855; J. A. Russell and L. Feldman Barrett, "Core Affect, Prototypical Emotional Episodes, and Other Things Called Emotion: Dissecting the Elephant," *Journal of Personality and Social Psychology,* 76, no. 5 (1999): 805–819; A. Tellegen, D. Watson, and L. A. Clark, "On the Dimensional and Hierarchical Structure of Affect," *Psychological Science,* 10 (1999): 297–309; D. Watson et al., "The Two General Activation Systems of Affect: Structural Findings, Evolutionary Considerations, and Psychobiological Evidence," *Journal of Personality and Social Psychology,* 76, no. 5 (1999): 820–838.

3. R. Adolphs and A. R. Damasio, "The Interaction of Affect and Cognition: A Neurobiological Perspective," *Handbook of Affect and Social Cognition,* ed. J. P. Forgas (Mahwah, NJ: Erlbaum, 2001), 27–49, 44.

4. G. A. Bonanno and T. J. Mayne, "The Future of Emotion Research," in *Emotions: Current Issues and Future Directions,* ed. T. J. Mayne and G. A. Bonanno (New York, London: Guilford Press, 2001), 398–410, 407.

5. P. C. Holland and M. Gallagher, "Amygdala Circuitry in Attentional and Representational Processes," *Trends in Cognitive Sciences,* 3 (1999): 65–73; J. E. LeDoux, *The Emotional Brain: The Mysterious Underpinnings of Emotional Life* (New York: Simon & Schuster, 1996); P. J. Whalen, "Fear, Vigilance, and Ambiguity: Initial Neuroimaging Studies of the Human Amygdala," *Current Directions in Psychological Science,* 7 (1998): 177–188.

6. K. N. Ochsner and L. Feldman Barrett, "A Multiprocess Perspective on the Neuroscience of Emotion," *Emotions: Current Issues and Future Directions,* ed. T. J. Mayne and G. A. Bonanno (New York: Guilford Press, 2001), 38–81, 60.

7. R. J. Davidson, "The Neuroscience of Affective Style," in *The New Cognitive Neurosciences,* ed. M. S. Gazzaniga, 2nd ed. (Cambridge, MA: MIT Press, 2000), 1149–1162.

8. J. A. Russell and L. Feldman Barrett, "Core Affect, Prototypical Emotional Episodes, and Other Things Called Emotion: Dissecting the Elephant," *Journal of Personality and Social Psychology,* 76, no. 5 (1999): 805–819.

9. K. N. Ochsner and L. Feldman Barrett, "A Multiprocess Perspective on the Neuroscience of Emotion," in *Emotions: Current Issues and Future Directions,* ed. T. J. Mayne and G. A. Bonanno (New York: Guilford Press, 2001), 38–81, 61.

10. Ibid., 45.

11. Ibid., 62.

12. For literature on genes, hormones, and violence, see, for example, P. C. Bernhardt, "Influences of Serotonin and Testosterone in Aggression and Dominance: Convergence with Social Psychology," *Current Directions in Psychological Science,* 6, no. 2 (1997): 44–48; A. Caspi et al., "Role of Genotype in the Cycle of Violence in Maltreated Children," *Science,* 297 (2002): 851–854; W. R. Clark and M. Grunstein,

Are We Hardwired? (New York: Oxford University Press, 2000); J. L. Fuller and W. R. Thompson, *Foundations of Behavior Genetics* (St. Louis, MO: Mosby, 2003); D. Hamer and P. Copeland, *Living with Our Genes: Why They Matter More Than You Think* (London: Pan Books, 2000).

13. For the link between masculinity and violence, see, for example, I. Breines, R. W. Connell, and I. Eide, eds., *Males Roles, Masculinities and Violence. A Culture of Peace Perspective* (Paris: UNESCO, 2000); R. W. Connell, *Masculinities* (Cambridge: Polity Press, 1995); R. W. Connell, "Teaching Boys: New Research on Masculinity, and Gender Strategies for Schools," *Teachers College Record*, 98, no. 2 (1996): 206–235; J. S. Goldstein, *War and Gender: How Gender Shapes the War Systems and Vice Versa* (Cambridge: Cambridge University Press, 2001); M. Kimmel, *Reducing Men's Violence: The Personal Meets the Political* (Oslo: Paper presented at the expert group meeting on "Male Roles and Masculinities in the Perspective of a Culture of Peace," Oslo, Norway, September 24–28, 1997); S. M. Whitehead, *Men and Masculinities: Key Themes and New Directions* (Cambridge: Polity Press, 2002); R. Wrangham and D. Peterson, *Demonic Males* (New York: Houghton Mifflin, 1996); M. Zalewski and J. Parpat, eds., *The "Man Question" in International Relations* (Boulder, CO: Westview, 1998). See also The Men's Studies Bibliography online at www.xyonline.net/mensbiblio.

14. S. E. Taylor et al., "Biobehavioral Responses to Stress in Females: Tend-and-Befriend, Not Fight-or-Flight," *Psychological Review*, 109, no. 4 (2002): 745–750. This may have an evolutionary background. While men were killed, women were often captured alive when communities were invaded and conquered. They may have adapted to this situation by developing a specific reaction to stress.

15. R. D. Petersen, *Understanding Ethnic Violence: Fear, Hatred, and Resentment in Twentieth Century Eastern Europe* (Cambridge: Cambridge University Press, 2002).

16. E. Fromm, *Escape from Freedom* (New York: Rinehart, 1941).

17. E. Becker, *The Denial of Death* (New York: Free Press, 1973).

18. See, for example, J. Greenberg, S. Solomon, and T. A. Pyszczynski, "The Role of Self-Esteem and Cultural Worldviews in the Management of Existential Terror," in *Advances in Experimental Social Psychology*, ed. M. P. Zanna (New York: Academic Press, 1997), and more recent publications related to the events of September 11, 2001, T. A. Pyszczynski, J. Greenberg, and S. Solomon, *In the Wake of 9/11: The Psychology of Terror* (Washington, DC: American Psychological Association, 2003).

19. Gautama Buddha, *The Dhammapada—The Path to the Truth*, Sukha Vagga, verse 201, retrieved from www.aimwell.org/Books/Suttas/Dhammapada/15-Sukha/15-sukha.html.

20. I. W. Charny, ed., *Encyclopedia of Genocide* (Santa Barbara, CA: ABC-CLIO, 1999).

21. S. J. Bartlett, *The Pathology of Man: A Study of Human Evil* (Springfield, IL: Thomas, 2005).

22. J. W. Jones, *Blood That Cries Out From the Earth: The Psychology of Religious Terrorism* (New York: Oxford University Press, 2008).

23. V. D. Volkan, "A Psychoanalytic Perspective on Intergroup Hatred," *Journal for the Psychoanalysis of Culture and Society*, 3, no. 1 (1998): 78–80.

24. R. J. Sternberg, "A Duplex Theory of Hate: Development and Application to Terrorism, Massacres, and Genocide," *Review of General Psychology*, 7, no. 3 (2003): 299–328. See also R. J. Sternberg, ed., *The Psychology of Hate* (Washington, DC: American Psychological Association, 2005).

25. S. Opotow and S. I. McClelland, "The Intensification of Hating: A Theory," *Social Justice Research*, 20, no. 1 (2007): 68.

26. S. Opotow, "Hate, Conflict, and Moral Exclusion," in *The Psychology of Hate*, ed. R. J. Sternberg (Washington, DC: American Psychological Association, 2005), 121.

27. S. Opotow, "Aggression and Violence," in *The Handbook of Conflict Resolution: Theory and Practice*, ed. M. Deutsch, P. T. Coleman, and E. C. Marcus, 2nd ed. (San Francisco: Jossey-Bass, 2006), 510.

28. A. T. Beck, *Prisoners of Hate: The Cognitive Basis of Anger, Hostility and Violence* (New York: Harper Collins, 1999).

29. E. Staub, *The Roots of Evil: The Origins of Genocide and Other Group Violence* (Cambridge: Cambridge University Press, 1989); E. Staub, *The Psychology of Good and Evil: Why Children, Adults, and Groups Help and Harm Others* (Cambridge: Cambridge University Press, 2003).

30. R. F. Baumeister, *Evil: Inside Human Cruelty and Violence* (New York: Freeman, 1996).

31. D. G. Dutton, E. O. Boyanowsky, and M. H. Bond, "Extreme Mass Homicide: From Military Massacre to Genocide," *Aggression and Violent Behavior*, 10 (2005): 437–473, Abstract.

32. T. J. Scheff, "Aggression, Hypermasculine Emotions and Relations: the Silence/Violence Pattern," *Irish Journal of Sociology*, 15, no. 1 (2006): 24–37, see www.soc.ucsb.edu/faculty/scheff/53.htm.

33. T. J. Scheff, "Aggression, Male Emotions and Relations: The Silence/Violence Pattern," Santa Barbara, CA, 2005, see www.soc.ucsb.edu/faculty/scheff/42.html.

34. H. B. Lewis, *Shame and Guilt in Neurosis* (New York: International Universities Press, 1971).

35. R. J. Eidelson and J. I. Eidelson, "Dangerous Ideas: Five Beliefs That Propel Groups toward Conflict," *American Psychologist*, 58, no. 3 (2003): 182–192.

36. See, for example, R. Benedict, *The Chrysanthemum and the Sword* (Boston: Houghton Mifflin, 1946). This book launched a debate among Japanese scholars over "shame culture" versus "guilt culture," which became so popularized that the two terms have become established as expressions in ordinary Japanese language.

37. S. J. Pharr, *Losing Face: Status Politics in Japan* (Berkeley: University of California Press, 1990).

38. H. Fung, "Becoming a Moral Child: The Socialization of Shame among Young Chinese Children," *Ethos*, 27, no. 2 (1999): 180–209; H. Fung and E. C.-H. Chen, "Across Time and beyond Skin: Self and Transgression in the Everyday Socialization of Shame among Taiwanese Preschool Children," *Social Development*, 10, no. 3 (2001): 420–437.

39. J. Li and K. W. Fischer, "Thought and Affect in American and Chinese Learners' Beliefs about Learning," in *Motivation, Emotion, and Cognition: Integrative Perspectives on Intellectual Functioning and Development*, ed. D. Y. Dai and R. J. Sternberg (Mahwah, NJ: Erlbaum, 2004), 385–418, 411.

Notes to Chapter 3

1. See I. J. Roseman, "Appraisals, Rather Than Unpleasantness or Muscle Movements, Are the Primary Determinants of Specific Emotions," *Emotion*, 4, no. 2

(2004): 145–150; C. A. Smith and L. D. Kirby, "Affect and Cognitive Appraisal Processes," in *Handbook of Affect and Social Cognition*, ed. J. P. Forgas (Mahwah, NJ: Erlbaum, 2001), 75–92; B. Weiner, *An Attributional Theory of Motivation and Emotion* (New York: Springer-Verlag, 1986); B. Weiner, *Judgments of Responsibility: A Foundation for a Theory of Social Conduct* (New York: Guilford Press, 1995).

2. J. M. Gottman, L. F. Katz, and C. Hooven, *Meta-Emotion: How Families Communicate Emotionally* (Mahwah, NJ: Erlbaum, 1997).

3. K. G. Allred, "Anger and Retaliation: Toward an Understanding of Impassioned Conflict in Organizations," in *Research on Negotiations in Organizations, vol. 7*, ed. R. J. Bies, R. J. Lewicki, and B. H. Sheppard (Greenwich, CT: JAI Press, 1999), 27–58; J. R. Averill, *Anger and Aggression: An Essay on Emotion* (New York: Springer-Verlag, 1982); J. R. Averill, "Illusions of Anger," in *Aggression and Violence: Social Interactionist Perspectives*, ed. R. B. Felson and J. T. Tedeschi (Washington, DC, 1993), 171–192.

4. See, among others, R. E. Nisbett and T. D. Wilson, "Telling More Than We Can Know: Verbal Reports on Mental Processes," *Psychological Review*, 84 (1977): 231–259; T. D. Wilson, *Strangers to Ourselves* (Cambridge, MA: Harvard University Press, 2002).

5. D. J. Bem, "Self-Perception Theory," *Advances in Experimental Social Psychology*, vol. 6, ed. L. Berkowitz (New York: Academic Press, 1972), 1–62. See also E. Shafir, I. Simonson, and A. Tversky, "Reason-Based Choice," *Cognition*, 49 (1993): 11–36.

6. Quoted in R. Jervis, "Understanding Beliefs," *Political Psychology*, 27, no. 5 (2006): 641–663, 657.

7. K. G. Allred, "Anger and Retaliation in Conflict: The Role of Attribution," in *The Handbook of Conflict Resolution: Theory and Practice*, ed. M. Deutsch and P. T. Coleman (San Francisco: Jossey-Bass, 2000), 236–255.

8. F. Heider, *The Psychology of Interpersonal Relations* (New York: Wiley, 1958).

9. E. E. Jones and K. E. Davis, "From Acts to Dispositions: The Attribution Process in Person Perception," *Advances in Experimental Social Psychology*, vol. 2, ed. L. Berkowitz (Orlando, FL: Academic Press, 1965); H. H. Kelley, "Attribution Theory in Social Psychology," *Nebraska Symposium on Motivation*, ed. D. Levine (Morristown: University of Nebraska Press, 1967).

10. E. E. Jones and V. A. Harris, "The Attribution of Attitudes," *Journal of Experimental Social Psychology*, 3 (1967): 1–24.

11. See, for example, L. D. Ross, "The Intuitive Psychologist and His Shortcomings: Distortions in the Attribution Process," in *Advances in Experimental Social Psychology*, vol. 10, ed. L. Berkowitz (Orlando, FL: Academic Press, 1977).

12. T. F. Pettigrew, "The Ultimate Attribution Error: Extending Allport's Cognitive Analysis of Prejudice," *Personality and Social Psychology Bulletin*, 5 (1979): 461–476. See also M. Hewstone, "The 'Ultimate Attribution Error'? A Review of the Literature on Intergroup Causal Attribution," *European Journal of Social Psychology*, 20 (1990): 311–335.

13. G. V. Bodenhausen, "Stereotypic Biases in Social Decision Making and Memory: Testing Process Models of Stereotype Use," *Journal of Personality and Social Psychology*, 55 (1988): 726–737.

14. I. L. Janis, *Groupthink: Psychological Studies of Policy Decisions and Fiascoes* (Boston: Houghton Mifflin, 1982).

15. See, for example, E. Stern and B. Sundelius, "The Essence of Groupthink," *Mershon International Studies Review*, 38, no. 1 (1994): 101–107; M. E. Turner and

A. R. Pratkanis, "Mitigating Groupthink by Stimulating Constructive Conflict," in *Using Conflict in Organizations*, ed. C. K. W. D. Dreu and E. v. d. Vliert (London: Sage, 1997), 53–71; P. Hart, E. K. Stern, and B. Sundelius, eds., *Beyond Groupthink: Political Group Dynamics and Foreign Policy-Making* (Ann Arbor: University of Michigan Press, 1997).

16. See M. J. Lerner, *The Belief in a Just World: A Fundamental Delusion* (New York: Plenum Press, 1980), and for his later work, M. J. Lerner, "The Justice Motive: Where Social Psychologists Found It, How They Lost It and Why They May Not Find It Again," *Personality and Social Psychology Review*, 7 (2003): 388–399.

17. L. D. Ross and J. T. Jost, "Fairness Norms and the Potential for Mutual Agreements Involving Majority and Minority Groups," in *Research on Managing Groups and Teams* (Vol. 2): *Groups in Their Context*, ed. M. A. Neale, E. A. Mannix, and R. Wageman (Greenwich, CT: JAI Press, 1999), 93–114.

18. O. Brafman and R. Brafman, *Sway: The Irresistible Pull of Irrational Behavior* (New York: Doubleday Business, 2008).

19. E. Goffman, *Frame Analysis: An Essay on the Organization of Experience* (New York: Harper and Row, 1974).

20. See, for example, L. D. Ross and R. E. Nisbett, *The Person and the Situation: Perspectives of Social Psychology* (Philadelphia: Temple University Press, 1991), and V. Liberman, S. M. Samuels, and L. D. Ross, "The Name of the Game: Predictive Power of Reputations versus Situational Labels in Determining Prisoner's Dilemma Game Moves," *Personality and Social Psychology Bulletin*, 30, no. 10 (2004): 1–11.

21. See, for example, B. Arfi, "Resolving the Trust Predicament: A Quantum Game-Theoretic Approach," *Theory and Decision*, 59, no. 2 (2005): 127–174; P. Slovic, "The Construction of Preference," *American Psychologist*, 50, no. 5 (1995): 364–371; E. W. Piotrowski and J. Sladkowski, "An Invitation to Quantum Game Theory," *International Journal of Theoretical Physics*, 42, no. 5 (2003): 1089–1099; M. Zak, "Quantum Decision-Maker," *Information Sciences*, 128 (2000): 199–215; and J. Zaller, *The Nature and Origins of Mass Opinion* (Cambridge: Cambridge University Press, 1992).

22. A. Wendt, *Social Theory as Cartesian Science: An Auto-Critique From a Quantum Perspective* (Columbus, OH: www.humiliationstudies.org/documents/Wendt AutoCritique.pdf, 2004), 36, an early text in preparation for S. Guzzini and A. Leander, *Constructivism and International Relations: Alexander Wendt and His Critics* (New York: Routledge, 2006).

23. M. Deutsch, *The Resolution of Conflict: Constructive and Destructive Processes* (New Haven, CT: Yale University Press, 1973), 367.

24. R. Axelrod, *The Evolution of Cooperation* (London: Penguin Books, 1990).

25. M. Deutsch, "A Personal Perspective on the Development of Social Psychology in the Twentieth Century," in *Reflections on 100 Years of Experimental Social Psychology*, ed. A. Rodriguez and R. V. Levine (New York: Basic Books, 1999), 1–34, 23.

26. See M. Deutsch, *Oppression and Conflict* (Skovde, Sweden: Plenary address given at the annual meetings of the International Society of Justice Research in Skovde, Sweden on June 17, 2002; retrieved November 20, 2002, from www.cpa .ca/epw/epw/Deutsch.pdf, 31.

27. See, for example, I. L. Janis and L. Mann, *Decision Making: A Psychological Analysis of Conflict, Choice, and Commitment* (New York: Free Press, 1977); R. Jervis,

R. N. Lebow, and J. G. Stein, *Psychology and Deterrence* (Baltimore, MD: Johns Hopkins University Press, 1985); or R. N. Lebow, *Between Peace and War: The Nature of International Crisis* (Baltimore, MD: Johns Hopkins University Press, 1981).

28. R. Jervis, "Understanding Beliefs," *Political Psychology*, 27, no. 5 (2006): 641–663, 654.

29. Marshall McLuhan is credited with having coined the phrase "global village" in 1959, after borrowing it from Wyndham Lewis; the term appeared in H. M. McLuhan, *The Gutenberg Galaxy: The Making of Typographic Man* (Toronto: University of Toronto Press, 1962).

Notes to Chapter 4

1. Celebrate Humanity campaign 2002, see www.olympic.org. Emphasis is added.

2. R. Rorty, *Contingency, Irony, and Solidarity* (Cambridge: Cambridge University Press, 1989), 92. I thank Howard Richards for making me aware of this quote.

3. T. L. Friedman, "The Humiliation Factor," *New York Times*, November 9, Section 4 (2003): 11.

4. A. Lazare, *On Apology* (New York: Oxford University Press, 2004), 262–263.

5. Please see www.dynamicsofconflict.iccc.edu.pl/index.php?page=home for an overview over the Peter Coleman's workgroup, and publications at www.tc .edu/icccr/research.html, and at www.tc.columbia.edu/icccr/centerPublica Coleman.html. See also www.beyondintractability.org.

6. P. T. Coleman, "Characteristics of Protracted, Intractable Conflict: Toward the Development of a Metaframework—I," *Peace and Conflict: Journal of Peace Psychology*, 9, no. 1 (2003): 1–37, 1.

7. Ibid., Abstract.

8. Ibid.; see also P. T. Coleman, "Paradigmatic Framing of Protracted, Intractable Conflict: Towards the Development of a Meta-Framework—II," *Peace and Conflict: Journal of Peace Psychology*, 10, no. 3 (2004): 197–235, and P. T. Coleman, "Conflict, Complexity, and Change: A Meta-Framework for Addressing Protracted, Intractable Conflicts—III," *Peace and Conflict: Journal of Peace Psychology*, 12, no. 4 (2006): 325–348.

9. L. Kriesberg, "Nature, Dynamics, and Phases of Intractability," in *Grasping the Nettle: Analyzing Cases of Intractable Conflict*, ed. C. A. Crocker, F. O. Hampson, and P. Aall (Washington, DC: U.S. Institute of Peace Press, 2005).

10. P. T. Coleman et al., "Intractable Conflict as an Attractor: A Dynamical Systems Approach to Conflict Escalation and Intractability," *American Behavioral Scientist*, 50 (2007): 14–54, retrieved on March 3, 2008, from abs.sagepub.com/cgi/ content/abstract/50/11/1454; M. Wessels and C. Monteiro, "Psychosocial Intervention and Post-War Reconstruction in Angola: Interweaving Traditional and Western Approaches," in *Peace, Conflict and Violence: Peace Psychology for the 21st Century*, ed. D. J. Christie, R. V. Wagner, and D. D. N. Winter (Upper Saddle River, NJ: Prentice Hall, 2001), 262–276; C. R. Mitchell, *Conflict, Social Change, and Conflict Resolution: An Enquiry* (Berlin: Berghof Research Center for Constructive Conflict Management, 2005), retrieved on March 3, 2008, from www.berghof-handbook .net/uploads/download/mitchell_handbook.pdf); and L. L. Putnam and T. Peterson, "The Edwards Aquifer Dispute: Shifting Frames in a Protracted Conflict," in

Making Sense of Intractable Environmental Conflicts: Concepts and Cases, ed. R. J. Lewicki, B. Gray, and M. Elliott (Washington, DC: Island Press, 2003).

11. P. T. Coleman, J. S. Goldman, and K. Kugler, *Emotional Intractability: The Effects of Emotional Roles on Aggression and Rumination in Conflict* (New York: International Center for Cooperation and Conflict Resolution, Teachers College, Columbia University, 2007), retrieved on December 19, 2007, from www.tc.columbia.edu/ICCCR/Documents/Coleman/PC_Emotinal_Intractability.pdf), 3, referring also to P. T. Coleman, "Characteristics of Protracted, Intractable Conflict: Toward the Development of a Metaframework—I," *Peace and Conflict: Journal of Peace Psychology*, 9, no. 1 (2003): 1–37; C. A. Crocker, F. O. Hampson, and P. Aall, eds., *Grasping the Nettle: Analyzing Cases of Intractable Conflict* (Washington, DC: U.S. Institute of Peace Press, 2005); T. L. Friedman, "The Humiliation Factor," *New York Times*, November 9, Section 4 (2003): 11; and J. M. Gottman, J. D. Murray, C. C. Swanson, R. Tyson, and K. R. Swanson, *The Mathematics of Marriage: Dynamic Non-Linear Models* (Cambridge, MA: MIT Press, 2005).

12. T. Webb, *Towards a Mature Shame Culture: Theoretical and Practical Tools for Personal and Social Growth* (Sidney: University of Western Sydney, doctoral dissertation, 2003).

13. W. G. Parrott, *Emotions in Social Psychology: Essential Readings* (Philadelphia, PA: Psychology Press, 2001).

14. J. L. Stamm, "The Meaning of Humiliation and Its Relationship to Fluctuations in Self-Esteem," *International Review of Psycho-Analysis*, 5 (1978): 425–433, 425.

15. P. Gilbert, "The Evolution of Social Attractiveness and Its Role in Shame, Humiliation, Guilt and Therapy," *British Journal of Medical Psychology*, 70, no. 2 (1997): 113–147, 134.

16. J. S. Goldman and P. T. Coleman, *How Humiliation Fuels Intractable Conflict: The Effects of Emotional Roles on Recall and Reactions to Conflictual Encounters* (New York: International Center for Cooperation & Conflict Resolution, Teachers College, Columbia University, 2005).

17. Adapted from T. Webb, *Towards a Mature Shame Culture: Theoretical and Practical Tools for Personal and Social Growth* (Sidney: University of Western Sydney, doctoral dissertation, 2003), 74.

18. S. S. Tomkins, *Affect Imagery and Consciousness* (volumes 1–4) (New York: Springer, 1962)

19. P. Ekman, W. V. Friesen, and P. C. Ellsworth, *Emotion in the Human Face: Guidelines for Research and Integration of Findings* (New York: Pergamon Press, 1972).

20. C. E. Izard, *The Psychology of Emotions.* (New York and London: Plenum Press, 1991).

21. C. Darwin, *The Expression of the Emotions in Man and Animals*, 3rd ed. (London: HarperCollins, 1872).

22. Adapted from W. G. Parrott, *Emotions in Social Psychology: Essential Readings* (Philadelphia, PA: Psychology Press, 2001).

23. P. T. Coleman, J. S. Goldman, and K. Kugler, *Emotional Intractability: The Effects of Emotional Roles on Aggression and Rumination in Conflict* (New York: International Center for Cooperation and Conflict Resolution, Teachers College, Columbia University, 2007), retrieved on December 19, 2007, from www.tc.columbia.edu/ICCCR/Documents/Coleman/PC_Emotinal_Intractability.pdf), 6–7.

24. Ibid., 28–29.

25. See, among others, S. S. Tomkins, *Affect Imagery and Consciousness* (volumes 1–4) (New York: Springer, 1962), and D. L. Nathanson, *Shame and Pride: Affect Sex and the Birth of the Self* (New York: Norton, 1992); shame has been addressed from a wide range of angles, see, for example, R. Dalziell, D. Parker, and I. Wright, eds., *Shame and the Modern Self* (Melbourne: Australian Scholarly Publishers, 1996); S. S. Dickerson and M. E. Kemeny, "When the Social Self Is Threatened: Shame, Physiology, and Health," *Journal of Personality*, 72 (2004): 1191–1216; S. M. Retzinger, *Violent Emotions: Shame and Rage in Marital Quarrels* (Newbury Park, CA: Sage, 1991); G. Taylor, *Pride, Shame and Guilt: Emotions of Self-Assessment* (Oxford: Clarendon Press, 1985); G. Taylor, "Shame, Integrity, and Self-Respect," *Dignity, Character, and Self-Respect*, ed. R. S. Dillon (New York: Routledge, 1995), 157–178; C. D. Schneider, *Shame, Exposure and Privacy* (New York: Norton, 1992); L. B. Smedes, *Shame and Grace: Healing the Shame We Don't Deserve* (San Francisco: HarperCollins, 1993); B. Williams, *Shame and Necessity* (Los Angeles: University of California Press, 1993).

26. HumanDHS, www.humiliationstudies.org/whoweare/don.php.

27. D. C. Klein, "The Humiliation Dynamic: Viewing the Task of Prevention from a New Perspective," *Journal of Primary Prevention*, 12, no. 2 (1991) and 3 (1992), Special issue, Section I: The humiliation dynamic, Section II: Those at risk of humiliation, Section III: Systemically related humiliation, Section IV: Dealing with humiliation.

28. L. M. Hartling and T. Luchetta, "Humiliation: Assessing the Impact of Derision, Degradation, and Debasement," *Journal of Primary Prevention*, 19, no. 5 (1999): 259–278. See also L. M. Hartling, *Humiliation: Real Pain, a Pathway to Violence* (Boston: Preliminary draft of a paper prepared for Round Table 2 of the 2005 Workshop on Humiliation and Violent Conflict, Columbia University, New York, December 15–16, 2005).

29. Personal communication, May 12, 2007.

30. Personal communication, January 25, 2008.

31. R. L. Hale, "The Role of Humiliation and Embarrassment in Serial Murder," *Psychology. A Journal of Human Behaviour*, 31, no. 2 (1994): 17–23.

32. C. Negrao, *Shame, Humiliation, and Childhood Sexual Abuse: Comparing Discrete and Clinical Theories of Emotion* (New York: Columbia University, doctoral dissertation, 2004).

33. See, among many, H. Silver and S. M. Miller, "From Poverty to Social Exclusion: Lessons from Europe," in *Poverty & Race in America: The Emerging Agendas*, ed. C. Hartman (Lexington, MA: Lexington Books, 2006), 57–70, or M. Sayler, *Humiliation and the Poor: A Study in the Management of Meaning* (Santa Barbara, CA: doctoral dissertation, Fielding Graduate Institute, 2004).

34. S. R. Pynchon, *Resisting Humiliation in Schooling: Narratives and Counter-Narratives* (Washington, DC: University of Washington, doctoral dissertation, 2005).

35. B. Benoliel, *Public Humiliation as a Mitigator in Criminal Sentencing* (Minneapolis, MN: Walden University, doctoral dissertation, 2006); see also J. Braithwaite, *Crime, Shame and Reintegration* (Cambridge: Cambridge University Press, 1989), and H. Zehr, *The Little Book of Restorative Justice* (Intercourse, PA: Good Books, 2002).

36. See, for example, M. R. Manning, *Individuation and Resilience in Older Women: How Awareness and Resolution of Culturally Induced Experiences of Shame and Humiliation Contribute to Intentional, Ongoing Development* (Santa Barbara, CA: Fielding Graduate University, doctoral dissertation, 2005).

37. H. B. Lewis, *Shame and Guilt in Neurosis* (New York: International Universities Press, 1971).

38. T. J. Scheff, *Bloody Revenge: Emotions, Nationalism and War* (Chicago: University of Chicago Press, 1990); T. J. Scheff, *Emotions, the Social Bond and Human Reality. Part/Whole Analysis* (Cambridge: Cambridge University Press, 1997); P. Masson, "When Soldiers Prefer Death to Humiliation," *Historia*, no. 596 (1996): 54–56; S. Vachon, "Passer de L'Appauvrissement à La Pauvreté Comme on Va de L'Humiliation à L'Humilité," *Voix et Images*, 18, no. 2 (1993): 382–387; V. V. Znakov, "The Comprehension of Violence and Humiliation Situations by Aggressive Adolescents," *Voprosy-Psikhologii*, January–February (1990): 20–27.

39. I. W. Charny, "A Personality Disorder of Excessive Power Strivings," *Israel Journal of Psychiatry*, 34, no. 1 (1997): 3–17.

40. J. Gilligan, *Violence: Our Deadly Epidemic and How to Treat It* (New York: Putnam, 1996).

41. See, among many others, A. Honneth, "Recognition and Moral Obligation," *Social Research*, 64, no. 1 (1997): 16–35, and A. Honneth, *The Struggle for Recognition: The Moral Grammar of Social Conflicts* (Cambridge: Polity Press, 1995), or Z. Bauman, "The Great War of Recognition," *Theory, Culture and Society*, 18, no. 2-643 (2001): 137–150.

42. M. Scheler, *Über Ressentiment und moralisches Werturteil* (Leipzig: Engelmann, 1912).

43. M. Scheler, *Zur Phänomenologie und Theorie der Sympathiegefühle und von Liebe und Haß* (Halle: Max Niemeyer, 1913).

44. L. Greenfeld, *Nationalism: Five Roads to Modernity* (Cambridge, MA: Harvard University Press, 1992); L. Greenfeld, "Nationalism and Modernity," *Social Research*, 63, no. 1 (1996): 3–40. Read also M. Hechter, "The Dynamics of Secession," *Acta Sociologica*, 35 (1992): 267–283, on the dynamics of secession.

45. I. Berlin, "The Bent Twig: On the Rise of Nationalism," in *The Crooked Timber of Humanity: Chapters in the History of Ideas*, ed. H. Hardy (London: Fontana Press, 1991), 238–261.

46. See, among others, D. Smith, *Globalization, the Hidden Agenda* (Cambridge: Polity Press, 2006), or D. Smith, "The Humiliating Organisation: The Functions and Disfunctions of Degradation," in *The Civilized Organisation*, ed. A. v. Iterson, W. Mastenbroek, T. Newton, and D. Smith (Amsterdam: Benjamin, 2002).

47. See, for example, S. J. Heine et al., "Is There a Universal Need for Positive Self-Regard?," *Psychological Review*, 106 (1999): 766–794.

48. C. Taylor, "The Politics of Recognition," in *Multiculturalism: Examining the Politics of Recognition*, ed. A. Gutman (Princeton, NJ: Princeton University Press, 1994).

49. C. Taylor, *The Ethics of Authenticity* (Cambridge, MA: Harvard University Press, 1990).

50. A. Maalouf, *In the Name of Identity: Violence and the Need to Belong* (New York: Arcade Publishing, 2001).

51. Tajfel's social identity theory proposes that the social part of our identity derives from the groups to which we belong. He suggests that we, by favoring attributes of our own groups over those of out-groups, acquire a positive sense of who we are and an understanding of how we should act toward ingroup and outgroup members. See H. Tajfel, *Human Groups and Social Categories: Studies in Social Psychology* (Cambridge: Cambridge University Press, 1981); H. Tajfel, C. Fraser, and J. M. F. Jaspars, *The Social Dimension: European Developments in Social Psychology* (Cambridge: Cambridge University Press, 1984); H. Tajfel and J. C. Turner, "The

Social Identity Theory of Intergroup Behavior," in *Psychology of Intergroup Relations*, ed. S. Worchel and W. G. Austin (Chicago: Neston-Hall, 1986), 204–227. For more literature, see, for example, D. Howitt and M. G. Billig, *Social Psychology: Conflicts and Continuities: An Introductory Textbook* (Milton Keynes: Open University Press, 1989); H. Tajfel, ed., *Differentiation between Social Groups: Studies in Intergroup Behavior* (London: Academic Press, 1978); H. Tajfel et al., "Social Categorization and Intergroup Behaviour," *European Journal of Social Psychology*, 1 (1971): 149–178; H. Tajfel, *Differentiation between Social Groups: Studies in the Social Psychology of Intergroup Relations* (London: European Association of Experimental Social Psychology, with Academic Press, 1978); H. Tajfel and Minority Rights Group, *The Social Psychology of Minorities* (London: Minority Rights Group, 1978); H. Tajfel, C. Fraser, and J. M. F. Jaspars, *The Social Dimension: European Developments in Social Psychology* (Cambridge: Cambridge University Press, 1984); J. C. Turner, "Towards a Cognitive Redefinition of the Social Group," in *Social Identity and Intergroup Relations*, ed. H. Tajfel (Cambridge: Cambridge University Press, 1982), 15–40.

52. See, for example, M. G. Billig, *Social Psychology and Intergroup Relations* (London: European Association of Experimental Social Psychology, with Academic Press, 1976); M. G. Billig, *Arguing and Thinking* (London: Cambridge University Press, 1987); M. G. Billig, S. Condor, D. Edwards, M. Gane, D. Middleton, and A. Radley, *Ideological Dilemmas. A Social Psychology of Everyday Thinking* (London: Sage, 1988); M. G. Billig, *Ideology and Opinions. Studies in Rhetorical Psychology* (London: Sage, 1991); M. G. Billig, *Banal Nationalism* (London: Sage, 1995); M. G. Billig, "Remembering the Particular Background of Social Identity Theory," in *Social Groups and Identities. Developing the Legacy of Henri Tajfel*, ed. W. P. Robinson (Oxford: Butterworth, Heinemann, 1996); M. G. Billig, "Politics as an Appearance and Reality Show: The Hermeneutics of Suspicion," in *Political Communications: The General Election Campaign of 2005*, ed. D. Wring, J. Green, R. Mortimore, and S. Atkinson (London: Palgrave Macmillan, 2007), 223–238; M. G. Billig, "Towards a Critique of the Critical: Editorial," *Discourse & Society*, 11, no. 3 (2000): 291–292, retrieved on August 24, 2006, from das.sagepub.com.

53. April 13–15, 2007, at the Institute of Discourse and Cultural Studies and Department of Applied Psychology, Zhejiang University, Hangzhou, China.

54. Lu Hsun; real name Zhou Shuren.

55. Lu Xun, *Call to Arms (Na Han)* (Beijing: Foreign Languages Press, 1981).

56. R. E. Nisbett and D. Cohen, *Culture of Honor: The Psychology of Violence in the South* (Boulder, CO: Westview Press, 1996).

57. B. Wyatt-Brown, *Southern Honor: Ethics and Behavior in the Old South* (New York: Oxford University Press, 1982).

58. W. I. Miller, *Humiliation and Other Essays on Honor, Social Discomfort, and Violence* (Ithaca, NY: Cornell University Press, 1993).

59. E. Lindner, *Making Enemies: Humiliation and International Conflict* (Westport, CT: Greenwood/Praeger Security International, 2006), 158–160.

60. R. Guha and G. C. Spivak, eds., *Selected Subaltern Studies* (New York: Oxford University Press, 1988).

61. A. Nandy, *Exiled at Home: Comprising At the Edge of Psychology, The Intimate Enemy, and Creating a Nationality* (New Delhi: Oxford University Press, 1998).

62. H.-G. Gadamer, *Truth and Method* (London: Sheed and Ward, 1989), discusses truth and method.

63. See literature about action research in the ejournal Action Research International, www.scu.edu.au/schools/gcm/ar/ari/arihome.html, and B. Atweh, S. Kemmis, and P. Weeks, *Action Research in Practice: Partnership for Social Justice in Education* (London: Routledge, 1998); N. Boyarsky and N. Murphy, *Action Research* (London: Black Dog, 1998); T. R. Carson and D. J. Sumara, *Action Research as a Living Practice* (New York: Lang, 1997); D. J. Greenwood and M. Levin, *Introduction to Action Research: Social Research for Social Change* (Thousand Oaks, CA: Sage, 1998); B. Gustavsen, "From Experiments to Network Building: Trends in the Use of Research for Reconstructing Working Life," *Human Relations*, 51, no. 3 (1998): 431–448; R. Kalleberg, *Action Research as Constructive Sociology* (Oslo: Institute for Social Research, 1989); A. J. Marrow, "Risks and Uncertainties in Action Research," *Journal of Social Issues*, 20, no. 3 (1964): 5–20; J. McNiff, *Action Research: Principles and Practice* (London: Routledge, 1992); G. E. Mills, *Action Research: A Guide for the Teacher Researcher* (Upper Saddle River, NJ: Merrill, 2000); P. Reason, ed., *Participation in Human Inquiry* (London: Sage, 1994); P. Reason and J. Rowan, *Human Inquiry: A Sourcebook of New Paradigm Research* (Chichester: Wiley, 1985); P. Reason, *Human Inquiry in Action: Developments in New Paradigm Research* (London: Sage, 1988); S. Srivastva and D. L. Cooperrider, *Appreciative Management and Leadership: The Power of Positive Thought and Action in Organizations* (San Francisco: Jossey-Bass, 1990); E. T. Stringer, *Action Research: A Handbook for Practitioners*, 2nd ed. (Thousand Oaks, CA: Sage, 1999); W. R. Torbert, *The Power of Balance: Transforming Self, Society, and Scientific Inquiry* (Newbury Park, CA: Sage, 1991); W. F. Whyte, *Participatory Action Research* (Newbury Park, CA: Sage, 1991); O. Zuber-Skerritt, *Action Research for Change and Development* (Aldershot: Avebury, 1991).

64. M. O'Neill, "Re-Imagining Diaspora through Ethno-Mimesis: Humiliation, Human Dignity and Belonging," in *Reimagining Diasporas: Transnational Lives and the Media*, ed. O. Guedes-Bailey, M. Georgiou, and R. Harindranath (London: Palgrave Macmillan, 2006).

65. For example, J. P. Tangney et al., "Shamed into Anger? The Relation of Shame and Guilt to Anger and Self-Reported Agression," *Journal of Personality and Social Psychology*, 62, no. 4 (1992): 669–675.

66. For example, J. R. Averill, "Studies on Anger and Aggression: Implications for Theories of Emotion," in *Emotions in Social Psychology: Essential Readings*, ed. W. G. Parrott (Philadelphia: Psychology Press, 2001), 337–352.

67. See, for example, M. H. Bond, "Culture and Collective Violence: How Good People, Usually Men, Do Bad Things," in *Are We Lost in Translations? On Intercultural Encounters in Treatment of Complex Trauma and PTSD*, ed. B. Drozdek and J. P. Wilson (New York: Springer, 2006).

68. See, for a recent publication, T. Masumoto et al., "A Typology of Facework Behaviors in Conflicts with Best Friends and Relative Strangers," *Communication Quarterly*, 4, no. 48 (2000): 397–419.

69. S. J. Pharr, *Losing Face: Status Politics in Japan* (Berkeley: University of California Press, 1990).

70. E. Goffman, *Stigma: Notes on the Management of Spoiled Identity* (Englewood Cliffs, NJ: Prentice Hall, 1953), E. Goffman, *Interaction Ritual: Essays in Face-to-Face Behavior* (Hawthorne: Aldine de Gruyter, 1967).

71. T. Millon, *Modern Psychopathology: A Biosocial Approach to Maladaptive Learning and Functioning* (Philadelphia: Saunders, 1969), T. Millon, *Theories of Psychopathology* (Philadelphia: Saunders, 1967).

72. L. Foo and G. Margolin, "A Multivariate Investigation of Dating Aggression," *Journal of Family Violence*, 10, no. 4 (1995): 351–377.

73. W. Mischel, A. L. De Smet, and E. Kross, "Self-Regulation in the Service of Conflict Resolution," in *The Handbook of Conflict Resolution: Theory and Practice*, ed. M. Deutsch and P. T. Coleman (San Francisco: Jossey-Bass, 2000), 256–275.

74. P. T. Coleman, J. S. Goldman, and K. Kugler, *Emotional Intractability: The Effects of Emotional Roles on Aggression and Rumination in Conflict* (New York: International Center for Cooperation and Conflict Resolution, Teachers College, Columbia University, 2007), retrieved on December 19, 2007, from www.tc.columbia.edu/ICCCR/Documents/Coleman/PC_Emotional_Intractability.pdf, 3.

75. A. Nadler, "Inter-Group Helping Relations as Power Relations: Maintaining or Challenging Social Dominance between Groups through Helping," *Journal of Social Issues*, 58, no. 3 (2002): 487–502. See also S. Rosen, "Perceived Inadequacy and Help-Seeking (Vol. II)," in *New Directions in Helping. Help-Seeking*, ed. B. M. De Paulo et al. (New York: Academic Press, 1983), 73–107. Kenneth Gergen and Mary Gergen write about the humiliating aspect of help-receiving in the mid-1970s, see their current work at www.swarthmore.edu/SocSci/kgergen1/text7.html. I owe this reference to Michael Harris Bond.

76. See, for example, M. B. Anderson, *Do No Harm: How Aid Can Support Peace—or War* (Boulder, CO: Lynne Rienner, 1999).

77. M. Maren, *The Road to Hell: The Ravaging Effects of Foreign Aid and International Charity* (New York: Free Press, 1997).

78. S. Karterud, *Om Forsoning* (Oslo: Lecture given at the Eitinger-seminaret 2001 "Hvordan forstå forsoningsprosesser: Fremmede og bremsende faktorer"). See also Jerrold Post's work on the profile of Saddam Hussein.

79. B. S. Steinberg, "Shame and Humiliation in the Cuban Missile Crisis. A Psychoanalytic Perspective," *Political Psychology*, 12, no. 4 (1991): 653–690, B. S. Steinberg, *Shame and Humiliation: Presidential Decision Making on Vietnam* (Montreal: McGill-Queen's, 1996).

80. See, among others, E. Staub, *The Psychology of Good and Evil: Why Children, Adults, and Groups Help and Harm Others* (Cambridge: Cambridge University Press, 2003); E. Staub, "The Roots of Evil: Social Conditions, Culture, Personality and Basic Human Needs," *Personality and Social Psychology Review*, 3, no. 3 (1999): 179–192.

81. A. Margalit, *The Decent Society* (Cambridge, MA: Harvard University Press, 1996).

82. A. Margalit, *The Ethics of Memory* (Cambridge, MA: Harvard University Press, 2002).

83. Ibid. See also Chapter 7, titled "The Humiliation Addiction" (pp. 127–140) in E. Lindner, *Making Enemies: Humiliation and International Conflict* (Westport, CT: Greenwood/Praeger Security International, 2006).

84. P. T. Coleman, J. S. Goldman, and K. Kugler, *Emotional Intractability: The Effects of Emotional Roles on Aggression and Rumination in Conflict* (New York: International Center for Cooperation and Conflict Resolution, Teachers College, Columbia University, 2007), retrieved on December 19, 2007, from www.tc.columbia.edu/ICCCR/Documents/Coleman/PC_Emotinal_Intractability.pdf, 9–12. See also P. T. Coleman, "Intractable Conflict," in *The Handbook of Conflict Resolution: Theory and Practice*, ed. M. Deutsch, P. T. Coleman, and E. C. Marcus, 2nd ed. (San Francisco: Jossey-Bass, 2006).

85. A. Nadler, "Social-Psychological Analysis of Reconciliation: Instrumental and Socio-Emotional Routes to Reconciliation," *Peace Education Worldwide: The Concepts, Underlying Principles, and Research*, ed. G. Salomon and B. Nevo (Mahwah, NJ: Erlbaum, 2002).

86. J. S. Goldman and P. T. Coleman, *How Humiliation Fuels Intractable Conflict: The Effects of Emotional Roles on Recall and Reactions to Conflictual Encounters* (New York: International Center for Cooperation and Conflict Resolution, Teachers College, Columbia University, 2005), 15–16. See also P. T. Coleman, K. Kugler, and J. S. Goldman, *The Privilege of Humiliation: The Effects of Social Roles and Norms on Immediate and Prolonged Aggression in Conflict* (New York: Paper submitted to the 20th annual conference of the International Association for Conflict Management, 2007).

87. V. D. Volkan, D. A. Julius, and J. V. Montville, eds., *The Psychodynamics of International Relationships. Vol II: Unofficial Diplomacy at Work* (Lexington, MA: Lexington Books, 1991).

88. V. D. Volkan, *Blind Trust: Large Groups and Their Leaders in Times of Crisis and Terror* (Charlottesville, VA: Pitchstone Publishing, 2004). See also V. D. Volkan, *Bloodlines: From Ethnic Pride to Ethnic Terrorism* (New York: Farrar, Straus and Giroux, 1997).

89. A. Banks and J. V. Jordan, "The Human Brain: Hardwired for Connections," *Research & Action Report*, 28, no. 2, Spring/Summer (2007): 8–11, retrieved on July 20, 2007, from www.wcwonline.org/joomla/index.php?option=com_content&task=view&id=1358&itemid=198.

90. N. I. Eisenberger and M. D. Lieberman, "Why It Hurts to Be Left Out: The Neurocognitive Overlap between Physical Pain and Social Pain," in *The Social Outcast: Ostracism, Social Exclusion, Rejection, and Bullying*, ed. K. Williams, J. P. Forgas, and W. v. Hippel (New York: Psychology Press, 2005), 109–127, 110.

91. V. S. Ramachandran, *Mirror Neurons and Imitation Learning as the Driving Force behind "the Great Leap Forward" in Human Evolution.* Edge Foundation, 2000, retrieved on August 14, 2006 from www.edge.org/documents/archive/edge69.html.

92. See also E. G. Lindner, *The Relevance of Humiliation Studies for the Prevention of Terrorism* (Budapest: Paper presented to the NATO Advanced Research Workshop Indigenous Terrorism: Understanding and Addressing the Root Causes of Radicalisation among Groups with an Immigrant Heritage in Europe, March 2008).

93. H. E. Albers, K. L. Huhman, and R. L. Meisel, "Hormonal Basis of Social Conflict and Communication," in *Hormones, Brain, and Behavior, vol. 1*, ed. D. W. Pfaff (Boston: Academic Press, 2002), 393–433; J. K. Kiecolt-Glaser et al., "Negative Behavior during Marital Conflict Is Associated with Immunological Down-Regulation," *Psychosomatic Medicine*, 55 (1993): 395–409; J. K. Kiecolt-Glaser et al., "Marital Conflict in Older Adults: Endocrinological and Immunological Correlates," *Psychosomatic Medicine*, 59 (1997): 339–349; B. N. Uchino, *Social Support and Physical Health: Understanding the Health Consequences of Relationships* (New Haven, CT: Yale University Press, 2004).

94. Didier Sornette, personal communication, May 26, 2005.

95. See www.humiliationstudies.org/publications/publications.php, where I attempt to provide access to related publications.

96. *Choice*, March 2007, see www.greenwood.com/catalog/C9109.aspx.

97. The Big Five, also known as the Five Factor Model (FFM), is among the most well-known models to organize the many different conceptions of personality that theorists have developed and that different tests measure. See, for example, L. M. Saulsman and A. C. Page, "The Five-Factor Model and Personality Disorder Empirical Literature: A Meta-Analytic Review," *Clinical Psychology Review, 23* (2004): 1055–1085.

98. Geert H. Hofstede has developed a classic systematization of culture dimensions and describes five dimensions of culture. See, for example, G. H. Hofstede, *Culture's Consequences: Comparing Values, Behaviors, Institutions, and Organizations across Nations,* 2nd ed. (Thousand Oaks, CA: Sage, 2001).

99. A. Wendt, "Why a World State Is Inevitable," *European Journal of International Relations,* 9, no. 4 (2003): 491–542, 510–511.

100. C. Taylor, *The Ethics of Authenticity* (Cambridge, MA: Harvard University Press, 1990).

101. See, for example, www.intractableconflict.org/docs/appendix_6.jsp.

102. See, among others, S. Haffner and G. Bateson, *Der Vertrag von Versailles. Mit Beiträgen von Sebastian Haffner, Gregory Bateson u. a.* (München: Matthes und Seitz, 1978); N. Elias, *The Germans. Power Struggles and the Development of Habitus in the Nineteenth and Twentieth Centuries [Studien über die Deutschen: Machtkämpfe und Habitusentwicklung im 19. und 20. Jahrhundert]* (Cambridge: Polity Press, 1996); T. J. Scheff, *Bloody Revenge: Emotions, Nationalism and War* (Chicago: University of Chicago Press, 1990); T. J. Scheff, "Hitler's Appeal: Alienation, Shame-Rage, and Revenge," in *Violence and Society: A Reader*, ed. M. Silberman (Upper Saddle River, NJ: Prentice Hall, 2003).

103. M. A. K. Matossian, "Ideologies of Delayed Industrialisation: Some Tensions and Ambiguities," in *Political Change in Underdeveloped Countries: Nationalism and Communism*, ed. J. H. Kautsky (New York: Wiley, 1962).

104. E. G. Lindner, *The Feeling of Being Humiliated: A Central Theme in Armed Conflicts. A Study of the Role of Humiliation in Somalia, and Great Lakes Region, between the Warring Parties, and in Relation to Third Intervening Parties. Outline of Research Project* (Oslo: University of Oslo, project description, published by Human Dignity and Humiliation Studies, 1996), www.humiliationstudies.org/whoweare/evelin02.php.

105. I thank Dagfinn Føllesdal for his support in formulating these questions.

106. See www.humiliationstudies.org/whoweare/evelin02.php.

107. HumanDHS, www.humiliationstudies.org.

108. See an interesting article on extreme mass homicide by D. G. Dutton, E. O. Boyanowsky, and M. H. Bond, "Extreme Mass Homicide: From Military Massacre to Genocide," *Aggression and Violent Behavior,* 10 (2005): 437–473.

Notes to Chapter 5

1. A. Onal, *Honour Killing: Stories of Men Who Killed* (London: Saqi Books, 2008). According to Stephanie Nebehay, " 'Honor Killings' of Women Said on Rise Worldwide," *Reuters Dispatch,* April 7 (2000), honor killings have been reported in Bangladesh, Britain, Brazil, Ecuador, Egypt, India, Israel, Italy, Jordan, Pakistan, Morocco, Sweden, Turkey, and Uganda. Nadera Shalhoub-Kevorkian, *Mapping and Analyzing the Landscape of Femicide in Palestine*, Research report submitted by the Women's Center for Legal Aid and Counseling (WCLAC) to UNIFEM, 2000, prefers to use the term *femicide*; see literature she uses in her work, such as

Notes

L. Abu-Odeh, "Crimes of Honor and the Construction of Gender in Arab Society," *Women and Sexuality in Muslim Society*, ed. P. Ilkkaracan (Istanbul: Women for Women's Human Rights, 2000), 363–380; S. Al-Khayyat, *Honour and Shame: Women in Modern Iraq* (London: Saqi, 1990); N. Baker, P. Gregware, and M. Cassidy, "Family Killing Fields: Honor Rationales in the Murder of Women," *Violence against Women*, 5, no. 2 (1999): 164–184; K. Polk, "Masculinity, Honour, and Confrontational Homicide?" in *Just Boys Doing Business? Men, Masculinities and Crime*, ed. T. Newburn and E. Stanko (London: Routledge and Kegan Paul, 1994); J. Radford and D. Russel, eds., *Femicide: The Politics of Woman Killing* (Buckingham: Open University Press, 1992); J. Hanmer, M. Hester, L. Kelly, and J. Radford, eds., *Women, Violence and Male Power: Feminist Activism, Research and Practice* (Buckingham: Open University Press, 1996); and K. Stout, "'Intimate Femicide': Effect of Legislation and Social Services," in *Femicide: The Politics of Woman Killing*, ed. J. Radford and D. Russel (Buckingham: Open University Press, 1992). One of the most empathetic presentations of the moral and emotional dilemmas entailed in honor killings is in Tatort, ARD, *Schatten der Angst*, 6 April 2008. *Tatort* ("Crime Scene") is a long-running German/Austrian, former Swiss, crime TV series.

2. Mohamad Mahathir, former Malaysian prime minister, is one of the advocators of the view that the claim that human rights are universal represents a humiliating form of imperialism through which powerful rich Western countries wish to dictate which rights they consider most important. However, clearly, although human rights arguments can be abused in bad faith and instrumentalized for inherently incompatible ends, this does not automatically entail that this abuse defines their essence.

3. See Chapter 4.

4. K. Mahbubani, *The New Asian Hemisphere: The Irresistible Shift of Global Power to the East* (New York: PublicAffairs, 2008).

5. See note 1 in the Introduction.

6. W. Ury, *Getting to Peace. Transforming Conflict at Home, at Work, and in the World* (New York: Viking, 1999).

7. Ibid., XVII.

8. See also C. L. Flinders, *Rebalancing the World: Why Women Belong and Men Compete and How to Restore the Ancient Equilibrium* (San Francisco: Harper, 2002), who conceptualizes human history in similar ways.

9. J. Haas, *Warfare and the Evolution of Culture* (Santa Fe, NM: Santa Fe Institute, 1998, Working papers 98-11-088), retrieved on November 15, 2002, from www.santafe.edu/sfi/publications/Working-Papers/98-10-088.pdf), 8.

10. J. Waller, *Becoming Evil: How Ordinary People Commit Genocide and Mass Killing* (Oxford: Oxford University Press, 2002).

11. F. Nietzsche, *On the Genealogy of Morals* (New York: Vintage Books, 1989/1887).

12. H. Morgenthau, *Scientific Man versus Power Politics* (Chicago: University of Chicago Press, 1946).

13. P. Giorgi, *The Origins of Violence by Cultural Evolution*, 2nd ed. (Brisbane: Minerva, 2001), downloadable from www.pierogiorgi.org/The-origins-of-violence-by-cultural-evolution.pdf, explains this point in detail.

14. Latin *circum* = around, *scribere* = to write, *circumscription* means limitation, enclosure, or confinement. The terms territorial or social circumscription address limitations in these respective areas.

15. P. J. Richerson, R. Boyd, and R. L. Bettinger, "The Origins of Agriculture as a Natural Experiment in Cultural Evolution" (Davis, CA: University of California, Center for Agricultural History, retrieved in November 2002 from www.des.ucdavis.edu/faculty/Richerson/Origins_Ag_IV3.htm, 1999)..

16. J. Diamond, *Guns, Germs, and Steel* (New York: Norton, 1997).

17. J. H. Herz, "Idealist Internationalism and the Security Dilemma," *World Politics,* 2 (1950): 157–180.

18. R. Jervis, R. N. Lebow, and J. G. Stein, *Psychology and Deterrence* (Baltimore, MD: Johns Hopkins University Press, 1985).

19. J. Snyder, "Perceptions of the Security Dilemma in 1914," in *Psychology and Deterrence,* ed. R. Jervis, R. N. Lebow, and J. G. Stein (Baltimore, MD: Johns Hopkins University Press, 1985), 153–179. See also J. Snyder and B. Walters, eds., *The Security Dilemma and Intervention in Civil Wars* (New York: Columbia University Press, 1999).

20. A. Collins, "State-Induced Security Dilemma Maintaining the Tragedy," *Cooperation and Conflict,* 39, no. 1 (2004): 27–44.

21. B. Posen, "The Security Dilemma and Ethnic Conflict," *Survival,* 35, no. 1 (1993): 27–47, and R. Hardin, *One for All: The Logic of Group Conflict* (Princeton, NJ: Princeton University Press, 1995).

22. See Joshua Goldstein, *War and Gender: How Gender Shapes the War Systems and Vice Versa* (Cambridge: Cambridge University Press, 2001), and how he links war and gender division.

23. One of Brazil's last uncontacted Indian tribes has been spotted in 2008 in the far western Amazon jungle near the Peruvian border, according to the National Indian Foundation (www.funai.gov.br).

24. See her most recent book, R. Eisler, *The Real Wealth of Nations: Creating a Caring Economics* (San Francisco: Berrett-Koehler, 2007).

25. Thucydides, *History of the Peloponnesian War* (The Internet Classics Archive at classics.mit.edu/Thucydides/pelopwar.html, 431), in the First Book, Chapter 3, about the Peloponnesian War. Thucydides was an early realist in international relations theory, as was Sun Tzu (or Sunzi, c. 544 B.C.–496 B.C.), the famous Chinese military strategist who wrote the *Art of War.*

26. D. Kagan, "Honor, Interest, and Nation-State," in *Honor among Nations,* ed. E. Abrams (Washington, DC: Ethics and Public Policy Center, 1998), or R. N. Lebow, "Fear, Interest, and Honour: Outlines of a Theory of International Relations," *International Affairs,* 82, no. 3, May (2006): 431–448.

27. P. Bourdieu, *Outline of a Theory of Practice* (Cambridge: Cambridge University Press, 1977).

28. Ibid., 11–12.

29. Research group in the Power of the Ruler and the Ideology of Rulership in Nordic Culture 800–1200, at the Centre for Advanced Study, 2007/2008, www.cas.uio.no/research/0708rulership/index.php.

30. G. Steinsland, *Myth and Power in the Cultural Transformation of the Nordic Countries from Viking to Medieval Age* (Oslo: Centre for Advanced Study at the Norwegian Academy of Science and Letters, Opening ceremony, September 4, 2007), Lecture by Professor Gro Steinsland, ILN, University of Oslo, Group leader at CAS, 2007/2008, retrieved on March 1, 2008, from www.cas.uio.no/research/0708rulership/lecture_040907.pdf.

31. Adapted from E. G. Lindner, "Were Ordinary Germans Hitler's 'Willing Executioners'? Or Were They Victims of Humiliating Seduction and Abandonment? The Case of Germany and Somalia," *IDEA: A Journal of Social Issues*, 5, no. 1 (2000), www.ideajournal.com/articles.php?id=31.

32. A. Hitler, *Mein Kampf* (London: Pimlico, original work published in 1925–26, 1999), 165.

33. Ibid., 167.

34. During my fieldwork in Germany (since childhood, due to being born into a highly traumatized family displaced from Silesia), I met many who confessed that they felt *raped* by Hitler, not *loved*.

35. W. I. Miller, *Humiliation and Other Essays on Honor, Social Discomfort, and Violence* (Ithaca, NY: Cornell University Press, 1993), 175, emphasis in original.

36. See the note explaining "emotion and the emergence of an individuated self" in Chapter 1.

37. As to human rights, see, among many others, M. A. Glendon, *A World Made New: Eleanor Roosevelt and the Universal Declaration of Human Rights* (New York: Random House, 2001); M. R. Ishay, *The History of Human Rights: From Ancient Times to the Globalization Era* (Berkeley: University of California Press, 2004); R. Jolly, L. Emmerij, D. Ghai, and F. Lapeyre, *UN Contributions to Development Thinking and Practice* (Bloomington: Indiana University Press, 2004); P. G. Lauren, *The Evolution of International Human Rights: Visions Seen*, 2nd ed. (Philadelphia: University of Pennsylvania Press, 2003); T. Lindholm, *The Emergence and Development of Human Rights: An Interpretation with a View to Cross-Cultural and Interreligious Dialogue* (Oslo: Norwegian Institute of Human Rights, 1997); J. W. Nickel, *Making Sense of Human Rights*, rev. ed. (Washington, DC: Georgetown University Press, 2004); R. Niezen, *A World beyond Difference: Cultural Identity in the Age of Globalization* (Malden, MA: Blackwell, 2004); K. Sellars, *The Rise and Rise of Human Rights* (Stroud: Sutton, 2002); G. Soros, *Open Society: Reforming Global Capitalism* (London: Little, Brown, 2000); C. Tomuschat, *Human Rights: Between Idealism and Realism* (Oxford: Oxford University Press, 2003).

38. See also the important work on the information age by Manuel Castells, *The Information Age: Economy, Society and Culture. The Rise of the Network Society*, vol. 1 (Cambridge, MA: Blackwell, 1996); M. Castells, *The Information Age: Economy, Society and Culture. The Power of Identity*, vol. 2 (Cambridge, MA: Blackwell, 1997); M. Castells, *The Information Age: Economy, Society and Culture. End of Millennium*, vol. 3 (Cambridge, MA: Blackwell, 1997).

39. See, for example, C. A. Lutz and L. Abu-Lughod, eds., *Language and the Politics of Emotion* (Cambridge: Cambridge University Press, 1990), L. Abu-Lughod, *Veiled Sentiments: Honour and Poetry in a Bedouin Society* (Berkeley: University of California Press, 1986).

40. C. J. Montiel, "Political Psychology of Nonviolent Democratic Transitions in Southeast Asia," *Journal of Social Issues*, 62, no. 1 (2006): 173–190, retrieved on August 14, 2007, from www.blackwell-synergy.com/doi/pdf/10.1111/j.1540-4560.2006.00445.x.

41. D. J. Christie, "What Is Peace Psychology the Psychology Of?," *Journal of Social Issues*, 62, no. 1 (2006): 1–17, retrieved on August 14, 2007, from www.blackwell-synergy.com/doi/pdf/10.1111/j.1540-4560.2006.00436.x, 13.

42. R. W. Fuller, *Somebodies and Nobodies: Overcoming the Abuse of Rank* (Gabriola Island, Canada: New Societies Publishers, 2003).

43. There is a vast amount of literature on globalization to draw on. See, for example, Z. Bauman, *Globalization: The Human Consequences* (Cambridge: Polity Press, 1998). For classic analyses in urban sociology, see Georg Simmel and his views on metropolitan life and its effects on the psyche. See, furthermore, M. R. Singer, *Intercultural Communication: A Perceptual Approach* (Englewood Cliffs, NJ: Prentice Hall, 1987), and M. Castells, *The Information Age: Economy, Society and Culture. The Power of Identity*, vol. 2 (Cambridge, MA: Blackwell, 1997).

44. Even though there is a connection between equality and equal dignity—the connection being "hidden" in the human rights stipulation that equal chances and enabling environments for all are necessary to protect human dignity.

45. E. G. Lindner, *Definitions of Terms as They Are Used in Lindner's Writing*, Human Dignity and Humiliation Studies, 2003. www.humiliationstudies.org/whoweare/evelin02.php.

46. G. Hardin, "The Tragedy of the Commons," *Science*, 162 (1968): 1243–1248.

47. D. Ariely, "The Cost of Social Norms: Why We Are Happy to Do Things but Not When We Are Paid to Do Them," in *Predictably Irrational: The Hidden Forces That Shape Our Decisions* (New York: HarperCollins, 2008), 67–88. See also the work by Lee D. Ross and his colleagues reported in Chapter 3. Their experiments show that people are willing to share resources equally.

48. P. L. Berger, "On the Obsolescence of the Concept of Honor," *Archives Européennes de Sociologie*, 11, no. 2 (1970): 339–347.

49. M. Heidegger, *Being and Time* (New York: Harper & Row, 1962), 260–274.

50. R. Fisher, W. Ury, and B. Patton, *Getting to Yes: Negotiating Agreement without Giving in* (New York: Houghton Mifflin, 1991).

51. G. A. Bonanno and J. T. Jost, "Conservative Shift among High-Exposure Survivors of the September 11th Terrorist Attacks," *Basic and Applied Social Psychology*, 28, no. 4 (2006): 311–323, Abstract.

52. Duchenne laughs and smiles involve activity in the orbicularis oculi muscles surrounding the eye and have been described by G. B. A. Duchenne de Bolougne, *The Mechanism of Human Facial Expression* (New York: Cambridge University Press, 1862). See also P. Ekman and W. V. Friesen, "Felt, False, and Miserable Smiles," *Journal of Nonverbal Behavior*, 6 (1982): 238–252, M. G. Frank, P. Ekman, and W. V. Friesen, "Behavioral Markers and the Recognizability of the Smile of Enjoyment," *Journal of Personality and Social Psychology*, 64 (1993): 83–93. Non-Duchenne expressions are smiles that lack both the contraction of the orbicularis muscles and the experience of positive emotion. They serve various functions, such as the communication of social politeness, deception, or appeasement.

53. See P. M. Rodriguez Mosquera, *Humiliation and Racism* (Perth, Australia: Paper Presented at the National Conference on Racism in Global Context, November 9–11, 2007, Murdoch University, 2007) for work on humiliation and racism.

54. D. Kagan, "Honor, Interest, and Nation-State," in *Honor among Nations*, ed. E. Abrams (Washington, DC: Ethics and Public Policy Center, 1998).

55. A. Koestler, *The Act of Creation* (New York: Macmillan, 1964), pp. 35–36.

56. M. Deutsch, *Oppression and Conflict* (Skovde, Sweden: Plenary address given at the annual meetings of the International Society of Justice Research in Skovde, Sweden on June 17, 2002), retrieved November 20, 2002, from www.cpa.ca/epw/epw/Deutsch.pdf, 35–36.

57. M. A. Fineman, *The Myth of Autonomy: A Theory of Dependency* (New York: New Press, 2004), 203.

58. Ibid., 31.

59. Personal communication, September 9, 2005.

60. See, for example, M. H. Bond, "Unity in Diversity: Orientations and Strategies for Building a Harmonious, Multicultural Society," in *Social Psychology and Cultural Context*, ed. J. Adamopoulos and Y. Kashima (Thousand Oaks, CA: Sage, 1998), 17–40, and J. A. Banks, P. Cookson, G. Gay, W. D. Hawley, J. J. Irvine, S. Nieto, J. W. Schofield, and W. G. Stephan, "Diversity within Unity: Essential Principles for Teaching and Learning in a Multicultural Society" (Seattle: Center for Multicultural Education, College of Education, University of Washington, Seattle, 2001), www.educ.washington.edu/coetestwebsite/pdf/DiversityUnity.pdf.

61. J. E. Bradshaw, *Healing the Shame That Binds You* (Deerfield Beach, FL: Health Communications, 2005).

62. See also E. G. Lindner, "The Concept of Human Dignity," in *Human Dignity: Concepts, Challenges and Solutions. The Case of Africa*, ed. H. Fischer and N. Quénivet (Berlin: Berliner Wissenschaftsverlag, 2008).

63. P. Gay, *The Enlightenment: An Interpretation* (New York: Norton, 1996).

64. R. S. Dillon, ed., *Dignity, Character, and Self-Respect* (New York: Routledge, 1995).

Notes to Chapter 6

1. G. Lakoff and M. Johnson, *Philosophy in the Flesh: The Embodied Mind and Its Challenge to Western Thought* (New York: Basic Books, 1999).

2. G. Kaufman, *The Psychology of Shame: Theory and Treatment of Shame-Based Syndromes* (New York: Springer, 1989).

3. J. E. Bradshaw, *Healing the Shame That Binds You* (Deerfield Beach, FL: Health Communications, 2005).

4. See D. Smith, "Organisations and Humiliation: Looking beyond Elias," *Organization*, 8, no. 3 (2001): 537–560, whom I thank for coining the words conquest/relegation/reinforcement/inclusion humiliation.

5. E. G. Lindner, "Humiliation—Trauma That Has Been Overlooked: An Analysis Based on Fieldwork in Germany, Rwanda/Burundi, and Somalia," *TRAUMATOLOGYe*, 7, no. 1 (2001): article 3 (32 pages), tmt.sagepub.com/cgi/content/abstract/7/1/43.

6. Adapted from D. Smith, "Organisations and Humiliation: Looking beyond Elias," *Organization*, 8, no. 3 (2001): 537–560, 543.

7. T. J. Scheff, personal communication, December 7, 2006. See also T. J. Scheff, "Shame and the Social Bond: A Sociological Theory," *Sociological Theory*, 18, no. 1 (2000): 84–99.

8. See J. P. Tangney, "Humility," in *Handbook of Positive Psychology*, ed. C. R. Snyder and S. J. Lopez (London: Oxford University Press, 2002), 411–419.

9. September 12–13, 2003, Maison des Sciences de l'Homme de l'Homme, Paris, www.humiliationstudies.org/whoweare/annualmeeting02.php.

10. See related work by H. Zehr, *Changing Lenses: A New Focus for Crime and Justice* (Scottdale, PA: Herald Press, 1990), H. Zehr, *The Little Book of Restorative Justice* (Intercourse, PA: Good Books, 2002).

11. T. Webb, *Working with Shame and Other Strong Emotions: Experiential Workshop Script from "Personal and Political Tools for Social Change" Course* (Sidney: Centre for Popular Education, University of Technology, 2005).

12. Tony Webb, personal communication, May 16, 2005.

13. See T. Webb, *Towards a Mature Shame Culture: Theoretical and Practical Tools for Personal and Social Growth* (Sidney: University of Western Sydney, PhD thesis, 2003), 196.

14. Interview with Andrew Denton, retrieved on July 4, 2007, from www.abc.net.au/tv/enoughrope/transcripts/s1968333.htm.

15. T. Webb, *Working with Shame and Other Strong Emotions: Experiential Workshop Script from "Personal and Political Tools for Social Change" Course* (Sidney: Centre for Popular Education, University of Technology, 2005), 14.

16. Ibid., 14.

17. Personal communication, May 16, 2008.

18. In an interview on November 15, 1997, in Oslo, Norway.

19. A Cambridge University study has found a direct link between the amount of money traders make and testosterone levels, see J. M. Coates and J. Herbert, "Endogenous Steroids and Financial Risk-Taking on a London Trading Floor," *Proceedings of the National Academy of Sciences*, 105, no. 16 (2008): 6167–6172, www.pnas.org/content/105/16/6167.full.pdf+html.

20. Linda Hartling writes (personal communication, July 22, 2007): "Perhaps, as Scheff seems to imply, 'some' working-class clients have more difficulty acknowledging 'shame' because their shame is actually humiliation (unjust degrading mistreatment)?! Perhaps members of the working classes have difficulty acknowledging shame because they have been beaten down by the daily humiliation and demoralization of living in a society that exploits the working class and the poor? Perhaps it is the upper social classes who are more likely in need of 'acknowledging their shame'?"

21. The International Panel of Eminent Personalities to Investigate the 1994 Genocide in Rwanda and the Surrounding Events, *Rwanda: The Preventable Genocide*. Retrieved on September 30, 2000, from www.oau-oua.org, 2000), chapter 16, paragraph 4.

22. See, for example, E. G. Lindner, "Humiliation and Reactions to Hitler's Seductiveness in Post-War Germany: Personal Reflections," *Social Alternatives*, 25, Special Issue: Humiliation and History in Global Perspectives, no. 1, (2006): 6–11; E. G. Lindner, "Were Ordinary Germans Hitler's 'Willing Executioners'? Or Were They Victims of Humiliating Seduction and Abandonment? The Case of Germany and Somalia," *IDEA: A Journal of Social Issues*, 5, no. 1 (2000), www.ideajournal.com/articles.php?id=31.

23. L. Festinger, *A Theory of Cognitive Dissonance* (Stanford, CA: Stanford University Press, 1957).

24. C. Tavris and E. Aronson, *Mistakes Were Made, but Not by Me: Why We Justify Foolish Beliefs, Bad Decisions, and Hurtful Acts* (Orlando, FL: Harcourt, 2007).

25. O. W. Holmes, "Contagiousness of Puerperal Fever," *New England Quarterly Journal of Medical Surgery*, 1 (1843): 503–530.

26. C. M. De Costa, "The Contagiousness of Childbed Fever": A Short History of Puerperal Sepsis and Its Treatment," *Medical Journal of Australia*, 177, no. 11/12 (2002): 668–671, retrieved on February 25, 2008, from www.mja.com.au/public/issues/177_11_021202/dec10354_fm.html#i1067496.

27. Ibid., quoting from R. W. Wertz and D. C. Wertz, *Lying-in: A History of Child-birth in America* (New York: New York Free Press, 1977).

28. R. W. Wertz and D. C. Wertz, *Lying-in: A History of Childbirth in America* (New York: New York Free Press, 1977).

29. C. Chen, *Chinese Children's Humiliation at School* (Minneapolis: University of Minnesota, doctoral dissertation, 2004).

Notes to Chapter 7

1. J. B. Miller, *Toward a New Psychology of Women*, 2nd ed. (Boston: Beacon Press, 1986).

2. A. Lazare, *On Apology* (New York: Oxford University Press, 2004), 164.

3. M. Deutsch, "Cooperation and Competition," in *The Handbook of Conflict Resolution: Theory and Practice*, ed. M. Deutsch and P. T. Coleman (San Francisco: Jossey-Bass, 2000), 21–40, 33.

4. P. H. Winne, "Key Issues in Modeling and Applying Research on Self-Regulated Learning," *Applied Psychology: An International Review*, 54 (2005): 232–238. See also R. F. Baumeister and K. D. Vohs, eds., *Handbook of Self-Regulation: Research, Theory, and Applications* (New York: Guilford Press, 2004).

5. D. Y. Dai, "Putting It All Together: Some Concluding Thoughts," in *Motivation, Emotion, and Cognition: Integrative Perspectives on Intellectual Functioning and Development*, ed. D. Y. Dai and R. J. Sternberg (Mahwah, NJ: Erlbaum, 2004), 419–432.

6. M. Csikszentmihalyi, *Creativity: Flow and the Psychology of Discovery and Invention* (New York: Harper Perennial, 1996).

7. G. Labouvie-Vief and M. M. González, "Dynamic Integration: Affect Optimization and Differentiation in Development," in *Motivation, Emotion, and Cognition: Integrative Perspectives on Intellectual Functioning and Development*, ed. D. Y. Dai and R. J. Sternberg (Mahwah, NJ: Erlbaum, 2004), 237–272.

8. G. A. Bonanno, "Emotion Self-Regulation," in *Emotions: Current Issues and Future Directions*, ed. T. J. Mayne and G. A. Bonanno (New York: Guilford Press, 2001), 251–285.

9. W. T. Powers, *Behavior: The Control of Perception* (Chicago: Aldine, 1973), W. T. Powers, *Making Sense of Behavior: The Meaning of Control* (New Canaan, CT: Benchmark, 1998).

10. C. S. Carver and M. F. Scheier, *Attention and Self-regulation: A Control Theory Approach to Human Behavior* (New York: Springer, 1981); C. S. Carver and M. F. Scheier, "Control Theory: A Useful Conceptual Framework for Personality—Social, Clinical and Health Psychology," *Psychological Bulletin*, 92 (1982): 111–135.

11. R. F. Baumeister, T. F. Heatherton, and D. M. Tice, *Losing Control: How and Why People Fail at Self-regulation* (New York: Academic Press, 1994); K. P. Leith and R. F. Baumeister, "Why Do Bad Moods Increase Self-Defeating Behavior?: Emotion, Risk-taking, and Self-regulation," *Journal of Personality and Social Psychology*, 71, no. 6 (1996): 1250–1267.

12. G. A. Bonanno, "Emotion Self-Regulation," in *Emotions: Current Issues and Future Directions*, ed. T. J. Mayne and G. A. Bonanno (New York: Guilford Press, 2001), 251–285, 257.

13. V. J. Marsick and A. Sauquet, "Learning through Reflection," in *The Handbook of Conflict Resolution: Theory and Practice*, ed. M. Deutsch and P. T. Coleman (San Francisco: Jossey-Bass, 2000), 382–399, 398.

14. For a comprehensive treatment, see, for example, M. J. Apter, *Motivational Styles in Everyday Life: A Guide to Reversal Theory* (Washington, DC: American Psychological Association, 2001).

15. D. Y. Dai, "Putting It All Together: Some Concluding Thoughts," in *Motivation, Emotion, and Cognition: Integrative Perspectives on Intellectual Functioning and Development*, ed. D. Y. Dai and R. J. Sternberg (Mahwah, NJ: Erlbaum, 2004), 419–432, 421.

16. H. C. Ellis and P. W. Ashbrook, "Resource Allocation Model of the Effects of Depressed Mood States on Memory," in *Affect, Cognition, and Social Behavior*, ed. K. Fiedler and J. P. Forgas (Toronto: Hogrefe, 1988), 25–43. For depression as functional adaptation, see R. M. Nesse, "Is Depression an Adaptation?," *Archives of General Psychiatry*, 57 (2000): 14–20, www-personal.umich.edu/%7Enesse/Articles/IsDepAdapt-ArchGenPsychiat-2000.pdf.

17. G. Mandler, *Mind and Body: Psychology of Emotion and Stress* (New York: Norton, 1984).

18. D. Y. Dai, "Putting It All Together: Some Concluding Thoughts," in *Motivation, Emotion, and Cognition: Integrative Perspectives on Intellectual Functioning and Development*, ed. D. Y. Dai and R. J. Sternberg (Mahwah, NJ: Erlbaum, 2004), 419–432, 422.

19. Ibid., 422. See also R. J. Sternberg and J. E. Davidson, eds., *The Nature of Insight* (Cambridge, MA: MIT Press, 1995); P. Thagard, "The Passionate Scientist: Emotion in Scientific Cognition," in *The Cognitive Basis of Science*, ed. P. Carruthers, S. Stich, and M. Siegal (Cambridge: Cambridge University Press, 2002), 235–250.

20. C. S. Dweck, J. A. Mangels, and C. Good, "Motivational Effects on Attention, Cognition, and Performance," in *Motivation, Emotion, and Cognition: Integrative Perspectives on Intellectual Functioning and Development*, ed. D. Y. Dai and R. J. Sternberg (Mahwah, NJ: Erlbaum, 2004), 41–56, 42, and J. Pascual-Leone and J. Johnson, "Affect, Self-Motivation, and Cognitive Development: A Dialectical Constructivist View," in *Motivation, Emotion, and Cognition: Integrative Perspectives on Intellectual Functioning and Development*, ed. D. Y. Dai and R. J. Sternberg (Mahwah, NJ: Erlbaum, 2004), 197–235, 222.

21. C. S. Dweck, J. A. Mangels, & C. Good, "Motivational Effects on Attention, Cognition, and Performance," in *Motivation, Emotion, and Cognition: Integrative Perspectives on Intellectual Functioning and Development*, ed. D. Y. Dai and R. J. Sternberg (Mahwah, NJ: Erlbaum, 2004), 41–56, 43.

22. M. Yoshikawa, *The "Double Swing" Model of Eastern-Western Intercultural Communication* (Honolulu, HI: Paper prepared for the Seminar on Communication Theory from Eastern and Western Perspectives, East-West Communication Institute, 1980), M. Yoshikawa, "The 'Double Swing' Model of Intercultural Communication Between the East and West," in *Communication Theory: Eastern and Western Perspectives*, ed. D. L. Kincaid (San Diego, CA: Academic Press, 1987), 319–329.

23. M. Buber, *I and Thou* (Edinburgh: Clark, translated from *Ich und Du*, Leipzig: Infelverlag, 1923, 1944); N. Nakayama, *Mujunteki Sosoku No Roni [The Logic of Soku]* (Kyoto,: Hyakka En, 1973), 24–29, as explained by E. I. Dow, *Approaching Intercultural Communication from the Space Between* (Tokyo: Seminar given at the 20th Annual Conference of the Society for Intercultural Education, Training, and Research [SIETAR] Japan, June 26, 2005, Rikkyo University).

24. See, for example, H. Masaaki, "The Road to a Theology of *Soku*," *Nanzan Bulletin*, 22 (1998): 59–74, paper written for the 10th Nanzan Symposium, "What does Christianity have to Learn from Buddhism? The Dialogue among Religions, Nanzan Institute for Religion & Culture, Nagoya, Japan, retrieved on May 29, 2008, from www.nanzan-u.ac.jp/SHUBUNKEN/publications/Bulletin_and_Shoho/pdf/ 22-Honda.pdf.

25. J. N. Martin, T. K. Nakayama, and L. A. Flores, "A Dialectical Approach to Intercultural Communication," in *Readings in Intercultural Communication: Experiences and Contexts*, ed. J. N. Martin, T. K. Nakayama, and L. A. Flores, 2nd ed. (Boston: McGraw-Hill, 2002), 3–13.

26. P. A. Levine, *Waking the Tiger: Healing Trauma* (Berkeley, CA: North Atlantic Books, 1997).

27. Quoted in T. J. Scheff, *Attachment, Attunement, Attraction: 24 Kinds of "Love"* (Santa Barbara, CA: www.soc.ucsb.edu/faculty/scheff/29.html, 2003), 10, an earlier and longer draft of T. J. Scheff, "What Is This Thing Called Love? The Three A's: Attachment, Attunement and Attraction," in *Goffman Unbound: A New Paradigm for Social Science*, ed. T. J. Scheff (Boulder, CO: Paradigm Publishers, 2006), 111–124.

28. Ibid., 10.

29. Ibid., 13.

30. W. Mischel and A. L. De Smet, "Self-Regulation in the Service of Conflict Resolution," in *The Handbook of Conflict Resolution: Theory and Practice*, ed. M. Deutsch and P. T. Coleman (San Francisco: Jossey-Bass, 2000), 256–275, 268. See on fear and fitness, I. M. Marks and R. M. Nesse, "Fear and Fitness: An Evolutionary Analysis of Anxiety Disorders," *Ethology and Sociobiology*, 15 (1994): 247–261, and R. M. Nesse, "Natural Selection and Fear Regulation Mechanisms," *Behavioral and Brain Sciences*, 18 (1995): 309–310.

31. A. Lutz et al., "Regulation of the Neural Circuitry of Emotion by Compassion Meditation: Effects of Meditative Expertise," *PLoS ONE*, 3, no. 3, March (2008): 1–10, retrieved on May 5, 2008, from www.plosone.org/article/fetchObjectAttachment .action;jsessionid=08EB0F78CE4390AF332000D85499E55C?uri=info%3Adoi%2F10 .1371%2Fjournal.pone.0001897&representation=PDF; R. J. Davidson et al., "Alterations in Brain and Immune Function Produced by Mindfulness Meditation," *Psychosomatic Medicine*, 65 (2003): 564–570; D. Goleman, *Destructive Emotions: A Scientific Dialogue with the Dalai Lama* (Westminster, MD: Bantam Books, 2004).

32. O. Flanagan, "Destructive Emotions," *Consciousness and Emotion*, 1, no. 2 (2000): 259–281.

33. D. Goleman, *Destructive Emotions: A Scientific Dialogue with the Dalai Lama* (Westminster, MD: Bantam Books, 2004), p. 356.

34. R. J. Lifton, *The Protean Self: Human Resilience in the Age of Fragmentation* (Chicago: University of Chicago Press, 1999).

35. See, for example, J. Kabat-Zin, *Wherever You Go, There You Are: Mindfulness, Meditation* (New York: Hyperion Books, 1994).

36. D. Goleman, *Destructive Emotions: A Scientific Dialogue with the Dalai Lama* (Westminster, MD: Bantam Books, 2004), 358. See also P. Ekman et al., "Buddhist and Psychological Perspectives on Emotions and Well-Being," *Current Directions in Psychological Science*, 14, no. 2 (2005): 59.

37. E. R. Borris, *The Healing Power of Forgiveness* (Fairfax, VA: Paper prepared for course on Reconciliation Processes, Institute of Conflict Analysis and Resolution, George Mason University, March 13–15, 2000).

38. See V. E. Frankl, *Der Mensch auf der Suche nach Sinn. Zur Rehumanisierung der Psychotherapie* (Freiburg im Breisgau: Herder, 1973); V. Frankl, *Der Wille zum Sinn. Ausgewählte Vorträge über Logotherapie* (Bern-Stuttgart-Wien: Hans Huber, 1972); V. Frankl, *Man's Search for Meaning: An Introduction to Logotherapy* (Boston, MA: Beacon Press, 1963).

39. See K. R. Speeth and I. Friedlander, *Gurdjieff—Seeker of the Truth* (New York: Harper Colophon Books, Harper & Row, 1980).

40. C. T. Tart, *Living the Mindful Life: A Handbook for Living in the Present Moment* (Boston: Shambhala, 1994).

41. D. R. Matsumoto, H. S. Yoo, and J. A. LeRoux, "Emotion and Intercultural Communication," in *Handbook of Applied Linguistics, Volume 7: Intercultural Communication*, ed. H. Kotthoff and H. Spencer-Oatley (Berlin: Mouton-de Gruyter Publishers, 2005), 18. See also the earlier discussion on the discomfort caused by cognitive dissonance, and the related tendency of self-justification.

42. Ibid., 18.

43. Ibid., 19, see also J. H. Wasilewski, "Interculturalists as Dragon-Riders," *Journal of Intercultural Communication, SIETAR Japan*, 4 (2001): 75–89.

44. J. H. Wasilewski, "Interculturalists as Dragon-Riders," *Journal of Intercultural Communication, SIETAR Japan*, 4 (2001): 75–89.

45. See, for example, M. Spett, "The Two Critical Components of All Psychotherapies: Experience the Emotion, Change the Cognition," *Newsletter of the New Jersey Association of Cognitive-Behavioral Therapists*, November (2004), retrieved on December 5, 2008, from www.nj-act.org/spett.html.

46. See ibid.

47. M. Ridley, *The Origins of Virtue: Human Instincts and the Evolution of Cooperation* (London: Penguin, 1996).

48. Robert Jervis writes, "The relationship between interests and ideas (and of course neither concept is unproblematic) is one of the oldest in social science and if Marx, Mannheim, and Weber could not settle it, I certainly cannot . . . Even if we believe in the existence of objective interests, they do not dictate all beliefs" (R. Jervis, "Understanding Beliefs," *Political Psychology*, 27, no. 5 [2006]: 641–663, 658).

49. R. Axelrod and W. D. Hamilton, "The Evolution of Cooperation," *Science*, 211 (1981): 1390–1396; R. Axelrod, *The Evolution of Cooperation* (New York: Basic Books, 1984).

50. M. Deutsch, "A Personal Perspective on the Development of Social Psychology in the Twentieth Century," in *Reflections on 100 Years of Experimental Social Psychology*, ed. A. Rodriguez and R. V. Levine (New York: Basic Books, 1999), 1–34, 19–20.

51. P. T. Coleman, and M. Deutsch, "Some Guidelines for Developing a Creative Approach to Conflict," in *The Handbook of Conflict Resolution: Theory and Practice*, ed. M. Deutsch and P. T. Coleman (San Francisco: Jossey-Bass, 2000), 355–365, 363.

52. D. W. Johnson, R. T. Johnson, and D. Tjosvold, "Constructive Controversy: The Value of Intellectual Opposition," in *The Handbook of Conflict Resolution: Theory and Practice*, ed. M. Deutsch and P. T. Coleman (San Francisco: Jossey-Bass, 2000), 65–85, 66.

53. C. R. Snyder, "Hope Theory: Rainbows in the Mind," *Psychological Inquiry*, 13, no. 4 (2002): 249–275, Abstract.

54. Ibid., 255.

55. S. T. Michael, "Hope Conquers Fear: Overcoming Anxiety and Panic Attacks," in *Handbook of Hope: Theory, Measures, and Applications*, ed. C. R. Snyder (San Diego, CA: Academic, 2000), 355–378; C. R. Snyder, "Hope, Goal Blocking Thoughts, and Test-Related Anxieties," *Psychological Reports*, 84 (1999): 206–208.

56. C. R. Snyder and K. Pulvers, "Dr. Seuss, the Coping Machine, and 'Oh, the Places You Will Go,'" in *Coping and Copers: Adaptive Processes and People*, ed. C. R. Snyder (New York: Oxford University Press, 2001), 3–29; A. L. Stanton and P. R. Snider, "Coping with a Breast Cancer Diagnosis: A Prospective Study," *Health Psychology*, 12 (1993): 16–23.

57. C. R. Snyder, "Hope Theory: Rainbows in the Mind," *Psychological Inquiry*, 13, no. 4 (2002): 249–275, 261.

58. Ibid., 252. See also the earlier discussion of the so-called Duchenne smile as a marker of good coping and favorable long-term adjustment.

59. Ibid., 253.

60. C. L. Rusting, "Personality as a Moderator of Affective Influences on Cognition," in *Handbook of Affect and Social Cognition*, ed. J. P. Forgas (Mahwah, NJ: Erlbaum, 2001), 371–391, 388; for the Affect Infusion Model (AIM), see J. P. Forgas, "Mood and Judgment: The Affect Infusion Model (AIM)," *Psychological Bulletin*, 117 (1995): 39–66.

61. C. R. Snyder, S. C. Sympson, S. T. Michael, and J. Cheavens, "The Optimism and Hope Constructs: Variants on a Positive Expectancy Theme," in *Optimism and Pessimism*, ed. E. C. Chang (Washington, DC: American Psychological Association, 2000), 103–124; C. R. Snyder, J. Cheavens, and S. C. Sympson, "Hope: An Individual Motive for Social Commerce," *Group Dynamics: Theory, Research, and Practice*, 1 (1997): 107–118; C. R. Snyder, *The Psychology of Hope: You Can Get There from Here* (New York: Free Press, 1994); C. R. Snyder, "Hope and Optimism," in *Encyclopedia of Human Behavior*, vol. 2, ed. V. S. Ramachandran (San Diego, CA: Academic, 1994), 535–542.

62. C. R. Snyder et al., "Preferences of High- and Low-Hope People for Self-Referential Input," *Cognition & Emotion*, 12 (1998): 807–823.

63. J. C. Brunstein, "Personal Goals and Subjective Well-Being: A Longitudinal Study," *Journal of Personality and Social Psychology*, 65 (1993): 1061–1070; B. R. Little, "Personal Projects Analysis: Trivial Pursuits, Magnificent Obsessions, and the Search for Coherence," in *Personality Psychology: Recent Trends and Emerging Directions*, ed. D. M. Buss and N. Cantor (New York: Springer-Verlag, 1989), 15–31.

64. S. Coopersmith, *The Antecedents of Self-Esteem* (San Francisco: Freeman, 1967), 4.

65. C. R. Snyder, "Hope Theory: Rainbows in the Mind," *Psychological Inquiry*, 13, no. 4 (2002): 249–275, 262.

66. Ibid., 253.

67. Ibid., 261.

68. L. A. Sagan, *The Health of Nations: The Causes of Sickness and Well-Being* (New York: Basic Books, 1987).

69. C. R. Snyder, "Hope Theory: Rainbows in the Mind," *Psychological Inquiry*, 13, no. 4 (2002): 185.

70. Ibid., 184.

71. See, for example, F. Gomes de Matos, "Language, Peace, and Conflict Resolution," in *The Handbook of Conflict Resolution: Theory and Practice*, ed. M. Deutsch, P. T. Coleman, and E. C. Marcus, 2nd ed. (San Francisco: Jossey-Bass, 2006), 158–175.

72. S. Ellison, *Taking the War Out of Our Words: The Art of Powerful Non-Defensive Communication* (Berkeley, CA: Bay Tree Publishing, 2003).

73. A. Miller, *For Your Own Good: Hidden Cruelty in Child-Rearing and the Roots of Violence* (London: Virago Press, 1983).

74. G. Lakoff and M. Johnson, *Philosophy in the Flesh: The Embodied Mind and Its Challenge to Western Thought* (New York: Basic Books, 1999), 313–314.

75. Ibid., 327.

76. T. W. Adorno, E. Frenkel-Brunswick, D. J. Levinson, and R. N. Sanford, *The Authoritarian Personality* (New York: Harper, 1950).

77. G. Lakoff and M. Johnson, *Philosophy in the Flesh: The Embodied Mind and Its Challenge to Western Thought* (New York: Basic Books, 1999), 316.

78. E. Lindner, *Gender and Humiliation: The Power of Dignity in Love, Sex and Parenthood* (Westport, CT: Greenwood/Praeger Security International, 2009).

79. See, for example, A. Nadler, T. Malloy, and J. D. Fisher, eds., *Social Psychology of Inter-Group Reconciliation: From Violent Conflict to Peaceful Co-Existence* (Oxford: Oxford University Press, 2008).

80. T. J. Mayne, "Emotions and Health," in *Emotions: Current Issues and Future Directions*, ed. T. J. Mayne and G. A. Bonanno (New York: Guilford Press, 2001), 361–397, 361.

81. B. L. Fredrickson and C. Branigan, "Positive Emotions," in *Emotions: Current Issues and Future Directions*, ed. T. J. Mayne and G. A. Bonanno (New York: Guilford Press, 2001), 123–151, 123.

82. B. L. Fredrickson and R. W. Levenson, "Positive Emotions Speed Recovery from the Cardiovascular Sequelae of Negative Emotions," *Cognition & Emotion*, 12, no. 2 (1998): 191–220.

83. B. L. Fredrickson, "What Good Are Positive Emotions?," *Review of General Psychology*, 2 (1998): 300–319.

84. J. T. Moskowitz, "Emotion and Coping," in *Emotions: Current Issues and Future Directions*, ed. T. J. Mayne and G. A. Bonanno (New York: Guilford Press, 2001), 311–336, 325.

85. J. Kuhl, "A Theory of Self-development: Affective Fixation and the STAR Model of Personality Disorders and Related Styles," in *Motivational Psychology of Human Development*, ed. J. Heckhausen (Amsterdam: Elsevier, 2000), 187–211; J. Kuhl and A. Fuhrmann, "Decomposing Self-regulation and Self-control: The Volitional Components Inventory," in *Life Span Perspectives in Motivation and Control*, ed. J. Heckhausen and C. S. Dweck (Mahwah, NJ: Erlbaum, 1998), 15–49.

86. J. Pascual-Leone and J. Johnson, "Affect, Self-Motivation, and Cognitive Development: A Dialectical Constructivist View," in *Motivation, Emotion, and Cognition: Integrative Perspectives on Intellectual Functioning and Development*, ed. D. Y. Dai and R. J. Sternberg (Mahwah, NJ: Erlbaum, 2004), 197–235, 224.

87. E. A. Linnenbrink and P. R. Pintrich, "Role of Affect in Cognitive Processing in Academic Contexts," in *Motivation, Emotion, and Cognition: Integrative Perspectives on Intellectual Functioning and Development*, ed. D. Y. Dai and R. J. Sternberg (Mahwah, NJ: Erlbaum, 2004), 57–88, 72.

88. R. Fisher and D. L. Shapiro, *Beyond Reason: Using Emotions as You Negotiate* (New York: Penguin, 2005).

89. W. B. Pearce, *Toward Communicative Virtuosity: A Meditation on Modernity and Other Forms of Communication* (Santa Barbara, CA: School of Human and Organization Development, Fielding Graduate University, 2005), 1.

90. Ibid., 2.

91. S. Sigman, "Toward Study of the Consequentiality (Not Consequences) of Communication," in *The Consequentiality of Communication*, ed. S. Sigman (Hillsdale, NJ: Erlbaum, 1995), 1–14.

92. W. T. Powers, *Behavior: The Control of Perception* (Chicago: Aldine, 1973); W. T. Powers, *Making Sense of Behavior: The Meaning of Control* (New Canaan, CT: Benchmark, 1998).

93. W. B. Pearce, *Communication and the Human Condition* (Carbondale: Southern Illinois University Press, 1989).

94. W. B. Pearce, *Toward Communicative Virtuosity: A Meditation on Modernity and Other Forms of Communication* (Santa Barbara, CA: School of Human and Organization Development, Fielding Graduate University, 2005), 1.

95. A. Naess, "Through Spinoza to Mahayana Buddhism or through Mahayana Buddhism to Spinoza?," in *Spinoza's Philosophy of Man: Proceedings of the Scandinavian Spinoza Symposium 1977*, ed. J. Wetlesen (Oslo: University of Oslo Press, 1978), 143.

96. W. Fox, "Intellectual Origins of the 'Depth' Theme in the Philosophy of Arne Naess," *Trumpeter*, 9, no. 2 (1992), retrieved on December 15, 2000, from trumpeter. athabascau.ca/archives/content/v9.2/fox2.html, 5.

97. W. Fox, *Toward a Transpersonal Ecology: Developing New Foundations for Environmentalism* (Boston: Shambhala, 1990), Chapters 4 and 5.

98. K. Weingarten, *Compassionate Witnessing and the Transformation of Societal Violence: How Individuals Can Make a Difference* (New York: Adapted from *Common Shock: Witnessing Violence Every Day—How We Are Harmed, How We Can Heal*, printed by arrangement with Dutton, a member of Penguin Group, and copyright (c) Kaethe Weingarten, 2003), 2.

99. I. Kogan, "Breaking the Cycle of Trauma: From the Individual to Society," *Mind and Human Interaction*, 11, no. 1 (2000): 2–10; V. D. Volkan, *Bloodlines: From Ethnic Pride to Ethnic Terrorism* (New York: Farrar, Straus and Giroux, 1997).

100. D. Bar-On, *The Legacy of Silence: Encounters with Children of the Third Reich* (Cambridge, MA: Harvard University Press, 1989); V. D. Volkan, "The Tree Model: A Comprehensive Psychopolitical Approach to Unofficial Diplomacy and the Reduction of Ethnic Tension," *Mind and Human Interaction*, 10, no. 3 (1999): 142–210.

101. K. Weingarten, *Compassionate Witnessing and the Transformation of Societal Violence: How Individuals Can Make a Difference* (New York: Adapted from *Common Shock: Witnessing Violence Every Day—How We Are Harmed, How We Can Heal*, printed by arrangement with Dutton, a member of Penguin Group, and copyright (c) Kaethe Weingarten, 2003), 16.

102. E. Ohnuki-Tierney, *Kamikaze, Cherry Blossoms, and Nationalisms: The Militarization of Aesthetics in Japanese History* (Chicago: University of Chicago Press, 2002), 182.

103. Ibid., 183.

104. Ibid., 170–171.

105. J. W. Dower, *Embracing Defeat: Japan in the Wake of World War II* (New York: Norton, 1999), 157.

106. Ibid., 157.

107. J. Dewey, *Democracy and Education* (New York: Free Press, 1916).

108. A neo-Kohlbergian view on moral reasoning (see also Jürgen Habermas and Karl Otto Apel) that describes a person who bases her moral standards on

principles that she herself has evaluated and that she accepts as inherently valid, regardless of society's opinion.

109. P. Freire, *Education for Critical Consciousness* (New York: Continuum, 1973).

110. E. Mustakova-Possardt, "Education for Critical Moral Consciousness," *Journal of Moral Education*, 33, no. 3, September (2004): 245–269.

111. E. Staub, *The Roots of Evil: The Origins of Genocide and Other Group Violence* (Cambridge: Cambridge University Press, 1989).

112. W. J. Freeman, *Societies of Brains: A Study in the Neuroscience of Love and Hate* (Hillsdale, NJ: Erlbaum, 1995).

113. N. Elias, *What Is Sociology?* (London: Hutchinson, 1978).

114. P. A. Stokes, *Homo Gubernator: Emotions and Human Self-Steering* (Dublin: Department of Sociology, University College Dublin, unpublished manuscript, 2005), 86.

115. S. Milgram, *Obedience to Authority* (New York: Harper & Row, 1974).

116. Ibid., 5–6.

117. S. P. Oliner and P. M. Oliner, *The Altruistic Personality: Rescuers of Jews in Nazi Europe* (New York: Free Press, 1988).

118. J. M. Gottman, "The Mathematics of Love: A Talk with John Gottman," *Edge*, 4.14.04 (2004), retrieved on December 5, 2007, from www.edge.org/3rd_culture/gottman05/gottman05_index.html.

119. J. Smedslund, *The Structure of Psychological Common Sense* (Mahwah, NJ: Erlbaum, 1997), 59–62 and 75–76.

120. I. Kant, *Lectures on Ethics [1775–1780]* (Indianapolis: Hackett, 1963), 126.

121. I. Kant, *Critique of Practical Reason* (Indianapolis: Bobbs-Merrill, 1956), 88.

122. R. S. Dillon, ed., *Dignity, Character, and Self-Respect* (New York: Routledge, 1995), 303.

123. F. Heider, *The Psychology of Interpersonal Relations* (New York: Wiley, 1958).

124. N. Tavuchis, *Mea Culpa: A Sociology of Apology and Reconciliation* (Stanford, CA: Stanford University Press, 1991).

125. J. Smedslund, "The Psychologic of Forgiving," *Scandinavian Journal of Psychology*, 32 (1991): 164–176.

126. A. J. Meier, "Conflict and the Power of Apologies," *Philologie im Netz*, 30 (2004): 1–17, revision and expansion of initial observations on conflict and apologies presented at the American Association for Applied Linguistics (AAAL), Stamford, Connecticut, 1999.

127. A. Lazare, *On Apology* (New York: Oxford University Press, 2004), 1.

128. P. T. Coleman, J. S. Goldman, and K. Kugler, *Emotional Intractability: The Effects of Emotional Roles on Aggression and Rumination in Conflict* (New York: International Center for Cooperation and Conflict Resolution. Teachers College, Columbia University, 2007), retrieved on December 19, 2007, from www.tc.columbia.edu/ICCCR/Documents/Coleman/PC_Emotinal_Intractability.pdf, 9–12.

129. N. H. Frijda, "Moods, Emotion Episodes, and Emotions," in *Handbook of Emotions*, ed. M. Lewis and J. M. Haviland (New York: Guilford Press, 1993), 381–404.

130. L. L. Martin and A. Tesser, "Some Ruminative Thoughts," in *Ruminative Thoughts: Vol. 11. Advances in Social Cognition*, ed. R. S. Wyer (Hillsdale, NJ: Erlbaum, 1996), 1–47.

131. M. A. Wheeler, D. A. T. Stuss, and E. Tulving, "Toward a Theory of Episodic Memory: The Frontal Lobes and Autonoetic Consciousness," *Psychological Bulletin*, 121 (1997): 331–354.

132. M. H. Bond, "Culture and Aggression—From Context to Coercion," *Personality and Social Psychology Review*, 8 (2004): 62–78, 67.

133. Ibid., 12.

134. Satoshi Nakagawa, personal communication from Jacqueline Wasilewski, June 25, 2005.

135. For related recent publications, see, for example, B. H. Lipton, *The Biology of Belief: Unleashing the Power of Consciousness, Matter, and Miracles* (Santa Rosa, CA: Elite Books, 2005).

136. W. James, "The Stream of Consciousness," in *Psychology*, ed. W. James (Cleveland & New York: World, 1892), retrieved on March 21, 2008, from psychclassics.yorku.ca/James/jimmy11.htm.

137. W. James, *Principles of Psychology* (2 vols.) (New York: Holt, 1890; reprinted Bristol: Thoemmes Press, 1999), retrieved on March 21, 2008 from psychclassics.asu.edu/James/Principles/index.htm, W. James, "Lectures IV and V: The Religion of Healthy Mindedness," in *The Varieties of Religious Experience: A Study of Human Nature* (New York: Longmans, Green, 1902; available as e-book from the Gutenberg Project, www.gutenberg.org/etext/621, retrieved on 12th April 2008).

138. P. Rozin and E. B. Royzman, "Negativity Bias, Negativity Dominance, and Contagion," *Personality and Social Psychology Review*, 5, no. 4 (2001): 296–320.

139. S. E. Taylor et al., "Biobehavioral Responses to Stress in Females: Tend-and-Befriend, Not Fight-or-Flight," *Psychological Review*, 109, no. 4 (2002): 745–750.

140. I thank Peter T. Coleman for reminding me of Gottman's work.

141. J. M. Gottman and R. W. Levenson, "The Timing of Divorce: Predicting When a Couple Will Divorce over a 14-Year Period," *Journal of Marriage and the Family*, 62, no. 3 (2000): 737–745.

142. J. M. Gottman and N. Silver, *The Seven Principles for Making Marriage Work* (New York: Crown, 1999), 11.

143. Ibid., 46.

144. J. B. Miller, "What Do We Mean by Relationships?," *Work in Progress, No. 22*, (Wellesley, MA: Stone Center Working Paper Series, 1986).

Notes to Chapter 8

1. As Kofi Annan is reported to have said.

2. M. G. Marshall, *Third World War: System, Process, and Conflict Dynamics* (Lanham, MD: Rowman and Littlefield, 1999).

3. R. H. Jackson, *Quasi-States, Sovereignty, International Relations and the Third World* (Cambridge: Cambridge University Press, 1990).

4. R. D. Kaplan, "The Coming Anarchy," *Atlantic Monthly*, February (1994): 44–76.

5. See, for example, the so-called minimal group paradigm: The mere fact that there are two distinct groups seems to suffice for people to favor their own group. See the reviews by H. Tajfel, "Social Psychology of Intergroup Relations," *Annual Review of Psychology*, 33 (1982): 1–39; M. B. Brewer and R. M. Kramer, "The Psychology of Intergroup Attitudes and Behavior," *Annual Review of Psychology*, 36 (1985): 219–243; and D. M. Messick and D. M. Mackie, "Intergroup Relations," *Annual Review of Psychology*, 40 (1989): 45–81. Research shows that the in-group favoring bias does not depend on competition. It occurs merely as a result of being a member

of a short-lived and arbitrarily formed group; for example, M. B. Brewer and M. Silver, "Ingroup Bias as a Function of Task Characteristics," *European Journal of Social Psychology*, 8 (1978): 393–400.

6. See, for more discussion, E. Lindner, *Making Enemies: Humiliation and International Conflict* (Westport, CT: Greenwood/Praeger Security International, 2006), 54, see also, for example, www.intractableconflict.org/docs/appendix_6.jsp.

7. M. Sherif and H. Cantril, *The Psychology of Ego-Involvements, Social Attitudes and Identifications* (New York: Wiley, 1947).

8. M. H. Bond, "Unity in Diversity: Orientations and Strategies for Building a Harmonious, Multicultural Society," in *Social Psychology and Cultural Context*, ed. J. Adamopoulos and Y. Kashima (Thousand Oaks, CA: Sage, 1998), 17–40, 32.

9. J. F. Dovidio, S. L. Gaertner, A. M. Isen, M. C. Rust, and P. Guerra, "Positive Affect, Cognition, and the Reduction of Intergroup Bias," in *Intergroup Cognition and Intergroup Behavior*, ed. C. Sedikides, J. Schopler, and C. A. Insko (Mahwah, NJ: Erlbaum, 1998), 337–366.

10. G. V. Bodenhausen, T. Mussweiler, S. Gabriel, and K. N. Moreno, "Affective Influences on Stereotyping and Intergroup Relations," in *Handbook of Affect and Social Cognition*, ed. J. P. Forgas (Mahwah, NJ: Erlbaum, 2001), 319–343, 323.

11. J. P. Lederach, *Building Peace: Sustainable Reconciliation in Divided Societies* (Washington, DC: U.S. Institute of Peace, 1997); J. P. Lederach, *The Moral Imagination: The Art and Soul of Building Peace* (Oxford: Oxford University Press, 2005).

12. H. C. Kelman, "Continuity and Change: My Life as a Social Psychologist," in *The Social Psychology of Group Identity and Social Conflict: Theory, Application, and Practice*, ed. A. H. Eagly, R. M. Baron, and V. L. Hamilton (Washington, DC: American Psychological Association, 2004), 233–275.

13. The contact hypothesis represents the "belief that interaction between individuals belonging to different groups will reduce ethnic prejudice and inter-group tension" (S. Ryan, "Peace-Building and Conflict Transformation," *Ethnic Conflict and International Relations* [Dartmouth: Dartmouth Publishing, 1995], see also www.intractableconflict.org/docs/appendix_6.jsp, 129–152, 131). See on cultural diffusion H. C. Triandis, *Culture and Social Behavior* (New York: McGraw-Hill, 1997).

14. W. G. Stephan, C. W. Stephan, and W. B. Gudykunst, "Anxiety in Intergroup Relations: A Comparison of Anxiety/Uncertainty Management Theory and Integrated Threat Theory," *International Journal of Intercultural Relations*, 23, no. 4 (1999): 613–628.

15. P. G. Devine, S. R. Evett, and K. A. Vasquez-Suson, "Exploring the Interpersonal Dynamics of Intergroup Contact," *Handbook of Motivation and Cognition*, vol. 3, ed. R. M. Sorrentino and E. T. Higgins (New York: Guilford Press, 1996), 423–464.

16. R. B. Zajonc, "Social Facilitation," *Science*, 149 (1965): 269–274; R. B. Zajonc, *The Selected Works of R. B. Zajonc* (Hoboken, NJ: Wiley, 2004).

17. D. A. Wilder and P. N. Shapiro, "Effects of Anxiety on Impression Formation in a Group Context: An Anxiety-Assimilation Hypothesis," *Journal of Experimental Social Psychology*, 25, no. 6 (1989): 481–499.

18. C. Taylor, "The Politics of Recognition," in *Multiculturalism: Examining the Politics of Recognition*, ed. A. Gutman (Princeton, NJ: Princeton University Press, 1994).

19. See note 1 in the Introduction.

20. As to the concept of nudging, see, R. Thaler and C. Sunstein, *Nudge: Improving Decisions about Health, Wealth and Happiness* (New Haven, CT: Yale University Press, 2008).

21. J. Goldstone and J. Ulfelder, "How to Construct Stable Democracies," *Washington Quarterly*, Winter 2004–5 (2005): 9–20, 9.

22. Ibid., 19–20.

23. Ibid., 20.

24. S. Milgram, *Obedience to Authority* (New York: Harper & Row, 1974), and P. G. Zimbardo, *The Power and Pathology of Imprisonment, Congressional Record*. (Serial no. 15, 1971-10-25), *Hearings before Subcommittee No. 3, of the Committee on the Judiciary, House of Representatives, Ninety-Second Congress, First Session on Corrections, Part II, Prisons, Prison Reform and Prisoner's Rights: California* (Washington, DC: Government Printing Office, 1971). See also P. G. Zimbardo, *The Lucifer Effect: Understanding How Good People Turn Evil* (New York: Random House, 2007).

25. In BBC World *HARDtalk* with Stephen Sackur on April 23, 2008.

26. German crime TV series are very different from those authored, for example, by Agatha Christie and her focus on the intellectual challenge in exposing a cold-blooded perpetrator (usually driven by greed) or the spotlight in many American series on good versus evil (with the courage required on the good side when facing evil being being visualized preferably by huge explosions and dangerous stunts).

27. J. B. Miller, "Forced Choices, False Choices," *Research & Action Report*, 27, no. 2, Spring/Summer (2006).

28. J. De Rivera, R. Kurrien, and N. Olsen, "Emotional Climates, Human Security, and Cultures of Peace," *Journal of Social Issues*, 63, no. 2, June (2007): 255–271, Abstract.

29. See, for example, europa.eu/scadplus/glossary/subsidiarity_en.htm.

30. J. Braithwaite, *Restorative Justice and Responsive Regulation* (Oxford: Oxford University Press, 2002).

31. W. T. Powers, *Behavior: The Control of Perception* (Chicago: Aldine, 1973); W. T. Powers, *Making Sense of Behavior: The Meaning of Control* (New Canaan, CT: Benchmark, 1998).

32. Ban Ki-Moon, "A Call to Global Leadership," presented at the 63rd session of the United Nations General Assembly, September 23, 2008, www.un.org/ga/63/generaldebate/sg.shtml.

33. E. M. Rogers, *Diffusion of Innovations* (New York: Free Press of Glencoe, 1962), describes how new ideas are carried forward by innovators, who convince early adopters, who in turn influence early majorities and may slide into loggerhead positions with laggards. I thank Barnett Pearce for making me aware of this literature. Read H. D. Lasswell and D. Lerner, eds., *World Revolutionary Elites: Studies in Coercive Ideological Movements* (Cambridge, MA: MIT Press, 1965). I thank Dennis Smith for this reference.

34. M. Gerzon, *GQ—Global Intelligence: Learning to Lead beyond Borders* (forthcoming), 1.

35. See, for example, research on expected utility theory, beginning with D. Bernoulli, "Exposition of a New Theory on the Measurement of Risk," *Econometrica*, 22, no. 1 (1954): 23-36 (original work published 1738); Paul J. H. Schoemaker, "The

Expected Utility Model: Its Variants, Purposes, Evidence and Limitations," *Journal of Economic Literature*, 20 (1982): 529–563; P. Anand, *Foundations of Rational Choice under Risk* (Oxford: Oxford University Press, 1993); or K. J. Arrow, "Uncertainty and the Welfare Economics of Medical Care," *American Economic Review*, 53 (1963): 941–973, and S. Plous, *The Psychology of Judgment and Decision Making* (New York: McGraw-Hill, 1993). Emotions and decision making has been studies by Alice M. Isen, see, for example, A. M. Isen and R. Patrick, "The Effect of Positive Feelings on Risk Taking: When the Chips Are Down," *Organizational Behavior and Human Decision Processes*, 31 (1983): 194–202, and A. M. Isen, "Some Perspectives on Positive Affect and Self-Regulation," *Psychological Inquiry*, 11, no. 3 (2000): 184–187. See also R. B. Zajonc, "Emotions," in *The Handbook of Social Psychology*, vol. 1, ed. D. T. Gilbert, S. T. Fiske, and G. Lindzey (Boston: McGraw-Hill, 1998), 591–632.

36. See, for example, G. Loewenstein et al., "Risk as Feelings," *Psychological Bulletin*, 127, no. 2 (2001): 267–286, Abstract.

37. T. S. Kuhn, *The Structure of Scientific Revolutions* (Chicago: University of Chicago Press, 1962), set the agenda of this topic.

38. Even though it was published in 1976, C. Argyris, *Increasing Leadership Effectiveness* (New York: Wiley, 1976), still remains a standard reference text.

39. See H. R. Markus and S. Kitayama, "Models of Agency: Sociocultural Diversity in the Construction of Action," *Nebraska Symposium on Motivation* (2004), and how they describe the cultural shaping of emotions as collective reality or core cultural ideas. They analyze the subjective reality of societies as flowing from their socioeconomic environment and institutional structures and examine how aspects of individual emotionality relate to this subjective reality. See, furthermore, W. B. Pearce and S. W. Littlejohn, *Moral Conflict: When Social Worlds Collide* (Newbury Park, CA: Sage, 1997), and R. Harré, ed., *The Social Construction of Emotions* (New York: Basil Blackwell, 1986).

40. C. W. Moore, *The Mediation Process: Practical Strategies for Resolving Conflict*, 2nd ed. (San Francisco: Jossey-Bass, 1996), identifies five kinds of conflict (p. 60): *relationship conflicts* (strong emotions, misperceptions or stereotypes, poor communication or miscommunication, repetitive negative behavior), *data conflicts* (lack of information, misinformation, different views on what is relevant, different interpretations of data, different assessment procedures), *interest conflicts* (perceived or actual competition over substantive [content] interests, procedural interests, psychological interests), *structural conflicts* (destructive patterns of behavior or interaction, unequal control, ownership, or distribution of resources, unequal power and authority, geographical, physical, or environmental factors that hinder cooperation, time constraints), and *value conflicts* (different criteria for evaluating ideas or behavior, exclusive intrinsically valuable goals, different ways of life, ideology, or religion). D. P. Fry and K. Björkvist, eds., *Cultural Variation in Conflict Resolution: Alternatives to Violence* (Mahwah, NJ: Erlbaum, 1997), focus on conflict and violence from a cross-cultural perspective. According to them, conflict is not tantamount with aggression but can be addressed in different ways: denying its very existence, negotiating a mutually desirable solution, compromising, threatening verbally, attacking physically, and appealing to a third party. Conflict strategies include contending (high concern for one's own outcomes and low concern for other's outcomes), problem solving (high concern for both one's own and other's outcomes), yielding (low concern for one's own and high concern for other's

outcomes), and avoiding (low concern for one's own and other's outcomes). Fry and Björkvist conclude that some cultures tend to favor one set of strategies, while others prefer another set of strategies. I thank Elizabeth Scheper for making me aware of the work carried out by Fry and Björkvist. Read, among others, L. J. Fisk and J. L. Schellenberg, *Patterns of Conflict: Paths to Peace* (Peterborough, ON: Broadview Press, 2000).

41. Political scientists P. Bachrach and M. S. Baratz, "The Two Faces of Power," *American Political Science Review,* 56 (1962): 947–952, were among the first to address power and conflict that is placed within the context of the civil rights movement in the United States of the 1960s. See also D. Keltner and R. J. Robinson, "Extremism, Power, and the Imagined Basis of Social Conflict," *Current Directions in Psychological Science,* 5 (1996): 101–105, who tested the hypothesis that within social disputes those partisans representing the status quo perceive their conflict less accurately than those seeking change, and that partisans seeking change typically are stereotyped as extremists.

42. See T. R. Gurr, *Why Men Rebel* (Princeton, NJ: Princeton University Press, 1970); T. R. Gurr, "Why Minorities Rebel: A Global Analysis of Communal Mobilization and Conflict since 1945," *International Political Science Review,* 14, no. 2 (1993): 161–201.

43. J. Collins, "Level 5 Leadership: The Triumph of Humility and Fierce Resolve," *Harvard Business Review,* January (2001): 68–76.

44. See www.selflessleadership.com.

45. J. L. Bower, "Solve the Succession Crisis by Growing Inside-Outside Leaders," *Harvard Business Review,* 85, no. 11, November (2007): 91–96.

46. L. Gratton and T. J. Erickson, "Eight Ways to Build Collaborative Teams," *Harvard Business Review,* 85, no. 11, November (2007): 100–109.

47. M. C. Gilbert, "The End of the Organization?," *Nonprofit Online News,* February 7 (2008), retrieved on February 24, 2008, from news.gilbert.org/EndOfOrg.

48. P. H. Ray and S. R. Anderson, *The Cultural Creatives: How 50 Million People Are Changing the World* (New York: Three Rivers Press, 2000), 234.

49. M. Gerzon, *Leading through Conflict: How Successful Leaders Transform Differences into Opportunities* (Boston: Harvard Business School Press, 2006).

50. R. Swedberg, *Economics and Sociology: Redefining Their Boundaries: Conversations with Economists and Sociologists* (Princeton, NJ: Princeton University Press, 1990).

51. B. Wyatt-Brown, *Southern Honor: Ethics and Behavior in the Old South* (New York: Oxford University Press, 1982), Chapter 4.

52. R. Jervis, "Understanding Beliefs," *Political Psychology,* 27, no. 5 (2006): 641–663, 644.

53. Ibid., 643.

54. Ibid.

55. See, among others, R. E. Nisbett and T. D. Wilson, "Telling More Than We Can Know: Verbal Reports on Mental Processes," *Psychological Review,* 84 (1977): 231–259; T. D. Wilson, *Strangers to Ourselves* (Cambridge, MA: Harvard University Press, 2002).

56. For a general discussion of motivated processing, see, for example, S. J. Spencer, S. Fein, M. P. Zanna, and J. M. Olson, eds., *Motivated Social Perception: The Ontario Symposium Volume 9* (Mahwah, NJ: Erlbaum, 2003).

57. "Suicide bombers" is a phrase we would use today; their operations, how-ever, were termed *tokkotai* operations in Japan, and in the West they became known as kamikaze operations.

58. E. Ohnuki-Tierney, *Kamikaze, Cherry Blossoms, and Nationalisms: The Militari-zation of Aesthetics in Japanese History* (Chicago: University of Chicago Press, 2002), 123.

59. N. Spivey, *How Art Made the World: How Humans Made Art and Art Made Us Human* (London: BBC Worldwide, 2005)

60. H. Arendt, *Eichmann in Jerusalem: A Report on the Banality of Evil* (New York: Viking Press, 1963).

61. W. Van Vuuren and I. Liebenberg, " 'Government by Illusion': The Legacy and Its Implications," in *The Hidden Hand, Covert Operations in South Africa*, ed. A. Minnaar, I. Liebenberg, and C. Schutte (Pretoria: Human Sciences Research Coun-cil, 1994), 25–43. I thank Zuzana Luckay for making me aware of these authors.

62. B. Wyatt-Brown, *Southern Honor: Ethics and Behavior in the Old South* (New York: Oxford University Press, 1982), Chapter 4.

63. By Corax (or Korax), along with Tisias. We know of the work of Corax from references made by later writers, such as Plato, Aristotle, and Cicero.

64. Even though Socrates held lectures, or *epideixis*, he preferred dialogue. The Socratic dialogues are a series of dialogues written by Plato and Xenophon in the form of discussions between Socrates and other persons of his time, or as discus-sions between Socrates's followers over his concept.

65. Plato made clear that merely being skilled in *techne*, or the craftsmanship of rhetoric, did not secure ethically sound outcomes.

66. Isocrates highlighted the need for sound timing, or *kairos*, meaning the "right or opportune moment."

67. Aristotle connected dialectic with rhetoric. In classical philosophy, dialectic is the exchange of theses and counterpropositions (antitheses) to arrive at a synthesis.

68. See, for example, E. Grassi, *Rhetoric as Philosophy: The Humanist Tradition* (University Park: Pennsylvania State University Press, 1980); E. Grassi, *Vico and Humanism: Essays on Vico, Heidegger, and Rhetoric* (New York: Peter Lang, 1990).

69. Grassi calls "external rhetorical speech," or "false speech," the superficial and mistaken definition of rhetoric as a technical art of persuasion."

70. Hugo de Sancto Victore, *The Didascalicon of Hugh of St. Victor: A Medieval Guide to the Arts* (New York: Columbia University Press, translated from the Latin with an introduction and notes by Jerome Taylor, 1961).

71. E. Durkheim, *The Evolution of Educational Thought: Lectures on the Formation and Development of Secondary Education in France* (London: Routledge & Kegan Paul, 1977).

72. See, for example, E. G. Lindner, "Dynamics of Humiliation in a Globalizing World," *International Journal on World Peace*, XXXIV, no. 3, September (2007): 15–52.

73. P. Burke, *A Social History of Knowledge: From Gutenberg to Diderot* (Cambridge: Polity Press, 2000).

74. W. J. Ong, *Ramus: Method, and the Decay of Dialogue: From the Art of Discourse to the Art of Reason* (Cambridge, MA: Harvard University Press, 1958).

75. Johann Gottfried von Herder, 1744–1803, Friedrich Schiller, 1759–1805, Johann Gottlieb Fichte, 1762–1814, Georg Wilhelm Friedrich Hegel, 1770–1831, Alexander von Humboldt, 1769–1859.

76. See, for example, for the discussion in Norway, Y. T. Nordkvelle, "Forelesningen Som Studentaktiv Undervisningsform–Et Argument Fra Undervisningens Kulturhistorie," *UNIPED*, 30, no. 1 (2007): 4–14, and A. Tjeldvoll, "Universitetspedagogisk Paradigmeskifte," *UNIPED*, 30, no. 1 (2007): 36–43.

77. E. G. Lindner, "The Educational Environment as a Place for Humiliating Indoctrination or Dignifying Empowerment," *Experiments in Education*, 36, Humiliation in the academic setting: A Special Symposium Issue, no. 3, March (2008): 51–60.

78. N. Elias, *The Civilizing Process (Volume 1: The History of Manners, Volume 2: State Formation and Civilization)* (Oxford: Blackwell, 1994) (he wrote the manuscript in 1939).

79. P. Bourdieu, *Outline of a Theory of Practice* (Cambridge: Cambridge University Press, 1977), 17.

80. C. Geertz, *Local Knowledge: Further Essays in Interpretive Anthropology* (New York: Basic Books, 1983), 75.

81. P. L. Berger and T. Luckmann, *The Social Construction of Reality: A Treatise in the Sociology of Knowledge* (Garden City, NY: Doubleday, 1966).

82. M. Foucault, *The Order of Things: An Archaeology of the Human Sciences* (New York: Pantheon Books, 1970. Original title *Les mots et les choses. Une archéologie des sciences humaines*. Paris: Gallimard, 1966).

83. Parsons integrates not only sociological concepts but also psychological, economic, political, and religious or philosophical components; see T. Parsons, *The Social System* (London: Routledge and Kegan Paul, 1951).

84. A. S. Palincsar, "Social Constructivist Perspectives on Teaching and Learning," *Annual Review of Psychology*, 49 (1998): 345–375.

85. M. Polanyi, *The Tacit Dimension* (New York: Anchor Books, 1967).

86. D. J. Bem, *Beliefs, Attitudes and Human Affairs* (Belmont, CA: Brooks/Cole, 1970).

87. S. T. Colbert, *The Colbert Report* Television show, October 17, 2005, http://www.colbertnation.com/the-colbert-report-videos/24039/october-17-2005/the-word—truthiness, 2005).

88. H. Mackay, *Why Don't People Listen? Solving the Communication Problem* (Sydney: Pan Macmillan Australia, 1994).

89. Y. Rogers, A. Rutherford, and P. A. Bibby, eds., *Models in the Mind: Theory, Perspective and Application* (London: Academic Press, 1992).

90. R. B. Zajonc, "Feeling and Thinking: Preferences Need No Inferences," *American Psychologist* 35 (1980): 151–175.

91. G. Lakoff, *Thinking Points: Communicating Our American Values and Vision* (New York: Farrar, Straus and Giroux, 2006), 25. See also www.rockridgeinstitute.org.

92. D. L. Nathanson, "What's a Script?," *Bulletin of The Tomkins Institute*, 3, Spring-Summer (1996): 1–4.

93. E. Berne, *What Do You Say After You Say Hello?* (New York: Bantam, 1972).

94. B. Anderson, *Imagined Communities* (London: Verso, 1991).

95. T. S. Kuhn, *The Structure of Scientific Revolutions* (Chicago: University of Chicago Press, 1962).

96. J. A. Bargh and E. L. Williams, "The Automaticity of Social Life," *Current Directions in Psychological Science*, 15, no. 1 (2006): 1–4.

97. M. Gladwell, *Blink: The Power of Thinking without Thinking* (New York: Little, Brown, 2005).

98. F. Strack and R. Deutsch, "Reflective and Impulsive Determinants of Social Behavior," *Personality and Social Psychology Review*, 8, no. 3 (2004): 220–247.

99. R. H. Fazio et al., "On the Automatic Activation of Attitudes," *Journal of Personality and Social Psychology*, 50, no. 2 (1986): 229–238, P. G. Devine, "Stereotypes and Prejudice: Their Automatic and Controlled Components," *Journal of Personality and Social Psychology*, 56, no. 1 (1989): 5–18. See also H. Nordtug, *Implicit Prejudice against Arab Immigrants* (Trondheim: Norwegian University of Science and Technology, master's thesis, 2008).

100. The "associative-propositional evaluation" model (APE) describes how implicit and explicit attitude change is guided by a distinction between associative and propositional processes—see B. Gawronski and G. V. Bodenhausen, "Associative and Propositional Processes in Evaluation: An Integrative Review of Implicit and Explicit Attitude Change," *Psychological Bulletin*, 132, no. 5 (2006): 692–731.

101. R. Barthes, *Mythologies* (London: Jonathan Cape, 1972), a collection of short essays, written one per month between 1954 and 1956, translated by Annette Lavers in 1972. See also work on ideology by T. Eagleton, *Ideology: An Introduction* (London: Verso, 1991).

102. P. Bourdieu, *Masculine Domination* (Stanford, CA: Stanford University Press, 2001), 2.

103. P. Bourdieu, *Algeria 1960: The Disenchantment of the World, the Sense of Honour, the Kabyle House or the World Reversed* (Cambridge/Paris: Cambridge University Press/Editions de la Maison des Sciences de l'Homme, 1979), vii.

104. P. Bourdieu, *Outline of a Theory of Practice* (Cambridge: Cambridge University Press, 1977), 22.

105. Ibid., 233.

106. Ibid., 171.

107. M. Foucault, *Discipline and Punish. The Birth of the Prison* (Harmondsworth: Allen Lane, 1977).

108. B. Faber, "Intuitive Ethics: Understanding and Critiquing the Role of Intuition in Ethical Decisions," *Technical Communication Quarterly*, 8, no. 2, Spring (1999): 189–202.

109. A. Giddens, *The Constitution of Society: Outline of the Theory of Structuration* (Berkeley: University of California Press, 1984).

110. N. Fairclough, *Discourse and Social Change* (Cambridge: Polity, 1992).

111. M. Foucault, "On Governmentality," *Ideology & Consciousness*, 6 (1979): 5–21; M. Foucault, "Governmentality," in *The Foucault Effect: Studies in Governmentality*, ed. G. Burchell, C. Gordon, and P. Miller (Chicago: University of Chicago Press, 1991), 87–104.

112. E. Lindner, *Making Enemies: Humiliation and International Conflict* (Westport, CT: Greenwood/Praeger Security International, 2006), 175.

113. J. Galtung, *Peace by Peaceful Means* (Oslo and London: International Peace Research Institute Oslo and Sage, 1996), 199.

114. R. Guha and G. C. Spivak, eds., *Selected Subaltern Studies* (New York: Oxford University Press, 1988).

115. J. Habermas, *The Theory of Communicative Action, Volume 2, System and Lifeworld: A Critique of Functionalist Reason* (Boston: Beacon Press, 1987).

116. P. H. Collins, *Black Feminist Thought: Knowledge, Consciousness, and the Politics of Empowerment* (New York: Routledge, 1991).

117. T. W. Adorno, E. Frenkel-Brunswick, D. J. Levinson, and R. N. Sanford, *The Authoritarian Personality* (New York: Harper, 1950).

118. A. Miller, *For Your Own Good: Hidden Cruelty in Child-Rearing and the Roots of Violence* (London: Virago Press, 1983).

119. G. Lakoff and M. Johnson, *Philosophy in the Flesh: The Embodied Mind and Its Challenge to Western Thought* (New York: Basic Books, 1999).

120. F. Fanon, *Black Skin, White Masks* (London: Pluto Press, 1986).

121. A. S. Reber, *The Penguin Dictionary of Psychology*, 2nd ed. (Harmondsworth: Penguin, 1995).

122. Ibid.

123. R. Guha and G. C. Spivak, eds., *Selected Subaltern Studies* (New York: Oxford University Press, 1988).

124. A. Nandy, *Exiled at Home: Comprising At the Edge of Psychology, The Intimate Enemy, and Creating a Nationality* (New Delhi: Oxford University Press, 1998).

125. E. Bernays, *Propaganda* (New York: Horace Liveright, 1928).

126. See also E. Clark, *The Want Makers: Inside the World of Advertising* (New York: Viking, 1988).

127. Four clips begin with www.youtube.com/watch?v=8aufuwMiKmE. See also humiliationstudies.org/intervention/design.php.

128. J. J. Gibson, "The Theory of Affordances: Toward an Ecological Psychology," in *Perceiving, Acting, and Knowing*, ed. R. Shaw and J. Bransford (Hillsdale, NJ: Erlbaum, 1977).

129. D. A. Norman, *The Psychology of Everyday Things* (New York: Basic Books, 1988).

130. P. R. Ehrlich and A. H. Ehrlich, *The Dominant Animal: Human Evolution and the Environment* (Washington, DC: Island Press, 2008).

131. J. Diamond, *Collapse: How Societies Choose to Fail or Succeed* (New York: Viking, 2005).

132. K. Kurokawa, P. C. Schmal, I. Flagge, and J. Visscher, eds., *Kisho Kurokawa: Metabolism and Symbiosis* (Berlin: Jovis, 2005).

133. See H. Tajfel and J. C. Turner, "The Social Identity Theory of Intergroup Behavior," in *Psychology of Intergroup Relations*, ed. S. Worchel and W. G. Austin (Chicago: Neston-Hall, 1986), 204–227 for a review of social identity theory.

134. M. B. Brewer and S. Roccas, "Social Identity Complexity," *Personality and Social Psychology Review*, 6 (2002): 88–106, show how membership in many different groups (multiple social identities) can lead to greater social identity complexity, which, in turn, can foster the development of superordinate social identities and global identity (making international identity more likely in individualist cultures). See also Shelly L. Chaiken's work, showing that people who are more open to discrepant evidence tend to make more accurate predictions; S. L. Chaiken, "Heuristic versus Systematic Information Processing and the Use of Source versus Message Cues in Persuasion," *Journal of Personality and Social Psychology*, 39 (1980): 752–766; S. L. Chaiken, D. H. Gruenfeld, and C. M. Judd, "Persuasion in Negotiations and Conflict Situations," in *The Handbook of Conflict Resolution: Theory and Practice*, ed. M. Deutsch and P. T. Coleman (San Francisco: Jossey-Bass, 2000), 144–165.

135. M. Serres, *The Troubadour of Knowledge* (Ann Arbor: University of Michigan Press, 1997).

136. M. Zembylas, "Of Troubadours, Angels, and Parasites: Reevaluating the Educational Territory in the Arts and Sciences through the Work of Michel Serres," *International Journal of Education & the Arts,* 3, no. 3, March 17 (2002), ijea.asu.edu/v3n3.

137. K. A. Appiah, "The Case for Contamination," *New York Times,* January 1 (2006), www.muhlenberg.edu/mgt/provost/frg/humanities/AppiahContamination.pdf.

138. E. Lévinas, "Responsibility for the Other," in *Ethics and Infinity: Conversations With Phillipe Nemo,* ed. E. Lévinas (Pittsburgh, PA: Duquesne University Press, 1985), 93–101.

139. W. Wintersteiner, *Pädagogik des Anderen: Bausteine für eine Friedenspädagogik in der Postmoderne (Pedagogy of the Other: Building Blocks for Peace Education in the Postmodern World)* (Münster: Agenda, 1999).

140. See www.tve.org/earthreport.

141. See www.irinnews.org/filmtv.aspx.

142. See www.queenrania.jo/default.aspx.

143. See www.synergos.org/globalgivingmatters/features/0506muslimwest.htm.

144. See www.data.org.

145. See humiliationstudies.org/intervention/events.php#peacestar.

Notes to Chapter 9

1. M. Kaku, *Parallel Worlds: A Journey through Creation, Higher Dimensions, and the Future of the Cosmos* (New York: Doubleday, 2005), 361.

2. D. A. Hamburg, *No More Killing Fields: Preventing Deadly Conflict* (Lanham, MD: Rowman and Littlefield, 2002).

3. D. A. Hamburg and B. A. Hamburg, *Learning to Live Together: Preventing Hatred and Violence in Child and Adolescent Development* (New York: Oxford University Press, 2004), 335.

4. Personal communication, May 28, 2008.

5. See A. Naess, *The Selected Works of Arne Naess, Volumes 1–10* (Dordrecht: Springer, 2005).

6. See, for example, V. V. Vaitheeswaran, *Power to the People: How the Coming Energy Revolution Will Transform an Industry, Change Our Lives, and Maybe Even Save the Planet* (New York: Farrar, Straus and Giroux, 2003).

7. D. J. Christie, "What Is Peace Psychology the Psychology Of?," *Journal of Social Issues,* 62, no. 1 (2006): 1–17, retrieved on August 14, 2007, from www.blackwell-synergy.com/doi/pdf/10.1111/j.1540-4560.2006.00436.x, 11.

8. I saw the play at the DR2 Theater in Union Square, NY.

9. Please see www.maskedtheplay.com/index_enter.html.

10. A. Margalit, *The Decent Society* (Cambridge, MA: Harvard University Press, 1996).

11. D. J. Christie, "What Is Peace Psychology the Psychology Of?," *Journal of Social Issues,* 62, no. 1 (2006): 1–17, retrieved on August 14, 2007, from www.blackwell-synergy.com/doi/pdf/10.1111/j.1540-4560.2006.00436.x, 3.

12. Ibid., 13.

13. M. Schwebel, "Realistic Empathy and Active Nonviolence Confront Political Reality," *Journal of Social Issues,* 62, no. 1 (2006): 191–208, retrieved on August 14, 2007, from www.blackwell-synergy.com/doi/pdf/10.1111/j.1540-4560.2006.00446.x.

14. J.-J. Rousseau, *Du Contrat Social ou Principes du Droit Politique* (Geneve: Archives de la Société Jean-Jacques Rousseau, Genève, 1762), retrieved March 6, 2003, from un2sg4.unige.ch/athena/rousseau/jjr_cont.html.

15. In BBC World's *HARDtalk* with Stephen Sackur on April 24, 2008.

16. R. Jervis, "Understanding Beliefs," *Political Psychology,* 27, no. 5 (2006): 641–663, 656.

17. F. Fukuyama, *The End of History and the Last Man* (New York: Avon Books, 1992), 163, 182.

18. A. Wendt, "Why a World State Is Inevitable," *European Journal of International Relations,* 9, no. 4 (2003): 491–542, 525.

19. See howardrichards.org/peace/component/option,com_frontpage/Itemid,1.

20. E. G. Lindner, "Avoiding Humiliation—From Intercultural Communication to Global Interhuman Communication," *Journal of Intercultural Communication, SIETAR Japan,* 10 (2007): 21–38.

21. See, for example, www.latinamericapress.org/article.asp?IssCode=&lanCode=1&artCode=5630.

22. E. G. Lindner, "What the World's Cultures Can Contribute to Creating a Sustainable Future for Humankind" (Oslo: Paper prepared for the 11th Annual Conference of Human Dignity and Humiliation Studies, www.humiliationstudies.org/whoweare/annualmeeting11.php), June 23–July 1, 2008, Norway, Human Dignity and Humiliation Studies), www.humiliationstudies.org/whoweare/evelin02.php#oslo08.

23. *Harmony* is a term writ large in Asia. China currently plans to develop a "Harmonious Society Measurement Standard," see, for example, www.chinacsr.com/2007/10/11/1744-china-plans-harmonious-society-measurement-standard.

24. In Europe, *social cohesion* is an important term. See the Joint Report on Social Protection and Social Inclusion (Commission proposal) at ec.europa.eu/employment_social/social_inclusion/news_en.htm, or the Joint Commission/Council Report, publication on February 22, 2007, at ec.europa.eu/employment_social/social_inclusion/jrep_en.htm.

25. S. Brittan, *An Ethical Foreign Policy?* (Cambridge, MA: Samuel Brittan: Hinton Lecture 24/11/99 at the Harvard School of Public Health, 1999), www.samuelbrittan.co.uk/spee6_p.html.

26. See, for example, M. J. Battle, *Reconciliation. The Ubuntu Theology of Desmond Tutu* (Cleveland, OH: Pilgrim Press, 1997).

27. J. B. Miller, "What Do We Mean by Relationships?," *Work in Progress, no. 22,* (Wellesley, MA: Stone Center Working Paper Series, 1986).

28. R. Otto, *Das Heilige: Über das Irrationale in der Idee des Göttlichen und sein Verhältnis zum Rationalen* (Breslau: Trewendt und Granier, 1917), *The Idea of the Holy,* English translation, 1950.

29. O. Ware, "Rudolph Otto's Idea of the Holy: A Reappraisal," *Heythrop Journal,* 48, no. 1, January (2007): 48–60.

30. See, for example, D. C. Klein and K. Morrow, *New Vision, New Reality: A Guide to Unleashing Energy, Joy, and Creativity in Your Life* (Center City, MN: Hazelden Information & Education Services, 2001), and more of his work at www.humiliationstudies.org/whoweare/don.php.

31. The avoidant personality was mentioned earlier.

32. K. R. Scherer, "Foreword," in *Emotions: Current Issues and Future Directions,* ed. T. J. Mayne and G. A. Bonanno (New York: Guilford Press, 2001), xiii–xv, xiv.

33. Ibid.

34. D. Keltner and J. Haidt, "Social Functions of Emotions," in *Emotions: Current Issues and Future Directions*, ed. T. J. Mayne and G. A. Bonanno (New York: Guilford Press, 2001), 192–213.

35. K. Waltz, *Theory of International Politics* (Reading, MA: Addison-Wesley, 1979).

36. R. O. Keohane, "International Liberalism Reconsidered," in *The Economic Limits to Modern Politics*, ed. J. Dunn (Cambridge: Cambridge University Press, 1990), 165–194.

37. D. Deudney, "Geopolitics and Change," in *New Thinking in International Relations Theory*, ed. M. W. Doyle and G. J. Ikenberry (Boulder, CO: Westview Press, 1999), 91–123; D. Deudney, "Regrounding Realism," *Security Studies*, 10, no. 1 (2000): 1–45.

38. R. Rorty, *Contingency, Irony, and Solidarity* (Cambridge: Cambridge University Press, 1989), 192. I thank Howard Richards for making me aware of this quote.

39. See the note explaining the origin of the term of the "global village" in Chapter 3.

40. A. Wendt, "Why a World State Is Inevitable," *European Journal of International Relations*, 9, no. 4 (2003): 491–542, 519.

41. Plotinus is considered to be the founder of neoplatonism. He developed a complex spiritual cosmology of three hypostases: the One, the Intelligence, and the Soul. The *Six Enneads* is the collection of writings of Plotinus, edited and compiled by his student Porphyry (c. 270 A.D.), and recently translated by Stephen MacKenna and B. S. Page, see Plotinus, S. MacKenna, and B. S. Page, *The Enneads*, 2nd ed. (London: Faber and Faber, 1956), or ccat.sas.upenn.edu/jod/texts/plotinus. See also Rudolf Otto and his quest to distill out what it is that connects all religions, namely, *The Idea of the Holy* (English translation in 1950), *Das Heilige: Über das Irrationale in der Idee des Göttlichen und Sein Verhältnis zum Rationalen* (Breslau: Trewendt und Granier, 1917).

42. G. Heard, *The Five Ages of Man* (New York: Julian Press, 1963).

43. M. Hollick, *The Science of Oneness: A Worldview for the Twenty-First Century* (Ropley, Hampshire: O-Books, 2006). I thank Sigurd Støren for making me aware of this book.

44. A. Wendt, *Social Theory of International Politics* (Cambridge: Cambridge University Press, 1999), 298–299. See also L.-E. Cederman, "Modeling the Democratic Peace as a Kantian Selection Process," *Journal of Conflict Resolution*, 45, no. 4 (2001): 470–502; the term *epigenesis* by A. Etzioni, "The Epigenesist of Political Communities at the International Level," *American Journal of Sociology*, 68, no. 4 (1963): 407–421, fits as well.

45. E. Boulding, *Building a Global Civic Culture: Education for an Interdependent World* (New York: Teachers College Press, 1988).

46. Wendt's stage three.

47. A. Wendt, "Why a World State Is Inevitable," *European Journal of International Relations*, 9, no. 4 (2003): 491–542, 520.

48. A. Wendt, *Why a World State Is Inevitable: Teleology and the Logic of Anarchy* (Chicago: University of Chicago, 2003), 4. Self-organization thinking is very interdisciplinary; for social psychology, see R. R. Vallacher and A. Nowak, "The Emergence of Dynamical Social Psychology," *Psychological Inquiry*, 8, no. 2 (1997): 73–99. See furthermore John S. Kauffman, *At Home in the Universe* (Oxford: Oxford

University Press, 1995), and B. Weber and D. Depew, "Natural Selection and Self-Organization," *Biology and Philosophy,* 11 (1996): 33–65, on its relationship to neo-Darwinism, as well as N. Luhmann, *Social Systems* (Stanford, CA: Stanford University Press, 1995); J. Epstein and R. Axtell, *Growing Artificial Societies: Social Science from the Bottom Up* (Cambridge, MA: MIT Press, 1996); U. Witt, "Self-Organization and Economics—What Is New?," *Structural Change and Economic Dynamics,* 8 (1997): 489–507; R. Marion, *The Edge of Organization: Chaos and Complexity Theories of Formal Social Systems* (Thousand Oaks, CA: Sage, 1999); and M. Macy and R. Willer, "From Factors to Actors: Computational Sociology and Agent-Based Modeling," *Annual Review of Sociology,* 28 (2002): 143–166. What cannot be subsumed in "the struggle for recognition" is the "logic of capital" (N. Fraser, "Rethinking Recognition," *New Left Review,* 3 [2000]: 107–120, N. Fraser and A. Honneth, *Redistribution or Recognition? A Political-Philosophical Exchange* [London: Verso, 2003]), however, also here, it is argued, a world state may be in the cards (C. Chase-Dunn and T. D. Hall, *Paradigms Bridged: Institutional Materialism and World-Systemic Evolution,* 2004, retrieved June 21, 2004, from csf.colorado.edu/ wsystems/archive/papers/c-d&hall/ssha97.htm; C. Chase-Dunn, "World State Formation: Historical Processes and Emergent Necessity," *Political Geography Quarterly,* 9, no. 2 [1990]: 108–130; M. Shaw, *Theory of the Global State* [Cambridge: Cambridge University Press, 2000]).

49. C. Nelder, "Envisioning a Sustainable Future," *BWZine (The Online Better World Magazine),* October/November/December (1996): 10.

50. P. H. Ray and S. R. Anderson, *The Cultural Creatives: How 50 Million People Are Changing the World* (New York: Three Rivers Press, 2000).

51. See the discussion at organizations as, for example, the World Bank, where *good governance* has become buzzwords after the failure of "helping" developing countries with financial and/or technical assistance. See, for example, J. E. Stiglitz, *Global Economic Prospects and the Developing Countries 1998/99: Beyond Financial Crisis* (New York: World Bank, 1998), www.worldbank.org/prospects/gep98-99/toc .htm, and J. E. Stiglitz, *Globalization and Its Discontents* (New York: Norton, 2003).

52. J. P. Baratta, *The Politics of World Federation: Vol. 1: The United Nations, U.N. Reform, Atomic Control. Vol. 2: From World Federalism to Global Governance* (Westport, CT: Praeger, 2004).

53. To name a small selection of publications, see J. Bunzl, *People-Centred Global Governance—Making It Happen!* (London: International Simultaneous Policy Organisation, 2008), available at www.simpol.org/en/books/PCGG.pdf; H.-J. Chang, *Bad Samaritans: Rich Nations, Poor Policies, and the Threat to the Developing World* (London: Random House, 2007); R. Eisler, *The Real Wealth of Nations: Creating a Caring Economics* (San Francisco: Berrett-Koehler, 2007); A. Etzioni, *The Common Good* (Cambridge: Polity, 2004); L. Gold, *The Sharing Economy: Solidarity Networks Transforming Globalisation* (Aldershot: Ashgate, 2004); J. Gray, *False Dawn: The Delusions of Global Capitalism* (London: Granta Books, 2002); H. Henderson and S. Sethi, *Ethical Markets: Growing the Green Economy* (White River Junction, VT: Chelsea Green, 2008); W. Hutton, *The Writing on the Wall: China and the West in the 21st Century* (London: Abacus, 2008); C. Karelis, *The Persistence of Poverty: Why the Economics of the Well-Off Can't Help the Poor* (New Haven, CT: Yale University Press, 2007); N. Klein, *The Shock Doctrine: The Rise of Disaster Capitalism* (New York: Metropolitan Books, 2007); R. Lane, *Loss of Happiness in Market Democracies* (New Haven,

CT: Yale University Press, 2001); P. Legrain, *Open World: The Truth about Globalisation* (London: Abacus, 2002); E. S. Reinert, *How Rich Countries Got Rich . . . And Why Poor Countries Stay Poor* (New York: Carroll & Graf, 2007); A. Sen, *Identity and Violence: The Illusion of Destiny* (New York: Norton, 2006); H. Silver and S. M. Miller, "From Poverty to Social Exclusion: Lessons from Europe," in *Poverty & Race in America: The Emerging Agendas*, ed. C. Hartman (Lexington, MA: Lexington Books, 2006), 57–70; J. E. Stiglitz, A. S. Edlin, and J. B. DeLong, eds., *The Economists' Voice: Top Economists Take on Today's Problems* (New York: Columbia University Press, 2008); G. Vaughan, ed., *Women and the Gift Economy: A Radically Different Worldview Is Possible* (Toronto: Innana Publications, 2007), retrieved on July 5, 2007, from www.gift-economy.com/womenand.html; R. G. Wilkinson, *The Impact of Inequality. How to Make Sick Societies Healthier* (London: Routledge, 2005). See also the new *Living Well* motto mentioned earlier.

54. H. Richards, "Socialism Is Good for Business," in *Solidaridad, Participacion, Transparencia* (Rosario, Argentina: Fundacion Estevez Boero, 2007), 22. This book has not yet been published in English. The full Spanish text can be found on line at lahoradelaetica.wordpress.com. This is an English translation of chapter 7. See also H. Richards and J. Swanger, *The Dilemmas of Social Democracies* (Lanham, MD: Rowman and Littlefield, 2006).

55. See A. P. Fiske, *Structures of Social Life: The Four Elementary Forms of Human Relations—Communal Sharing, Authority Ranking, Equality Matching, Market Pricing* (New York: Free Press, 1991).

56. See, for example, F. S. Heffermehl, ed., *Peace Is Possible* (Geneva: International Peace Bureau with the support of UNESCO, 2001).

57. See www.un.org/millenniumgoals.

58. For literature on relative deprivation and causal attribution, apart from F. Heider, *The Psychology of Interpersonal Relations* (New York: Wiley, 1958), H. H. Kelley, "The Processes of Causal Attribution," *American Psychologist*, 28, no. 107 (1973): 128, and I. Walker and T. F. Pettigrew, "Relative Deprivation Theory: An Overview and Conceptual Critique," *British Journal of Social Psychology*, 23 (1984): 301–310, see also I. Choi, R. E. Nisbett, and A. Norenzayan, "Causal Attribution across Cultures: Variation and Universality," *Psychological Bulletin*, 125 (1999): 47–63, F. J. Crosby, P. Muehrer, and G. Loewenstein, "Relative Deprivation and Explanation: Models and Concepts," in *Relative Deprivation and Assertive Action. The Ontario Symposium*, ed. J. M. Olson, M. P. Zanna, and P. Hernan (Hillsdale, NJ: Erlbaum, 1986), 214–237; M. Fine, A. Burns, Y. A. Payne, and M. E. Torre, *Civics Lessons: The Color and Class of Betrayal* (New York: Social/Personality Psychology, Graduate Center, CUNY, 2002); or C. W. Leach, N. Snider, and A. Iyer, "'Poisoning the Consciences of the Fortunate': The Experience of Relative Advantage and Support for Social Equality," in *Relative Deprivation: Specification, Development, and Integration*, ed. I. Walker and H. J. Smith (Cambridge: Cambridge University Press, 2001), 136–163, just to name a few out of a large body of literature. W. G. Runciman, *Relative Deprivation and Social Justice: A Study of Attitudes to Social Inequality in Twentieth-Century England* (London: Routledge & Keagan Paul, 1966), differentiates egoistic and fraternal deprivation. Egoistical deprivation arises when an individual feels disadvantaged relative to other individuals; fraternal deprivation occurs when a person feels his group is disadvantaged in relation to another group. N. J. Colletta and M. L. Cullen, *Violent Conflict and the Transformation of*

Social Capital: Lessons from Cambodia, Rwanda, Guatemala, and Somalia (Washington, DC: World Bank, 2000), make the argument that private investment increases social cohesion. However, this claim may be questioned. I thank Elizabeth E. Scheper for making me aware of this literature and the counterargument. Investment may also lead to the opposite of social cohesion, particularly when investment creates inequalities that are perceived as illegitimate. In that case, investment could even lead to feelings of humiliation and resentment.

59. H. B. Lewis, *Shame and Guilt in Neurosis* (New York: International Universities Press, 1971).

60. Interviews in March 2004 in Israel.

61. See, for example, L. Klaveras, "Political Realism: A Culprit for the 9/11 Attacks," *Harvard International Review*, 26 (Europe), no. 3 (2004), retrieved on February 29, 2008, from hir.harvard.edu/articles/1252/1, explaining the virtues of liberalism over realism in the aftermath of the 9/11 attacks.

62. See, for example, B. Richardson, "A New Realism: A Realistic and Principled Foreign Policy," *Foreign Affairs*, 87, no. 1 (2008): 142–154, governor of New Mexico, and candidate for the Democratic presidential nomination, discussing "a new realism." See also E. G. Lindner, "Dynamics of Humiliation in a Globalizing World," *International Journal on World Peace*, XXXIV, no. 3, September (2007): 15–52.

63. See www.wto.org/english/tratop_e/dda_e/dda_e.htm. In June 2007, negotiations within the Doha Round broke down at a conference in Potsdam, as a major impasse occurred between the United States, the European Union, India, and Brazil. The main disagreements rage over opening up agricultural and industrial markets in various countries and how to cut rich nation farm subsidies.

64. A. Bandura, "Mechanisms of Moral Disengagement," in *Origins of Terrorism: Psychologies, Ideologies, Theologies, States of Mind*, ed. W. Reich (New York, Washington, DC: Cambridge University Press, Woodrow Wilson International Center for Scholars, 1990), 161–191, A. Bandura, "Moral Disengagement in the Perpetration of Inhumanities," *Personality and Social Psychology Review*, 3, no. 3 (1999): 193–209.

65. See also L. D. Ross and A. Ward, "Psychological Barriers to Dispute Resolution," *Advances in Experimental Social Psychology*, 27 (1995): 255–304; L. D. Ross, "Reactive Devaluation in Negotiation and Conflict Resolution," in *Barriers to the Negotiated Resolution of Conflict*, ed. K. J. Arrow, R. H. Mnookin, L. D. Ross, A. Tversky, and R. Wilson (New York: Norton, 1995).

66. E. G. Lindner, *Disasters as a Chance to Implement Novel Solutions That Highlight Attention to Human Dignity* (Boston: Panel contribution to the International Conference on Rebuilding Sustainable Communities for Children and Their Families after Disasters, convened by Adenrele Awotona, Founder and Director of the Center for Rebuilding Sustainable Communities after Disasters, College of Public and Community Service, University of Massachusetts, November 16–19, 2008).

67. The work done by D. Sornette, "2050: The End of the Growth Era?," in *Why Stock Markets Crash: Critical Events in Complex Financial Systems* (Princeton, NJ: Princeton University Press, 2003), 355–418 on entrepreneurial risks at ETH Zurich, for example, has a telling title.

68. See humiliationstudies.org/whoweare/evelin.php.

69. E. Boulding, *New Understandings of Citizenship: Path to a Peaceful Future?* (Boston: Boston Research Center Resources, retrieved on July 10, 2007, from /69.36.178.127/ebrf_paper.html, 2001).

70. D. T. Gilbert, *Stumbling on Happiness* (New York: Knopf, 2006).

71. E. G. Lindner, *Lebensqualität im ägyptisch-deutschen Vergleich: Eine Interkulturelle Untersuchung an drei Berufsgruppen (Ärzte, Journalisten, Künstler)* (Hamburg: Department of Psychological Medicine, University of Hamburg, doctoral dissertation in medicine, 1994).

72. See also M. Walker and W. Rosen, *How Connections Heal: Stories from Relational-Cultural Therapy* (Wellesley, MA: Guilford Press, 2004).

REFERENCES

Abu-Lughod, L. *Veiled Sentiments: Honour and Poetry in a Bedouin Society.* Berkeley: University of California Press, 1986.

Abu-Odeh, L. "Crimes of Honor and the Construction of Gender in Arab Society." *Women and Sexuality in Muslim Society.* Edited by Pinar Ilkkaracan, 363–380. Istanbul: Women for Women's Human Rights, 2000.

Adolphs, R. and A. R. Damasio. "The Interaction of Affect and Cognition: A Neurobiological Perspective." *Handbook of Affect and Social Cognition.* Edited by Joseph P. Forgas, 27–49. Mahwah, NJ: Erlbaum, 2001.

Adorno, T. W., E. Frenkel-Brunswick, D. J. Levinson, and R. N. Sanford. *The Authoritarian Personality.* New York: Harper, 1950.

Albers, H. E., K. L. Huhman, and R. L. Meisel. "Hormonal Basis of Social Conflict and Communication." *Hormones, Brain, and Behavior, Vol. 1.* Edited by Donald W. Pfaff, 393–433. Boston: Academic Press, 2002.

Al-Khayyat, S. *Honour and Shame: Women in Modern Iraq.* London: Saqi, 1990.

Allen, P. G. *The Sacred Hoop: Recovering the Feminine in American Indian Traditions.* Boston: Beacon Press, 1992.

Allred, K. G. "Anger and Retaliation in Conflict: The Role of Attribution." *The Handbook of Conflict Resolution: Theory and Practice.* Edited by Morton Deutsch and Peter T. Coleman, 236–255. San Francisco: Jossey-Bass, 2000.

Allred, K. G. "Anger and Retaliation: Toward an Understanding of Impassioned Conflict in Organizations." *Research on Negotiations in Organizations. Vol. 7.* Edited by Robert J. Bies, Roy J. Lewicki, and Blair H. Sheppard, 27–58. Greenwich, CT: JAI Press, 1999.

Amini, F., R. Lannon, and T. Lewis. *A General Theory of Love.* New York: Vintage, 2001.

Anand, P. *Foundations of Rational Choice Under Risk.* Oxford: Oxford University Press, 1993.

Anderson, B. *Imagined Communities*. London: Verso, 1991.

Anderson, M. B. *Do No Harm: How Aid Can Support Peace—or War*. Boulder, CO: Lynne Rienner, 1999.

Appiah, K. A. "The Case for Contamination." *New York Times* January 1, 2006, www.muhlenberg.edu/mgt/provost/frg/humanities/AppiahContamination .pdf.

Apter, M. J. *Motivational Styles in Everyday Life: A Guide to Reversal Theory*. Washington, DC: American Psychological Association, 2001.

Archer, M. S., R. Bhaskar, A. Collier, T. Lawson, and A. Norrie, eds. *Critical Realism: Essential Readings Roy Bhaskar, Andrew Collier, Tony Lawson, and Alan Norrie*. London: Routledge, 1998.

Arendt, H. *Eichmann in Jerusalem: A Report on the Banality of Evil*. New York: Viking Press, 1963.

Arfi, B. "Resolving the Trust Predicament: A Quantum Game-Theoretic Approach." *Theory and Decision* 59, no. 2 (2005): 127–174.

Argyris, C. *Increasing Leadership Effectiveness*. New York: Wiley, 1976.

Ariely, D. "The Cost of Social Norms: Why We Are Happy to Do Things but Not When We Are Paid to Do Them." *Predictably Irrational: The Hidden Forces That Shape Our Decisions*, 67–88. New York: HarperCollins, 2008.

Arnold, M. B. *Emotion and Personality*. New York: Columbia University Press, 1960.

Arrow, K. J. "Uncertainty and the Welfare Economics of Medical Care." *American Economic Review* 53 (1963): 941–973.

Atweh, B., S. Kemmis, and P. Weeks. *Action Research in Practice: Partnership for Social Justice in Education*. London: Routledge, 1998.

Augoustinos, M. "Ideology, False Consciousness and Psychology." *Theory & Psychology* 9, no. 3 (1999): 295–312.

Averill, J. R. *Anger and Aggression: An Essay on Emotion*. New York: Springer-Verlag, 1982.

Averill, J. R. "Illusions of Anger." *Aggression and Violence: Social Interactionist Perspectives*. Edited by Richard B. Felson and James T. Tedeschi, 171–192. Washington, DC: American Psychological Association, 1993.

Averill, J. R. "Studies on Anger and Aggression: Implications for Theories of Emotion." *Emotions in Social Psychology: Essential Readings*. Edited by W. G. Parrott, 337–352. Philadelphia: Psychology Press, 2001.

Averill, J. R. "The Emotions: An Integrative Approach." *Handbook of Personality Psychology*. Edited by Robert Hogan, John Johnson, and Stephen Briggs. San Diego, CA: Academic Press, 1997.

Axelrod, R. *The Evolution of Cooperation*. New York: Basic Books, 1984.

Axelrod, R. *The Evolution of Cooperation*. London: Penguin Books, 1990.

Axelrod, R. and W. D. Hamilton. "The Evolution of Cooperation." *Science* 211 (1981): 1390–1396.

Bachrach, P. and M. S. Baratz. "The Two Faces of Power." *American Political Science Review* 56 (1962): 947–952.

Badiou, A. *Ethics: An Essay on the Understanding of Evil*. London: Verso, 2001.

Baker, N., P. Gregware, and M. Cassidy. "Family Killing Fields: Honor Rationales in the Murder of Women." *Violence Against Women* 5, no. 2 (1999): 164–184.

Bandura, A. "Mechanisms of Moral Disengagement." *Origins of Terrorism: Psychologies, Ideologies, Theologies, States of Mind*. Edited by Walter Reich, 161–191.

New York, Washington, DC: Cambridge University Press, Woodrow Wilson International Center for Scholars, 1990.

Bandura, A. "Moral Disengagement in the Perpetration of Inhumanities." *Personality and Social Psychology Review* 3, no. 3 (1999): 193–209.

Banks, A. and J. V. Jordan. "The Human Brain: Hardwired for Connections." *Research & Action Report* 28, no. 2, Spring/Summer (2007): 8–11, retrieved on July 20, 2007, from www.wcwonline.org/joomla/index.php?option=com_content&task=view&id=1358&itemid=198.

Banks, J. A., P. Cookson, G. Gay, W. D. Hawley, J. J. Irvine, S. Nieto, J. W. Schofield, and W. G. Stephan. *Diversity within Unity: Essential Principles for Teaching and Learning in a Multicultural Society*. Seattle: Center for Multicultural Education, College of Education, University of Washington, 2001, www.educ.washington.edu/coetestwebsite/pdf/DiversityUnity.pdf.

Baratta, J. P. *The Politics of World Federation: Vol. 1: The United Nations, U.N. Reform, Atomic Control. Vol. 2: From World Federalism to Global Governance*. Westport, CT: Praeger, 2004.

Bargh, J. A. and E. L. Williams. "The Automaticity of Social Life." *Current Directions in Psychological Science* 15, no. 1 (2006): 1–4.

Bar-On, D. *The Legacy of Silence: Encounters with Children of the Third Reich*. Cambridge, MA: Harvard University Press, 1989.

Barry, B. and R. L. Oliver. "Affect in Dyadic Negotiation: A Model and Proposition." *Organizational Behavior and Human Decision Processes* 70 (1996): 175–187.

Barthes, R. *Mythologies*. London: Jonathan Cape, 1972 (a collection of short essays, written one per month between 1954 and 1956, translated by Annette Lavers in 1972).

Bartlett, S. J. *The Pathology of Man: A Study of Human Evil*. Springfield, IL: Charles C. Thomas, 2005.

Barušs, I. "Can We Consider Matter as Ultimate Reality? Some Fundamental Problems with a Materialist Interpretation of Reality." *Ultimate Reality and Meaning: Interdisciplinary Studies in the Philosophy of Understanding* 16, no. 3–4 (1993): 245–254.

Barušs, I. "The Art of Science: Science of the Future in Light of Alterations of Consciousness." *Journal of Scientific Exploration* 15, no. 1 (2001): 57–68.

Bateson, G. *Steps to an Ecology of Mind*. Scranton, PA: Chandler, 1972.

Batson, C. D., L. L. Shaw, and K. C. Oleson. "Differentiating Affect, Mood, and Emotion: Toward Functionally Based Conceptual Distinctions." *Review of Personality and Social Psychology: Vol. 13. Emotion*. Edited by Margaret S. Clark, 294–326. Newbury Park, CA: Sage, 1992.

Battle, M. J. *Reconciliation. The Ubuntu Theology of Desmond Tutu*. Cleveland, OH: Pilgrim Press, 1997.

Bauman, Z. *Globalization: The Human Consequences*. Cambridge: Polity Press, 1998.

Bauman, Z. "The Great War of Recognition." *Theory, Culture and Society* 18, no. 2-643 (2001): 137–150.

Baumeister, R. F. *Evil: Inside Human Cruelty and Violence*. New York: Freeman, 1996.

Baumeister, R. F. and K. D. Vohs, eds. *Handbook of Self-Regulation: Research, Theory, and Applications*. New York: Guilford Press, 2004.

Baumeister, R. F., T. F. Heatherton, and D. M. Tice. *Losing Control: How and Why People Fail at Self-regulation*. New York: Academic Press, 1994.

Baumeister, R. F. and M. R. Leary. "The Need to Belong: Desire for Interpersonal Attachments as a Fundamental Human Motivation." *Motivational Science: Social and Personality Perspectives.* Edited by Tory E. Higgins and Arie W. Kruglanski, 24–49. Philadelphia: Taylor and Francis, 2000.

Beck, A. T. *Prisoners of Hate: The Cognitive Basis of Anger, Hostility and Violence.* New York: HarperCollins, 1999.

Becker, E. *The Denial of Death.* New York: Free Press, 1973.

Bem, D. J. *Beliefs, Attitudes and Human Affairs.* Belmont, CA: Brooks/Cole, 1970.

Bem, D. J. "Self-Perception Theory." *Advances in Experimental Social Psychology, Vol. 6.* Edited by Leonard Berkowitz, 1–62. New York: Academic Press, 1972.

Benedict, R. *The Chrysanthemum and the Sword.* Boston: Houghton Mifflin Company, 1946.

Benoliel, B. *Public Humiliation as a Mitigator in Criminal Sentencing.* Minneapolis, MN: Walden University, doctoral dissertation, 2006.

Berger, P. L. "On the Obsolescence of the Concept of Honor." *Archives Européennes De Sociologie* 11, no. 2 (1970): 339–347.

Berger, P. L. and T. Luckmann. *The Social Construction of Reality: A Treatise in the Sociology of Knowledge.* Garden City, NY: Doubleday, 1966.

Berlin, I. "The Bent Twig: On the Rise of Nationalism." *The Crooked Timber of Humanity: Chapters in the History of Ideas.* Edited by Henry Hardy, 238–261. London: Fontana Press, 1991.

Bernays, E. *Propaganda.* New York: Horace Liveright, 1928.

Berne, E. *What Do You Say after You Say Hello?* New York: Bantam, 1972.

Bernhardt, P. C. "Influences of Serotonin and Testosterone in Aggression and Dominance: Convergence with Social Psychology." *Current Directions in Psychological Science* 6, no. 2, April (1997): 44–48.

Bernoulli, D. "Exposition of a New Theory on the Measurement of Risk." *Econometrica* 22, no. 1 (1954): 23–36.

Besnier, N. "The Politics of Emotion in Nukulaelae Gossip." *Everyday Conceptions of Emotion.* Edited by James A. Russell, Jose M. Fernández-Dols, Antony S. R. Manstead, and Jane C. Wellenkamp, 221–240. Dordrecht: Kluwer Academic, 1995.

Billig, M. G. *Arguing and Thinking.* London: Cambridge University Press, 1987.

Billig, M. G. *Banal Nationalism.* London: Sage, 1995.

Billig, M. G. *Ideology and Opinions. Studies in Rhetorical Psychology.* London: Sage, 1991.

Billig, M. G. "Politics as an Appearance and Reality Show: The Hermeneutics of Suspicion." *Political Communications: The General Election Campaign of 2005.* Edited by Dominic Wring, Green Jane, Roger Mortimore, and Simon Atkinson, 223–238. London: Palgrave Macmillan, 2007.

Billig, M. G. "Remembering the Particular Background of Social Identity Theory." *Social Groups and Identities. Developing the Legacy of Henri Tajfel.* Edited by W. P. Robinson. Oxford: Butterworth, Heinemann, 1996.

Billig, M. G. *Social Psychology and Intergroup Relations.* London: Published in cooperation with the European Association of Experimental Social Psychology by Academic Press, 1976.

Billig, M. G. "Towards a Critique of the Critical: Editorial." *Discourse & Society* 11, no. 3 (2000): 291–292, retrieved on August 24, 2006, from das.sagepub.com.

Billig, M. G., S. Condor, D. Edwards, M. Gane, D. Middleton, and A. Radley. *Ideological Dilemmas. A Social Psychology of Everyday Thinking.* London: Sage, 1988.

Blakeslee, S. "Cells That Read Minds." *New York Times,* January 10, 2006, Section F, Column 2, Science Desk, retrieved on January 10, 2006, from www.nytimes.com/2006/01/10/science/10mirr.html?ei=5088&en=4b525f923a669928&ex=1294549200&partner=rssnyt&emc=rss&pagewanted=print.

Bodenhausen, G. V. "Emotions, Arousal, and Stereotypic Judgments: A Heuristic Model of Affect and Stereotyping." *Affect, Cognition, and Stereotyping.* Edited by Diane M. Mackie and David L. Hamilton, 13–37. San Diego, CA: Academic Press, 1993.

Bodenhausen, G. V. "Stereotypic Biases in Social Decision Making and Memory: Testing Process Models of Stereotype Use." *Journal of Personality and Social Psychology* 55 (1988): 726–737.

Bodenhausen, G. V., T. Mussweiler, S. Gabriel, and K. N. Moreno. "Affective Influences on Stereotyping and Intergroup Relations." *Handbook of Affect and Social Cognition.* Edited by Joseph P. Forgas, 319–343. Mahwah, NJ: Erlbaum, 2001.

Bonanno, G. A. "Emotion Self-Regulation." *Emotions: Current Issues and Future Directions.* Edited by Tracy J. Mayne and George A. Bonanno, 251–285. New York: Guilford Press, 2001.

Bonanno, G. A. and J. T. Jost. "Conservative Shift among High-Exposure Survivors of the September 11th Terrorist Attacks." *Basic and Applied Social Psychology* 28, no. 4 (2006): 311–323.

Bonanno, G. A. and T. J. Mayne. "Preface." *Emotions: Current Issues and Future Directions.* Edited by Tracy J. Mayne and George A. Bonanno, xvii–xx. New York: Guilford Press, 2001.

Bonanno, G. A. and T. J. Mayne. "The Future of Emotion Research." *Emotions: Current Issues and Future Directions.* Edited by Tracy J. Mayne and George A. Bonanno, 398–410. New York: Guilford Press, 2001.

Bond, M. H. "Culture and Aggression—From Context to Coercion." *Personality and Social Psychology Review* 8 (2004): 62–78.

Bond, M. H. "Culture and Collective Violence: How Good People, Usually Men, Do Bad Things." *Are We Lost in Translations? On Intercultural Encounters in Treatment of Complex Trauma and PTSD.* Edited by Boris Drozdek and John P. Wilson. New York: Springer, 2006.

Bond, M. H. "Unity in Diversity: Orientations and Strategies for Building a Harmonious, Multicultural Society." *Social Psychology and Cultural Context.* Edited by John Adamopoulos and Yoshihisa Kashima, 17–40. Thousand Oaks, CA: Sage, 1998.

Borris, E. R. *The Healing Power of Forgiveness.* Fairfax, VA: Paper prepared for course on Reconciliation Processes, Institute of Conflict Analysis and Resolution, George Mason University, March 13–15, 2000.

Boulding, E. *Building a Global Civic Culture: Education for an Interdependent World.* New York: Teachers College Press, 1988.

Boulding, E. *New Understandings of Citizenship: Path to a Peaceful Future?* Boston, MA: Boston Research Center Resources, retrieved on July 10, 2007, from 69.36.178.127/ebrf_paper.html, 2001.

Bourdieu, P. *Algeria 1960: The Disenchantment of the World, the Sense of Honour, the Kabyle House or the World Reversed.* Cambridge/Paris: Cambridge University Press/Editions de la Maison des Sciences de l'Homme, 1979.

Bourdieu, P. *Masculine Domination*. Stanford, CA: Stanford University Press, 2001.

Bourdieu, P. *Outline of a Theory of Practice*. Cambridge: Cambridge University Press, 1977.

Bourke, J. "How to Seek Shelter When It's Raining Fear." *International Herald Tribune*, February 8. 2005, www.commondreams.org/views05/0208-26.htm.

Bower, J. L. "Solve the Succession Crisis by Growing Inside-Outside Leaders." *Harvard Business Review* 85, no. 11, November (2007): 91–96.

Bowlby, J. *Attachment and Loss*. New York: Basic Books, 1969.

Boyarsky, N. and N. Murphy. *Action Research*. London: Black Dog, 1998.

Bradley, F. H. *Appearance and Reality: A Metaphysical Essay*. New York: Macmillan, 1893.

Bradshaw, J. E. *Healing the Shame That Binds You*. Expanded and updated ed. Deerfield Beach, FL: Health Communications, 2005.

Brafman, O. and R. Brafman. *Sway: The Irresistible Pull of Irrational Behavior*. New York: Doubleday Business, 2008.

Braithwaite, J. *Crime, Shame and Reintegration*. Cambridge: Cambridge University Press, 1989.

Braithwaite, J. *Restorative Justice and Responsive Regulation*. Oxford: Oxford University Press, 2002.

Breines, I., R. W. Connell, and I. Eide, eds. *Males Roles, Masculinities and Violence. A Culture of Peace Perspective*. Paris: UNESCO, 2000.

Brewer, M. B. and M. Silver. "Ingroup Bias as a Function of Task Characteristics." *European Journal of Social Psychology* 8 (1978): 393–400

Brewer, M. B. and S. Roccas. "Social Identity Complexity." *Personality and Social Psychology Review* 6 (2002): 88–106.

Brewer, M. B. and R. M. Kramer. "The Psychology of Intergroup Attitudes and Behavior." *Annual Review of Psychology* 36 (1985): 219–243.

Brittan, S. *An Ethical Foreign Policy?* Cambridge, MA: Samuel Brittan: Hinton Lecture 24/11/99 at the Harvard School of Public Health, 1999, www.samuelbrittan.co.uk/spee6_p.html.

Brothers, L. *Friday's Footprint: How Society Shapes the Human Mind*. New York: Oxford University Press, 1997.

Bruner, J. S. *Acts of Meaning*. Cambridge, MA: Harvard University Press, 1990.

Brunstein, J. C. "Personal Goals and Subjective Well-Being: A Longitudinal Study." *Journal of Personality and Social Psychology* 65 (1993): 1061–1070.

Buber, M. *I and Thou*. Edinburgh: Clark, translated from *Ich und Du*, Leipzig: Infelverlag, 1923, 1944.

Bunzl, J. *People-Centred Global Governance—Making It Happen!* London: International Simultaneous Policy Organisation, 2008, www.simpol.org/en/books/PCGG.pdf.

Burke, P. *A Social History of Knowledge: From Gutenberg to Diderot*. Cambridge: Polity Press, 2000.

Cacioppo, J. T. and G. G. Berntson, eds. *Essays in Social Neuroscience*. Cambridge, MA: MIT Press, 2004.

Cacioppo, J. T., G. G. Berntson, R. Adolphs, C. S. Carter, R. J. Davidson, M. K. McClintock, B. S. McEwen, M. J. Meaney, D. L. Schacter, E. M. Sternberg, S. S. Suomi, and S. E. Taylor, eds. *Foundations in Social Neuroscience*. Cambridge, MA: MIT Press, 2002.

Cacioppo, J. T., W. L. Gardner, and G. G. Berntson. "The Affect System Has Parallel and Integrative Processing Components: Form Follows Function." *Journal of Personality and Social Psychology* 76, no. 5 (1999): 839–855.

Carson, T. R. and D. J. Sumara. *Action Research as a Living Practice.* New York: Lang, 1997.

Carver, C. S. and M. F. Scheier. *Attention and Self-regulation: A Control Theory Approach to Human Behavior.* New York: Springer, 1981.

Carver, C. S. and M. F. Scheier. "Control Theory: A Useful Conceptual Framework for Personality—Social, Clinical and Health Psychology." *Psychological Bulletin* 92 (1982): 111–135.

Caspi, A., T. E. Moffitt, J. Mill, J. Martin, I. W. Craig, A. Taylor, and R. Poulton. "Role of Genotype in the Cycle of Violence in Maltreated Children." *Science* 297, August (2002): 851–854.

Castells, M. *The Information Age: Economy, Society and Culture. End of Millennium* (Vol. 3). Cambridge, MA; Oxford: Blackwell, 1997.

Castells, M. *The Information Age: Economy, Society and Culture. The Power of Identity* (Vol. 2). Cambridge, MA; Oxford: Blackwell, 1997.

Castells, M. *The Information Age: Economy, Society and Culture. The Rise of the Network Society* (Vol. 1). Cambridge, MA; Oxford: Blackwell, 1996.

Cederman, L.-E. "Modeling the Democratic Peace as a Kantian Selection Process." *Journal of Conflict Resolution* 45, no. 4 (2001): 470–502.

Chaiken, S. L. "Heuristic versus Systematic Information Processing and the Use of Source versus Message Cues in Persuasion." *Journal of Personality and Social Psychology* 39 (1980): 752–766.

Chaiken, S. L., D. H. Gruenfeld, and C. M. Judd. "Persuasion in Negotiations and Conflict Situations." *The Handbook of Conflict Resolution: Theory and Practice.* Edited by Morton Deutsch and Peter T. Coleman, 144–165. San Francisco: Jossey-Bass, 2000.

Chang, H.-J. *Bad Samaritans: Rich Nations, Poor Policies, and the Threat to the Developing World.* London: Random House, 2007.

Charny, I. W. "A Personality Disorder of Excessive Power Strivings." *Israel Journal of Psychiatry* 34, no. 1 (1997): 3–17.

Charny, I. W., ed. *Encyclopedia of Genocide.* Santa Barbara, CA: ABC-CLIO, 1999.

Chase-Dunn, C. "World State Formation: Historical Processes and Emergent Necessity." *Political Geography Quarterly* 9, no. 2 (1990): 108–130.

Chase-Dunn, C. and T. D. Hall. *Paradigms Bridged: Institutional Materialism and World-Systemic Evolution.* Retrieved June 21, 2004, from csf.colorado.edu/wsystems/archive/papers/c-d&hall/ssha97.htm, 2004.

Chen, C. *Chinese Children's Humiliation at School.* Minneapolis: University of Minnesota, doctoral dissertation, 2004.

Choi, I., R. E. Nisbett, and A. Norenzayan. "Causal Attribution across Cultures: Variation and Universality." *Psychological Bulletin* 125 (1999): 47–63.

Christie, D. J. "What Is Peace Psychology the Psychology of?" *Journal of Social Issues* 62, no. 1 (2006): 1–17, retrieved on August 14, 2007, from www.blackwell-synergy.com/doi/pdf/10.1111/j.1540-4560.2006.00436.x.

Clark, E. *The Want Makers: Inside the World of Advertising.* New York: Viking, 1988.

Clark, W. R. and M. Grunstein. *Are We Hardwired?* New York: Oxford University Press, 2000.

Coates, J. M. and J. Herbert. "Endogenous Steroids and Financial Risk-Taking on a London Trading Floor." *Proceedings of the National Academy of Sciences* 105, no. 16 (2008): 6167–6172, www.pnas.org/content/105/16/6167.full.pdf+html.

Colbert, S. T. *The Colbert Report.* Television show, October 17, 2005, http://www .colbertnation.com/the-colbert-report-videos/24039/october-17-2005/the-word—truthiness, 2005.

Coleman, P. T. "Characteristics of Protracted, Intractable Conflict: Toward the Development of a Metaframework—I." *Peace and Conflict: Journal of Peace Psychology* 9, no. 1 (2003): 1–37.

Coleman, P. T. "Conflict, Complexity, and Change: A Meta-Framework for Addressing Protracted, Intractable Conflicts—III." *Peace and Conflict: Journal of Peace Psychology* 12, no. 4 (2006): 325–348.

Coleman, P. T. "Intractable Conflict." *The Handbook of Conflict Resolution: Theory and Practice*, 2nd ed. Edited by Morton Deutsch, Peter T. Coleman, and Eric C. Marcus. San Francisco: Jossey-Bass, 2006.

Coleman, P. T. "Paradigmatic Framing of Protracted, Intractable Conflict: Towards the Development of a Meta-Framework—II." *Peace and Conflict: Journal of Peace Psychology* 10, no. 3 (2004): 197–235.

Coleman, P. T., J. S. Goldman, and K. Kugler. *Emotional Intractability: The Effects of Emotional Roles on Aggression and Rumination in Conflict.* New York: International Center for Cooperation and Conflict Resolution. Teachers College, Columbia University, 2007, retrieved on December 19, 2007, from www.tc.columbia.edu/ ICCCR/Documents/Coleman/PC_Emotinal_Intractability.pdf.

Coleman, P. T., R. R. Vallacher, A. Nowak, and L. Bui-Wrzosinska. "Intractable Conflict As an Attractor: A Dynamical Systems Approach to Conflict Escalation and Intractability." *American Behavioral Scientist* 50 (2007): 14–54, retrieved on March 3, 2008, from abs.sagepub.com/cgi/content/abstract/50/11/1454.

Coleman, P. T., and M. Deutsch. "Some Guidelines for Developing a Creative Approach to Conflict." *The Handbook of Conflict Resolution: Theory and Practice.* Edited by Morton Deutsch and Peter T. Coleman, 355–365. San Francisco: Jossey-Bass, 2000.

Coleman, P. T., K. Kugler, and J. S. Goldman. *The Privilege of Humiliation: The Effects of Social Roles and Norms on Immediate and Prolonged Aggression in Conflict.* New York: Paper submitted to the 20th annual conference of the International Association for Conflict Management, 2007.

Colletta, N. J. and M. L. Cullen. *Violent Conflict and the Transformation of Social Capital: Lessons from Cambodia, Rwanda, Guatemala, and Somalia.* Washington, DC: World Bank, 2000.

Collins, A. "State-Induced Security Dilemma Maintaining the Tragedy." *Cooperation and Conflict* 39, no. 1 (2004): 27–44.

Collins, J. "Level 5 Leadership: The Triumph of Humility and Fierce Resolve." *Harvard Business Review* January (2001): 68–76.

Collins, P. H. *Black Feminist Thought: Knowledge, Consciousness, and the Politics of Empowerment.* New York: Routledge, 1991.

Conlan, T. D. *In Little Need of Divine Intervention: Takezaki Suenaga's Scrolls of the Mongol Invasions of Japan.* Ithaca, NY: East Asia Program, Cornell University, 2001.

Connell, R. W. *Masculinities.* Cambridge: Polity Press, 1995.

Connell, R. W. "Teaching Boys: New Research on Masculinity, and Gender Strategies for Schools." *Teachers College Record* 98, no. 2 (1996): 206–235.

Coopersmith, S. "The Antecedents of Self-Esteem." San Francisco: Freeman, 1967.

Coser, L. A. *Masters of Sociological Thought: Ideas in Historical and Social Context*, 2nd ed. Fort Worth, TX: Harcourt Brace Jovanovich, 1977.

Crocker, C. A., F. O. Hampson, and P. Aall, eds. *Grasping the Nettle: Analyzing Cases of Intractable Conflict*. Washington, DC: U.S. Institute of Peace Press, 2005.

Crosby, F. J., P. Muehrer, and G. Loewenstein. "Relative Deprivation and Explanation: Models and Concepts." *Relative Deprivation and Assertive Action. The Ontario Symposium*. Edited by James M. Olson, Mark P. Zanna, and P. Hernan, 214–237. Hillsdale, NJ: Erlbaum, 1986.

Csikszentmihalyi, M. *Creativity: Flow and the Psychology of Discovery and Invention*. New York: Harper Perennial, 1996.

Dai, D. Y. "Putting It All Together: Some Concluding Thoughts." *Motivation, Emotion, and Cognition: Integrative Perspectives on Intellectual Functioning and Development*. Edited by David Y. Dai and Robert J. Sternberg, 419–432. Mahwah, NJ: Erlbaum, 2004.

Dai, D. Y. and R. J. Sternberg. "Beyond Cognitivism: Toward an Integrated Understanding of Intellectual Functioning and Development." *Motivation, Emotion, and Cognition: Integrative Perspectives on Intellectual Functioning and Development*. Edited by David Y. Dai and Robert J. Sternberg, 3–40. Mahwah, NJ: Erlbaum, 2004.

Dalziell, R., D. Parker, and I. Wright, eds. *Shame and the Modern Self*. Melbourne: Australian Scholarly Publishers, 1996.

Damasio, A. R. "A Neurobiology for Consciousness." *Neural Correlates of Consciousness*. Edited by Thomas Metzinger, 111–120. Cambridge, MA: MIT Press, 2000.

Damasio, A. R. *Descartes' Error. Emotion, Reason and the Human Brain*. New York: Avon Books, 1994.

Damasio, A. R. *Looking for Spinoza: Joy, Sorrow, and the Feeling Brain*. Orlando, FL: Harcourt, 2003.

Damasio, A. R. *The Feeling of What Happens: Body and Emotion in the Making of Consciousness*. New York: Harcourt Brace, 1999.

Danner, M. "America Defeated: How Terrorists Turned a Superpower's Strengths Against Itself." *Alternet* March 26 (2008), www.alternet.org/story/80547.

Darwin, C. *The Expression of the Emotions in Man and Animals*, 3rd ed. London: HarperCollins, 1872.

Davidson, R. J. "The Neuroscience of Affective Style." *The New Cognitive Neurosciences*, 2nd ed. Edited by Michael S. Gazzaniga, 1149–1162. Cambridge, MA: MIT Press, 2000.

Davidson, R. J., J. Kabat-Zinn, J. Schumacher, M. Rosenkranz, D. Muller, S. F. Santorelli, F. Urbanowski, A. Harrington, K. Bonus, and J. F. Sheridan. "Alterations in Brain and Immune Function Produced by Mindfulness Meditation." *Psychosomatic Medicine* 65 (2003): 564–570.

De Costa, C. M. " 'The Contagiousness of Childbed Fever': A Short History of Puerperal Sepsis and Its Treatment." *Medical Journal of Australia* 177, no. 11/12 (2002): 668–671, retrieved on February 25, 2008, from www.mja.com.au/public/issues/177_11_021202/dec10354_fm.html#i1067496.

De Rivera, J., R. Kurrien, and N. Olsen. "Emotional Climates, Human Security, and Cultures of Peace." *Journal of Social Issues* 63, no. 2, June (2007): 255–271.

Deikman, A. J. *The Observing Self: Mysticism and Psychotherapy*. Boston: Beacon Press, 1982.

Derrida, J. "Of Grammatology." Baltimore, MD: Johns Hopkins University Press, 1976 (translation from the original French edition *De la grammatologie* first published in 1967).

Deudney, D. "Geopolitics and Change." *New Thinking in International Relations Theory*. Edited by Michael W. Doyle and G. J. Ikenberry, 91–123. Boulder, CO: Westview Press, 1999.

Deudney, D. "Regrounding Realism." *Security Studies* 10, no. 1 (2000): 1–45.

Deutsch, M. "A Personal Perspective on the Development of Social Psychology in the Twentieth Century." *Reflections on 100 Years of Experimental Social Psychology*. Edited by A. Rodriguez and R. V. Levine, 1–34. New York: Basic Books, 1999.

Deutsch, M. "Cooperation and Competition." *The Handbook of Conflict Resolution: Theory and Practice*. Edited by Morton Deutsch and Peter T. Coleman, 21–40. San Francisco: Jossey-Bass, 2000.

Deutsch, M. *Oppression and Conflict*. Skovde, Sweden: Plenary address given at the annual meetings of the International Society of Justice Research in Skovde, Sweden on June 17, 2002, retrieved November 20, 2002, from www.cpa.ca/epw/epw/Deutsch.pdf.

Deutsch, M. *The Resolution of Conflict: Constructive and Destructive Processes*. New Haven, CT: Yale University Press, 1973.

Devine, P. G. "Stereotypes and Prejudice: Their Automatic and Controlled Components." *Journal of Personality and Social Psychology* 56, no. 1 (1989): 5–18.

Devine, P. G., S. R. Evett, and K. A. Vasquez-Suson. "Exploring the Interpersonal Dynamics of Intergroup Contact." *Handbook of Motivation and Cognition, Vol. 3*. Edited by Richard M. Sorrentino and E. T. Higgins, 423–464. New York: Guilford Press, 1996.

Dewey, J. *Democracy and Education*. New York: Free Press, 1916.

Dewey, J. "The Theory of Emotion (I) Emotional Attitudes." *Psychological Review* 1 (1894): 553–569.

Dewey, J. "The Theory of Emotion (Ll) The Significance of Emotions." *Psychological Review* 2 (1895): 13–32.

Diamond, J. *Collapse: How Societies Choose to Fail or Succeed*. New York: Viking, 2005.

Diamond, J. *Guns, Germs, and Steel*. New York: Norton, 1997.

Dickerson, S. S. and M. E. Kemeny. "When the Social Self Is Threatened: Shame, Physiology, and Health." *Journal of Personality* 72 (2004): 1191–1216.

Dillon, R. S., ed. *Dignity, Character, and Self-Respect*. New York: Routledge, 1995.

Dovidio, J. F., S. L. Gaertner, A. M. Isen, M. C. Rust, and P. Guerra. "Positive Affect, Cognition, and the Reduction of Intergroup Bias." *Intergroup Cognition and Intergroup Behavior*. Edited by Constantine Sedikides, John Schopler, and Chester A. Insko, 337–366. Mahwah, NJ: Erlbaum, 1998.

Dow, E. I. *Approaching Intercultural Communication from the Space Between*. Tokyo: Seminar given at the 20th Annual Conference of the Society for Intercultural Education, Training, and Research (SIETAR) Japan, June 26 2005, Rikkyo University.

Dower, J. W. *Embracing Defeat: Japan in the Wake of World War II*. New York: Norton, 1999.

Duchenne de Bolougne, G. B. A. *The Mechanism of Human Facial Expression*. New York: Cambridge University Press, 1862.

Dunbar, R. I. M. "The Social Brain Hypothesis." *Evolutionary Anthropology* 6 (1998): 178–190.

Durkheim, E. *The Evolution of Educational Thought: Lectures on the Formation and Development of Secondary Education in France.* London: Routledge & Kegan Paul, 1977.

Dutton, D. G., E. O. Boyanowsky, and M. H. Bond. "Extreme Mass Homicide: From Military Massacre to Genocide." *Aggression and Violent Behavior* 10 (2005): 437–473.

Dweck, C. S., J. A. Mangels, and C. Good. "Motivational Effects on Attention, Cognition, and Performance." *Motivation, Emotion, and Cognition: Integrative Perspectives on Intellectual Functioning and Development.* Edited by David Y. Dai and Robert J. Sternberg, 41–56. Mahwah, NJ: Erlbaum, 2004.

Eagleton, T. *Ideology: An Introduction.* London: Verso, 1991.

Edelman, G. M. "Memory and the Individual Soul: Against Silly Reductionism." *Nature's Imagination: The Frontiers of Scientific Vision.* Edited by John Cornwell, 200–206. Oxford: Oxford University Press, 1995.

Ehrlich, P. R. and A. H. Ehrlich. *The Dominant Animal: Human Evolution and the Environment.* Washington, DC: Island Press, 2008.

Eidelson, R. J. and J. I. Eidelson. "Dangerous Ideas: Five Beliefs That Propel Groups Toward Conflict." *American Psychologist* 58, no. 3 (2003): 182–192.

Eisenberger, N. I. and M. D. Lieberman. "Why It Hurts to Be Left Out: The Neurocognitive Overlap between Physical Pain and Social Pain." *The Social Outcast: Ostracism, Social Exclusion, Rejection, and Bullying.* Edited by Kipling Williams, Joseph P. Forgas, and William v. Hippel, 109–127. New York: Psychology Press, 2005.

Eisler, R. *The Chalice and the Blade: Our History, Our Future.* London: Unwin Hyman, 1987.

Eisler, R. *The Real Wealth of Nations: Creating a Caring Economics.* San Francisco: Berrett-Koehler, 2007.

Ekman, P. "An Argument for Basic Emotions." *Cognition and Emotion* 6 (1992): 169–200.

Ekman, P. "Are There Basic Emotions?" *Psychological Review* 99, no. 3, July (1992): 550–553.

Ekman, P., R. J. Davidson, M. Ricard, and B. A. Wallace. "Buddhist and Psychological Perspectives on Emotions and Well-Being." *Current Directions in Psychological Science* 14, no. 2 (2005): 59

Ekman, P., W. V. Friesen, and P. C. Ellsworth. *Emotion in the Human Face: Guidelines for Research and Integration of Findings.* New York: Pergamon Press, 1972.

Ekman, P. and W. V. Friesen. "Felt, False, and Miserable Smiles." *Journal of Nonverbal Behavior* 6 (1982): 238–252.

Ekman, P. and R. J. Davidson. *The Nature of Emotion: Fundamental Questions.* New York: Oxford University Press, 1994.

Ekman, P., W. V. Friesen, and P. C. Ellsworth. "What Emotion Categories or Dimensions Can Observers Judge from Facial Behavior?" *Emotion in the Human Face,* 2nd ed. Edited by Paul Ekman, 39–55. Cambridge: Cambridge University Press, 1982.

Elias, N. *The Civilizing Process (Volume 1: The History of Manners, Volume 2: State Formation and Civilization).* Oxford: Blackwell, 1994.

Elias, N. *The Germans. Power Struggles and the Development of Habitus in the Nineteenth and Twentieth Centuries [Studien über die Deutschen: Machtkämpfe und*

Habitusentwicklung im 19. und 20. Jahrhundert]. Cambridge: Polity Press, 1996 (original work published in German 1989).

Elias, N. *What Is Sociology?* London: Hutchinson, 1978.

Elison, J. and S. Harter. "Humiliation: Causes, Correlates, and Consequences." *The Self-Conscious Emotions: Theory and Research.* Edited by Jessica L. Tracy, Richard W. Robins, and June P. Tangney, 310–329. New York: Guilford Press, 2007.

Ellis, H. C. and P. W. Ashbrook. "Resource Allocation Model of the Effects of Depressed Mood States on Memory." *Affect, Cognition, and Social Behavior.* Edited by Klaus Fiedler and Joseph P. Forgas, 25–43. Toronto: Hogrefe, 1988.

Ellison, S. *Taking the War Out of Our Words: The Art of Powerful Non-Defensive Communication.* Berkeley, CA: Bay Tree Publishing, 2003.

Elster, J. *Alchemies of the Mind: Rationality and the Emotions.* Cambridge: Cambridge University Press, 2003.

Elster, J. "Emotion and Action." *Thinking about Feeling: Contemporary Philosophers on Emotions.* Edited by Robert Solomon. New York: Oxford University Press, 2003.

Elster, J. *Strong Feelings: Emotion, Addiction, and Human Behavior.* Cambridge, MA: MIT Press, 1999.

Epstein, J. and R. Axtell. *Growing Artificial Societies: Social Science from the Bottom Up.* Cambridge, MA: MIT Press, 1996.

Etzioni, A. *The Common Good.* Cambridge: Polity, 2004.

Etzioni, A. "The Epigenesist of Political Communities at the International Level." *American Journal of Sociology* 68, no. 4 (1963): 407–421.

Faber, B. "Intuitive Ethics: Understanding and Critiquing the Role of Intuition in Ethical Decisions." *Technical Communication Quarterly* 8, no. 2, Spring (1999): 189–202.

Fairclough, N. *Discourse and Social Change.* Cambridge: Polity, 1992.

Fanon, F. *Black Skin, White Masks.* London: Pluto Press, 1986.

Fazio, R. H., D. M. Sanbonmatsu, M. C. Powell, and F. R. Kardes. "On the Automatic Activation of Attitudes." *Journal of Personality and Social Psychology* 50, no. 2 (1986): 229–238.

Fehr, E., U. Fischbacher, and M. Kosfeld. *Neuroeconomic Foundation of Trust and Social Preferences.* London: Centre for Economic Policy Research, 2005.

Fehr, E., M. Naef, and K. Schmidt. *The Role of Equality and Efficiency in Social Preferences.* London: Centre for Economic Policy Research, 2005.

Feldman Barrett, L. "The Future of Emotion Research." *Affect Scientist* 12 (1998): 6–8.

Feldman Barrett, L. and J. A. Russell. "The Structure of Current Affect: Controversies and Emerging Consensus." *Current Directions in Psychological Science* 8 (1999): 10–14.

Festinger, L. *A Theory of Cognitive Dissonance.* Stanford, CA: Stanford University Press, 1957.

Fine, M., A. Burns, Y. A. Payne, and M. E. Torre. *Civics Lessons: The Color and Class of Betrayal.* New York: Social/Personality Psychology, The Graduate Center, CUNY, 2002.

Fineman, M. A. *The Myth of Autonomy: A Theory of Dependency.* New York: New Press, 2004.

Fischer, K. W. and J. P. Tangney. "Introduction: Self-Conscious Emotions and the Affect Revolution: Framework and Overview." *Self-Conscious Emotions: The*

Psychology of Shame, Guilt, Embarrassment, and Pride. Edited by Kurt W. Fischer and June P. Tangney, 3–24. New York: Guilford Press, 1995.

Fisher, R., W. Ury, and B. Patton. *Getting to Yes: Negotiating Agreement without Giving in.* New York: Houghton Mifflin, 1991.

Fisher, R. and D. L. Shapiro. *Beyond Reason: Using Emotions as You Negotiate.* New York: Penguin, 2005.

Fisher-Yoshida, B. "Coaching to Transform Perspective." *Transformative Learning in Action.* Edited by Jack Mezirow and Edward W. Taylor. San Francisco: Jossey-Bass, 2008.

Fisk, L. J. and J. L. Schellenberg. *Patterns of Conflict: Paths to Peace.* Peterborough, ON: Broadview Press, 2000.

Fiske, A. P. *Structures of Social Life: The Four Elementary Forms of Human Relations—Communal Sharing, Authority Ranking, Equality Matching, Market Pricing.* New York: Free Press, 1991.

Flanagan, O. "Destructive Emotions." *Consciousness and Emotion* 1, no. 2 (2000): 259–281.

Flinders, C. L. *Rebalancing the World: Why Women Belong and Men Compete and How to Restore the Ancient Equilibrium.* San Francisco: Harper, 2002.

Føllesdal, D. *How Can We Use Arguments in Ethics?* Oslo: Presentation at Det Norske Vitenskaps-Akademi [Norwegian Academy of Science], January 30, 1996.

Føllesdal, D. "Husserl on Evidence and Justification." *Edmund Husserl and the Phenomenological Tradition: Essays in Phenomenology. Proceedings of a Lecture Series in the Fall of 1985, in Studies in Philosophy and the History of Philosophy.* Edited by Robert Sokolowski, 107–129. Washington, DC: Catholic University of America Press, 1988.

Føllesdal, D. *Intersubjectivity and Ethics in Husserl's Phenomenology.* Oslo: Seminar organised by the Norwegian Ethics Programme at the Research Council of Norway, February 19–24, 1996.

Foo, L. and G. Margolin. "A Multivariate Investigation of Dating Aggression." *Journal of Family Violence* 10, no. 4 (1995): 351–377.

Forgas, J. P. "Feeling and Thinking: Summary and Integration." *Feeling and Thinking: The Role of Affect in Social Cognition.* Edited by Joseph P. Forgas, 387–406. New York: Cambridge University Press, 2000.

Forgas, J. P. "Introduction: Affect and Social Cognition." *Handbook of Affect and Social Cognition.* Edited by Joseph P. Forgas, 1–24. Mahwah, NJ: Erlbaum, 2001.

Forgas, J. P. "Mood and Judgment: The Affect Infusion Model (AIM)." *Psychological Bulletin* 117 (1995): 39–66.

Foucault, M. *Discipline and Punish. The Birth of the Prison.* Harmondsworth: Allen Lane, 1977.

Foucault, M. "Governmentality." *The Foucault Effect: Studies in Governmentality.* Edited by Graham Burchell, Colin Gordon, and Peter Miller, 87–104. Chicago: University of Chicago Press, 1991.

Foucault, M. "On Governmentality." *Ideology & Consciousness* 6 (1979): 5–21.

Foucault, M. *The Order of Things: An Archaeology of the Human Sciences.* New York: Pantheon Books. Original title *Les mots et les choses. Une archéologie des sciences humaines.* Paris: Gallimard, 1966, 1970.

Fox, W. "Intellectual Origins of the "Depth" Theme in the Philosophy of Arne Naess." *Trumpeter* 9, no. 2 (1992), retrieved on December 15, 2000, from trumpeter.athabascau.ca/archives/content/v9.2/fox2.html.

Fox, W. *Toward a Transpersonal Ecology: Developing New Foundations for Environmentalism*. Boston: Shambhala, 1990.

Frank, M. G., P. Ekman, and W. V. Friesen. "Behavioral Markers and the Recognizability of the Smile of Enjoyment." *Journal of Personality and Social Psychology* 64 (1993): 83–93.

Frankl, V. E. *Der Mensch auf der Suche nach Sinn. Zur Rehumanisierung der Psychotherapie*. Freiburg im Breisgau: Herder, 1973.

Frankl, V. *Der Wille zum Sinn. Ausgewählte Vorträge über Logotherapie*. Bern-Stuttgart-Wien: Hans Huber, 1972.

Frankl, V. *Man's Search for Meaning: An Introduction to Logotherapy*. Boston: Beacon Press, 1963.

Fraser, N. "Rethinking Recognition." *New Left Review* 3 (2000): 107–120.

Fraser, N. and A. Honneth. *Redistribution or Recognition? A Political-Philosophical Exchange*. London: Verso, 2003.

Fredrickson, B. L. "What Good Are Positive Emotions?" *Review of General Psychology* 2 (1998): 300–319.

Fredrickson, B. L. and C. Branigan. "Positive Emotions." *Emotions: Current Issues and Future Directions*. Edited by Tracy J. Mayne and George A. Bonanno, 123–151. New York: Guilford Press, 2001.

Fredrickson, B. L. and R. W. Levenson. "Positive Emotions Speed Recovery from the Cardiovascular Sequelae of Negative Emotions." *Cognition & Emotion* 12, no. 2 (1998): 191–220.

Freeman, W. J. *Societies of Brains: A Study in the Neuroscience of Love and Hate*. Hillsdale, NJ: Erlbaum, 1995.

Freire, P. *Education for Critical Consciousness*. New York: Continuum, 1973.

Friedman, T. L. "The Humiliation Factor." *New York Times* November 9, 2003, Section 4, 11.

Frijda, N. H. "Moods, Emotion Episodes, and Emotions." *Handbook of Emotions*. Edited by Michael Lewis and Jeannette M. Haviland, 381–404. New York: Guilford Press, 1993.

Frijda, N. H. "The Laws of Emotion." *American Psychologist* 43 (1988): 349–358.

Frijda, N. H. *The Laws of Emotion*. Hillsdale, NJ: Erlbaum, 2006.

Frijda, N. H. *The Emotions*. Cambridge: Cambridge University Press, 1986.

Frijda, N. H., P. Kuipers, and E. ter Schure. "Relations among Emotion, Appraisal, and Emotional Action Readiness." *Journal of Personality and Social Psychology* 57, no. 2, August (1989): 212–228.

Frijda, N. H. and B. Mesquita. "The Social Roles and Functions of Emotions." *Emotion and Culture: Empirical Studies of Mutual Influence*. Edited by Shinobu Kitayama and Hazel R. Markus, 51–87. Washington, DC: American Psychological Association, 1994.

Frith, C. D. and D. Wolpert, eds. *The Neuroscience of Social Interaction: Decoding, Influencing, and Imitating the Actions of Others*. Oxford: Oxford University Press, 2004.

Fromm, E. *Escape from Freedom*. New York: Rinehart, 1941.

Fromm, E. *To Have or to Be?* New York: Harper and Row, 1976.

Fry, D. P. and K. Björkvist, eds. *Cultural Variation in Conflict Resolution: Alternatives to Violence*. Mahwah, NJ: Erlbaum, 1997.

Frydenberg, E. *Morton Deutsch: A Life and Legacy of Mediation and Conflict Resolution*. Brisbane: Australian Academic Press, 2005.

Fukuyama, F. *The End of History and the Last Man*. New York: Avon Books, 1992.

Fuller, J. L. and W. R. Thompson. *Foundations of Behavior Genetics*. St. Louis, MO: Mosby, 2003.

Fuller, R. W. *Somebodies and Nobodies: Overcoming the Abuse of Rank*. Gabriola Island, Canada: New Societies Publishers, 2003.

Fung, H. "Becoming a Moral Child: The Socialization of Shame among Young Chinese Children." *Ethos* 27, no. 2 (1999): 180–209.

Fung, H. and E. C.-H. Chen. "Across Time and Beyond Skin: Self and Transgression in the Everyday Socialization of Shame among Taiwanese Preschool Children." *Social Development* 10, no. 3 (2001): 420–437.

Gadamer, H.-G. *Truth and Method*. London: Sheed and Ward, 1989.

Galtung, J. *Peace by Peaceful Means*. Oslo and London: PRIO (International Peace Research Institute Oslo) and Sage, 1996.

Galtung, J., C. G. Jacobsen, K. F. Brand-Jacobsen, and F. Tschudi. *Searching for Peace: The Road to TRANSCEND*. London: Pluto Press in association with TRANSCEND, 2000.

Gawronski, B. and G. V. Bodenhausen. "Associative and Propositional Processes in Evaluation: An Integrative Review of Implicit and Explicit Attitude Change." *Psychological Bulletin* 132, no. 5 (2006): 692–731.

Gay, P. *The Enlightenment: An Interpretation*. New York: Norton, 1996.

Geertz, C. *Local Knowledge: Further Essays in Interpretive Anthropology*. New York: Basic Books, 1983.

Gergen, K. J. "Technology and the Self: From the Essential to the Sublime." *Constructing the Self in a Mediated World*. Edited by Grodin and Lindlof London: Sage, 1996, draft of chapter retrieved January 6, 2000, from www.swarthmore .edu/SocSci/kgergen1/text11.html.

Gerzon, M. *GQ—Global Intelligence: Learning to Lead beyond Borders*. Forthcoming.

Gerzon, M. *Leading through Conflict: How Successful Leaders Transform Differences into Opportunities*. Boston: Harvard Business School Press, 2006.

Gibson, J. J. "The Theory of Affordances: Toward an Ecological Psychology." *Perceiving, Acting, and Knowing*. Edited by Robert Shaw and John Bransford Hillsdale, NJ: Erlbaum, 1977.

Giddens, A. *The Constitution of Society: Outline of the Theory of Structuration*. Berkeley: University of California Press, 1984.

Gilbert, D. T. *Stumbling on Happiness*. New York: Knopf, 2006.

Gilbert, M. C. "The End of the Organization?" *Nonprofit Online News*, February 7, 2008, retrieved on February 24, 2008, from news.gilbert.org/EndOfOrg.

Gilbert, P. "The Evolution of Social Attractiveness and Its Role in Shame, Humiliation, Guilt and Therapy." *British Journal of Medical Psychology* 70, no. 2 (1997): 113–147.

Gilligan, J. *Violence: Our Deadly Epidemic and How to Treat It*. New York: Putnam, 1996.

Giorgi, P. *The Origins of Violence by Cultural Evolution*, 2nd ed. Brisbane, Australia: Minerva, 2001, www.pierogiorgi.org/The-origins-of-violence-by-cultural-evolution.pdf.

Gladwell, M. *Blink: The Power of Thinking without Thinking*. New York: Little, Brown, 2005.

Glendon, M. A. *A World Made New: Eleanor Roosevelt and the Universal Declaration of Human Rights*. New York: Random House, 2001.

Goffman, E. *Frame Analysis: An Essay on the Organization of Experience.* New York: Harper and Row, 1974.

Goffman, E. *Interaction Ritual: Essays in Face-to-Face Behavior.* Hawthorne: Aldine de Gruyter, 1967.

Goffman, E. *Stigma: Notes on the Management of Spoiled Identity.* Englewood Cliffs, NJ: Prentice Hall, 1953.

Gold, L. *The Sharing Economy: Solidarity Networks Transforming Globalisation.* Aldershot: Ashgate, 2004.

Goldman, J. S. and P. T. Coleman. *How Humiliation Fuels Intractable Conflict: The Effects of Emotional Roles on Recall and Reactions to Conflictual Encounters.* New York: International Center for Cooperation & Conflict Resolution, Teachers College, Columbia University, 2005.

Goldstein, J. S. *War and Gender: How Gender Shapes the War Systems and Vice Versa.* Cambridge: Cambridge University Press, 2001.

Goldstone, J. and J. Ulfelder. "How to Construct Stable Democracies." *Washington Quarterly* Winter 2004–5 (2005): 9–20.

Goldstone, J. *Conflict among Civilizations 500 BC–2030 AD.* Oslo: Paper presented at the 11th Annual Meeting of Humiliation Studies in Norway, June 23–July 1, 2008.

Goleman, D. *Destructive Emotions: A Scientific Dialogue with the Dalai Lama.* Westminster, MD: Bantam Books, 2004.

Goleman, D. *Emotional Intelligence.* New York: Bantam Books, 1995.

Gomes de Matos, F. "Language, Peace, and Conflict Resolution." *The Handbook of Conflict Resolution: Theory and Practice,* 2nd ed. Edited by Morton Deutsch, Peter T. Coleman, and Eric C. Marcus, 158–175. San Francisco: Jossey-Bass, 2006.

Gottman, J. M. "The Mathematics of Love: A Talk with John Gottman." *Edge* 4.14.04 (2004), retrieved on December 5, 2007, from www.edge.org/3rd_culture/gottman05/gottman05_index.html.

Gottman, J. M., J. D. Murray, C. C. Swanson, R. Tyson, and K. R. Swanson. *The Mathematics of Marriage: Dynamic Non-Linear Models.* Cambridge, MA: MIT Press, 2005.

Gottman, J. M., L. F. Katz, and C. Hooven. *Meta-Emotion: How Families Communicate Emotionally.* Mahwah, NJ: Erlbaum, 1997.

Gottman, J. M. and N. Silver. *The Seven Principles for Making Marriage Work.* New York: Crown, 1999.

Gottman, J. M. and R. W. Levenson. "The Timing of Divorce: Predicting When a Couple Will Divorce over a 14-Year Period." *Journal of Marriage and the Family* 62, no. 3 (2000): 737–745.

Grassi, E. *Rhetoric as Philosophy: The Humanist Tradition.* University Park: Pennsylvania State University Press, 1980.

Grassi, E. *Vico and Humanism: Essays on Vico, Heidegger, and Rhetoric.* New York: Peter Lang, 1990.

Gratton, L. and T. J. Erickson. "Eight Ways to Build Collaborative Teams." *Harvard Business Review* 85, no. 11, November (2007): 100–109.

Gray, J. *False Dawn: The Delusions of Global Capitalism.* London: Granta Books, 2002.

Gray, J. A. *The Neuropsychology of Anxiety.* Oxford: Oxford University Press, 1982.

Greenberg, J., S. Solomon, and T. A. Pyszczynski. "The Role of Self-Esteem and Cultural Worldviews in the Management of Existential Terror." *Advances in Experimental Social Psychology.* Edited by Mark P. Zanna. New York: Academic Press, 1997.

Greenfeld, L. "Nationalism and Modernity." *Social Research* 63, no. 1 (1996): 3–40.

Greenfeld, L. *Nationalism: Five Roads to Modernity.* Cambridge, MA: Harvard University Press, 1992.

Greenwood, D. J. and M. Levin. *Introduction to Action Research: Social Research for Social Change.* Thousand Oaks, CA: Sage, 1998.

Guha, R. and G. C. Spivak, eds. *Selected Subaltern Studies.* New York: Oxford University Press, 1988.

Gurr, T. R. *Why Men Rebel.* Princeton, NJ: Princeton University Press, 1970.

Gurr, T. R. "Why Minorities Rebel: A Global Analysis of Communal Mobilization and Conflict since 1945." *International Political Science Review* 14, no. 2 (1993): 161–201.

Gustavsen, B. "From Experiments to Network Building: Trends in the Use of Research for Reconstructing Working Life." *Human Relations* 51, no. 3 (1998): 431–448.

Guzzini, S. and A. Leander. *Constructivism and International Relations: Alexander Wendt and His Critics.* New York: Routledge, 2006

Haas, J. *Warfare and the Evolution of Culture.* Santa Fe, NM: Santa Fe Institute, Working papers 98-11-088, 1998, retrieved on November 15, 2002, from www.santafe.edu/sfi/publications/Working-Papers/98-10-088.pdf.

Habermas, J. *The Theory of Communicative Action, Volume 2, System and Lifeworld: A Critique of Functionalist Reason.* Boston: Beacon Press, 1987.

Haffner, S. and G. Bateson. *Der Vertrag von Versailles. Mit Beiträgen von Sebastian Haffner, Gregory Bateson u. a.* München: Matthes und Seitz, 1978.

Hale, R. L. "The Role of Humiliation and Embarrassment in Serial Murder." *Psychology. A Journal of Human Behaviour* 31, no. 2 (1994): 17–23.

Hamburg, D. A. *No More Killing Fields: Preventing Deadly Conflict.* Lanham, MD: Rowman and Littlefield, 2002.

Hamburg, D. A. and B. A. Hamburg. *Learning to Live Together: Preventing Hatred and Violence in Child and Adolescent Development.* New York: Oxford University Press, 2004.

Hamer, D. and P. Copeland. *Living with Our Genes: Why They Matter More Than You Think.* London: Pan Books, 2000.

Hanmer, J., M. Hester, L. Kelly, and J. Radford, eds. *Women, Violence and Male Power: Feminist Activism, Research and Practice.* Buckingham: Open University Press, 1996.

Hardin, G. "The Tragedy of the Commons." *Science* 162 (1968): 1243–1248.

Hardin, R. *One for All: The Logic of Group Conflict.* Princeton, NJ: Princeton University Press, 1995.

Harré, R., ed. *The Social Construction of Emotions.* New York: Basil Blackwell, 1986.

Hart, P., E. K. Stern, and B. Sundelius, eds. *Beyond Groupthink: Political Group Dynamics and Foreign Policy-Making.* Ann Arbor: University of Michigan Press, 1997.

Hartling, L. M. *Humiliation: Real Pain, a Pathway to Violence.* Boston: Preliminary draft of a paper prepared for Round Table 2 of the 2005 Workshop on Humiliation and Violent Conflict, Columbia University, New York, December 15–16, 2005.

Hartling, L. M. "Prevention through Connection: A Collaborative Response to Women's Substance Abuse." *Work in Progress, No. 103.* Wellesley, MA: Stone Center Working Papers Series, 2003.

Hartling, L. M. "Strengthening Resilience in a Risky World: It Is All About Relationships." *Work in Progress, No. 101.* Wellesley, MA: Stone Center Working Papers Series, 2003.

Hartling, L. M. and T. Luchetta. "Humiliation: Assessing the Impact of Derision, Degradation, and Debasement." *Journal of Primary Prevention* 19, no. 5 (1999): 259–278.

Hartling, L. M. and E. Sparks. "Relational-Cultural Practice: Working in a Nonrelational World." *Work in Progress, No. 97*. Wellesley, MA: Stone Center Working Papers Series, 2000.

Hartling, L. M. and J. Ly. "Relational References: A Selected Bibliography of Research, Theory, and Applications." *Work in Progress, No. 7*. Wellesley, MA: Stone Center Working Papers Series, 2000.

Hayashi, K. "Current Intercultural Issues and Challenges in Japanese Business Interfaces: Blending Theory and Practice." *Management Japan* 35 (2003), www.iijnet.or.jp/imaj/mj/hayashi35.pdf.

Heard, G. *The Five Ages of Man*. New York: Julian Press, 1963.

Hechter, M. "The Dynamics of Secession." *Acta Sociologica* 35 (1992): 267–283.

Heffermehl, F. S., ed. *Peace Is Possible*. Geneva: International Peace Bureau (IPB) with the support of UNESCO, 2001.

Heidegger, M. *Being and Time*. New York: Harper & Row, 1962.

Heider, F. *The Psychology of Interpersonal Relations*. New York: Wiley, 1958.

Heine, S. J., D. R. Lehman, H. R. Markus, and S. Kitayama. "Is There a Universal Need for Positive Self-Regard?" *Psychological Review* 106 (1999): 766–794.

Henderson, H. and S. Sethi. *Ethical Markets: Growing the Green Economy*. White River Junction, VT: Chelsea Green, 2008.

Herz, J. H. "Idealist Internationalism and the Security Dilemma." *World Politics* 2 (1950): 157–180.

Hewstone, M. "The 'Ultimate Attribution Error'? A Review of the Literature on Intergroup Causal Attribution." *European Journal of Social Psychology* 20 (1990): 311–335.

Hitler, A. *Mein Kampf*. London: Pimlico, original work published in 1925–26, 1999.

Hofstede, G. H. *Culture's Consequences: Comparing Values, Behaviors, Institutions, and Organizations Across Nations*, 2nd ed. Thousand Oaks, CA: Sage, 2001.

Holland, P. C. and M. Gallagher. "Amygdala Circuitry in Attentional and Representational Processes." *Trends in Cognitive Sciences* 3 (1999): 65–73.

Hollick, M. *The Science of Oneness: A Worldview for the Twenty-First Century*. Ropley, Hampshire: O-Books, 2006.

Holmes, O. W. "Contagiousness of Puerperal Fever." *New England Quarterly Journal of Medical Surgery* 1 (1843): 503–530.

Honneth, A. "Recognition and Moral Obligation." *Social Research* 64, no. 1 (1997): 16–35.

Honneth, A. *The Struggle for Recognition: The Moral Grammar of Social Conflicts*. Cambridge: Polity Press, 1995.

Hopkin, M. "How We Judge the Thoughts of Others: Brain Division Could Help Explain Stereotyping, Religious Conflict and Racism." *Nature* (2008), retrieved on April 28, 2008, from www.nature.com/news/2008/080317/full/news.2008.677.html.

Howitt, D. and M. G. Billig. *Social Psychology: Conflicts and Continuities: An Introductory Textbook*. Milton Keynes: Open University Press, 1989.

Hudnall, A. C. and E. G. Lindner. "Crisis and Gender: Addressing the Psychosocial Needs of Women in International Disasters." *Handbook of International*

Disaster Psychology (Vol 4): Interventions with Special Needs Populations. Edited by Gilbert Reyes and Gerard A. Jacobs, 1–18. Westport, CT: Greenwood/Praeger, 2005.

Hugo de Sancto Victore. *The Didascalicon of Hugh of St. Victor: A Medieval Guide to the Arts.* New York: Columbia University Press, translated from the Latin with an introduction and notes by Jerome Taylor, 1961.

Hume, D. "A Treatise of Human Nature, Book 2: Of the Passions, Part 3: Of the Will and Direct Passions." *The Complete Works and Correspondence of David Hume.* Charlottesville, VA: InteLex, 1996.

Hutton, W. *The Writing on the Wall: China and the West in the 21st Century.* London: Abacus, 2008.

Iacoboni, M., R. P. Woods, M. Brass, H. Bekkering, J. C. Mazziotta, and G. Rizzolatti. "Cortical Mechanisms of Human Imitation." *Science* 286, no. 5449 (1999): 2526–2528.

Insel, T. R. and R. D. Fernald. "How the Brain Processes Social Information: Searching for the Social Brain." *Annual Review of Neuroscience* 27 (2004): 697–722.

Isen, A. M. "Some Perspectives on Positive Affect and Self-Regulation." *Psychological Inquiry* 11, no. 3 (2000): 184–187.

Isen, A. M. and R. Patrick. "The Effect of Positive Feelings on Risk Taking: When the Chips Are Down." *Organizational Behavior and Human Decision Processes* 31 (1983): 194–202.

Ishay, M. R. *The History of Human Rights: From Ancient Times to the Globalization Era.* Berkeley: University of California Press, 2004.

Izard, C. E. "Basic Emotions, Relations among Emotions, and Emotion-Cognition Relations." *Psychological Review* 99, no. 3, July (1992): 561–565.

Izard, C. E. "Human Emotions." New York: Plenum Press, 1977.

Izard, C. E. *Patterns of Emotion: A New Analysis of Anxiety and Depression.* San Diego, CA: Academic Press, 1972.

Izard, C. E. *The Face of Emotion.* New York: Appleton-Century-Crofts, 1971.

Izard, C. E. *The Psychology of Emotions.* New York: Plenum Press, 1991.

Jackson, R. H. *Quasi-States, Sovereignty, International Relations and the Third World.* Cambridge: Cambridge University Press, 1990.

Jackson, W. A. "Dualism, Duality and the Complexity of Economic Institutions." *International Journal of Social Economics* 26, no. 4 (1999): 545–558, retrieved on March 26, 2008, from www.emeraldinsight.com/Insight/ViewContentServlet?Filename=Published/EmeraldFullTextArticle/Pdf/0060260406.pdf.

James, W. "Lectures IV and V: The Religion of Healthy Mindedness." *The Varieties of Religious Experience: A Study of Human Nature.* New York: Longmans, Green, 1902; retrieved on April 12, 2008, as e-book from the Gutenberg Project, www.gutenberg.org/etext/621.

James, W. *Principles of Psychology* (2 Vols.). New York: Holt, 1890 (reprinted Bristol: Thoemmes Press, 1999), retrieved on March 21, 2008, from psychclassics.asu.edu/James/Principles/index.htm.

James, W. *Selected Writing (The Varieties of Religious Experience).* New York: BookoftheMonth Club, 1997.

James, W. *The Principles of Psychology (Vol. 1).* New York: Dover, 1950.

James, W. "The Stream of Consciousness." *Psychology.* Edited by William James. Cleveland: World, 1892, retrieved on March 21, 2008, from psychclassics.yorku.ca/James/jimmy11.htm.

James, W. "What Is an Emotion?" *Mind* 9 (1884): 188–205.

Janis, I. L. *Groupthink: Psychological Studies of Policy Decisions and Fiascoes*. Boston: Houghton Mifflin, 1982.

Janis, I. L. and L. Mann. *Decision Making: A Psychological Analysis of Conflict, Choice, and Commitment*. New York: Free Press, 1977.

Jervis, R. "Understanding Beliefs." *Political Psychology* 27, no. 5 (2006): 641–663.

Jervis, R., R. N. Lebow, and J. G. Stein. *Psychology and Deterrence*. Baltimore, MD: Johns Hopkins University Press, 1985.

Johnson, D. W., R. T. Johnson, and D. Tjosvold. "Constructive Controversy: The Value of Intellectual Opposition." *The Handbook of Conflict Resolution: Theory and Practice*. Edited by Morton Deutsch and Peter T. Coleman, 65–85. San Francisco: Jossey-Bass, 2000.

Jolly, R., L. Emmerij, D. Ghai, and F. Lapeyre. *UN Contributions to Development Thinking and Practice*. Bloomington: Indiana University Press, 2004.

Jones, E. E. and K. E. Davis. "From Acts to Dispositions: The Attribution Process in Person Perception." *Advances in Experimental Social Psychology, Vol. 2*. Edited by Leonard Berkowitz. Orlando, FL: Academic Press, 1965.

Jones, E. E. and V. A. Harris. "The Attribution of Attitudes." *Journal of Experimental Social Psychology* 3 (1967): 1–24.

Jones, J. W. *Blood That Cries Out From the Earth: The Psychology of Religious Terrorism*. New York: Oxford University Press, 2008.

Jordan, J. V. and L. M. Hartling. "New Developments in Relational-Cultural Theory." *Rethinking Mental Health and Disorder*. Edited by Mary Ballou and Laura Brown, 48–70. New York: Guilford Press, 2002.

Jordan, J. V., M. Walker, and L. M. Hartling. *The Complexity of Connection*. New York: Guilford Press, 2004.

Kabat-Zin, J. *Wherever You Go, There You Are: Mindfulness, Meditation*. New York: Hyperion Books, 1994.

Kagan, D. "Honor, Interest, and Nation-State." *Honor among Nations*. Edited by Elliot Abrams. Washington, DC: Ethics and Public Policy Center, 1998.

Kahneman, D. *Daniel Kahneman: The Sveriges Riksbank Prize in Economic Sciences in Memory of Alfred Nobel 2002*. Stockholm: Nobel Foundation, 2002, retrieved on Januay 7, 2007, from nobelprize.org/nobel_prizes/economics/laureates/2002/kahneman-autobio.html.

Kaku, M. *Parallel Worlds: A Journey through Creation, Higher Dimensions, and the Future of the Cosmos*. New York: Doubleday, 2005.

Kalleberg, R. *Action Research as Constructive Sociology*. Oslo: Institute for Social Research, 1989.

Kant, I. *Critique of Practical Reason*. Indianapolis: Bobbs-Merrill, 1956.

Kant, I. *Lectures on Ethics [1775–1780]*. Indianapolis: Hackett, 1963.

Kaplan, R. D. "The Coming Anarchy." *Atlantic Monthly* February (1994): 44–76.

Karelis, C. *The Persistence of Poverty: Why the Economics of the Well-Off Can't Help the Poor*. New Haven, CT: Yale University Press, 2007.

Karterud, S. *Om Forsoning*. Oslo: Lecture given at the Eitinger-seminaret 2001 "Hvordan forstå forsoningsprosesser: Fremmede og bremsende faktorer."

Katz, J., ed. *One: Essential Writings on Nonduality*. Boulder, CO: Sentient, 2007.

Kauffman, S. *At Home in the Universe*. Oxford: Oxford University Press, 1995.

Kaufman, G. *The Psychology of Shame: Theory and Treatment of Shame-Based Syndromes.* New York: Springer, 1989.

Kelley, H. H. "Attribution Theory in Social Psychology." *Nebraska Symposium on Motivation.* Edited by David Levine. Morristown: University of Nebraska Press, 1967.

Kelley, H. H. "The Processes of Causal Attribution." *American Psychologist* 28, no. 107 (1973): 128.

Kelman, H. C. "Continuity and Change: My Life as a Social Psychologist." *The Social Psychology of Group Identity and Social Conflict: Theory, Application, and Practice.* Edited by Alice H. Eagly, Reuben M. Baron, and V. L. Hamilton, 233–275. Washington, DC: American Psychological Association, 2004.

Keltner, D. and J. Haidt. "Social Functions of Emotions at Four Levels of Analysis." *Cognition & Emotion* 13, no. 5 (1999): 505–521.

Keltner, D. and R. J. Robinson. "Extremism, Power, and the Imagined Basis of Social Conflict." *Current Directions in Psychological Science* 5 (1996): 101–105.

Keltner, D. and J. Haidt. "Social Functions of Emotions." *Emotions: Current Issues and Future Directions.* Edited by Tracy J. Mayne and George A. Bonanno, 192–213. New York: Guilford Press, 2001.

Kemper, T. D. "Sociological Models in the Explanation of Emotions." *Handbook of Emotions.* Edited by Michael Lewis and Jeannette M. Haviland, 41–51. New York: Guilford Press, 1993.

Keohane, R. O. "International Liberalism Reconsidered." *The Economic Limits to Modern Politics.* Edited by John Dunn, 165–194. Cambridge: Cambridge University Press, 1990.

Keysers, C. and V. Gazzola. "Towards a Unifying Neural Theory of Social Cognition." *Progress in Brain Research, Vol. 156.* Edited by Silke Anders, Gabriele Ende, Markus Junghofer, Johanna Kissler, and Dirk Wildgruber Amsterdam: Elsevier, 2006, www.bcn-nic.nl/txt/people/publications/keysersgazzolapbr.pdf.

Kiecolt-Glaser, J. K., R. Glaser, J. T. Cacioppo, R. C. MacCallum, M. A. Snydersmith, and C. Kim. "Marital Conflict in Older Adults: Endocrinological and Immunological Correlates." *Psychosomatic Medicine* 59, (1997): 339–349.

Kiecolt-Glaser, J. K., W. B. Malarkey, M. Chee, T. Newton, J. T. Cacioppo, H. Y. Mao, and R. Glaser. "Negative Behavior during Marital Conflict Is Associated with Immunological Down-Regulation." *Psychosomatic Medicine* 55 (1993): 395–409.

Kim, Y. Y. and B. D. Ruben. "Intercultural Transformation: A Systems Theory." *International and Intercultural Communication Annual* 12, (1988): 299–321.

Kimmel, M. *Reducing Men's Violence: The Personal Meets the Political.* Paper presented at the expert group meeting on Male Roles and Masculinities in the Perspective of a Culture of Peace, Oslo, Norway, September 24–28 1997.

Kimmel, M. *The Gendered Society.* Oxford: Oxford University Press, 2000.

Klaveras, L. "Political Realism: A Culprit for the 9/11 Attacks." *Harvard International Review* 26 (Europe), no. 3 (2004), retrieved on February 29, 2008, from hir .harvard.edu/articles/1252/1.

Klein, D. C. "The Humiliation Dynamic: Viewing the Task of Prevention from a New Perspective." *Journal of Primary Prevention* 12, no. 2/1991 and 3/1992, Special issue, Section I: The humiliation dynamic, Section II: Those at risk of humiliation, Section III: Systemically related humiliation, Section IV: Dealing with humiliation (1991).

Klein, D. C. and K. Morrow. *New Vision, New Reality: A Guide to Unleashing Energy, Joy, and Creativity in Your Life*. Center City, MN: Hazelden Information & Education Services, 2001.

Klein, N. *The Shock Doctrine: The Rise of Disaster Capitalism*. New York: Metropolitan Books, 2007.

Koestler, A. *The Act of Creation*. New York: Macmillan, 1964.

Kogan, I. "Breaking the Cycle of Trauma: From the Individual to Society." *Mind and Human Interaction* 11, no. 1 (2000): 2–10.

Kriesberg, L. "Nature, Dynamics, and Phases of Intractability." *Grasping the Nettle: Analyzing Cases of Intractable Conflict*. Edited by Chester A. Crocker, Fen Osler Hampson, and Pamela Aall. Washington, DC: U.S. Institute of Peace Press, 2005.

Krippendorff, Ekkehart. *Staat und Krieg. Die historische Logik politischer Unvernunft*. Frankfurt: Suhrkamp Verlag, 1985.

Kuhl, J. "A Theory of Self-development: Affective Fixation and the STAR Model of Personality Disorders and Related Styles." *Motivational Psychology of Human Development*. Edited by Jutta Heckhausen, 187–211. Amsterdam: Elsevier, 2000.

Kuhl, J. and A. Fuhrmann. "Decomposing Self-regulation and Self-control: The Volitional Components Inventory." *Life Span Perspectives in Motivation and Control*. Edited by Jutta Heckhausen and Carol S. Dweck, 15–49. Mahwah, NJ: Erlbaum, 1998.

Kuhn, T. S. *The Structure of Scientific Revolutions*. Chicago: University of Chicago Press, 1962.

Kurokawa, K, P. C. Schmal, I. Flagge, and J. Visscher, eds. *Kisho Kurokawa: Metabolism and Symbiosis*. Berlin: Jovis, 2005.

Labouvie-Vief, G. and M. M. González. "Dynamic Integration: Affect Optimization and Differentiation in Development." *Motivation, Emotion, and Cognition: Integrative Perspectives on Intellectual Functioning and Development*. Edited by David Y. Dai and Robert J. Sternberg, 237–272. Mahwah, NJ: Erlbaum, 2004.

Lakoff, G. *Thinking Points: Communicating Our American Values and Vision*. New York: Farrar, Straus and Giroux, 2006.

Lakoff, G. and M. Johnson. *Philosophy in the Flesh: The Embodied Mind and Its Challenge to Western Thought*. New York: Basic Books, 1999.

Lane, R. *Loss of Happiness in Market Democracies*. New Haven, CT: Yale University Press, 2001.

Lasswell, H. D. and D. Lerner, eds. *World Revolutionary Elites: Studies in Coercive Ideological Movements*. Cambridge, MA: MIT Press, 1965

Lauren, P. G. *The Evolution of International Human Rights: Visions Seen*, 2nd ed. Philadelphia: University of Pennsylvania Press, 2003.

Lawson, T. *Economics and Reality*. London: Routledge, 1997.

Lazare, A. *On Apology*. New York: Oxford University Press, 2004.

Lazarus, R. S. *Emotion and Adaptation*. New York: Oxford University Press, 1991.

Leach, C. W., N. Snider, and A. Iyer. "'Poisoning the Conscienses of the Fortunate': The Experience of Relative Advantage and Support for Social Equality." *Relative Deprivation: Specification, Development, and Integration*. Edited by Iain Walker and Heather J. Smith, 136–163. Cambridge: Cambridge University Press, 2001.

Lebow, R. N. *Between Peace and War: The Nature of International Crisis*. Baltimore, MD: Johns Hopkins University Press, 1981.

Lebow, R. N. "Fear, Interest, and Honour: Outlines of a Theory of International Relations." *International Affairs* 82, no. 3, May (2006): 431–448.

Lederach, J. P. *Building Peace: Sustainable Reconciliation in Divided Societies.* Washington, DC: U.S. Institute of Peace, 1997.

Lederach, J. P. *The Moral Imagination: The Art and Soul of Building Peace.* Oxford: Oxford University Press, 2005.

LeDoux, J. E. *The Emotional Brain: The Mysterious Underpinnings of Emotional Life.* New York: Simon & Schuster, 1996.

LeDoux, J. E., L. M. Romanski, and A. E. Xagoraris. "Indelibility of Subcortical Emotional Memories." *Journal of Cognitive Neuroscience* 1 (1989): 238–243.

Legrain, P. *Open World: The Truth about Globalisation.* London: Abacus, 2002.

Leith, K. P. and R. F. Baumeister. "Why Do Bad Moods Increase Self-Defeating Behavior?: Emotion, Risk-taking, and Self-regulation." *Journal of Personality and Social Psychology* 71, no. 6 (1996): 1250–1267.

Lerner, M. J. *The Belief in a Just World: A Fundamental Delusion.* New York: Plenum Press, 1980.

Lerner, M. J. "The Justice Motive: Where Social Psychologists Found It, How They Lost It and Why They May Not Find It Again." *Personality and Social Psychology Review* 7 (2003): 388–399.

LeShan, L. *The Psychology of War: Comprehending Its Mystique and Its Madness.* Chicago: Noble Press, 1992.

Leupnitz, D. A. and S. Tulkin. "The Cybernetic Epistemology of Gestalt Therapy." *Psychotherapy: Theory, Research & Practice* 17, no. 2 (1980): 153–157, retrieved on March 27, 2008, from psycnet.apa.org/index.cfm?fa=main.showContent&id=1980-30800-001&view=fulltext&format=pdf.

Levenson, R. W. "The Intrapersonal Functions of Emotion." *Cognition & Emotion* 13, no. 5 (1999): 481–504.

Leventhal, H. and K. R. Scherer. "The Relationship of Emotion to Cognition: A Functional Approach to a Semantic Controversy." *Cognition and Emotion* 1 (1987): 3–28.

Lévinas, E. "Responsibility for the Other." *Ethics and Infinity: Conversations With Phillipe Nemo.* Edited by Emmanuel Lévinas, 93–101. Pittsburgh, PA: Duquesne University Press, 1985.

Levine, P. A. *Waking the Tiger: Healing Trauma.* Berkeley, CA: North Atlantic Books, 1997.

Levy, H. S. *The Lotus Lovers: The Complete History of the Curious Erotic Custom of Footbinding in China.* Buffalo, NY: Prometheus Books, 1992.

Lewis, H. B. *Shame and Guilt in Neurosis.* New York: International Universities Press, 1971.

Lewis, M. and L. Michalson. *Children's Emotions and Moods: Developmental Theory and Measurement.* New York: Plenum Press, 1983.

Lewis, M. and J. M. Haviland. *Handbook of Emotions.* New York: Guilford Press, 1993.

Lewis, M. D. "Emotional Self-organization at Three Time Scales." *Emotion, Development, and Self-organization: Dynamic Systems Approaches to Emotional Development.* Edited by Marc D. Lewis and Isabela Granic, 37–69. New York: Cambridge University Press, 2000.

Li, J. and K. W. Fischer. "Thought and Affect in American and Chinese Learners' Beliefs about Learning." *Motivation, Emotion, and Cognition: Integrative Perspectives on Intellectual Functioning and Development*. Edited by David Y. Dai and Robert J. Sternberg, 385–418. Mahwah, NJ: Erlbaum, 2004.

Liberman, V., S. M. Samuels, and L. D. Ross. "The Name of the Game: Predictive Power of Reputations versus Situational Labels in Determining Prisoner's Dilemma Game Moves." *Personality and Social Psychology Bulletin* 30, no. 10 (2004): 1–11.

Lifton, R. J. *The Protean Self: Human Resilience in the Age of Fragmentation*. Chicago: University of Chicago Press, 1999.

Lindholm, T. *The Emergence and Development of Human Rights: An Interpretation with a View to Cross-Cultural and Interreligious Dialogue*. Oslo: Norwegian Institute of Human Rights, 1997.

Lindner, E. G. "Avoiding Humiliation—From Intercultural Communication to Global Interhuman Communication." *Journal of Intercultural Communication, SIETAR Japan* 10 (2007): 21–38.

Lindner, E. G. *Definitions of Terms as They Are Used in Lindner's Writing*. Human Dignity and Humiliation Studies, 2003, www.humiliationstudies.org/whoweare/evelin02.php.

Lindner, E. G. *Disasters as a Chance to Implement Novel Solutions That Highlight Attention to Human Dignity*. Boston: Panel contribution to the International Conference on Rebuilding Sustainable Communities for Children and Their Families after Disasters, convened by Adenrele Awotona, Founder and Director of the Center for Rebuilding Sustainable Communities after Disasters, College of Public and Community Service, University of Massachusetts, Boston, , November 16–19, 2008.

Lindner, E. G. "Dynamics of Humiliation in a Globalizing World." *International Journal on World Peace* 34, no. 3, September (2007): 15–52.

Lindner, E. G. "Dynamics of Humiliation in a Globalizing World." *International Journal on World Peace* XXXIV, no. 3, September (2007): 15–52.

Lindner, E. G. "Emotion and Conflict: Why It Is Important to Understand How Emotions Affect Conflict and How Conflict Affects Emotions." *The Handbook of Conflict Resolution: Theory and Practice*, 2nd ed. Edited by Morton Deutsch, Peter T. Coleman, and Eric C. Marcus, 268–293. San Francisco: Jossey-Bass, 2006.

Lindner, E. G. *Gender and Humiliation: The Power of Dignity in Love, Sex and Parenthood*. Westport, CT: Greenwood/Praeger Security International, 2009.

Lindner, E. G. "Healing the Cycles of Humiliation: How to Attend to the Emotional Aspects of 'Unsolvable' Conflicts and the Use of 'Humiliation Entrepreneurship.'" *Peace and Conflict: Journal of Peace Psychology* 8, no. 2 (2002): 125–138, www.informaworld.com/smpp/ftinterface~content=a785828772~fulltext=713240930.

Lindner, E. G. "Humiliation and Global Terrorism: How to Overcome It Nonviolently." *Encyclopedia of Life Support Systems (EOLSS), Theme 6.120: Nonviolent Alternatives for Social Change*. Edited by Ralph Summy. Oxford: Developed under the Auspices of the UNESCO, EOLSS Publishers, 2007, www.eolss.net.

Lindner, E. G. "Humiliation and Reactions to Hitler's Seductiveness in Post-War Germany: Personal Reflections." *Social Alternatives* 25, Special Issue: Humiliation and History in Global Perspectives, no. 1, First Quarter (2006): 6–11.

Lindner, E. G. "Humiliation and the Human Condition: Mapping a Minefield." *Human Rights Review* 2, no. 2 (2001): 46–63.

Lindner, E. G. "Humiliation, Killing, War, and Gender." *The Psychology of Resolving Global Conflicts: From War to Peace. Volume 1: Nature vs. Nurture.* Edited by Mari Fitzduff and Chris E. Stout, 137–174. Westport, CT: Greenwood/Praeger Security International, 2006.

Lindner, E. G. "Humiliation or Dignity: Regional Conflicts in the *Global Village*." *International Journal of Mental Health, Psychosocial Work and Counselling in Areas of Armed Conflict* 1, no. 1, January (2003): 48–63, www.transnational.org/forum/meet/2002/Lindner_RegionalConflicts.html.

Lindner, E. G. "Humiliation, Trauma, and Trauma Recovery in a Globalizing World." *Peacebuilding for Traumatized Societies.* Edited by Barry Hart. Lanham, MD: University Press of America, 2008.

Lindner, E. G. "Humiliation—Trauma That Has Been Overlooked: An Analysis Based on Fieldwork in Germany, Rwanda/Burundi, and Somalia." *TRAUMA-TOLOGYe* 7, no. 1 (2001), tmt.sagepub.com/cgi/content/abstract/7/1/43.

Lindner, E. G. "In Times of Globalization and Human Rights: Does Humiliation Become the Most Disruptive Force?" *Journal of Human Dignity and Humiliation Studies* 1, no. 1, March (2007), www.humilliationstudies.upeace.org.

Lindner, E. G. *Lebensqualität im ägyptisch-deutschen Vergleich: Eine Interkulturelle Untersuchung an drei Berufsgruppen (Ärzte, Journalisten, Künstler).* Hamburg: Department of Psychological Medicine, University of Hamburg, doctoral dissertation in Medicine, 1994.

Lindner, E. *Making Enemies: Humiliation and International Conflict.* Westport, CT: Greenwood/Praeger Security International, 2006.

Lindner, E. G. "The Concept of Human Dignity." *Human Dignity: Concepts, Challenges and Solutions. The Case of Africa.* Edited by Horst Fischer and Noelle Quénivet. Berlin: Berliner Wissenschaftsverlag, 2008.

Lindner, E. G. "The Educational Environment as a Place for Humiliating Indoctrination or Dignifying Empowerment." *Experiments in Education* 37, Humiliation in the academic setting: A Special Symposium Issue, no. 3, March (2008): 51–60.

Lindner, E. G. *The Feeling of Being Humiliated: A Central Theme in Armed Conflicts. A Study of the Role of Humiliation in Somalia, and Great Lakes Region, Between the Warring Parties, and in Relation to Third Intervening Parties. Outline of Research Project.* Oslo: University of Oslo, project description, published by Human Dignity and Humiliation Studies, 1996, www.humiliationstudies.org/whoweare/evelin02.php.

Lindner, E. G. *The Psychology of Humiliation: Somalia, Rwanda/Burundi, and Hitler's Germany.* Oslo: University of Oslo, Department of Psychology, doctoral dissertation, 2000.

Lindner, E. G. *The Relevance of Humiliation Studies for the Prevention of Terrorism.* Budapest,: Paper presented to the NATO Advanced Research Workshop Indigenous Terrorism: Understanding and Addressing the Root Causes of Radicalisation among Groups with an Immigrant Heritage in Europe, March 7–9, 2008.

Lindner, E. G. "Were Ordinary Germans Hitler's 'Willing Executioners'? Or Were They Victims of Humiliating Seduction and Abandonment? The Case of Germany and Somalia." *IDEA: A Journal of Social Issues* 5, no. 1 (2000), www.ideajournal.com/articles.php?id=31.

Lindner, E. G. *What the World's Cultures Can Contribute to Creating a Sustainable Future for Humankind.* Oslo: Paper prepared for the 11th Annual Conference of Human Dignity and Humiliation Studies (HumanDHS, www.humiliationstudies.org/

whoweare/annualmeeting11.php), June 23– July 1, 2008, Norway, Human Dignity and Humiliation Studies, www.humiliationstudies.org/whoweare/evelin02.php#oslo08.

Lindner, E. G., N. R. Walsh, and J. Kuriansky. "Humiliation or Dignity in the Israeli-Palestinian Conflict." *Terror in the Holy Land, Inside the Anguish of the Israeli-Palestinian Conflict.* Edited by Judy Kuriansky, 123–131. Westport, CT: Greenwood/Praeger Security International, 2006.

Linnenbrink, E. A. and P. R. Pintrich. "Role of Affect in Cognitive Processing in Academic Contexts." *Motivation, Emotion, and Cognition: Integrative Perspectives on Intellectual Functioning and Development.* Edited by David Y. Dai and Robert J. Sternberg, 57–88. Mahwah, NJ: Erlbaum, 2004.

Lipton, B. H. *The Biology of Belief: Unleashing the Power of Consciousness, Matter, and Miracles.* Santa Rosa, CA: Elite Books, 2005.

Little, B. R. "Personal Projects Analysis: Trivial Pursuits, Magnificent Obsessions, and the Search for Coherence." *Personality Psychology: Recent Trends and Emerging Directions.* Edited by David M. Buss and Nancy Cantor, 15–31. New York: Springer-Verlag, 1989.

Loewenstein, G., E. U. Weber, C. K. Hsee, and N. Welch. "Risk as Feelings." *Psychological Bulletin* 127, no. 2 (2001): 267–286.

Loux, M. J. *Metaphysics: A Contemporary Introduction,* 3rd ed. London: Routledge, 2006.

Lu, X. *Call to Arms (Na Han).* Beijing: Foreign Languages Press, 1981.

Luhmann, N. *Social Systems.* Stanford, CA: Stanford University Press, 1995.

Lutz, A., J. Brefczynski-Lewis, T. Johnstone, and R. J. Davidson. "Regulation of the Neural Circuitry of Emotion by Compassion Meditation: Effects of Meditative Expertise." *PLoS ONE* 3, no. 3, March (2008): 1–10, retrieved on May 5, 2008, from www.plosone.org/article/fetchObjectAttachment.action;jsessionid=08EB0F78CE4390AF332000D85499E55C?uri=info%3Adoi%2F10.1371%2Fjournal.pone.0001897&representation=PDF.

Lutz, C. A. and L. Abu-Lughod, eds. *Language and the Politics of Emotion.* Cambridge: Cambridge University Press, 1990.

Maalouf, A. *In the Name of Identity: Violence and the Need to Belong.* New York: Arcade Publishing, 2001.

Mackay, H. *Why Don't People Listen? Solving the Communication Problem.* Sydney: Pan Macmillan Australia, 1994.

MacLean, P. D. *A Triune Concept of the Brain and Behavior: Hincks Memorial Lectures.* Toronto,: University of Toronto Press, 1973.

Macy, M. and R. Willer. "From Factors to Actors: Computational Sociology and Agent-Based Modeling." *Annual Review of Sociology* 28 (2002): 143–166.

Mahbubani, K. "The New Asian Hemisphere: The Irresistible Shift of Global Power to the East." New York: PublicAffairs, 2008.

Mandler, G. *Mind and Body: Psychology of Emotion and Stress.* New York: Norton, 1984.

Manning, M. R. *Individuation and Resilience in Older Women: How Awareness and Resolution of Culturally Induced Experiences of Shame and Humiliation Contribute to Intentional, Ongoing Development.* Santa Barbara, CA: Fielding Graduate University, doctoral dissertation, 2005.

Marcus, G. E. "The Psychology of Emotion and Politics." *Oxford Handbook of Political Psychology.* Edited by David O. Seares, Leonie Huddy, and Robert Jervis, 182–221. New York: Oxford University Press, 2003.

Maren, M. *The Road to Hell: The Ravaging Effects of Foreign Aid and International Charity*. New York: Free Press, 1997.

Margalit, A. *The Decent Society*. Cambridge, MA: Harvard University Press, 1996.

Margalit, A. *The Ethics of Memory*. Cambridge, MA: Harvard University Press, 2002.

Marion, R. *The Edge of Organization: Chaos and Complexity Theories of Formal Social Systems*. Thousand Oaks, CA: Sage, 1999.

Marks, I. M. and R. M. Nesse. "Fear and Fitness: An Evolutionary Analysis of Anxiety Disorders." *Ethology and Sociobiology* 15 (1994): 247–261.

Markus, H. R. and S. Kitayama. "Models of Agency: Sociocultural Diversity in the Construction of Action." *Nebraska Symposium on Motivation* (2004).

Marrow, A. J. "Risks and Uncertainties in Action Research." *Journal of Social Issues* 20, no. 3 (1964): 5–20.

Marshall, M. G. *Third World War: System, Process, and Conflict Dynamics*. Lanham, MD: Rowman and Littlefield, 1999.

Marsick, V. J. and A. Sauquet. "Learning through Reflection." *The Handbook of Conflict Resolution: Theory and Practice*. Edited by Morton Deutsch and Peter T. Coleman 382–399. San Francisco: Jossey-Bass, 2000.

Martin, J. N., T. K. Nakayama, and L. A. Flores. "A Dialectical Approach to Intercultural Communication." *Readings in Intercultural Communication: Experiences and Contexts*, 2nd ed. Edited by Judith N. Martin, Thomas K. Nakayama, and Lisa A. Flores, 3–13. Boston: McGraw-Hill, 2002.

Martin, L. L. and A. Tesser. "Some Ruminative Thoughts." *Ruminative Thoughts: Vol. 11. Advances in Social Cognition*. Edited by Robert S. Wyer, 1–47. Hillsdale, NJ: Erlbaum, 1996.

Masaaki, H. "The Road to a Theology of *Soku*." *Nanzan Bulletin* 22 (1998): 59–74, paper written for the 10th Nanzan Symposium, "What does Christianity have to Learn from Buddhism? The Dialogue Among Religions, Nanzan Institute for Religion & Culture, Nagoya, Japan, retrieved on May 29, 2008, from www.nanzan-u.ac.jp/SHUBUNKEN/publications/Bulletin_and_Shoho/pdf/22-Honda.pdf.

Masson, P. "When Soldiers Prefer Death to Humiliation." *Historia*, no. 596 (1996): 54–56.

Masumoto, T., J. G. Oetzel, J. Takai, S. Ting-Toomey, and Y. Yokochi. "A Typology of Facework Behaviors in Conflicts with Best Friends and Relative Strangers." *Communication Quarterly* 4, no. 48 (2000): 397–419.

Matossian, M. A. K. "Ideologies of Delayed Industrialisation: Some Tensions and Ambiguities." *Political Change in Underdeveloped Countries: Nationalism and Communism*. Edited by John H. Kautsky. New York: Wiley, 1962.

Matsumoto, D. R., H. S. Yoo, and J. A. LeRoux. "Emotion and Intercultural Communication." *Handbook of Applied Linguistics, Volume 7: Intercultural Communication*. Edited by Helga Kotthoff and Helen Spencer-Oatley. Berlin: Mouton–de Gruyter, 2005.

Mayer, E. L. *Extraordinary Knowing: Science, Skepticism, and the Inexplicable Powers of the Human Mind*. New York: Bantam Books, 2007.

Mayne, T. J. "Emotions and Health." *Emotions: Current Issues and Future Directions*. Edited by Tracy J. Mayne and George A. Bonanno, 361–397. New York: Guilford Press, 2001.

Mayne, T. J. and G. A. Bonanno, eds. *Emotions: Current Issues and Future Directions*. New York: Guilford Press, 2001.

Mayne, T. J. and J. Ramsey. "The Structure of Emotion: A Nonlinear Dynamic Systems Approach." *Emotions: Current Issues and Future Directions*. Edited by Tracy J. Mayne and George A. Bonanno, 1–37. New York: Guilford Press, 2001.

McDermott, R. "The Feeling of Rationality: The Meaning of Neuroscientific Advances for Political Science." *Perspectives on Politics* 2 (2004): 691–706.

McDougall, W. *An Introduction to Social Psychology*. Boston: Luce, 1926.

McElreath, R. and R. Boyd. *Mathematical Models of Social Evolution: A Guide for the Perplexed*. Chicago: University of Chicago Press, 2007.

McLuhan, H. M. *The Gutenberg Galaxy: The Making of Typographic Man*. Toronto: University of Toronto Press, 1962.

McNeill, D. *Gesture and Thought*. Chicago: University of Chicago Press, 2005.

McNiff, J. *Action Research: Principles and Practice*. London: Routledge, 1992.

Meier, A. J. "Conflict and the Power of Apologies." *Philologie Im Netz* 30 (2004): 1–17, revision and expansion of initial observations on conflict and apologies presented at the American Association for Applied Linguistics (AAAL), Stamford, CT, 1999.

Mesquita, B. "Culture and Emotion: Different Approaches to the Question." *Emotions: Current Issues and Future Directions*. Edited by Tracy J. Mayne and George A. Bonanno, 214–250. New York: Guilford Press, 2001.

Messick, D. M. and D. M. Mackie. "Intergroup Relations." *Annual Review of Psychology* 40 (1989): 45–81.

Mezirow, J. *Transformative Dimensions of Adult Learning*. San Francisco: Jossey-Bass, 1991.

Michael, S. T. "Hope Conquers Fear: Overcoming Anxiety and Panic Attacks." *Handbook of Hope: Theory, Measures, and Applications*. Edited by C. R. Snyder, 355–378. San Diego, CA: Academic, 2000.

Milgram, S. *Obedience to Authority*. New York: Harper & Row, 1974.

Miller, J. B. "Forced Choices, False Choices." *Research & Action Report* 27, no. 2, Spring/Summer (2006).

Miller, A. *For Your Own Good: Hidden Cruelty in Child-Rearing and the Roots of Violence*. London: Virago Press, 1983.

Miller, J. B. *Toward a New Psychology of Women*, 2nd ed. Boston: Beacon Press, 1986.

Miller, J. B. "What Do We Mean by Relationships?" *Work in Progress, No. 22*. Wellesley, MA: Stone Center Working Paper Series, 1986.

Miller, J. B. and I. P. Stiver. *The Healing Connection: How Women Form Relationships in Therapy and in Life*. Boston: Beacon Press, 1997.

Miller, W. I. *Humiliation and Other Essays on Honor, Social Discomfort, and Violence*. Ithaca, NY: Cornell University Press, 1993.

Millon, T. *Modern Psychopathology: A Biosocial Approach to Maladaptive Learning and Functioning*. Philadelphia: Saunders, 1969.

Millon, T. *Theories of Psychopathology*. Philadelphia: Saunders, 1967.

Mills, G. E. *Action Research: A Guide for the Teacher Researcher*. Upper Saddle River, NJ: Merrill, 2000.

Mischel, W. and A. L. De Smet. "Self-Regulation in the Service of Conflict Resolution Walter Aaron L." *The Handbook of Conflict Resolution: Theory and Practice*. Edited by Morton Deutsch and Peter T. Coleman, 256–275. San Francisco: Jossey-Bass, 2000.

Mitchell, C. R. *Conflict, Social Change, and Conflict Resolution: An Enquiry*. Berlin: Berghof Research Center for Constructive Conflict Management, 2005, retrieved on March 3, 2008, from www.berghof-handbook.net/uploads/download/ mitchell_handbook.pdf.

Montiel, C. J. "Political Psychology of Nonviolent Democratic Transitions in Southeast Asia." *Journal of Social Issues* 62, no. 1 (2006): 173–190, retrieved on August 14, 2007, from www.blackwell-synergy.com/doi/pdf/10.1111/j.1540-4560.2006 .00445.x.

Moore, C. W. *The Mediation Process: Practical Strategies for Resolving Conflict*, 2nd ed. San Francisco: Jossey-Bass, 1996.

Morgenthau, H. *Scientific Man versus. Power Politics*. Chicago: University of Chicago Press, 1946.

Morris, W. N. "A Functional Analysis of the Role of Mood in Affective Systems." *Review of Personality and Social Psychology: Vol 13. Emotion*. Edited by Margaret S. Clark, 256–293. Newbury Park, CA: Sage, 1992.

Moskowitz, J. T. "Emotion and Coping." *Emotions: Current Issues and Future Directions*. Edited by Tracy J. Mayne and George A. Bonanno, 311–336. New York: Guilford Press, 2001.

Mosse, G. L. *The Image of Man: The Creation of Modern Masculinity*. New York: Oxford University Press, 1996.

Mowrer, O. H. *Learning Theory and Behavior*. New York: Wiley, 1960.

Munch, R. and N. J. Smelser, eds. *Theory of Culture*. Berkeley: University of California Press, 1992.

Mustakova-Possardt, E. "Education for Critical Moral Consciousness." *Journal of Moral Education* 33, no. 3, September (2004): 245–269.

Nadler, A. "Inter-Group Helping Relations as Power Relations: Maintaining or Challenging Social Dominance between Groups through Helping." *Journal of Social Issues* 58, no. 3 (2002): 487–502.

Nadler, A. "Social-Psychological Analysis of Reconciliation: Instrumental and Socio-Emotional Routes to Reconciliation." *Peace Education Worldwide: The Concepts, Underlying Principles, and Research*. Edited by Gavriel Salomon and Baruch Nevo. Mahwah, NJ: Erlbaum, 2002.

Nadler, A., T. Malloy, and J. D. Fisher, eds. *Social Psychology of Inter-Group Reconciliation: From Violent Conflict to Peaceful Co-Existence*. Oxford: Oxford University Press, 2008.

Naess, A. *The Selected Works of Arne Naess, Volumes 1–10*. Dordrecht: Springer, 2005.

Naess, A. "Through Spinoza to Mahayana Buddhism or through Mahayana Buddhism to Spinoza?" *Spinoza's Philosophy of Man: Proceedings of the Scandinavian Spinoza Symposium 1977*. Edited by Jon Wetlesen. Oslo: University of Oslo Press, 1978.

Nagata, A. L. "Bodymindfulness for Skillful Communication." *Rikkyo Intercultural Communication Review* 5 (2007): 61–76.

Nagata, A. L. *Somatic Mindfulness and Energetic Presence in Intercultural Communication: A Phenomenological/Hermeneutic Exploration of Bodymindset and Emotional Resonance*. Dissertation Abstracts International, 62/(12), 5999B. (UMI No.3037968), 2002.

Nakayama, N. *Mujunteki Sosoku No Roni [The Logic of Soku]*. Kyoto: Hyakka En, 1973.

Nandy, A. *Exiled at Home: Comprising: At the Edge of Psychology, The Intimate Enemy, Creating a Nationality*. New Delhi: Oxford University Press, 1998.

Nathanson, D. L. *Shame and Pride: Affect Sex and the Birth of the Self.* New York: Norton, 1992.

Nathanson, D. L. "What's a Script?" *Bulletin of The Tomkins Institute* 3, Spring–Summer (1996): 1–4.

Neal, Peter M., G. Watts, and E. Calhoun. (1995). *Action Research.* Alexandria, VA: Association for Supervision and Curriculum Development.

Nebehay, S. "'Honor Killings' of Women Said on Rise Worldwide." *Reuters Dispatch* April 7 (2000).

Negrao, C. *Shame, Humiliation, and Childhood Sexual Abuse: Comparing Discrete and Clinical Theories of Emotion.* New York: Columbia University, doctoral dissertation, 2004.

Nelder, C. "Envisioning a Sustainable Future." *BWZine (The Online Better World Magazine)* October/November/December (1996).

Nelson, A. *Living the Wheel: Working with Emotion, Terror, and Bliss through Imagery.* York Beach, ME: Samuel Weiser, 1993.

Nesse, R. M. "Is Depression an Adaptation?" *Archives of General Psychiatry* 57 (2000): 14–20, www-personal.umich.edu/%7Enesse/Articles/IsDepAdapt-ArchGenPsychiat-2000.pdf.

Nesse, R. M. "Natural Selection and Fear Regulation Mechanisms." *Behavioral and Brain Sciences* 18 (1995): 309–310.

Nickel, J. W. *Making Sense of Human Rights.* Revised ed. Washington, DC: Georgetown University Press, 2004.

Nietzsche, F. *On the Genealogy of Morals.* New York: Vintage Books, 1989.

Niezen, R. *A World Beyond Difference: Cultural Identity in the Age of Globalization.* Malden, MA: Blackwell, 2004.

Nisbett, R. E. and D. Cohen. *Culture of Honor: The Psychology of Violence in the South.* Boulder, CO: Westview Press, 1996.

Nisbett, R. E. and T. D. Wilson. "Telling More Than We Can Know: Verbal Reports on Mental Processes." *Psychological Review* 84 (1977): 231–259.

Nordkvelle, Y. T. "Forelesningen Som Studentaktiv Undervisningsform—Et Argument Fra Undervisningens Kulturhistorie." *UNIPED* 30, no. 1 (2007): 4–14.

Nordtug, H. *Implicit Prejudice against Arab Immigrants.* Trondheim: Norwegian University of Science and Technology, master's thesis, 2008.

Norman, D. A. *The Psychology of Everyday Things.* New York: Basic Books, 1988.

Oatley, K. and P. N. Johnson-Laird. "Towards a Cognitive Theory of Emotions." *Cognition & Emotion* 1 (1987): 29–50.

Ochsner, K. N. and L. F. Barrett. "A Multiprocess Perspective on the Neuroscience of Emotion." *Emotions: Current Issues and Future Directions.* Edited by Tracy J. Mayne and George A. Bonanno, 38–81. New York: Guilford Press, 2001.

Ohnuki-Tierney, E. *Kamikaze, Cherry Blossoms, and Nationalisms: The Militarization of Aesthetics in Japanese History.* Chicago: University of Chicago Press, 2002.

Oliner, S. P. and P. M. Oliner. *The Altruistic Personality: Rescuers of Jews in Nazi Europe.* New York: Free Press, 1988.

Onal, A. *Honour Killing: Stories of Men Who Killed.* London: Saqi Books, 2008.

O'Neill, M. "Re-Imagining Diaspora through Ethno-Mimesis: Humiliation, Human Dignity and Belonging." *Reimagining Diasporas: Transnational Lives and the Media.* Edited by Olga Guedes-Bailey, Myria Georgiou, and Ramaswami Harindranath. London: Palgrave Macmillan, 2006.

Ong, W. J. *Ramus: Method, and the Decay of Dialogue: From the Art of Discourse to the Art of Reason*. Cambridge, MA: Harvard University Press, 1958.

Opotow, S. "Aggression and Violence." *The Handbook of Conflict Resolution: Theory and Practice*, 2nd ed. Edited by Morton Deutsch, Peter T. Coleman, and Eric C. Marcus. San Francisco: Jossey-Bass, 2006.

Opotow, S. "Hate, Conflict, and Moral Exclusion." *The Psychology of Hate*. Edited by Robert J. Sternberg. Washington, DC: American Psychological Association, 2005.

Opotow, S. and S. I. McClelland. "The Intensification of Hating: A Theory." *Social Justice Research* 20, no. 1, March (2007): 68.

Ortony, A. and T. J. Turner. "What's Basic about Basic Emotions?" *Psychological Review* 97 (1990): 315–331.

Otto, R. *Das Heilige: Über das Irrationale in der Idee des Göttlichen und sein Verhältnis zum Rationalen*. Breslau: Trewendt und Granier, 1917.

Palincsar, A. S. "Social Constructivist Perspectives on Teaching and Learning." *Annual Review of Psychology* 49 (1998): 345–375.

Panksepp, J. "A Critical Role for 'Affective Neuroscience' in Resolving What Is Basic about Basic Emotions." *Psychological Review* 99, no. 3, July (1992): 554–560.

Panksepp, J. *Affective Neuroscience: The Foundations of Human and Animal Emotions*. New York: Oxford University Press, 1998.

Panksepp, J. "Toward a General Psychobiological Theory of Emotions." *Behavioral and Brain Sciences* 5 (1982): 407–467.

Parkinson, B. *Ideas and Realities of Emotions*. London: Routledge, 1995.

Parrott, W. G. *Emotions in Social Psychology: Essential Readings*. Philadelphia: Psychology Press, 2001.

Parsons, T. *The Social System*. London: Routledge and Kegan Paul, 1951.

Pascal, B. *Pensées*. Harmondsworth: Penguin Books, 1966, original work published in 1643.

Pascual-Leone, J. and J. Johnson. "Affect, Self-Motivation, and Cognitive Development: A Dialectical Constructivist View." *Motivation, Emotion, and Cognition: Integrative Perspectives on Intellectual Functioning and Development*. Edited by David Y. Dai and Robert J. Sternberg, 197–235. Mahwah, NJ: Erlbaum, 2004.

Pearce, W. B. *Communication and the Human Condition*. Carbondale: Southern Illinois University Press, 1989.

Pearce, W. B. *Toward Communicative Virtuosity: A Meditation on Modernity and Other Forms of Communication*. Santa Barbara, CA: School of Human and Organization Development, Fielding Graduate University, 2005.

Pearce, W. B. and S. W. Littlejohn. *Moral Conflict: When Social Worlds Collide*. Newbury Park, CA: Sage, 1997.

Petersen, R. D. *Understanding Ethnic Violence: Fear, Hatred, and Resentment in Twentieth Century Eastern Europe*. Cambridge: Cambridge University Press, 2002.

Pettigrew, T. F. "The Ultimate Attribution Error: Extending Allport's Cognitive Analysis of Prejudice." *Personality and Social Psychology Bulletin* 5 (1979): 461–476.

Pettit, P. *Republicanism: A Theory of Freedom and Government*. Oxford: Clarendon Press, 1997.

Pfeiffer, T., C. Rutte, T. Killingback, M. Taborsky, and S. Bonhöfer. "Evolution of Cooperation by Generalized Reciprocity." *Proceedings of the Royal Society of London, Series B* 272 (2005): 1115–1120, retrieved on July 8, 2007, from www.journals.royalsoc.ac.uk/content/u47987fqkfy74u7p/fulltext.pdf.

Pharr, S. J. *Losing Face: Status Politics in Japan.* Berkeley: University of California Press, 1990.

Philippot, P. and A. Schaefer. "Emotion and Memory." *Emotions: Current Issues and Future Directions.* Edited by Tracy J. Mayne and George A. Bonanno, 82–121. New York: Guilford Press, 2001.

Piaget, J. *Intelligence and Affectivity: Their Relationship during Child Development.* Palo Alto, CA: Annual Reviews, 1981.

Piaget, J. *The Origins of Intelligence in Children.* New York: International University Press, 1950.

Pinker, S. *The Blank Slate: The Modern Denial of Human Nature.* London: Allen Lane, 2001.

Piotrowski, E. W. and J. Sladkowski. "An Invitation to Quantum Game Theory." *International Journal of Theoretical Physics* 42, no. 5 (2003): 1089–1099.

Plotinus, S. MacKenna, and B. S. Page. *The Enneads,* 2nd ed. London: Faber and Faber, 1956.

Plous, S. *The Psychology of Judgment and Decision Making.* New York: McGraw-Hill, 1993.

Plutchik, R. "A General Psychoevolutionary Theory of Emotion." *Emotion: Theory, Research, and Experience: Vol. 1. Theories of Emotion.* Edited by Robert Plutchik and Henry Kellerman, 3–31. New York: Academic Press, 1980.

Polanyi, M. *The Tacit Dimension.* New York: Anchor Books, 1967.

Polk, K. "Masculinity, Honour, and Confrontational Homicide?" *Just Boys Doing Business? Men, Masculinities and Crime.* Edited by Tim Newburn and Elizabeth Stanko. London/New York: Routledge and Kegan Paul, 1994.

Porges, S. W. "Emotion: An Evolutionary By-Product of the Neural Regulation of the Autonomic Nervous System." *The Integrative Neurobiology of Cognition.* Edited by C. S. Carter, I. I. Lederhendler, and Brian Kirkpatrick, 62–77. Annals of the New York Academy of Sciences, Volume 807. New York: New York Academy of Sciences, 1997.

Posen, B. "The Security Dilemma and Ethnic Conflict." *Survival* 35, no. 1 (1993): 27–47.

Powers, W. T. *Behavior: The Control of Perception.* Chicago: Aldine, 1973.

Powers, W. T. *Making Sense of Behavior: The Meaning of Control.* New Canaan, CT: Benchmark, 1998.

Putnam, L. L. and T. Peterson. "The Edwards Aquifer Dispute: Shifting Frames in a Protracted Conflict." *Making Sense of Intractable Environmental Conflicts: Concepts and Cases.* Edited by Roy J. Lewicki, Barbara Gray, and Michael Elliott. Washington, DC: Island Press, 2003.

Pynchon, S. R. *Resisting Humiliation in Schooling: Narratives and Counter-Narratives.* Washington, DC: University of Washington, doctoral dissertation, 2005.

Pyszczynski, T. A., J. Greenberg, and S. Solomon. *In the Wake of 9/11: The Psychology of Terror.* Washington, DC: American Psychological Association, 2003.

Pyszczynski, T. A., J. Greenberg, and S. Solomon. "Toward a Dialectical Analysis of Growth and Defensive Motives." *Psychological Inquiry* 11 (2000): 301–305.

Radford, J. and D. Russel, eds. *Femicide: The Politics of Woman Killing.* Buckingham: Open University Press, 1992.

Ramachandran, V. S. *Mirror Neurons and Imitation Learning as the Driving Force Behind "the Great Leap Forward" in Human Evolution.* Edge Foundation, 2000, retrieved on August 14, 2006, from www.edge.org/documents/archive/edge69 .html.

Ray, P. H. and S. R. Anderson. *The Cultural Creatives: How 50 Million People Are Changing the World.* New York: Three Rivers Press, 2000.

Reason, P. *Human Inquiry in Action: Developments in New Paradigm Research.* London: Sage, 1988.

Reason, P., ed. *Participation in Human Inquiry.* London: Sage, 1994.

Reason, P. and J. Rowan. *Human Inquiry: A Sourcebook of New Paradigm Research.* Chichester: Wiley, 1985.

Reber, A. S. *The Penguin Dictionary of Psychology,* 2nd ed. Harmondsworth: Penguin, 1995.

Reddy, W. M. *The Navigation of Feeling: A Framework for the History of Emotions.* Port Chester, NY: Cambridge University Press, 2001.

Reinert, E. S. *How Rich Countries Got Rich . . . And Why Poor Countries Stay Poor.* New York: Carroll & Graf, 2007.

Retzinger, S. M. *Violent Emotions: Shame and Rage in Marital Quarrels.* Newbury Park, CA: Sage, 1991.

Richards, H. *Foucault and the Future.* Richmond, IN: unpublished work in progress, 2007.

Richards, H. "Socialism Is Good for Business." *Solidaridad, Participacion, Transparencia.* Rosario, Argentina: Fundacion Estevez Boero, 2007, lahoradelaetica.wordpress.com.

Richards, H. and J. Swanger. *The Dilemmas of Social Democracies.* Lanham, MD: Rowman and Littlefield, 2006.

Richardson, B. "A New Realism: A Realistic and Principled Foreign Policy." *Foreign Affairs* 87, no. 1 (2008): 142–154.

Richerson, P. J., R. Boyd, and R. L. Bettinger. *The Origins of Agriculture as a Natural Experiment in Cultural Evolution.* Davis, CA: University of California, Center for Agricultural History, 1999, retrieved in November 2002, from www.des.ucdavis .edu/faculty/Richerson/Origins_Ag_IV3.htm.

Ridley, M. *The Origins of Virtue: Human Instincts and the Evolution of Cooperation.* London: Penguin, 1996.

Rizzolatti, G. and L. Craighero. "The Mirror-Neuron System." *Annual Review of Neuroscience* 27 (2004): 169–192.

Rodriguez Mosquera, P. M. *Humiliation and Racism.* Perth, Australia: Paper presented at The National Conference on Racism in Global Context, November 9–11, 2007, Murdoch University.

Rogers, E. M. *Diffusion of Innovations.* New York: Free Press of Glencoe, 1962.

Rogers, Y., A. Rutherford, and P. A. Bibby, eds. *Models in the Mind: Theory, Perspective and Application.* London: Academic Press, 1992.

Rorty, R. *Contingency, Irony, and Solidarity.* Cambridge: Cambridge University Press, 1989.

Roseman, I. J. "Appraisals, Rather Than Unpleasantness or Muscle Movements, Are the Primary Determinants of Specific Emotions." *Emotion* 4, no. 2, June (2004): 145–150.

Rosen, S. "Perceived Inadequacy and Help-Seeking (Vol. II)." *New Directions in Helping. Help-Seeking.* Edited by B. M. De Paulo and et al., 73–107. New York: Academic Press, 1983.

Rosenberg, E. L. "Levels of Analysis and the Organization of Affect." *Review of General Psychology* 2 (1998): 247–270.

Rosenwein, B. H. *Anger's Past: The Social Uses of an Emotion in the Middle Ages.* Ithaca, NY: Cornell University Press, 1998.

Ross, L. D. "Reactive Devaluation in Negotiation and Conflict Resolution." *Barriers to the Negotiated Resolution of Conflict.* Edited by Kenneth J. Arrow, Robert H. Mnookin, Lee D. Ross, Amos Tversky, and Robert Wilson. New York: Norton, 1995.

Ross, L. D. "The Intuitive Psychologist and His Shortcomings: Distortions in the Attribution Process." *Advances in Experimental Social Psychology. Vol. 10.* Edited by Leonard Berkowitz. Orlando, FL: Academic Press, 1977.

Ross, L. D. and J. T. Jost. "Fairness Norms and the Potential for Mutual Agreements Involving Majority and Minority Groups." *Research on Managing Groups and Teams (Vol. 2): Groups in Their Context.* Edited by Margaret A. Neale, Elizabeth A. Mannix, and Ruth Wageman, 93–114. Greenwich, CT: JAI Press, 1999.

Ross, L. D. and A. Ward. "Psychological Barriers to Dispute Resolution." *Advances in Experimental Social Psychology* 27 (1995): 255–304.

Ross, L. D. and R. E. Nisbett. *The Person and the Situation: Perspectives of Social Psychology.* Philadelphia: Temple University Press, 1991.

Rousseau, J.-J. *Du Contrat Social ou Principes du Droit Politique.* Geneve: Archives de la Société Jean-Jacques Rousseau, 1762, retrieved on March 6, 2003, from / un2sg4.unige.ch/athena/rousseau/jjr_cont.html.

Rozin, P. and E. B. Royzman. "Negativity Bias, Negativity Dominance, and Contagion." *Personality and Social Psychology Review* 5, no. 4 (2001): 296–320.

Runciman, W. G. *Relative Deprivation and Social Justice: A Study of Attitudes to Social Inequality in Twentieth-Century England.* London: Routledge & Keagan Paul, 1966.

Russell, J. A. "Cultural Variations in Emotions: A Review." *Psychological Bulletin* 112, no. 2 (1991): 179–204.

Russell, J. A. and L. F. Barrett. "Core Affect, Prototypical Emotional Episodes, and Other Things Called Emotion: Dissecting the Elephant." *Journal of Personality and Social Psychology* 76, no. 5 (1999): 805–819.

Rusting, C. L. "Personality as a Moderator of Affective Influences on Cognition." *Handbook of Affect and Social Cognition.* Edited by Joseph P. Forgas, 371–391. Mahwah, NJ: Erlbaum, 2001.

Ryan, S. "Peace-Building and Conflict Transformation." *Ethnic Conflict and International Relations,* 129–152. Dartmouth: Dartmouth Publishing, 1995, see also www.intractableconflict.org/docs/appendix_6.jsp.

Sagan, L. A. *The Health of Nations: The Causes of Sickness and Well-Being.* New York: Basic Books, 1987.

Saulsman, L. M. and A. C. Page. "The Five-Factor Model and Personality Disorder Empirical Literature: A Meta-Analytic Review." *Clinical Psychology Review* 23 (2004): 1055–1085.

Saurette, P. "You Dissin Me? Humiliation and Post 9/11 Global Politics." *Review of International Studies* 32 (2006): 495–522.

Sayler, M. *Humiliation and the Poor: A Study in the Management of Meaning.* Santa Barbara, CA: doctoral dissertation, Fielding Graduate Institute, 2004.

Scheff, T. J. *Aggression, Male Emotions and Relations: The Silence/Violence Pattern.* Santa Barbara, CA, 2005, www.soc.ucsb.edu/faculty/scheff/42.html.

Scheff, T. J. *Attachment, Attunement, Attraction: 24 Kinds of "Love."* Santa Barbara, CA: www.soc.ucsb.edu/faculty/scheff/29.html, 2003.

Scheff, T. J. *Bloody Revenge: Emotions, Nationalism and War.* Chicago: University of Chicago Press, 1990.

Scheff, T. J. *Emotions, the Social Bond and Human Reality. Part/Whole Analysis.* Cambridge: Cambridge University Press, 1997.

Scheff, T. J. "Hitler's Appeal: Alienation, Shame-Rage, and Revenge." *Violence and Society: A Reader.* Edited by Matthew Silberman. Upper Saddle River, NJ: Prentice Hall, 2003.

Scheff, T. J. "Shame and the Social Bond: A Sociological Theory." *Sociological Theory* 18, no. 1 (2000): 84–99.

Scheff, T. J. *Strategies for the Social Science of Emotion.* St. Barbara, CA, 2004, www.soc.ucsb.edu/faculty/scheff/31.html.

Scheff, T. J. *Toward a Web of Concepts: The Case of Emotions and Affects.* St. Barbara, CA, 2004, www.soc.ucsb.edu/faculty/scheff/41.html.

Scheff, T. J. "Aggression, Hypermasculine Emotions and Relations: the Silence/ Violence Pattern." *Irish Journal of Sociology* 15, no. 1 (2006): 24–37, see www.soc.ucsb.edu/faculty/scheff/53.htm.

Scheff, T. J. "What Is This Thing Called Love? The Three A's: Attachment, Attunement and Attraction." *Goffman Unbound: A New Paradigm for Social Science.* Edited by Thomas J. Scheff, 111–124. Boulder, CO: Paradigm, 2006.

Scheler, M. *Über Ressentiment und moralisches Werturteil.* Leipzig: Engelmann, 1912.

Scheler, M. *Zur Phänomenologie und Theorie der Sympathiegefühle und von Liebe und Haß.* Halle: Max Niemeyer, 1913.

Schelling, F. W. J. v. *System des transcendentalen Idealismus.* Tübingen: Cotta, 1800.

Schelling, F. W. J. v. *System of Transcendental Idealism.* New 1993 ed. Charlottesville: University Press of Virginia, 1978.

Scherer, K. R. "Foreword." *Emotions: Current Issues and Future Directions.* Edited by Tracy J. Mayne and George A. Bonanno, xiii–xv. New York: Guilford Press, 2001.

Scherer, K. R. "On the Nature and Function of Emotion: A Component Process Approach." *Approaches to Emotion.* Edited by Klaus R. Scherer and Paul Ekman, 293–318. Hillsdale, NJ: Erlbaum, 1984.

Schneider, C. D. *Shame, Exposure and Privacy.* New York: Norton, 1992.

Schoemaker, Paul J. H. "The Expected Utility Model: Its Variants, Purposes, Evidence and Limitations." *Journal of Economic Literature* 20 (1982): 529–563.

Schwarz, N. "Warmer and More Social: Recent Developments in Cognitive Social Psychology." *Annual Review of Sociology* 24 (1998): 239–264.

Schwarz, N. and G. L. Clore. "Feelings and Phenomenal Experiences." *Social Psychology: Handbook of Basic Principles.* Edited by E. T. Higgins and Arie W. Kruglanski, 433–465. New York: Guilford Press, 1996.

Schwarz, N., D. Kahneman, and E. Diener, eds. *Well-Being: The Foundations of Hedonic Psychology.* New York: Russell Sage Foundation, 1999.

Schwebel, M. "Realistic Empathy and Active Nonviolence Confront Political Reality." *Journal of Social Issues* 62, no. 1 (2006): 191–208, retrieved on August 14, 2007, from www.blackwell-synergy.com/doi/pdf/10.1111/j.1540-4560.2006.00446.x.

Seligman, M. E. P. *Authentic Happiness: Using the New Positive Psychology to Realize Your Potential for Lasting Fulfillment.* New York: Free Press, 2002.

Sellars, K. *The Rise and Rise of Human Rights*. Stroud: Sutton, 2002.

Sen, A. *Identity and Violence: The Illusion of Destiny*. New York: Norton, 2006.

Serres, M. *The Troubadour of Knowledge*. Ann Arbor: University of Michigan Press, 1997.

Shafir, E., I. Simonson, and A. Tversky. "Reason-Based Choice." *Cognition* 49 (1993): 11–36.

Shalhoub-Kevorkian, N. *Mapping and Analyzing the Landscape of Femicide in Palestine*. Research report submitted by the Women's Center for Legal Aid and Counseling (WCLAC) to UNIFEM, 2000.

Shaw, M. *Theory of the Global State*. Cambridge: Cambridge University Press, 2000.

Sherif, M. and H. Cantril. *The Psychology of Ego-Involvements, Social Attitudes and Identifications*. New York: Wiley, 1947.

Siegel, D. J. *The Developing Mind: Toward a Neurobiology of Interpersonal Experience*. New York: Guilford Press, 1999.

Sigman, S. "Toward Study of the Consequentiality (Not Consequences) of Communication." *The Consequentiality of Communication*. Edited by Stuart Sigman, 1–14. Hillsdale, NJ: Erlbaum, 1995.

Silver, H. and S. M. Miller. "From Poverty to Social Exclusion: Lessons from Europe." *Poverty and Race in America: The Emerging Agendas*. Edited by Chester Hartman, 57–70. Lexington, MA: Lexington Books, 2006.

Singer, M. R. *Intercultural Communication: A Perceptual Approach*. Englewood Cliffs, NJ: Prentice Hall, 1987.

Slovic, P. "The Construction of Preference." *American Psychologist* 50, no. 5 (1995): 364–371.

Smedes, L. B. *Shame and Grace: Healing the Shame We Don't Deserve*. San Francisco: HarperCollins, 1993.

Smedslund, J. "Are Frijda's 'Laws of Emotion' Empirical?" *Cognition & Emotion* 6, no. 6 (1992): 435–456.

Smedslund, J. *Dialogues about a New Psychology*. Chagrin Falls, OH: Taos Institute, 2004.

Smedslund, J. "From Hypothesis-Testing Psychology to Procedure-Testing Psychologic." *Review of General Psychology* 6, no. 1 (2002): 51–72.

Smedslund, J. *Psycho-Logic*. Berlin: Springer, 1988.

Smedslund, J. "Social Representations and Psychologic." *Culture & Psychology* 4, no. 4 (1998): 435–454.

Smedslund, J. "The Psychologic of Forgiving." *Scandinavian Journal of Psychology* 32 (1991): 164–176.

Smedslund, J. *The Structure of Psychological Common Sense*. Mahwah, NJ: Erlbaum, 1997.

Smith, C. A. and L. D. Kirby. "Affect and Cognitive Appraisal Processes." *Handbook of Affect and Social Cognition*. Edited by Joseph P. Forgas, 75–92. Mahwah, NJ: Erlbaum, 2001.

Smith, D. *Globalization, the Hidden Agenda*. Cambridge: Polity Press, 2006.

Smith, D. "Organisations and Humiliation: Looking beyond Elias." *Organization* 8, no. 3 (2001): 537–560.

Smith, D. "The Humiliating Organisation: The Functions and Disfunctions of Degradation." *The Civilized Organisation*. Edited by Ad v. Iterson, Willem Mastenbroek, Tim Newton, and Dennis Smith. Amsterdam: Benjamin, 2002.

Smith, M. B., J. S. Bruner, and R. W. White. *Opinions and Personality.* New York: Wiley, 1956.

Snyder, C. R. "Hope and Optimism." *Encyclopedia of Human Behavior, Vol. 2.* Edited by Vilayanur S. Ramachandran, 535–542. San Diego, CA: Academic, 1994.

Snyder, C. R. "Hope, Goal Blocking Thoughts, and Test-Related Anxieties." *Psychological Reports* 84 (1999): 206–208.

Snyder, C. R. "Hope Theory: Rainbows in the Mind." *Psychological Inquiry* 13, no. 4 (2002): 249–275.

Snyder, C. R. *The Psychology of Hope: You Can Get There From Here.* New York: Free Press, 1994.

Snyder, C. R. and K. Pulvers. "Dr. Seuss, the Coping Machine, and 'Oh, the Places You Will Go.'" *Coping and Copers: Adaptive Processes and People.* Edited by C. R. Snyder, 3–29. New York: Oxford University Press, 2001.

Snyder, C. R., J. Cheavens, and S. C. Sympson. "Hope: An Individual Motive for Social Commerce." *Group Dynamics: Theory, Research, and Practice* 1 (1997): 107–118.

Snyder, C. R., A. B. LaPointe, J. J. Crowson Jr., and S. Early. "Preferences of High- and Low-Hope People for Self-Referential Input." *Cognition & Emotion* 12 (1998): 807–823.

Snyder, C. R., S. C. Sympson, S. T. Michael, and J. Cheavens. "The Optimism and Hope Constructs: Variants on a Positive Expectancy Theme." *Optimism and Pessimism.* Edited by E. C. Chang, 103–124. Washington, DC: American Psychological Association, 2000.

Snyder, J. "Perceptions of the Security Dilemma in 1914." *Psychology and Deterrence.* Edited by Robert Jervis, Richard N. Lebow, and Janice G. Stein, 153–179. Baltimore, MD: Johns Hopkins University Press, 1985.

Snyder, J. and B. Walters, eds. *The Security Dilemma and Intervention in Civil Wars.* New York: Columbia University Press, 1999.

Sornette, D. "2050: The End of the Growth Era?" *Why Stock Markets Crash: Critical Events in Complex Financial Systems,* 355–418. Princeton, NJ: Princeton University Press, 2003.

Soros, G. *Open Society: Reforming Global Capitalism.* London: Little, Brown, 2000.

Speeth, K. R. and I. Friedlander. *Gurdjieff—Seeker of the Truth.* New York: Harper Colophon Books, Harper & Row, 1980.

Spencer, R. "A Comparison of Relational Psychologies." *Work in Progress, No. 5.* Wellesley, MA: Stone Center Working Paper Series, 2000.

Spencer, S. J., S. Fein, M. P. Zanna, and J. M. Olson, eds. *Motivated Social Perception: The Ontario Symposium Volume 9.* Mahwah, NJ: Erlbaum, 2003.

Spett, M. "The Two Critical Components of All Psychotherapies: Experience the Emotion, Change the Cognition." *Newsletter of the New Jersey Association of Cognitive-Behavioral Therapists* November (2004), retrieved on December 5, 2008, from www.nj-act.org/spett.html.

Spivey, N. *How Art Made the World: How Humans Made Art and Art Made Us Human.* London: BBC Worldwide, 2005.

Srivastva, S. and D. L. Cooperrider. *Appreciative Management and Leadership: The Power of Positive Thought and Action in Organizations.* San Francisco: Jossey-Bass, 1990.

Stamm, J. L. "The Meaning of Humiliation and Its Relationship to Fluctuations in Self-Esteem." *International Review of Psycho-Analysis* 5 (1978): 425–433.

Stanton, A. L. and P. R. Snider. "Coping with a Breast Cancer Diagnosis: A Prospective Study." *Health Psychology* 12 (1993): 16–23.

Staub, E. "The Psychology of Bystanders, Perpetrators, and Heroic Helpers." *International Journal of Intercultural Relations* 17 (1993): 315–341.

Staub, E. *The Psychology of Good and Evil: Why Children, Adults, and Groups Help and Harm Others.* Cambridge: Cambridge University Press, 2003.

Staub, E. "The Roots of Evil: Social Conditions, Culture, Personality and Basic Human Needs." *Personality and Social Psychology Review* 3, no. 3 (1999): 179–192.

Staub, E. *The Roots of Evil: The Origins of Genocide and Other Group Violence.* Cambridge: Cambridge University Press, 1989.

Stearns, C. Z. and P. N. Stearns. *Anger: The Struggle for Emotional Control in America's History.* Chicago: University of Chicago Press, 1986.

Steinberg, B. S. "Shame and Humiliation in the Cuban Missile Crisis. A Psychoanalytic Perspective." *Political Psychology* 12, no. 4 (1991): 653–690.

Steinberg, B. S. *Shame and Humiliation: Presidential Decision Making on Vietnam.* Montreal: McGill-Queen's, 1996.

Steinsland, G. *Myth and Power in the Cultural Transformation of the Nordic Countries From Viking to Medieval Age.* Oslo: Centre for Advanced Study (CAS) at the Norwegian Academy of Science and Letters, Opening ceremony, September 4, 2007, Lecture by Professor Gro Steinsland, ILN, University of Oslo, Group leader at CAS, 2007/2008, retrieved on March 1, 2008, from www.cas.uio.no/research/0708rulership/lecture_040907.pdf.

Stephan, W. G., C. W. Stephan, and W. B. Gudykunst. "Anxiety in Intergroup Relations: A Comparison of Anxiety/Uncertainty Management Theory and Integrated Threat Theory." *International Journal of Intercultural Relations* 23, no. 4 (1999): 613–628.

Stern, E. and B. Sundelius. "The Essence of Groupthink." *Mershon International Studies Review* 38, no. 1 (1994): 101–107.

Sternberg, R. J. "A Duplex Theory of Hate: Development and Application to Terrorism, Massacres, and Genocide." *Review of General Psychology* 7, no. 3 (2003): 299–328.

Sternberg, R. J., ed. *The Psychology of Hate.* Washington, DC: American Psychological Association, 2005.

Sternberg, R. J. and J. E. Davidson, eds. *The Nature of Insight.* Cambridge, MA: MIT Press, 1995.

Stiglitz, J. E. *Global Economic Prospects and the Developing Countries 1998/99: Beyond Financial Crisis.* New York: World Bank, 1998, www.worldbank.org/prospects/gep98-99/toc.htm.

Stiglitz, J. E. *Globalization and Its Discontents.* New York: Norton, 2003.

Stiglitz, J. E., A. S. Edlin, and J. B. DeLong, eds. *The Economists' Voice: Top Economists Take on Today's Problems.* New York: Columbia University Press, 2008.

Stokes, P. A. *Homo Gubernator: Emotions and Human Self-Steering.* Dublin: Department of Sociology, University College Dublin, unpublished manuscript, 2005.

Stout, K. " 'Intimate Femicide': Effect of Legislation and Social Services." *Femicide: The Politics of Woman Killing.* Edited by Jill Radford and Diana Russel Buckingham, England: Open University Press, 1992.

Strack, F. and R. Deutsch. "Reflective and Impulsive Determinants of Social Behavior." *Personality and Social Psychology Review* 8, no. 3 (2004): 220–247.

Stringer, E. T. *Action Research: A Handbook for Practitioners*, 2nd ed. Thousand Oaks, CA: Sage, 1999.

Sun, R., ed. *Cognition and Multi-Agent Interaction: From Cognitive Modeling to Social Simulation*. Cambridge: Cambridge University Press, 2006.

Swedberg, R. *Economics and Sociology: Redefining Their Boundaries: Conversations with Economists and Sociologists*. Princenton, NJ: Princeton University Press, 1990.

Tajfel, H. *Differentiation between Social Groups: Studies in the Social Psychology of Intergroup Relations*. London: Published in cooperation with European Association of Experimental Social Psychology by Academic Press, 1978.

Tajfel, H. *Human Groups and Social Categories: Studies in Social Psychology*. Cambridge: Cambridge University Press, 1981.

Tajfel, H. "Social Psychology of Intergroup Relations." *Annual Review of Psychology* 33 (1982): 1–39.

Tajfel, H., C. Flament, M. G. Billig, and R. P. Bundy. "Social Categorization and Intergroup Behaviour." *European Journal of Social Psychology* 1 (1971): 149–178.

Tajfel, H., C. Fraser, and J. M. F. Jaspars. *The Social Dimension: European Developments in Social Psychology*. Cambridge: Cambridge University Press, 1984.

Tajfel, H. and J. C. Turner. "The Social Identity Theory of Intergroup Behavior." *Psychology of Intergroup Relations*. Edited by Stephen Worchel and William G. Austin, 204–227. Chicago: Neston-Hall, 1986.

Tajfel, H. and Minority Rights Group. *The Social Psychology of Minorities*. London: Minority Rights Group, 1978.

Tajfel, H., ed. *Differentiation between Social Groups: Studies in Intergroup Behavior*. London: Academic Press, 1978.

Tangney, J. P. "Humility." *Handbook of Positive Psychology*. Edited by C. R. Snyder and Shane J. Lopez, 411–419. London: Oxford University Press, 2002.

Tangney, J. P., P. Wagner, C. Fletcher, and R. Gramzow. "Shamed into Anger? The Relation of Shame and Guilt to Anger and Self-Reported Agression." *Journal of Personality and Social Psychology* 62, no. 4 (1992): 669–675.

Tart, C. T. *Living the Mindful Life: A Handbook for Living in the Present Moment*. Boston: Shambhala, 1994.

Tavris, C. and E. Aronson. *Mistakes Were Made, but Not by Me: Why We Justify Foolish Beliefs, Bad Decisions, and Hurtful Acts*. Orlando, FL: Harcourt, 2007.

Tavuchis, N. *Mea Culpa: A Sociology of Apology and Reconciliation*. Stanford, CA: Stanford University Press, 1991.

Taylor, C. *The Ethics of Authenticity*. Cambridge: Harvard University Press, 1990.

Taylor, C. "The Politics of Recognition." *Multiculturalism: Examining the Politics of Recognition*. Edited by Amy Gutman. Princeton, NJ: Princeton University Press, 1994.

Taylor, G. *Pride, Shame and Guilt: Emotions of Self-Assessment*. Oxford: Clarendon Press, 1985.

Taylor, G. "Shame, Integrity, and Self-Respect." *Dignity, Character, and Self-Respect*. Edited by Robin S. Dillon, 157–178. New York, London: Routledge, 1995.

Taylor, S. E., L. C. Klein, B. P. Lewis, T. L. Gruenewald, R. A. R. Gurung, and J. A. Updegraff. "Biobehavioral Responses to Stress in Females: Tend-and-Befriend, Not Fight-or-Flight." *Psychological Review* 109, no. 4 (2002): 745–750.

Tellegen, A., D. Watson, and L. A. Clark. "On the Dimensional and Hierarchical Structure of Affect." *Psychological Science* 10 (1999): 297–309.

Thagard, P. "The Passionate Scientist: Emotion in Scientific Cognition." *The Cognitive Basis of Science*. Edited by Peter Carruthers, Stephen Stich, and Michael Siegal, 235–250. Cambridge: Cambridge University Press, 2002.

Thaler, R. and C. Sunstein. *Nudge: Improving Decisions about Health, Wealth and Happiness*. New Haven, CT: Yale University Press, 2008.

The International Panel of Eminent Personalities to Investigate the 1994 Genocide in Rwanda and the Surrounding Events. *Rwanda: The Preventable Genocide*, 2000. Retrieved on September 30, 2000, from www.oau-oua.org.

Thucydides. *History of the Peloponnesian War*. The Internet Classics Archive at classics.mit.edu/Thucydides/pelopwar.html, 431.

Tjeldvoll, A. "Universitetspedagogisk Paradigmeskifte." *UNIPED* 30, no. 1 (2007): 36–43.

Tomkins, S. S. *Affect Imagery and Consciousness (Volumes I–IV)*. New York: Springer, 1962.

Tomkins, S. S. "Affect Theory." *Approaches to Emotion*. Edited by Klaus R. Scherer and Paul Ekman, 163–195. Hillsdale, NJ: Erlbaum, 1984.

Tomuschat, C. *Human Rights: Between Idealism and Realism*. Oxford: Oxford University Press, 2003.

Tooby, J. and L. Cosmides. "The Past Explains the Present: Emotional Adaptations and the Structure of Ancestral Environments." *Ethology and Sociobiology* 11 (1990): 375–424.

Torbert, W. R. *The Power of Balance: Transforming Self, Society, and Scientific Inquiry*. Newbury Park, CA: Sage, 1991.

Triandis, H. C. *Culture and Social Behavior*. New York: McGraw-Hill, 1997.

Tuchman, B. W. *The March of Folly: From Troy to Vietnam*. New York: Knopf, 1984.

Turner, J. C. "Towards a Cognitive Redefinition of the Social Group." *Social Identity and Intergroup Relations*. Edited by Henri Tajfel, 15–40. Cambridge: Cambridge University Press, 1982.

Turner, M. E. and A. R. Pratkanis. "Mitigating Groupthink by Stimulating Constructive Conflict." *Using Conflict in Organizations*. Edited by Carsten K. W. D. Dreu and Evert v. d. Vliert, 53–71. London: Sage, 1997.

Turner, T. J. and A. Ortony. "Basic Emotions: Can Conflicting Criteria Converge?" *Psychological Review* 99, no. 3, July (1992): 566–571.

Uchino, B. N. *Social Support and Physical Health: Understanding the Health Consequences of Relationships*. New Haven, CT: Yale University Press, 2004.

Ueno, C. *Nationalism and Gender*. Melbourne: Trans Pacific Press, 2004.

Umilta, M. A., E. Kohler, V. Gallese, L. Fogassi, L. Fadiga, C. Keysers, and G. Rizzolatti. " 'I Know What You Are Doing': A Neurophysiological Study." *Neuron* 31 (2001): 155–165.

Ury, W. *Getting to Peace. Transforming Conflict at Home, at Work, and in the World*. New York: Viking, 1999.

Vachon, S. "Passer De L'Appauvrissement à La Pauvreté Comme on Va De L'Humiliation à L'Humilité." *Voix Et Images* 18, no. 2 (1993): 382–387.

Vaitheeswaran, V. V. *Power to the People: How the Coming Energy Revolution Will Transform an Industry, Change Our Lives, and Maybe Even Save the Planet*. New York: Farrar, Straus and Giroux, 2003.

Vallacher, R. R. and A. Nowak. "The Emergence of Dynamical Social Psychology." *Psychological Inquiry* 8, no. 2 (1997): 73–99.

Van Vuuren, W. and I. Liebenberg. " 'Government by Illusion': The Legacy and Its Implications." *The Hidden Hand, Covert Operations in South Africa.* Edited by Anthony Minnaar, Ian Liebenberg, and Charl Schutte, 25–43. Pretoria: Human Sciences Research Council, 1994.

Vaughan, G., ed. *Women and the Gift Economy: A Radically Different Worldview Is Possible.* Toronto: Innana Publications, 2007, retrieved on July 5, 2007, from www .gift-economy.com/womenand.html.

Vidal, G. and Parini, J., eds. *The Selected Essays of Gore Vidal.* Toronto: Doubleday, 2008.

Volkan, V. D. "A Psychoanalytic Perspective on Intergroup Hatred." *Journal for the Psychoanalysis of Culture and Society* 3, no. 1 (1998): 78–80.

Volkan, V. D. *Blind Trust: Large Groups and Their Leaders in Times of Crisis and Terror.* Charlottesville, VA: Pitchstone Publishing, 2004.

Volkan, V. D. *Bloodlines: From Ethnic Pride to Ethnic Terrorism.* New York: Farrar, Straus and Giroux, 1997.

Volkan, V. D. "The Tree Model: A Comprehensive Psychopolitical Approach to Unofficial Diplomacy and the Reduction of Ethnic Tension." *Mind and Human Interaction* 10, no. 3 (1999): 142–210.

Volkan, V. D., D. A. Julius, and J. V. Montville, eds. *The Psychodynamics of International Relationships. Vol II: Unofficial Diplomacy at Work.* Lexington, MA: Lexington Books, 1991.

Vygotsky, L. S. *Mind in Society: The Development of Higher Psychological Processes.* Cambridge, MA: Harvard University Press, 1978.

Walker, I. and T. F. Pettigrew. "Relative Deprivation Theory: An Overview and Conceptual Critique." *British Journal of Social Psychology* 23 (1984): 301–310.

Walker, M. and W. Rosen. *How Connections Heal: Stories from Relational-Cultural Therapy.* Wellesley, MA: Guilford Press, 2004.

Waller, J. *Becoming Evil: How Ordinary People Commit Genocide and Mass Killing.* Oxford: Oxford University Press, 2002.

Waltz, K. *Theory of International Politics.* Reading, MA: Addison-Wesley, 1979.

Ware, O. "Rudolph Otto's Idea of the Holy: A Reappraisal." *Heythrop Journal* 48, no. 1, January (2007): 48–60.

Wasilewski, J. H. "Interculturalists as Dragon-Riders." *Journal of Intercultural Communication, SIETAR Japan* 4 (2001): 75–89.

Watson, D., L. A. Clark, and A. Tellegen. "Development and Validation of Brief Measures of Positive and Negative Affect: The PANAS Scales." *Journal of Personality and Social Psychology* 54 (1988): 1063–1070.

Watson, D., D. Wiese, J. Vaidya, and A. Tellegen. "The Two General Activation Systems of Affect: Structural Findings, Evolutionary Considerations, and Psychobiological Evidence." *Journal of Personality and Social Psychology* 76, no. 5 (1999): 820–838.

Watson, J. B. *Behaviorism.* Chicago: University of Chicago Press, 1930.

Webb, T. *Towards a Mature Shame Culture: Theoretical and Practical Tools for Personal and Social Growth.* Sydney: University of Western Sydney, doctoral dissertation, 2003.

Webb, T. *Working with Shame and Other Strong Emotions: Experiential Workshop Script from "Personal and Political Tools for Social Change" Course.* Sydney: Centre for Popular Education, University of Technology, 2005.

Weber, B. and D. Depew. "Natural Selection and Self-Organization." *Biology and Philosophy* 11 (1996): 33–65.

Weiner, B. *An Attributional Theory of Motivation and Emotion.* New York: Springer-Verlag, 1986.

Weiner, B. *Judgments of Responsibility: A Foundation for a Theory of Social Conduct.* New York: Guilford Press, 1995.

Weiner, B. and S. Graham. "An Attributional Approach to Emotional Development." *Emotions, Cognition, and Behavior.* Edited by Carroll E. Izard, Jerome Kagan, and Robert B. Zajonc, 167–191. New York: Cambridge University Press, 1984.

Weingarten, K. *Compassionate Witnessing and the Transformation of Societal Violence: How Individuals Can Make a Difference.* New York: Adapted from *Common Shock: Witnessing Violence Every Day—How We Are Harmed, How We Can Heal*, printed by arrangement with Dutton, a member of Penguin Group, 2003.

Wendt, A. *Social Theory of International Politics.* Cambridge: Cambridge University Press, 1999

Wendt, A. *Social Theory As Cartesian Science: An Auto-Critique From a Quantum Perspective.* Columbus, OH: Retrieved on December 31, 2004, www.humiliation-studies.org/documents/WendtAutoCritique.pdf, 2004.

Wendt, A. "Why a World State Is Inevitable." *European Journal of International Relations* 9, no. 4 (2003): 491–542.

Wendt, A. *Why a World State Is Inevitable: Teleology and the Logic of Anarchy.* Chicago: University of Chicago, 2003.

Wertz, R. W. and D. C. Wertz. *Lying-in: A History of Childbirth in America.* New York: Free Press, 1977.

Wesselss, M. and C. Monteiro. "Psychosocial Intervention and Post-War Reconstruction in Angola: Interweaving Traditional and Western Approaches." *Peace, Conflict and Violence: Peace Psychology for the 21st Century.* Edited by Daniel J. Christie, Richard V. Wagner, and Deborah D. N. Winter, 262–276. Upper Saddle River, NJ: Prentice Hall, 2001.

Whalen, P. J. "Fear, Vigilance, and Ambiguity: Initial Neuroimaging Studies of the Human Amygdala." *Current Directions in Psychological Science* 7 (1998): 177–188.

Wheeler, G. *Beyond Individualism: Toward a New Understanding of Self, Relationship & Experience.* Hillsdale, NJ: Analytic Press, 2000.

Wheeler, M. A., D. A. T. Stuss, and E. Tulving. "Toward a Theory of Episodic Memory: The Frontal Lobes and Autonoetic Consciousness." *Psychological Bulletin* 121 (1997): 331–354.

White, R. K. *Fearful Warriors: A Psychological Profile of U.S.-Soviet Relations.* New York: Free Press, 1984.

Whitehead, S. M. *Men and Masculinities: Key Themes and New Directions.* Cambridge: Polity Press, 2002.

Whyte, W. F. *Participatory Action Research.* Newbury Park, CA: Sage, 1991.

Wicker, B., C. Keysers, J. Plailly, J.-P. Royet, V. Gallese, and G. Rizzolatti. "Both of Us Disgusted in My Insula: The Common Neural Basis of Seeing and Feeling Disgust." *Neuron* 40, no. 3 (2003): 655–664.

Wierzbicka, A. "Human Emotions: Universal or Culture Specific?" *American Anthropologist* 88 (1986): 584–594.

Wierzbicka, A. and J. Harkins, eds. *Emotions in Crosslinguistic Perspective.* Berlin: Mouton de Gruyter, 2001.

Wilber, K. *No Boundary.* Boston: Shambhala, 1979.

Wilder, D. A. and P. N. Shapiro. "Effects of Anxiety on Impression Formation in a Group Context: An Anxiety-Assimilation Hypothesis." *Journal of Experimental Social Psychology* 25, no. 6 (1989): 481–499.

Wilkinson, R. G. *The Impact of Inequality. How to Make Sick Societies Healthier.* London: Routledge, 2005.

Williams, B. *Shame and Necessity.* Los Angeles: University of California Press, 1993.

Wilson, T. D. *Strangers to Ourselves.* Cambridge, MA: Harvard University Press, 2002.

Winne, P. H. "Key Issues in Modeling and Applying Research on Self-Regulated Learning." *Applied Psychology: An International Review* 54 (2005): 232–238.

Winter, D. D. N. *Ecological Psychology: Healing the Split between Planet and Self.* New York: HarperCollins, 1996.

Wintersteiner, W. *Pädagogik des Anderen: Bausteine für eine Friedenspädagogik in der Postmoderne (Pedagogy of the Other: Building Blocks for Peace Education in the Postmodern World).* Münster: Agenda, 1999.

Witt, U. "Self-Organization and Economics—What Is New?" *Structural Change and Economic Dynamics* 8 (1997): 489–507.

Wittine, B. "Jungian Analysis and Nondual Wisdom." *Sacred Mirror: Nondual Wisdom & Psychotherapy.* Edited by John J. Prendergast, Peter Fenner, and Sheila Krystal, 268–289. New York: Paragon House, 2003.

Wrangham, R. and D. Peterson. *Demonic Males.* New York: Houghton Mifflin, 1996.

Wyatt-Brown, B. *Southern Honor: Ethics and Behavior in the Old South.* New York: Oxford University Press, 1982.

Yoshikawa, M. "The 'Double Swing' Model of Intercultural Communication between the East and West." *Communication Theory: Eastern and Western Perspectives.* Edited by D. L. Kincaid, 319–329. San Diego, CA: Academic Press, 1987.

Yoshikawa, M. *The "Double Swing" Model of Eastern-Western Intercultural Communication.* Honolulu: Paper prepared for the Seminar on Communication Theory from Eastern and Western Perspectives, East-West Communication Institute, 1980.

Zajonc, R. B. "Emotions." *The Handbook of Social Psychology, Vol 1.* Edited by Daniel T. Gilbert, Susan T. Fiske, and Gardner Lindzey, 591–632. Boston: McGraw-Hill, 1998.

Zajonc, R. B. "Feeling and Thinking: Preferences Need No Inferences." *American Psychologist* 35 (1980): 151–175.

Zajonc, R. B. "Social Facilitation." *Science* 149 (1965): 269–274.

Zajonc, R. B. *The Selected Works of R. B. Zajonc.* Hoboken, NJ: Wiley, 2004.

Zak, M. "Quantum Decision-Maker." *Information Sciences* 128 (2000): 199–215.

Zalewski, M. and J. Parpat, eds. *The "Man Question" in International Relations.* Boulder, CO: Westview, 1998.

Zaller, J. *The Nature and Origins of Mass Opinion.* Cambridge: Cambridge University Press, 1992.

Zehr, H. *Changing Lenses: A New Focus for Crime and Justice.* Scottdale, PA: Herald Press, 1990.

Zehr, H. *The Little Book of Restorative Justice.* Intercourse, PA: Good Books, 2002.

Zeilinger, A., M. Plüss, and R. Hügli. *Spooky Action and Beyond: Viennese Physicist Anton Zeilinger Talks about Teleportation, the Information Stored in a Human Being and Freedom in Physics.* Berlin: Perlentaucher Medien, signandsight.com, 2006, retrieved on April 16, 2008, from www.signandsight.com/features/614.html.

Zembylas, M. "Of Troubadours, Angels, and Parasites: Reevaluating the Educational Territory in the Arts and Sciences through the Work of Michel Serres." *International Journal of Education & the Arts* 3, no. 3, March 17 (2002), ijea.asu .edu/v3n3.

Zimbardo, P. G. *The Lucifer Effect: Understanding How Good People Turn Evil.* New York: Random House, 2007.

Zimbardo, P. G. *The Power and Pathology of Imprisonment. Congressional Record. (Serial No. 15, 1971-10-25). Hearings Before Subcommittee No. 3, of the Committee on the Judiciary, House of Representatives, Ninety-Second Congress, First Session on Corrections, Part II, Prisons, Prison Reform and Prisoner's Rights: California.* Washington, DC: Government Printing Office, 1971.

Znakov, V. V. "The Comprehension of Violence and Humiliation Situations by Aggressive Adolescents." *Voprosy-Psikhologii* January–February (1990): 20–27.

Zuber-Skerritt, O. *Action Research for Change and Development.* Aldershot: Avebury, 1991.

Index

About the Author

EVELIN LINDNER is Founding Director of Human Dignity and Humiliation Studies and Lecturer at the International Center for Cooperation and Conflict Resolution, at Columbia University. She is also Senior Lecturer in Psychology at the University of Oslo. Her earlier book, *Making Enemies: Humiliation and International Conflict* (Praeger, 2006), was named an Outstanding Academic Title 2007.